Manxland's King of Music

The Life and Times of Harry Wood

Manxland's King of Music

The Life and Times of Harry Wood

Maurice Powell

Published by
Lily Publications,
PO Box 33
Ramsey
Isle of Man, British Isles
IM99 4LP

Printed and bound by Words and Spaces, Douglas

Cover design: Ruth Sutherland

ISBN 978-1-911177-46-3

For my parents

Manxland's King of Music,
1868 - 1938.

Manxland's King of Music
The Life and Times of Harry Wood

Contents

by the same author

ENCORE! The Story of the Isle of Man Symphony Orchestra

A Very Gifted Manx Lady, the life and career of Kathleen Rydings

Manx Musical Worthies: A Supplement to New Manx Worthies: Florrie Forde, John Edward Quayle, Edward Quayle, Oliver Gaggs, F. C. Poulter, Charles Fox Jr, Kathleen Rydings.

Several articles on aspects of the Manx entertainment and tourist industry including 'Has Anybody Here Seen Kelly; 'The Isle of Man Festival of Britain pageants 1951'; 'Let's Have a Song About the Isle of Man', 'A Trip to Manxland'; 'Florrie Forde at the Derby Castle 1900-39'; 'Mr Craine's Oratorio'; 'A rale Manx Concert'; 'The Origins of Hi! Kelly'; 'Tipperary and the Isle of Man, New Evidence', and 'The Imperial Viennese Orchestra at the Villa Marina Kursaal'.
(See manxmusic.com and the Manx National Heritage Manuscript Collection MS 13670.)

Foreword

I was born in Douglas into a boarding house family in 1951 at a time when the Isle of Man's fabled visiting industry was still a mainstay of the Manx economy.

I am lucky to have personal memories of the crowded promenades and the packed beaches, the donkey rides and the Punch and Judy at the bottom of Broadway. The coach tours and the steam trains running to Ramsey and, above all, the entertainment. White City, the Derby Castle, the Palace Ballroom and the Palace Theatre, the Villa Marina and the Gaiety Theatre, all running at full capacity with variety shows, dance bands, comedy acts and music hall turns night after night throughout the long summer months.

But what I remember, marvellous as it was, is a mere shadow of what it was like earlier in the century when more than 650,000 holiday makers would arrive in one season expecting to be fed, watered and entertained in royal style, and they weren't disappointed.

The roll call of artistes that visited the Island through these years is extraordinary, and there must have been palpable excitement on the boats as they brought tens of thousands of visitors in Irish Week, Scots Week, and the Wakes Weeks, all wondering which of the great stars would be here on the Island - would it be Vesta Tilley, was Wilkie Baird here this week, have we missed Florrie Forde?

These appearances inspired a huge corpus of songs about the Isle of Man. We've all heard of *Flanagan* and *Has Anybody Here Seen Kelly?* but those are just two of dozens and dozens of songs written especially about Douglas and the Island. No other seaside resort in Britain can boast of anything like this. Every night the bands and orchestras struck up for the dancing, for variety acts, for classical concerts and for some of the world's greatest singers. Douglas was known throughout Britain as presenting the best in entertainment, in launching new songs and dance tunes, and for setting the standards for the season's hits.

At the very centre of this, for nearly fifty years, was a short, plump, jovial man, with rounded spectacles and a trim moustache, who conducted the orchestras, arranged endless songs and dance tunes and engaged the artists; someone who could genuinely be called Manxland's King of Music.

His name was Harry Wood.

His family came from Yorkshire, and although he wasn't born in the

Island he quickly adopted it as his home and spent almost his entire working life here, making an immeasurable contribution to Manx music.

Whilst his more famous brother, Haydn, became known throughout the world as a composer of light music - perhaps his most enduring song is *Roses of Picardy* - Harry carved his career out on the Island, starting as a violinist in the seasonal orchestras and eventually rising to be a conductor, impresario, composer, confidante of artistes and publishers alike, and as much a fixture of the Manx musical scene as any of the regular places of entertainment.

Although born in Essex, Maurice Powell lived for more than twenty years in Yorkshire, no more than thirty miles from Slaithwaite, the birth place of Harry Wood. He has devoted long hours to researching many aspects of Manx music and has hugely increased our knowledge of an aspect of Island culture that had long been forgotten. Maurice brings to life the extraordinary years when Douglas was thronged by trippers enjoying an endless variety of entertainment. Through his research we meet many of the characters that made an appearance in the Isle of Man and we learn about the genius at the centre of it all, Harry Wood.

One surprising aspect that comes to light is that, despite being at the absolute forefront of the entertainment world, presenting the latest songs and dances, Harry Wood also found time to dip into the rich seam of traditional Manx music. He wrote countless arrangements of Manx airs and composed whole shows based on Manx themes. At a time when the Island's traditional way of life might have seemed under threat from a huge influx of tourists, Harry made sure that Manx music, at least, was treasured and brought to as wide a pubic as possible.

This carefully researched and stylishly written book makes an important contribution to the field of Manx studies whilst, at the same time, being an extremely entertaining read.

Charles Guard
Onchan, August 2018

Introduction

A portly man of middle height and middle years strolls leisurely along Loch Promenade, Douglas, Isle of Man. The year is 1904, and it is just after twelve o'clock on a Monday morning on a warm day in the August of the third full summer season of the Edwardian age. The fresh air and sunshine come as a relief following the morning's two-hour rehearsal with the Palace Grand Orchestra and Miss Florrie Forde with her new song 'Down at the Old Bull and Bush'.

The promenade is crowded as the summer season is well and truly underway with holiday makers having arrived in force for their annual holidays. He pauses now and then, allowing occasional jostling groups of likely lads to surge past him. Parasol-carrying girls wait idly for the 'male' boats to disgorge fresh batches of keen, young would-be 'mashers', and the fruit and flower sellers move among the crowds competing with the stallholders in enticing the visitors to purchase their wares. More annoyingly, aggressive touts vie with each other to extort carriage fares from the visitors, and woe betide the visitor who fails to 'haggle' effectively or agree a fare before commencing their journey.

He listens abstractedly to a colourful group of minstrels and, in the distance, to an Italian organ grinder churning out an indistinct tune as well-dressed couple dashes across the promenade with a sing-song shout of 'Hi Kelly!' in an attempt to attract a carriage driver. He scans the thronged beach with its wheeled bathing machines, donkeys and Punch and Judy show which has attracted a small crowd of children. To his right in the far distance he can just make out the Jubilee Clock and the area around Victoria Pier and the Harbour Commissioner's Building. A steamer has docked, and another, maybe from Fleetwood or Liverpool, belching smoke, waits outside the harbour for its turn to dock and disembark its expectant visitors. To his left, at the foot of Onchan Head at the end of the recently developed Queen's Promenade with its Electric Tram terminus, he glimpses a sight he knows only too well, the imposing and recently re-furbished Derby Castle entertainment complex with its new Opera House. To his right, in the middle distance, dominating the promenade, is the new grand Palace Ballroom, his base of operations, re-opened just the year before after the fire of 1902. Towering above are the white castellated walls of the Falcon Cliff Hotel, next to which a Monstre Ballroom once stood where, sixteen years earlier as a young summer visitor, he had played his first violin solo in Douglas.

As he takes one last admiring glance at the impressive sweep of Douglas Bay, the relaxed hubbub of the chattering holiday makers intrudes upon his reverie. He recognises their accents, mainly from the northern industrial towns of England, Manchester and Liverpool, and yes, from his own home too, the districts in West Yorkshire around Huddersfield. Amiable and fascinating though their snatches of conversation are, his ear is tuned not so much to what they are saying, but to what they are whistling and humming, notably in the case of one group of Lancashire lasses singing lustily as, arms linked, they skip excitedly by. He jots down the titles of a few popular songs he recognises, and moving swiftly with short, purposeful strides along the Queen's Promenade, he crosses the busy thoroughfare and enters his home at number 1, Marathon Terrace.

He urgently searches in his extensive library for the music for the songs he has heard in order that they will be included in the week's dance programmes, arranged and inserted into his newest up-to-date lancers. His sisters – both accomplished musicians and honorary assistant librarians - will ensure that the orchestral parts will be inserted into the musicians' folders so that they will appear on their music stands for a second brief rehearsal later that week. On such a fine day, other 'spies' - music publishers or their emissaries - will also have been out and about among the crowds making a special note of the 'catches' or 'hits' of the season which would then be heard in many theatres all over England during the coming pantomime season.

~

Meet Harry Wood, one of the best-known and most popular figures in Douglas, known as 'Manxland's King of Music', a one-man musical power-house: composer, arranger, 'fixer', performer and teacher, overall musical director of the Palace & Derby Castle Company, and our guide though nearly fifty years of musical entertainment on the Isle of Man. It is through his diaries, recollections and reminiscences that I hope to recapture something of the energy and excitement of the golden age of holiday entertainment on 'The Leisure Isle'.

Although anything approaching a comprehensive study of the entertainment industry on the Island is beyond the scope of this book, Harry Wood was such an important figure that I shall be looking at the dancing programmes and the variety shows at the Falcon Cliff, the Marina

Pavilion, the Derby Castle and the Palace Ballroom and Coliseum – and, in passing, the plays, operas and operettas at the Gaiety and Grand Theatres - the Minstrel and Pierrot shows, the Sunday Sacred Concerts, Harry Wood's students' concerts, the Manx Music Festival, the Celtic concerts, the Homecomers' concerts and the outdoor entertainments on Douglas Head, at Belle Vue, Laxey Glen Gardens, Glen Helen and elsewhere.

~

Harry Wood first visited the Isle of Man in 1884 during a period of profound change, when the rise in tourism became a flood of holiday makers which contributed significantly to the Island's economy. He was at the forefront of everything that was new in popular dance music and song, and contributed enormously to the development and flowering of sacred and 'classical' concerts on the Island where the greatest artistes appeared: Clara Butt, Nellie Melba, Paul Robeson and John McCormack to name just a handful. He also played a significant part in helping to preserve, popularise and propagate traditional Manx music.

He was *the* major figure in the musical life of the Isle of Man from the late 1880s until just before the Second World War, when Douglas was known as 'the birthplace of popular song'. We shall see how Harry Wood, together with music publishers such as Bert Feldman and Francis, Day & Hunter, and huge variety artistes such as Florrie Forde, secured the Island's popularity by ensuring that the most up-to-date popular songs and dances were 'tried out' here every summer.

Harry's life encompasses the rise and flowering of that delightful and once again popular genre we know as British Light Music, a genre that his younger brother Haydn Wood was to contribute to so elegantly, particularly in his orchestral works based on traditional Manx melodies. He lived and worked through the full flowering of the music hall age; the rise of variety and revue; the hey-day of the waltz, schottische, polka and lancers and the coming of the jazz age and the new dance crazes, the fox-trot and tango, the one-step and the two-step; the peak of the silent film era and the rapid advance of the 'talkies'.

~

Harry Wood's musical contemporaries included Edward German; Lionel Monckton, the composer of the popular Edwardian musical, *The Arcadians*; and Leslie Stuart, the composer of the popular song, *The Lily of Laguna*, and

Scott Joplin. Of greater significance were Elgar, Vaughan Williams, Granville Bantock, Rachmaninov and Hamish McCunn, the composer of the popular tone-poem *The Land of the Mountain and the Flood.*

His other close contemporaries included Tsar Nicholas II; Marie Dressler, theatre and film actress; Scott Joplin, pianist and composer of piano Rags; Amelia Earhart, aviatrix; Robert Falcon Scott, of the Antarctic; Vittorio Monti, the composer of the famous *Csárdás* for violin; Patty Hill Smith, the composer of 'Happy Birthday'; and Charles Rennie Mackintosh, architect, illustrator and designer. The year of his birth also witnessed the serialization of Wilkie Collins' *The Moonstone*; the premiers of Offenbach's *La Belle Hélène*, Brahms' *Requiem*, Wagner's *Die Meistersinger*, Grieg's piano concerto and Bruch's first violin concerto; and the opening of the Gaiety Theatre in London's West End with a burlesque on Meyerbeer's gothic shocker *Robert the Devil*, entitled *The Nun, the Dun and the Son of a Gun*, a variety of lampooning musical extravaganza that Harry Wood would become all too familiar with. Benjamin Disraeli became Prime Minister for the second time.

The death of Harry Wood on Christmas Day 1938, the start of WWII less than a year later and the death of Florrie Forde in 1940, were events that signalled the end of an era. Tourism picked up again after the war with some 168,000 visitors coming to the Island even in 1945, and by 1947 visitor numbers had reached a very respectable 600,000. A new era in the story of entertainment on the Isle of Man had dawned, with new music and new men; but that, as they say, is another story.

~

Beyond the musical directors, the great variety and concert artistes and the managers of the grand entertainment venues, the heroes and heroines of this story are the Manx people themselves. For as Arthur Quayle Moore, the theatre correspondent of the *Mona's Herald* perceptively wrote in 1933:

> Anyone who spends most of his time among amusement-seekers from various parts of the British Isles, must come to the conclusion that Manx people are the severest critics to be found anywhere. When it comes to the criticising of a concert the opinions heard are usually sound, for no one will deny the Manxman his knowledge of, or instinct for, what is good, bad or indifferent in music.

Acknowledgements

In the writing of this book I have been fortunate to benefit from the help, advice and encouragement of a number of friends, musical colleagues and enthusiasts for the Island's entertainment history, who showed great interest in the project from the earliest days of my researches. My very special thanks must go to the following:

Miles Cowsill of Lily Publications, whose experience, advice and encouragement smoothed the path to publication. He also generously granted me access to the Keig Collection of photographs of the Island.

Charles Guard, historian, composer, film-maker and friend who was ever ready to offer advice and encouragement and freely let me draw on his knowledge of Manx social, political and cultural history. Charles undertook the exacting role of laying out the book, sympathetic and meticulous editor-in-chief, and generously wrote the Foreword.

The Staff of Manx National Heritage and the Manx Museum, and the staff of the Public Records Office. I am grateful for the help and courtesy of the staff of both institutions, upon whose resources I have been happily reliant throughout.

The publication of this book has been supported by Culture Vannin, and I wish to further convey my thanks to their staff, principally the Director, Dr Breesha Maddrell and Dr Chloë Woolley, the Manx Music Development Officer, who were unfailingly encouraging and patiently dealt with my many enquiries, particularly those concerning both Harry and Haydn Wood's important engagement with traditional Manx music.

Sue Woolley, for nearly thirty years the northern news reporter for the Isle of Man Times, local historian and folklorist, scrupulously proof-read each chapter as it appeared, and the entire book when completed, and offered a wealth of stimulating ideas and insights too numerous to mention. More to the point, she kept me focused on the central story of Harry Wood's career when I would happily have wandered down the many enticing byways of the period.

Caron Harrison, author and friend, whose keen editorial eye and strict adherence to the rules and intricacies of English grammar contributed to making my sometimes wayward style more intelligible.

Sheila Powell, whose constant support, patience and enthusiasm for the book helped to clarify many issues in the story, and thus played an important role in seeing it through to fruition.

Marjorie Cullerne, curator and custodian of the Haydn Wood Music Library and Archive, Victoria, Vancouver Island, BC, Canada, the most important collection of surviving material concerning the Wood family, which she freely made available to me during a delightful three-week stay at her home in 2015.

My heartfelt gratitude to you all, and to many others who were kind enough to take an interest in my endeavours. Needless to say, all factual errors and omissions are entirely my own.

Maurice Powell,
Ramsey, August 2018.

Picture Acknowledgements

The author wishes to acknowledge the generosity of the following libraries, archives and private collectors for permission to use images, photographs and other illustrations:

The Haydn Wood Music Library and Archive (HWMLA), by kind permission of the founder, custodian and archivist Marjorie Cullerne: Frontispiece, p. 2, 3, 4, 32, 43, 50, 52, 69, 79, 91, 95, 116, 117, 146, 148, 150, 158, 165, 173, 175, 187, 203, 205, 206, 226, 227, 235, 242, 258, 278, 279, 285, 287, 295.

The Keig Collection by kind permission of Miles Cowsill, Lily Publications: p.11, 15, 29, 30, 77, 103, 133, 137, 139, 144, 182, 209, 219, 261.

The Midwood collection by kind permission of Les Clarke: P. 26, 92, 214, 248.

Manx National Heritage Photographic Archive: P. 18, 21, 46, 57, 63, 108, 123, 124, 199, 208, 244, 263, 303.

The Victoria and Albert Museum, London: P. 119, 159, 237,

Many images, taken from old newspapers and magazines, or photographs whose origin is unknown, were sadly in poor condition. Blemishes caused by the ravages of time have as far as possible been removed, and the images enlarged or reduced in size specially for this book. All other images and photographs are either in the public domain, from the author's own collection of Victorian and Edwardian postcards, song sheets, posters and images of variety and concert artistes, or from private collectors who wish to remain anonymous.

Chapter 1

Beginnings in Yorkshire and the Isle of Man

1868-85

Harry Wood's first visit to Douglas, Isle of Man, was recorded in a terse entry in his engagements diary on 14th July 1884: 'Went to the Isle of Man on a visit'.

A visitor from Ireland who spent five days on the Island at that time described Douglas as 'gay and fashionable'. The writer was enchanted by 'the loveliness of the bay, the semi-circular sweep of sand and shingle, the lofty boarding houses', and the surrounding 'crescent of mountains'. He was captivated by the Derby Castle 'with its lovely grounds lit by long lines of coloured lanterns', and believed that when lit up by the rising sun the bay 'could be compared to the Bay of Naples'.

Harry's Douglas debut as a young concert violinist took place during the afternoon of 18th July, 1884, and was recorded in a second brief entry in his engagements diary: 'Played at a concert at Falcon Cliff, Douglas. I played a solo, Delphin Alard's *Fantasia on Un Ballo in Maschera*'.

The following day the *Isle of Man Times* reported that there had been 'several solos by members of the band', although Harry's contribution was not singled out for special mention. It was the inauspicious first step towards a fifty year career on the Island as a violinist, violin teacher, orchestral leader and ultimately musical director of the most enduring and successful entertainment company on the Island, the Palace & Derby Castle Company.

~

Harry Wood was born at the Lewisham Hotel,[1] Slaithwaite, near Huddersfield, West Yorkshire, on 20th October, 1868, and was baptised on 15th November. He was the fifth child of Clement and Sabra Wood, his elder brother, John William[2] having been born in 1857, and eldest sister, Mary Hannah,[3] in 1862. An un-named son was stillborn in 1865, and another son, George, born in 1867, survived only three years.

Known locally as 'Slawit, 'Slowit' or 'Slathwaite', Slaithwaite[4] today is a quiet, thriving post-industrial town of some 5,000 people - described in one current guide as 'a true Yorkshire grit mill town' - and lies within the Metropolitan Borough of Kirklees in the valley of the river Colne.

The Lewisham Hotel, Slaithwaite.

Historically part of the West Riding of Yorkshire and formerly part of the Earl of Dartmouth's estates, the town is straddled by a railway viaduct, and bisected by a canal[5] and the river Colne, both of which run in parallel through the town.

At the time of Harry Wood's birth, Slaithwaite was more of an industrial village than an industrial town, though even by the 1820s there were several large cotton mills and woollen factories which employed a considerable number of people. In *Slaithwaite Notes of the Past and Present*,[6] John Sugden compared Slaithwaite in the mid-nineteenth century very favourably with the neighbouring villages of Marsden, Golcar and Linthwaite, and stated that:

> this neighbourhood has always been noted for its devotion to this pleasing art (music), both vocal and instrumental.

~

Slaithwaite in the 1880s.

Clement Wood.

Sabra Wood.

Harry's father, Clement, born in 1833, was the third child of John Wood, born around 1800, and Sophia Schofield, born in 1804. Sophia was the daughter of John Schofield of the Harp Inn, Slaithwaite, of whom we shall hear much more shortly, and Betty Beevor. Harry's mother, Sabra Sykes, born 21st June, 1836 at the Old Hall, Slaithwaite, was the daughter of Daniel Sykes (born in 1797), a Slaithwaite cotton twister, and a farmer of land rented from Lord Dartmouth,[7] and Elizabeth 'Betty' Clay, a bread baker and cotton piecer.[8] Her name, Sabra, pronounced 'Saybrah', was very rare in England before the 1930s, and may derive from a Hebrew name meaning 'to rest', or an older Arabic name meaning 'patience'. Harry was proud of his forebears, whom he described as 'farmers, mill owners and publicans', and retained a strong life-long affection for the town of his birth.

Slaithwaite band outside the Harp Inn.

Music at the Harp Inn

Beyond their names, little is known of Harry's grandparents, John and Sophia Wood, but his maternal great-grandfather, John Schofield,[9] was a very well-known and respected local figure. He was the celebrated first landlord of the well-known Harp Inn opposite the Parish Church, where he was the unpaid organist for over 50 years.

John Sugden refers to him thus:

> . . . Mr Schofield of the Harp Inn . . . stands out boldest in that far-distant time as one of the most eminent men in the neighbourhood, possessing such influence as to bring all the musical celebrities of the period to the large room at the Harp Inn for rehearsals, reunions etc.

Among the most notable musical artistes that appeared in the upper room at the Harp Inn early in her career before she became renowned throughout the north of England, was the famous Yorkshire soprano, Mrs Sunderland.[10] Sugden paid her the following tribute:

> The Yorkshire 'Queen of Song' . . . then Miss Sykes, the most promising girl of the period, with a natural talent far above the average, a perseverance irresistible, and a modesty characteristic of her genius. Miss Sykes (later Mrs Sunderland) was always welcome at the Harp Inn, and, no matter whether as a visitor or vocalist, she was always the most favoured artist that ever entered the town, and most appreciated.

John Schofield was also the founder, in 1819, of the first reed band in

Slaithwaite, the precursor of the later Slaithwaite Brass and Reed Band which rehearsed in the upper room at the Harp Inn 'under the laithe and mistal', and 'played jolly old songs with the villagers with jugs of ale'. Harry recalled as a child finding some six-keyed flutes, a yellowing clarinet and a valveless trumpet that belonged to the old band, which eventually found their way from the Harp Inn to a cupboard 'in the top room at the Lewisham Hotel', 'which we boys soon discovered and played around with'. Some of the concerts at the Harp Inn were larger in scale. Harry Wood maintained that his younger brother Haydn was given his illustrious name because Clement Wood had attended a performance of Haydn's Creation at the inn just prior to his birth.[11]

The Woods of Slaithwaite.

Clement Wood's life before he became the landlord of the Lewisham Hotel can only be glimpsed through brief, sometimes conflicting references. He lived for a time with his grandparents at the Harp Inn, but moved to the Lewisham Hotel, Station Road, Slaithwaite in 1853 following the death at only 23 years of age of Humphrey Wood.[12] The 1861 census, however, describes him as a 'commercial clerk', living with his aunt, Maria Anne Schofield in Mallingfield. Clement Wood was an educated man, an amateur musician, and from 1862 acted as the First Clerk to the Local Board, drawing up wills for Slaithwaite residents. Earlier, he had worked either as a pupil-teacher, or trained as a school teacher, at the National School, and according to John Sykes,[13] he was 'a favourite with the scholars but not with the master'.

When Clement Wood married Sabra Sykes on 15th August, 1865, at the Huddersfield Registry Office, three of their children had already been born: John William, 1857, Mary Hannah, 1862 and a son, stillborn in November 1865. They settled in at the Lewisham Hotel, a thriving establishment with at least one room large enough to accommodate the various feasts, functions, gatherings and band practices that were part of the weekly merry-go-round. The 1871 census describes Clement as an 'Inn Keeper at the Lewisham Hotel', a licensed victualler and publican. It was there, in the upper room, that he presided over the practises of the very same band formed many years before by his grandfather at the Harp Inn.

~

The Wood's were an expanding family. We have briefly met Harry's brother John William, and his sister Mary Hannah, but eight more children would be born into the family: George, born in 1867 who died in 1870; Sophia, born in 1870; Daniel, born in 1873; Hubert, born in 1874, who survived less than six months; Elizabeth, born in 1876, who died in 1880, barely three years of age; Eliza Beevor – sometimes given as Beaver - known as Elise, born in 1878, who became an accomplished pianist and accompanist; Adeline, born in 1880; Haydn, born in 1882, the most famous and naturally gifted of the talented Wood family, and the youngest of them all, Tom, born in around 1883, who died in infancy.

Thus, of the thirteen children born to Clement and Sabra Wood, five died either shortly after birth, in infancy or before their childhood had barely begun. Yet behind these dark statistics Harry recalled years later that his parents were a happy couple. In his engagement diary Harry recorded that in addition to the family, there was at one time a live-in girl and possibly two female servants.

~

Harry's only surviving diary, his engagement diary,[14] though mainly recording his musical activities, does occasionally lift the veil on his family life. We learn that Clement Wood was a freemason, a founder of the Colne Valley Masonic Lodge whose meetings were held at the Lewisham Hotel, and that he owned some hay fields and a gig.

We also learn something of the local annual holidays such as the Colne Valley Wakes which traditionally took place in August, preceded by the Slaithwaite Feast,[15] thought to be an ancient tradition in honour of St. James, the patron saint of Slaithwaite Church. There were street attractions and local shop keepers' stalls selling 'treacle beer and parkin pigs with current eyes and penny muffins'. Barrel organs, hurdy-gurdies, merry-go-rounds, swing boats, monkeys and performing bears were in evidence to encourage people to spend their money locally instead of heading for the seaside resorts. We also learn that Harry was a cricket enthusiast; one of the earliest entries in his diary records 'a cricket club entertainment at the Slaithwaite National School'.

Young Harry enjoyed good health but could never have been described as having an athletic build, being a 'chubby' lad, not much given to taking part in local sporting activities or undertaking long energetic tramps over the surrounding moors. The earliest-known photograph of him, taken during his eighteenth year, already shows the portly, slightly heavy-jowled figure who would become one of the most recognisable personalities in the Isle of Man.

Musical Apprenticeship

Harry tells us in the second entry of his diary, that he had his proper first violin lesson with Sam Moore of Huddersfield in 1878, at the age of nine, and played in public for the first time two months later at the Holthead Sunday School Anniversary. He probably had some sort of violin tuition earlier, perhaps under his father's guidance, and from John Sugden, who appended an intriguing note to his reminiscences of a concert at the Palace, Douglas in 1903, in his book, Slawit in the Sixties, in which Harry, Daniel and Haydn Wood all took part: 'I was largely the means of Harry Wood being a fiddler . . . '

In 1881 or '82 Harry became a pupil of George Haddock of Leeds, one of the best-known and influential violin teachers in the north of England and a highly respected orchestral leader and conductor.[16] Harry's engagements diary records regular lessons with Haddock, sometimes in Leeds and sometimes in Bradford, up to the end of 1884, although some lessons were missed through illness, and on one occasion because he was helping his father with the haymaking.

In April 1882, Harry took part in what may have been George Haddock's first Annual Students' Orchestral Concert at the Church Institute, Bradford, with an orchestra of some fifty young string players, conducted by Haddock himself, during which Harry played a violin solo. These students' concerts may well have been the inspiration for Harry's own future annual students' concerts. The following year he was invited to play a solo at the students' concert, and contributed a spectacular Tarantella. The Bradford Observer noted that:

> Master Harry Wood of Slaithwaite followed with (a) violin solo . . . in which the instrumentalist not only displayed a wonderful power of execution but brought out a fine clear tone. He has greatly improved since last year, and ought to make his mark.

George Haddock clearly recognised Harry as a budding concert violinist, and gave him some of the most challenging solo violin pieces in the repertoire to study: Mendelssohn's violin concerto, the air varies of de Beriot, Paganini's *Carnival de Venice* and his Douglas calling card Delphin Alard's *Fantasia on Un Ballo in Maschera*. In September 1883 he first records taking formal music theory lessons with a Mr S. Backhausen in Huddersfield, and on 14th December, he notes that there was no violin lesson that day because of a Trinity College of Music theory examination which he passed with honours in the junior division.

Slaithwaite Spa Baths and Leisure Grounds.

Clement and Sabra Wood hosted many local events held at the Lewisham Hotel, and many of them featured music. It was at this time that Harry formed his own House Band, sometimes known as the Quadrille Band, consisting of three or four players, who regularly played at the hotel on Sunday evenings and provided music for many local events. One such event was recorded in the *Huddersfield Daily Chronicle* on 25th May, 1882: a supper, with several sittings, for around 300 people on the day of the annual opening of the Slaithwaite Spa Baths and Leisure Grounds.[17] After 'full justice being done to the good fare being provided by Mr Clement Wood', Harry's band played on the croquet lawn for guests to 'trip the light fantastic toe'. Harry was soon in demand as a popular local violin soloist and band leader and his diary increasingly mentions several 'minor engagements . . . mill parties and balls' without giving any details. On 15th October, 1882, there occurred a happy family event, namely the marriage of Harry's sister Mary Hannah to Francis Cullerne, which was followed on the 17th by a large celebration at the Paragon Hotel, Huddersfield.

The young orchestral leader in Operetta-land

In March 1882, the thirteen-year-old Harry's career took a significant step forward when he was engaged as a violinist at the Huddersfield Theatre Royal and Opera House for a modest run of an anti-Mormon idyll-drama, *The Danites*. The following week there were six performances of

Huddersfield Theatre Royal and Opera House.

Les Cloches de Corneville, (*The Chimes* or *Bells of Normandy*) Planquette's melodious and colourful opera comique, one of the most popular French operettas of all time. That year, Harry took part in no fewer than fifty-three performances of twenty different pantomimes, operettas, musical comedies and comic operas.

Theatre orchestras, whether permanently attached to a particular theatre, or ad-hoc, 'fit-up' bands recruited from local musicians, had to be versatile as the repertoire could range from a run of Gounod's opera *Faust* or a play by Shakespeare, Goldsmith or Sheridan, to an operetta by Offenbach or Gilbert and Sullivan, a burlesque or pantomime. From his position in the first violins Harry doubtless soaked up a myriad of impressions and took careful note of how subtle orchestral effects could be achieved with a moderate sized orchestra, and how to write appropriate incidental music. These skills would later be put to brilliant use with his own orchestras and productions in the Isle of Man.

~

In March 1883, Harry played five solo violin pieces at a promenade concert in Stockton-on-Tees, and was engaged as a violinist in an orchestra of some ten players for a short season. On July 9th, Harry received a telegram from J.W. White, Manager of the Theatre Royal and Opera House, Huddersfield, engaging him again to play in the theatre orchestra.

In his diary, he noted that at the first rehearsal for Planquette's new operetta *Rip van Winkle*, there was not enough room in the pit for all the players, so he sat in the stalls and carefully noted all the 'cuts' and other directions requested by the conductor in his violin part.

The engagement diary tells us that sometime in 1884, Harry, now almost 16, began teaching the violin with two local pupils, Sam Wild from Lewthwaite and John Cowgill from Marsden. A third pupil, Joseph Wood, received his second lesson. Early in May, two more pupils were taken on: a Miss A.J. Armitage[18] and Joseph Shaw. Later that month, Harry paid a bill to a local music shop for £1 8s 6d for 'two little bows, box of strings, instruction book and music stand', which indicates that some of his pupils were young children.

An interlude in Manxland

Harry did not record how his first brief excursion to the Isle of Man in 1884 came about, although a number of possibilities present themselves. His teacher George Haddock may have had a contact on the Island, but more likely the invitation to play a solo in the famous Falcon Cliff 'Monstre Pavilion' may have come via Sydney Ward, a conductor at the Theatre Royal, Huddersfield, whose brother, Edgar Ward, was the musical director at the Falcon Cliff Hotel and Pleasure Grounds.[19] It seems likely that at the age of fifteen he was accompanied by a family member, and his obituary in December, 1938, seems to confirm this: 'Harry Wood came to the Island as a boy with his father Clement Wood . . .' What is certain is that he caught the 1pm sailing from The Prince's Landing Stage, Liverpool, to Douglas, with a sailing time in fair weather of four-and-a-half hours.

A preview of the 1884 summer season in the *Isle of Man Times* announced that a 'splendid band' of some 12-15 musicians would be under the directorship of Mr Edgar Ward, 'who was so appreciated last year'. The Falcon Cliff orchestra, or 'band' as it was more commonly referred to, played for the afternoon promenade concerts, during which the doors of the huge pavilion would be opened in fine weather to enable the promenaders in the beautiful grounds to hear the music. The evening's entertainment opened with a demonstration of transformation dancing (whereby a dancer alters their image and character) by Le Petite Rosie, after which the band – 'the finest band out of London' - played for dancing until 11pm.

~

The Falcon Cliff Pavillion

Although Harry was already the veteran of many operettas, burlesques, plays and musical shows, it was the first time he had shared the concert platform with some of the biggest names in the world of variety entertainment. Among the artistes performing at the 'Cliff' that season was the Lancashire comedian Lester Barrett,[20] one of the most popular resident entertainers in Douglas at this time and for many years to come, and Bessie Bellwood,[21] 'Queen of the Halls', famous for her broad humour, 'rollicking' style and racy sketches. She often impersonated a factory girl, typically dressed in multi-coloured skirts, and sang the new song that launched her career, *Wotcher 'Ria*!

Elsewhere in Douglas, the repertoire would have had a very familiar feel: *Iolanthe* at the Grand Theatre; *Fun on the Bristol*, 'an American oddity', at the Gaiety Theatre followed by the 'outrageously funny' burlesque *Fra Diavolo*, a 'send up' of Auber's popular opera comique. The Derby Castle – the main competitor of the Falcon Cliff – presented dancing every night of the week, firework nights and variety acts, such as the daring child trick cyclists Lotto, Lilo and Otto; The Masonic Hall featured a minstrel show and the Victoria Baths presented an 'aquatic entertainment' during which Professor Bibbero – 'the Human Fish' – ate, drank, wrote and smoked under water. The dance sensation of the season was the new waltz *Endenia*, by the local composer and conductor F. C. Poulter, who would become one of Harry's closest colleagues.

A week later Harry was back in his seat in the orchestra pit of the Grand Theatre, Huddersfield, for a short run of the farce *The Little Vixen*, and rehearsing for the burlesque, *Queen of Arts*. On 25th July, he was in Leeds for a lesson with George Haddock, and no doubt embroiled in a post mortem of his recent performance of Alard's *Fantasia* in Douglas. Did he for one moment imagine that he would return to the Isle of Man the following year for a full summer season at the Falcon Cliff, let alone sense that he would spend the rest of his career in Douglas as the most popular musical director in the Island's history?

~

Harry was soon swept up in a relentless round of operas and operettas, burlesques and plays and local engagements, relieved on 20th October when he and Clement Wood both celebrated their birthdays: Harry was sixteen and his father was fifty-one. Inevitably perhaps, Harry's increasingly busy schedule caused a rift with the management of the Theatre Royal. Things began to come to a head in late October, a typically crowded and eventful period of tight schedules and local band engagements, when he occasionally had to rush to the Theatre Royal for the last act of the current play or operetta. He resigned from the Theatre Royal on 1st November, 1884, 'as Mr Liversedge the conductor would not let me leave the theatre for a night or so to attend concerts etc'. Harry clearly found it difficult to say 'no' when invited to play, particularly if the invitation was from a local organisation he had known all his life. This agreeable characteristic was one that would particularly endear him to the Manx public.

Harry did not remain without theatre work and local engagements for long, for on 20th December he received a telegram from J. Sydney Jones, the conductor at the Grand Theatre, Leeds, engaging him as a first violinist for a ten-week run of the pantomime *Bo Peep* with Wilson Barrett's Company.[22] Harry records that the show was 'a tremendous success', and that by the time it closed in early March 1885, the pantomime had been seen by over 100,000 people, many of whom had travelled by excursion train to witness it.

Harry returns to the Isle of Man

The year 1885 would be a momentous one in the fortunes of the Wood family, yet it started ordinarily enough. *Bo Peep* closed in Leeds in early March, and after bidding farewell to his band colleagues, Harry journeyed to Stockton-on-Tees to stay with a friend for a week, returning to Slaithwaite on 17th March in time to hear the great violinist Carrodus give a recital in the Town Hall, Huddersfield. His diary records a number of minor engagements with the house band during April and May, and he also noted that his father became Worshipful Master at his Masonic Lodge.

On 23rd May, 1885, the *Isle of Man Times* declared:

> TO-DAY we enter the threshold of the visiting season . . . Douglas is immensely popular as a watering-place, and its popularity . . . seems to be annually increasing.

Two day earlier, the seventeen-year-old Harry Wood left home at 9.30am by train for Liverpool and sailed to the Isle of Man where he had an engagement as leader and soloist of the large orchestra under the conductorship of Edgar Ward at the Falcon Cliff Castle.

There was great optimism about the coming season. The *Isle of Man Times* continued:

> Bathing and boating are unsurpassed, accommodation without rival in any summer resort of equal size. The Promenade with its long, graceful curve . . . is almost without parallel. The beauties of the Island are much appreciated during the day; in the evening the two principal attractions of the Falcon Cliff and the Derby Castle – despite never being a 'Winter Gardens' – offer a rare combination of the natural and the artistic. Douglas was never so capable of affording (such) varied and extensive accommodation and entertainment for all classes of visitors.

Lodging-house keepers were hoping for a bumper season and were endeavouring to under-cut each other in fierce competition. All-in-all, the annual 'feverish expectation' could be felt all over the Island. No-one, it seemed, had taken any heed of the cautionary words expressed by an *Isle of Man Examiner* reporter the previous June:

> . . . the town – the entire country – is far too dependent on the results of the season . . . too much is at stake for all eggs to be in one basket.
>
> If the Island ever lost its reputation as a pleasant watering-hole, he warned, both town and country would lose and suffer a loss of prosperity 'and would sink into a worse poverty than fell upon them on the collapse of the great smuggling trade of the last century'.

Tens of thousands of eager pleasure-seekers from Lancashire,

Yorkshire and Cheshire headed for the Island and upon arrival were 'startled by the loveliness of the bay', which when lit up 'with electricity at night', presented a panorama unequalled in many visitors' experience. The entertainment to be enjoyed at the Falcon Cliff and the Derby Castle included afternoon concerts, familiar variety artists from the North of England, and dancing every evening.

Visitors were warned about the 'menace' of the Douglas 'car' (carriage) drivers and their aggressive touting for hire. A correspondent from the *Warrington Guardian* advised holiday-makers to 'walk as much as possible' so as to avoid the 'extortions of the car drivers', whose object seemed to be - in modern parlance- to 'rip-off the punter'. Some hotels were highly praised and commended: the Peveril, the Villiers and the Athol where 'attention and civility' went hand-in hand with 'good value, even for the slenderest purse'.

Douglas was beginning to assert its position as an up-and-coming health and entertainment resort, the equal of many in England. If only the visitors 'of the better classes' could be encouraged to come to the Island during the months of May and June, when the late spring and early summer weather brought out 'all its traditionary verdure and beauty'.

The Douglas entertainment venues in 1885

There are very few photographs of the Falcon Cliff Hotel and Pleasure Grounds and the 'Monstre' Dance Pavilion, and none of the interior. The white, castellated hotel and huge pavilion dominated the Douglas skyline – the promenades were as yet undeveloped – in a way that the Derby Castle complex, 'The Hall by the Sea', and the later Palace and Coliseum, despite their imposing grandeur and beautiful grounds and gardens, never could.

The history of the Falcon Cliff complex is confusing, and along with the Derby Castle, the Castle Mona Palace and the other entertainment venues on the Island, has yet to be fully explored. We first hear of the Falcon Cliff – originally a local bank manager's private residence - as an entertainment venue from an announcement in *Mona's Herald* in February 1877, that states that the 'Falcon Cliff is about to be converted into a Hotel and Recreation Ground'. The same newspaper reported further developments in April, when a new 'running path' was to be opened by a Grand Athletic Festival on Whit-Tuesday. 'A first class band will be engaged for the occasion'.

There is no mention at this early date of a pavilion or dance hall so if

The Palace Ballroom.

dancing took place at the Falcon Cliff at this early date, then it may have been accommodated on some sort of outdoor dance floor, or in a marquee, such as the Monstre Marquee, referred to in *Mona's Herald* in a reminiscence in 1882, which apparently held three thousand dancers. We next hear of the Falcon Cliff Castle Hotel and Pleasure Grounds Company Limited, in the *Manx Sun* in August 1883, when a Grand Opening Gala and Fête Day was advertised for Bank Holiday Monday. The Monstre Pavilion was mentioned for the first time, together with billiard rooms in the hotel, concerts, dancing and fireworks all 'at people's prices' during the day and evening. The Pavilion itself was a glass, iron and wooden building of enormous proportions, with a dancing area of 7,000 square feet, a large stage, balcony and two bars. The stage fittings were said to 'rank in excellence with many provincial theatres', and the scenery, 'worthy of any stage in the Kingdom'. Glazed throughout with tinted glass, and illuminated by gas jets, the building was also light and airy.

~

The invitation to join the Falcon Cliff band for the 1885 summer season could have been issued when Harry was on the Island the previous

July. However, he makes no mention of such an exciting offer in his diary, so it is more likely that the offer came as late as March. The season began inauspiciously, as his diary entry for 22nd May confirms: '8.00pm rehearsal cancelled as some players missed the boat!'

The orchestra that Harry was to lead consisted of twenty-two musicians and was essentially a typical theatre band of the type familiar to him in Yorkshire. The *Isle of Man Times'* season preview described Edgar Ward's Falcon Cliff Band in the following glowing terms:

> . . . the Champion Band of the Island . . . and has greatly improved upon their performances of last year, both in their selections and when playing for dancing. Mr Ward has a number of clever instrumentalists under his control and there is no doubt that the band will be one of the best on the Island after a few weeks work. 'A very great number of people attend the concerts here'.

Harry's first full day with the Falcon Cliff band was 23rd May, and a routine for the summer was quickly established: afternoon concerts from 3–5pm; playing for dancing in the evenings from 7.45 until 10.45pm. The popular afternoon concerts were said to be 'of high merit', and featured good instrumentalists and singers, although according to one observer, they were not always well-patronised other than by 'ladies who clearly considered music merely as an adjunct to incessant knitting'. In an article in the *Isle of Man Times* towards the end of his career Harry recollected that for the evening dances 'there was no Master of Ceremonies . . the musical director would take requests from the dance floor and rang the changes between the popular dances of the season'. The players would have to have been 'on their toes' to quickly find the music for each request from a large stock of pieces on their music stands.

At the next afternoon concert he played two solos, de Beriot's *11th Air varie* and Paganini's Variations on a *Carnival of Venice*. The format of the first day was repeated on 26th and 27th, but on 28th : '. . . there were some sports held at the Falcon Cliff grounds . . . and our orchestra played out in the open air. The sports went off splendidly. After they were over we adjourned to the Pavilion and I had to play a solo, I got very loudly encored. Played for dancing at night . . .' This familiar pattern of afternoon concerts and evening dancing resumed on 29th, and on 30th he made the following entry in his diary: '. . . received my (first) wage from Mr Edgar Ward, the conductor. Played for dancing at night'.

Variety artists and concert artistes appeared during the afternoons and evenings, and Harry mentions some of the most popular ones in his diary. The Yorkshire humorist G. W. Nicholson was in residence and entertained the audiences with his new song *Those Girls at the School at the End of the Street*, and with his impersonation of a working class Lancashire lad. 'A clever man at his business' reported the *Manx Sun*. The celebrated tenor, J. B. Saunderson, appeared at the afternoon concerts, and 'was very much appreciated'. There were, of course, some breaks in the routine such as rest days, excursions around the Island, visits to new friends, visits from family and occasional concerts and impromptu rehearsals away from the Pavilion.

Harry Wood's Engagements Diary

Harry's diary entries are nearly all brief and to the point. He was, of course, still a teenage lad, albeit an extremely talented one, not a budding diarist of distinction, and was writing neither for posterity nor for publication. Although his entries were intended to be little more than *aides memoire*, one wishes he had been more expansive, and left us more details of the concerts he took part in, the musical director Edgar Ward, and first-hand impressions of artistes such as G. H. Snazelle,[23] a popular baritone, raconteur and all-round entertainer with an international reputation as a showman; John Sims Reeve, whom Harry describes as 'the greatest living tenor', nearing the end of his career, but still a hugely influential artist and one of the foremost singers of the mid-Victorian age; Edward de Jong,[24] the Manchester flute virtuoso and conductor, whose career would also become part of the Island's cultural story; and many other lesser-known performers, mostly forgotten now.

I have selected just a few of the more interesting entries in order to give a flavour of Harry Wood's life on the Isle of Man during his first summer season:

> **2nd June:** Mr de Jong a very celebrated flautist, who is conductor of a large orchestra in Manchester, came to the Falcon Cliff and would have me play a solo. I did so and pleased him very much.
>
> **7th June**: Had a beautiful drive to Glen Helen along with Mr Smyth, Mr Alfred Bray and son, of Meltham, and Mr John Varley of Slaithwaite. He told me my father and mother, and all my brothers and sisters were in good health.

As far as is known, these were the first of Harry's Yorkshire friends to

George H Wood.

visit him in Douglas.

> **Sunday 14th June**: Went to church in the morning, and in the afternoon had tea with Mr (G. H.) Wood, Manager of the Isle of Man Railway Company. One of his daughters plays the piano very well. We played a number of solos together. I enjoyed myself very well. I am liking the Isle of Man very well indeed. It is such a beautiful place.
>
> **Sunday 21st June**: Went to church in the morning. At night, Mr Ward our conductor, Mr Armstrong, our second-violinist, Mr Reid, violoncello and myself practised Beethoven's quartets at the house of the former. We had a very good practice.
>
> **Sunday 28th June**: Six of our band men had a little boat and we had a row to Port Skillion adjoining Douglas. Some of them had a bathe.

Douglas Head, with access from rowing boats, small harbour ferries, an incline railway, the Douglas Head Hotel, Minstrel and other concert parties, light house and the Marine Drive tramway, was a favourite area for holiday-makers, and Port Skillion became a popular bathing creek.

> **30th June:** Played de Beriot's 5th Air varie as solo. My sister Mary Hannah accompanied me on the piano.

Tynwald Day, 5th July was a holiday, and his mother, sisters Mary Hannah, Sophia, Elise and Adeline, and 'my little brother Haydn' were on the Island and enjoying the lovely weather.

> **Sunday 12th July:** . . . a beautiful walk with mother and the children.

> **14th July:** Played de Beriot's 1st concerto with band accompaniment at the daily concert.

The family returned to Yorkshire on 15th July. Harry played the de Beriot concerto again on 17th, and on Sunday 19th the orchestra played 'Farmer's celebrated Mass in Bb at the Catholic Chapel', an immensely popular sacred work that was performed on several occasions before the end of the summer. Edgar Ward and the Falcon Cliff orchestra clearly enjoyed a close relationship with the Catholic Church in Douglas for on Sunday 20th September the orchestra joined the church choir for a performance of a Mozart mass.

> **Sunday 26th July:** A very great number of people have attended the Falcon Cliff so far . . . it is the most popular place of entertainment in the Isle of Man.

> **1st August:** About 3000 people at 1/- each passed the turnstiles . . .

As the hotel and boarding house keepers of Douglas had hoped, 1885 was turning out to be an exceptional year for visitors.

'I am liking the Isle of Man very much'.

The summer season had reached its peak, but there were still many interesting concerts and excursions to report on:

> **Sunday 2nd August:** Our band gave a Sacred Concert on the Iron Pier. It was very successful. We are going to continue giving them. A very great number of people attend the concerts here, as they are very good.

> **3rd August:** We had splendid bicycle races at the Falcon Cliff course today . . . there was some splendid racing (foot racing or athletics) . . . the champions of the world were running. During the races our band were playing in the concert in the Pavilion and we played at

night for dancing. Over 7000 passed the turnstiles.

The following day was wet, and the sports were cancelled. Edward de Jong brought a concert party to the Falcon Cliff on 5th August, which Harry referred to as 'the main day of season'. The 6th, though, was 'a beautiful day', and the band played in the grounds for the bicycle races.

De Jong's group performed again on 7th August, and on Sunday 9th, the sacred concert at the Iron Pier featured an excerpt from Rossini's *Stabat Mater* during which Harry played a violin solo. 'I arranged the accompaniment for band myself', he proudly added.

~

Sabra and Clement Wood visited the Island for the second time from 14th - 28th August. On this occasion they were accompanied by Harry's younger brother Daniel, twelve years of age and already a talented flautist, who played a piccolo solo, *The Blue Bells of Scotland* before a very large audience at a Falcon Cliff afternoon concert.

> **25th August:** Eleven of our band set out . . . at 7am for Ramsey in a wagonette to give a concert at the pier (The Queen's Pier). We had a splendid drive. In fact it is considered the nicest drive on the Isle of Man. There is some splendid scenery on the route.

On 31st August five hundred people attended the races at the Falcon Cliff course and on 4th September G.H. Snazelle gave his final concert of the season, his benefit evening. Harry performed the favourite showpiece, Alard's Fantasia on themes from *Un Ballo in Maschera* on the 10th, the piece he played at his Falcon Cliff debut the previous year. The musical director Edgar Ward paid the band their wages which included an extra amount for four concerts at the Catholic Church.

On 13th September Harry had tea and supper with G. H. Wood and his family, and on the 17th, the band enjoyed a 'splendid' supper which concluded with a presentation of a decorative baton to Edgar Ward.

The benefit night for the Manager of the Falcon Cliff, Mr Stokes, took place on 22nd September. The last night of the season was the 26th, and on the 28th a benefit concert for Edgar Ward took place. Harry noted: 'I was very successful with my solos'.

Over forty years later, in 1927, the Douglas-born tenor William Kewley reminisced in the *Examiner* about his nearly sixty years as a local chorister and soloist. He recalled the Falcon Cliff during Edgar Ward's time there as musical director, and his 1885 benefit concert at the Grand Theatre, and

The earliest known photograph of Harry Wood shows him standing at end of the back row of Frank Heslop's orchestra holding his violin.

noted that 'Master Harry Wood, solo violin' took part.

The final entry in Harry Wood's engagements diary was on 30th September: 'Came home from the Isle of Man, all our family very well at home'.

~

At some stage during the Wood family's summer visits, a momentous decision was arrived at, for Clement and Sabra decided to move permanently to the Isle of Man. How this decision came about Harry does not reveal in his diary, nor do we find out in subsequent diary entries, family correspondence or even Harry's own later recollections of his years on the Island. Whatever the circumstances, at some point during the summer of 1885, the idea of moving to the Isle of Man took hold and became a reality. Clement and Sabra could see that Harry was making a name for himself even during his first full season, and that there were many opportunities on the Island for playing engagements, and probably teaching, even after the close of the season. Perhaps Clement had been quietly investigating the opportunities on the Island for an experienced publican and hotel owner, particularly one who was anticipating taking things a little easier in a less hectic environment, and in a beautiful location.

Chapter 2

'Cometh the hour, cometh the man'[1]

1886-91

At this distance in time the precise course of events during the weeks and months following Harry Wood's return from the Isle of Man in September 1885 can only be guessed at. However, in an article in the *Isle of Man Times* from September 1931, he recalled that before his appointment at the Falcon Cliff in the summer of 1886, he was engaged as the leader and musical director of La Comedie Anglais, Maggie Morton's famous theatrical touring company, and toured throughout England, Wales and Ireland with a wide variety of plays ranging from Shakespeare to light comedies and pantomimes. This engagement is confirmed by Sykes:[2]

> During the winter of 1885, he went on tour in Ireland and Wales as solo violinist and leader of the orchestra, with Miss Maggie Morton's La Comedie Anglais Company afterwards returning to Douglas, wither his parents had in the meantime moved.

A letter preserved in the Victoria and Albert Museum Theatres Collection from 1883 reveals that Maggie Morton was the actor-manager of the company that bore her name, that the company enjoyed a reputation 'from Land's End to John O'Groats' and was in its fifth uninterrupted year of the Grand Pantomime *Robinson Crusoe*. Harry fondly remembered his time in Ireland, with performances in Dublin, Belfast, Cork, Londonderry, Killarney, Waterford, Limerick and Wexford, and in a later, undated newspaper cutting, referred to this period as his 'holiday in Dear Ould Ireland'.

During this period Harry was still living at the Lewisham Hotel in Slaithwaite - now under the management of his sister Mary Hannah and her husband Francis Cullerne - between engagements and tours. We do not know the exact date when Clement and Sabra Wood moved to the Isle of Man, but the evidence of two letters is suggestive. The first is from Sydney Jones at the Grand Theatre, Leeds to Clement Wood:

> Xmas, 1885.
> Dear Sir
> May I depend on your son for the pantomime to commence on Monday December 21st. Yours truly

The second, again undated, from Clement Wood to Harry, presumably a day-or-so later:

> My Dear Son
> This has just come by post from Mr Jones rather it was past (*sic*) on from the Lewisham. I think it will be best for you to reply to it yourself as you will best know your wishes and intentions. Write to him immediately . . .
> Your affectionate father

These letters seem to suggest that Harry's parents were in Douglas before Christmas 1885, presumably looking for another hotel or public house to take on, but does not confirm that they were permanently residing there at that time. Both of the above letters have boat and train times to the Island and partial lists of clothing pencilled in the margins, which may suggest that Clement and Sabra made a series of exploratory journeys to the Island. It is not known whether Harry played under Sydney Jones for the Leeds pantomime that winter as there are no further engagement diaries extant. Sometime during this period of upheaval, though, he found time to take his final violin examination, and gained maximum marks.

'Our little Manx nation'.

What was the Isle of Man like in 1886, and what was it about the Island that so attracted Clement and Sabra Wood, that they chose to move there, leaving a flourishing hotel, family and friends behind in Slaithwaite? By the mid-1880s there was much for the islanders to be proud of in the midst of a period of unprecedented growth, expansion and prosperity after years of slow growth in the principal industries of fishing, agriculture and mining. Arguably the single most important improvement to the Island's infrastructure was the development of the harbours and piers, and the consequent expansion of the Steam Packet services which fuelled a burgeoning tourist new industry that would – during the summer months at least – transform the Island's economy and herald a number of significant social and cultural changes. Douglas was thriving (347,968 visitors came to the Island in 1887), its population was steadily growing and would constitute 30% of the Island's total population by the end of the decade.

The Lieutenant Governor, Sir Spencer Walpole,[3] was a highly popular and well-respected figure and 'one of the ablest rulers the Island has ever experienced'. He was also a first-rate administrator and financier, whose eleven years in office witnessed important measures to reduce public debt and improvements in education and local government. The future looked promising as the vigorous Victorian spring of the Island's entertainment era headed relentlessly towards its Edwardian high summer!

There were of course negative aspects to these generally positive changes in the Island's fortunes. Once considered a genteel watering place favoured by the 'higher class' traveller seeking to embrace the comparative solitude of the Island, the wild romantic scenery and the quaint customs and folklore, the changes in the character of Douglas in particular, annually besieged by hordes of pleasure-seeking summer 'trippers' from the northern industrial towns, became a cause for concern. It was even suggested that the development of the pleasure grounds at the Falcon Cliff and Derby Castle was to blame for bringing a 'lower class' of visitor to the Island, principally textile workers, all of them determined to get the most out of their week's holiday.

There was also more considered disquiet expressed, in that by adapting so eagerly to rapid economic and social changes, the Island was becoming too dependent on the ten-week holiday season. These were precisely the same sentiments - 'too many eggs in one basket' - expressed in 1885, but there were other genuine, deeply-felt reservations and fears for the future of the soul of the Island, summed up most eloquently by perhaps Manxland's greatest author, Hall Caine:[4]

It has become too English of late. The change has been sudden . . . God forbid that I should grudge the factory hand his breath of the sea and glimpse of gorse-bushes; but I know what price we are paying that we may entertain him.[11]

Disenchantment with the behaviour of the crowds in Douglas in particular was not new. As early as 1877 the Loch Promenade was described as:

> a place of assemblage for itinerant characters of all kinds and practices . . . street preachers, German Bands, songsters, touters for boats, tract distributors and various other sources of annoyance have it in full force for the discomfort chiefly of our visitors, by their impudent importunities or disgusting or disgraceful noises or remarks.

'Vaterland hear it. I make zee Manxman and ze forinjeer to fly'.[5]

From this distance in time, it may seem that the nuisance caused principally by German bands on the promenades and in the streets of Douglas, is hardly an issue serious enough to devote many words to, but

A German band in Ramsey.

in fact, German bands, together with minstrel groups, hurdy-gurdy players and organ-grinders were a persistent source of annoyance to residents and visitors alike for many years. Referred to disparagingly in local newspapers as 'travelling musicians' or 'mendicants' (beggars) and 'their brother professors with the dark faces', their presence on the Island was often questioned, particularly as visiting English bands were always welcome and much appreciated.

The bands in question were not the small, colourful Tyrolean oompah bands beloved of picturesque Bavarian villages today, but rather, scruffily attired groups of itinerant musicians, well-integrated into the world of Britain's wandering street performers. Like dreadful harbingers of the summer season to come, they descended upon the town in May well before Whit-week, and from early morning until late at night, punctuated the holiday atmosphere of Douglas with their incessant noise. The musicians were often second-rate in quality and often the remnants of minor theatre bands. Their performances consisted of poorly played, raucous and out-of-

Italian organ grinder.

tune renderings of *Der Wacht am Rhein, Hi! Kelly, The Death of Nelson* and even the *Hallelujah* chorus! The pestered and deafened visitors and Douglas residents had much to grumble at.

It was not just the German Bands that destroyed the peace of the promenades, as 'Spex' in the *Isle of Man Times* observed in 1885:

> We are stormed by the rabble from Germany with reeds and brass, the canaille of France with catgut and accordions, and the lazaroni of Italy with poisoned ice creams and hokey pokey.[6] Is there no relief, no calm secluded spot about town to escape from the maddening din?' "From early morn to dewy eve", and far into the night, goes the vile brassy competition of rival bands . . . '

Handle-turning Italian piano organists - street organ-grinders and hurdy-gurdy players - 'the greasy grinders' as they were sometimes referred to, were second only to the German bands in nuisance-value, and were memorably numbered among Ko-Ko's potential victims in *The Mikado*: '... the piano-organist, I've got him on the list'.

Although Douglas Town Commissioners' Promenades Committee received several letters each season from groups requesting permission to perform in the town, the itinerant bands seldom sought such permission and the Commissioners had no power to remove nuisance groups, unless they caused an obstruction or an individual householder complained of the noise.` However, in 1894 some sort of order was imposed and a measure of 'peace and solemnity' restored to the streets and promenades as a new law requiring street performers to obtain a licence came into force. Harry left no impressions of street entertainments in Douglas during the 1880s and '90s although he probably recalled the ragged groups of German musicians that could be heard in the Colne Valley of his youth, setting up in competition with his father's Slaithwaite band.

'A propensity for drunkenness'.

Sometime in April 1886 Clement Wood was granted the licence of the Black Lion Hotel,[7] on the North Quay, Douglas, after 'the most satisfactory certificates of character from Huddersfield and elsewhere in the applicant's favour' had been produced. The Black Lion was situated on the site of the present day St. Matthew's Church on the corner of Ridgeway Street, not far from the British Hotel, where Crooked Lane - one of a maze of dark, narrow, ill-paved thoroughfares described in Henry Hanby Hay's poem *One by the Sea-Boy* as 'a dozen cart-wide, elbow-bending lanes' - once emerged onto North Quay. It was a large, three-storey structure, whose upper two floors had five windows each, and over whose front entrance was a large gas lamp.

The inner harbour was very much the working commercial end of the quay, and old photographs show two-and three-masted coasters and schooners unloading tanned hides, bricks, timber from the Baltic and beer, or loading coal onto horse-drawn carts or into the warehouses, many of which have long been demolished. Always a noisy, bustling and smelly place, full of jostling crowds and carts, it was never more so than when the fishing boats had docked and were unloading their catches on the ground near the Market Place. Large paddle steamers would tie up in the lower harbour at the Red Pier near the Imperial Hotel, waiting for the tide to turn. During the winter, the Steam Packet's vessels and harbour ferries would lie up at the Tongue, undergoing re-painting and general maintenance, and when the fishing fleet was in it was sometimes possible

The Black Lion hotel with its ornate lamp above the entrance door.

to walk across the harbour on their decks. It was all a far cry from that other Douglas, the watering place, with its broad and colourful promenades, attractive gardens and brightly lit entertainment venues.

By the mid-1880s, the Isle of Man had acquired the reputation as 'par excellence the land of boarding houses'; according to the *Isle of Man Examiner* in 1886, however, Douglas had also acquired the unenviable reputation as 'a town of public houses with all the experienced temptations of evils of such places'. The strictly teetotal Douglas Coffee Palace, built as a reaction to the excessive drunkenness associated with the area, stood 'gallant and lonely amidst a sea of alcohol', and was a popular meeting place. The Black Lion itself had a reputation for being 'noisy and boisterous', and even the few months that Clement Wood was the landlord were not without a certain amount of controversy. In August, one Thomas Collins was fined 10 shillings and costs for being on licensed premises at the Black Lion during illegal hours, and in September, Clement Wood himself was charged with having kept his premises open on a Sunday.

The north quay, Douglas.

A Magnificent Orchestral Band.

There are tantalizing references to the Falcon Cliff orchestra in the local newspapers between Whit-week and start of the summer season proper in 1886. The *Manx Sun* reported that the voyage from Liverpool to Douglas on the paddle steamer Tynwald:

> . . . was enlivened by an excellent treat, The Falcon Cliff Band conducted by Mr Ball[8] played a short but enjoyable programme of music, followed by solos from George Barton, tenor and Mr Snazelle, baritone. £1. 2s 6d was collected for the Hospital and handed over to Capt. Gibson.

No doubt the musicians and singers welcomed the opportunity presented by a calm crossing and a captive audience to 'warm up' for the summer season with an impromptu concert.

On 25th March the new manager of the Falcon Cliff, William

George H Snazelle.

Lawrence, wrote to Harry inviting him to join the Falcon Cliff band under their musical director Dick Ball. The band contributed enormously to the growing success of the entertainment complex, and according to the *Manx Sun*, was a great improvement on the previous year. Many of the musicians performed solos at the afternoon promenade concerts, and were all recognised as 'thorough masters on their instruments'. The band was led by a Mr F. H. Haynes (or Haines), who also performed duty as the official accompanist, plus three further violinists, one viola player, one 'cellist and one double bass player. The woodwind players consisted of one of each of flute, clarinet, oboe and bassoon, with a brass complement of two cornets and trombone, and one percussionist.

Harry is not listed among the musicians during the early part of the season probably because he was still in Ireland with Maggie Morton's touring company, but in August is mentioned as a violin soloist in the singer and entertainer G. H. Snazelle's benefit concert. The next time we hear of him is in the *Manx Sun*'s review of an afternoon concert in September, when the violin solo in the introduction to Dick Ball's *Falcon Cliff Polka*, 'was well played by Mr Wood . . . the audience were charmed with it'. From these brief references, we may conclude that Harry was not

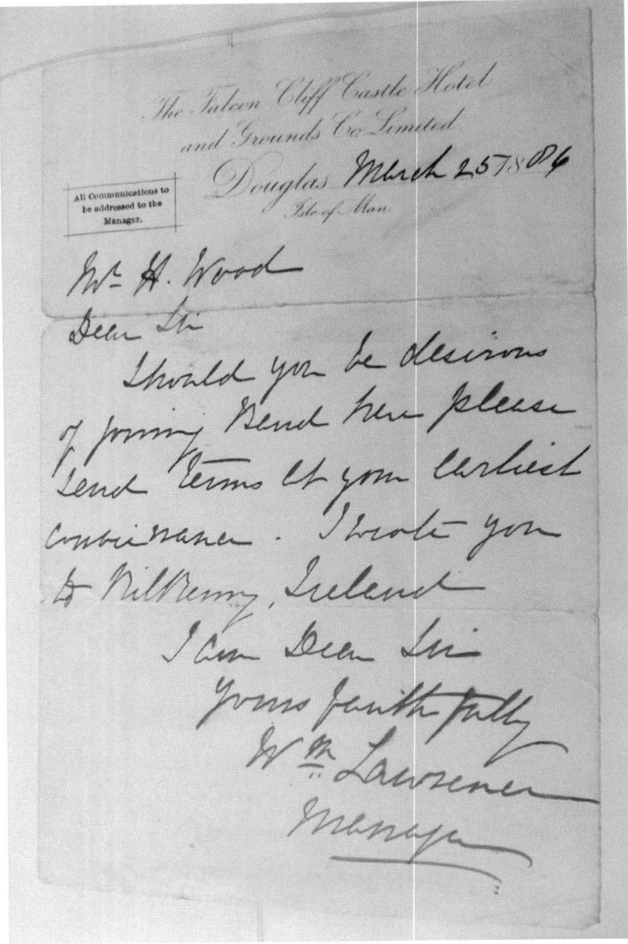

The Falcon Cliff Castle Hotel
and Grounds Co Limited
Douglas March 25th 86
Isle of Man

All Communications to be addressed to the Manager.

Mr H. Wood
Dear Sir
Should you be desirous
of joining Band here please
send terms at your earliest
convenience. I wrote you
to Kilkenny, Ireland
I am Dear Sir
Yours faithfully
Wm Lawrence
Manager

Enquiry from the Falcon Cliff.

available to play for the entire 1886 summer season, and was probably not able to join the Falcon Cliff orchestra until mid-August at the earliest.

At the end of the season one reviewer claimed that the Douglas concerts were coming up to the standards of Harrogate, Scarborough, Blackpool and Buxton. Gone were the days when concert programmes were changed only once a week; the Derby Castle led the way by introducing a fresh concert programme each afternoon, and as a consequence no less than thirty singers were engaged that season. The Falcon Cliff was not slow to bring its programmes up to date and to engage better quality artists.

'This popular and excellently managed resort'.

The 1886 season started on Monday 1st June with the opening of the Falcon Cliff Castle and Pleasure Grounds, and although Whit-week was both late and cold, there was an enticing mixture of entertainments on offer. The afternoon promenade concerts in the pavilion - Ballad Concerts, or 'Grand Afternoon Ballad Concerts' - featured a blend of pleasant, easy-to-listen-to light classical pieces, instrumental solos and vocal items, 'free from music hall inanities', with an average attendance of around four hundred. The programmes customarily commenced with a popular overture, such as Balfe's *The Bohemian Girl*, Adam's bright and tuneful *La Reine d'un Jour*, Nicolai's *The Merry Wives of Windsor* and the newest operettas such as Planquette's *Rip van Winkle* or Suppe's *Light Cavalry*, and concluded with a march, often *The War March of the Priests* from Mendelssohn's *Athalia* or Michaelis' stirring march-medley *Turkish Patrol*. Occasionally a more serious and dramatic overture would find its way onto a programme including Mozart's *Don Giovanni* and Verdi's *Ernani*.

After the overtures, and selections from operas and operettas, with the best-loved numbers woven into a continuous concert-piece, were essential to the success of the afternoon concerts, and among the most popular were those taken from Gilbert and Sullivan and Offenbach. The concert waltz[9] was also an indispensible ingredient for a gentle afternoon's listening such as Chassaigne's sparkling *Falka*, Liddell's new waltz *The Maid of the Mill* and the ever-popular waltzes of Waldteufel. Short novelty or descriptive pieces such as Koenig's *Post Horn Galop*, Michaelis' charming pastoral idyll *The Forge in the Forest* and Dick Ball's own *Fantasia on National Airs* were all were performed 'in first class style' by a band that 'was sure to gain a great name this season'.

~

Concert artistes, overwhelmingly singers, were a huge draw, and it was customary to engage new, often young and not yet established singers, at the beginning and end of each season. One young artist who first appeared at the Falcon Cliff Pavilion in 1885, the Wolverhampton-born contralto Elizabeth Dews,[10] was engaged every year until 1897, and again in 1907. So popular was Miss Dews, that she was awarded her own benefit concert at the end of her six week engagement, the longest engagement of any concert artist at the Falcon Cliff up to that time. She received an ovation for her rendering of Frederick Cowen's poignant ballad *The Better*

Miss Elizabeth Dews.

Land at one of her first appearances, and acceded to the audience's persistent demands for encores with what was arguably the most famous ballad of the nineteenth century: Sir Henry Bishop's *Home! Sweet Home!*

The tenor Charles Chilley - from the Royal Italian Opera House, Covent Garden, and the Crystal Palace concerts - performed Balfe's parlour war-horse *Come into the Garden, Maud* during this, his debut season on the Island; Kendal Thompson performed Braham's stirring ballad *The Death of Nelson*[11] on a number of occasions, and the Lancashire tenor, George Barton, the resident tenor that season, introduced a new setting of the poem, *Ellan Vannin* by Dr Fred W. Friend,[12] destined to be forever linked with the Isle of Man.

The baritone, G. H. Snazelle, a most charismatic performer, made a welcome return to the Falcon Cliff, and delighted audiences with his singing of such favourites as *The Good Old Temeraire* and popular recitations such as *The Old Clock on the Stairs.* Sometimes billed as 'England's greatest baritone' - he was hardly that - he was nevertheless a fine actor and raconteur and always attracted 'a very large attendance'. Edward Grimes, a genuinely fine baritone, sang Stanford's setting of the old Irish song *Father O'Flynn,* and Lindon Travers, whose three week Island debut commenced at the end of June, gave Stanford's *The Soldier's*

Goodbye in 'a fine, rich baritone', and *The Midshipmite*, Stephen Adam's affecting nautical ballad.

~

In addition to the afternoon promenade concerts, there was dancing to the newest waltzes, polkas and lancers every evening in the Monstre Pavilion on the 'finest waxed dance floor in the Kingdom'. An innovation that soon proved to be popular was the engagement of Peter Wright, a prominent Scottish Dancing Master, as the Master of Ceremonies, who appeared each evening in full highland costume, followed by a resident comedian such as G. W. Nicholson, a popular comedian from the previous season, billed as 'an eccentric vocalist', who entertained the dancers during the intervals between dances. He was followed by the more controversial T. N. Hartley who regaled the crowd with his 'musical eccentricities, fund of humour and witty and clever sayings'. Reactions were mixed, though, when it came to his 'comical nigger' or 'black and white entertainment'; as one reviewer observed '. . . a clever artist in his way, but his way does not happen to be our way'.

The Falcon Cliff 'Grand Orchestral Band' was also engaged to play for George Barton's Sunday evening concerts, sometimes known as Sacred Concerts, which normally took place in the Assembly Rooms on Loch Promenade. The first of these concerts - precursors of the later, highly popular Sunday Sacred Concerts from the Palace, Falcon Cliff and the Derby Castle - took place at the height of the season in July and featured solo singers and instrumental soloists from the orchestra, including Harry.

Harry becomes established

''arry and his sweatheart',[13] likewise 'the Yorkshire and Midland counties masher', were the 'rather common objects on the beach' during the overcrowded holiday month of August. These remarks constituted the opening salvos of a mixed review of the Douglas summer season from the *Scottish News*, reprinted in the *Isle of Man Times* at the end of September. The writer, whilst acknowledging the beauties of the Island and the opportunities to enjoy its charming sights by waggonette, railway and steamer excursions, found 'the German Band nuisance, the smell of bad liquors . . . and the desecration of Douglas Head every afternoon by vendors, negro melodists' and the 'scum of the visitors' indulging in 'flirtation, silly joking and horseplay . . . decidedly and disagreeably in the ascendant'.

Our Harry, though, was rapidly establishing himself as a dependable, young local solo violinist, and took part in a number of concerts after the summer season was over. Early in November he played two virtuoso showpieces at the Masonic Hall, Douglas, after which the critic reported that 'such violin playing is not often heard here'. His playing brought forth 'such hearty applause' that an encore was demanded, and Harry complied with one of his favourite pieces, Prosper Sainton's *Variations on Home! Sweet Home!* Further appearances in November are typical of the kind of event that Harry, ever adaptable and obliging, was invited to play at. On Hollantide Fair Day he directed a small band that provided music for an Orange Tea Meeting and Ball, and later that month he added to his reputation by playing at the third of a series of St. Matthews' Popular Entertainments in the church hall. The *Manx Sun* declared that 'he and his fiddle know each other well'.

On Wednesday 22nd December 1886, Clement Wood died suddenly at the age of fifty-three years, and was buried in Kirk Braddan churchyard on Christmas Day. He had been ailing for some time, his health probably undermined by the relentless hours and hard physical work demanded of those in the public house and hotel trade. That afternoon Harry fulfilled an engagement to play at a Christmas Day Festival at the specially decorated Centenary Hall in Peel. And we may easily imagine his feelings on that day, although Harry himself did not record them. Clement had experienced the Island at its best in the summer of 1885, and in 1886 had witnessed Harry beginning to carve out a career for himself. Perhaps he dreamed of an easier life away from the damp climate of semi-industrial Slaithwaite, and he gambled that in such beautiful surroundings his health would improve, and he would be able to bring all the energy and sociability of an experienced 'mine host' to bear at the Black Lion. It was not to be. Many years later Haydn Wood honoured his father by giving his setting of Isaac Watt's hymn *My Saviour, My Almighty Friend* the name 'Clement'.

~

The year 1887 was the first year that Harry was engaged as a violinist in Douglas as a permanent resident, rather than as a visiting summer musician. The year began with several engagements at various local events, including the annual parochial tea at St. Matthews Church at which his younger brother Daniel, then aged fifteen, made his Douglas concert debut in a flute solo.

In March came the news that Dick Ball would be replaced at the Falcon Cliff by the ebullient Oliver Gaggs,[14] popularly known as 'Genial

Oliver Gaggs', something of a showman, a flautist with the Hallé Orchestra early in his career, and a musical director who would leave an indelible mark in the story of the Island's entertainment industry. An 'efficient band' with Gaggs 'in sole and complete control of the music', was promised, with leading players from the Hallé Orchestra, de Jong's Manchester Concerts and the Carl Rosa Opera Company among the ranks.

Harry would not have expected to be engaged to join the Falcon Cliff band under Gaggs, as it was customary for each newly appointed musical director to engage his own players, musicians already known to them, and in fact the players in the Falcon Cliff band were nearly all new to Douglas. However, he was quickly 'snapped' up' as repetiteur violinist by Charles Reynolds,[15] in his second year as conductor at the rival Derby Castle, known as 'The Hall by the Sea' or 'Mona's Crystal Palace', and was never again associated with the Falcon Cliff. The move to the Derby Castle would prove to be both fortuitous and prophetic in view of his future career on the Island. Charles Reynolds was also a fine oboist, 'the greatest oboe player of his generation', the experienced musical director of orchestras at Buxton, Scarborough, Southport, Eastbourne and Blackpool,[16] and the composer of attractive topical waltzes, polkas and gallops.

~

Under Oliver Gaggs' direction the Falcon Cliff season went from strength to strength, even without Harry in the orchestra. His keenly anticipated dances and novelty pieces included the *Snaefell Galop*, the *Fantasie Galop* and *The Lifeboat Resue*, 'with wonderful storm effects'. The 'hit' of the season was the vocal polka, *Hi! Kelly*, which was played at 9.40 each evening,[17] and always encored. The popularity of the *Hi! Kelly* polka ultimately created a demand for 'Kelly' songs featuring the ubiquitous Kelly and his escapades on and off the Island.

The opening line of Harry's *Cavalcade*[18] tells us that:

> The most popular tune in Douglas was the vocal polka *Hi! Kelly*, composed by Oliver Gaggs . . . when playing this polka the musicians shout Hi! Kelly Hi! Kelly just before the trio, in which they sing:
>
> Hi! Kelly, Hi! Kelly Hi! Kelly bring your boat.
> Hi! Kelly let's quickly get afloat.
> Each fresh'ning breeze shall echo loud, as we skim o'er the bay,
> Hi! Kelly Hi! Kelly the burden of our lay.

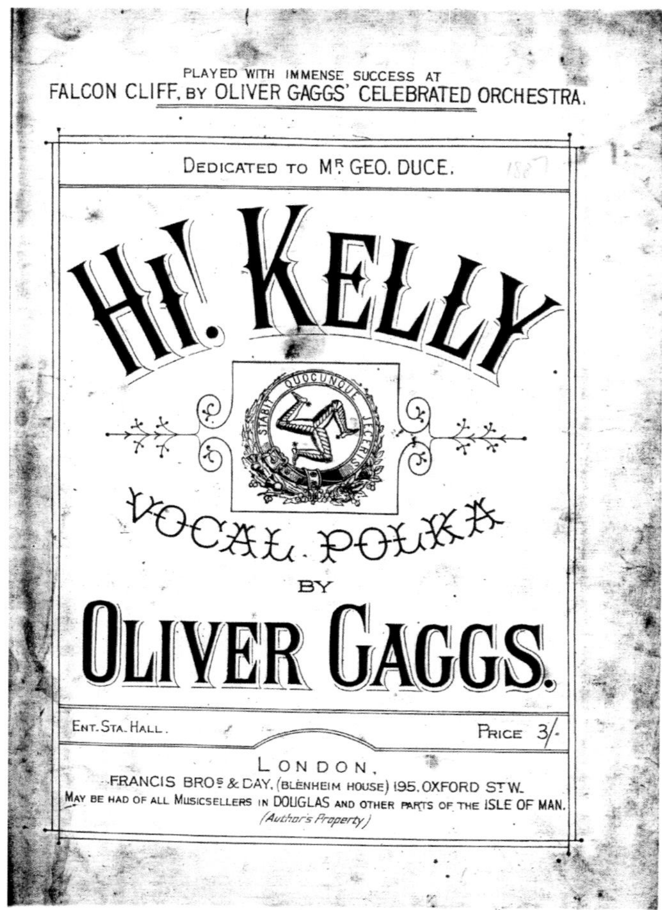

The call or greeting of Hi! Kelly quickly caught on in Douglas, and by the height of the season could be heard everywhere. Even fifty years later, Harry noted that 'if a visitor required assistance, and shouts Hi! Kelly, a boatman or porter magically appears'. Local businessmen were not slow to recognise that the popular new 'catch words' could be used to their advantage. In 1889, Little & Cooper's, shoemakers of Strand Street, headed their newspaper advertisement with: 'Hi! Kelly, look at my boots'.

The Derby Castle opening afternoon concert of the 1887 season commenced with the overture from Weber's spooky opera *Der Freischutz* and continued with a selection from Sullivan's newest operetta, *Ruddigore*. There were trombone, flute, oboe, clarinet and cornet solos and a violin duet played by Harry and the orchestra's leader John Daly. Attendances at the promenade concerts continued to be rated as fair even after the Whit-week visitors had left and the season progressed into the so-called slack period before the official start of the season in July. That year Herr Barcza's *Blue Hungarian Band* appeared for the first time at a promenade concert and was immediately re-engaged for August, thus allowing the Derby Castle to announce that there would be 'Two Bands Daily' until the end of the month. This proved to be a shrewd plan, as by August, the dance floor at the Derby Castle was very crowded every evening, making 'the enjoyment of a good round dance impossible'. A temporary outside dancing platform was hastily laid in order to accommodate the overflow from the ballroom.

The first concert artiste to be engaged that season was the soprano Madame Marie Sutton who sang Bishop's Shakespearean ballad *Should He Upbraid*, Sullivan's *The Lost Chord*, the stupendously popular ballad that the composer himself believed he never equalled, and an aria from Meyerbeer's opera *Robert le Diable*. She proved to be so popular that she was re-engaged for a further period, and was given the honour of performing E. Bach's Jubilee song, *Long Live Victoria*. Other singers from the Carl Rosa Opera Company and the Albert Hall and St James' Hall concerts in London appeared later in the season, and by the end of August three to four thousand music-lovers were attending the afternoon promenade concerts.

~

Popular though the afternoon promenade concerts were, by far the largest numbers of visitors attended the dances each evening, which commenced at 7.30pm and ended at 11.00pm. Waltzes, polkas, lancers, galops and quadrilles predominated, and every musical director was expected to compose new fashionable and topical dances each season. At the end of each week, a special evening took place where the dances were selected from those most popular with the audiences.[19] Novelty items also proved immensely popular, such as the *Polka Inferno* with 'lightning and realistic effects'. The climax of Charles Reynolds' benefit concert on Friday 9th September was truly spectacular as the combined forces of the Derby Castle Orchestra, the Castletown Brass Band and the visiting Eastbourne Military Band performed the *British Army Quadrille*, complete with piper in full costume. Together with a firing party, the total number of performers under Reynolds' direction exceeded seventy.

'The most successful season ever'

There is no doubt that the 1887 summer season exceeded all expectations as far as visitor numbers were concerned. It was estimated that there was an increase of over eight thousand visitors over the previous year and last minute visitors often found that there were no lodgings available. According to one newspaper, some holiday makers resorted to sleeping in fields of corn. Queen Victoria's Jubilee on 20th and 21st June saw processions both large and small in most towns and villages organised by local groups of Oddfellows and Rechabites, churches and schools, and at the Derby Castle, a Floral and Horticulture Show was held.

As autumn drew on the local newspapers indulged themselves in the inevitable seasonal post-mortems which, predictably, produced very mixed views. The success of any summer season was easily measured if you were the manager of the Falcon Cliff or Derby Castle, a hotel or boarding-house owner, a shopkeeper or cafe owner, the Steam Packet Company, the Tram Company or one of the thousands of local people who relied heavily for their livelihood on a large influx of holiday makers. For those Manxmen who were involved in non-commercial activities, the success of the holiday period was less easily gauged, and there was considerable disquiet expressed at the effect of great numbers of visitors invading the Island.

In Notes and Observations by Wayfarer, a *Manx Sun* correspondent paints a less attractive portrait of Douglas during the height of the season. The proliferation of street musicians on the promenades continued to be a particular nuisance, and local businesses and legitimate traders complained that the by-laws were not being enforced with consistency as the touts were 'being allowed to get away with anything!' The attractions at Douglas Head were not being properly regulated by the Town Commissioners; some female holiday-makers were displaying their 'bumps' too readily, and some of the songs being sung had 'unsavoury words'. Particularly distasteful were the 'loafers', who sat on the sea walls spitting tobacco onto the promenades. The 'natives', Wayfarer suggested, 'were over-thronged'. Manxland was 'rapidly getting 'Arryized'.

As the last of the visitors began to leave the Island, the management of the Derby Castle began to ponder the quieter winter months. One novel idea to keep the complex in use, was to host fortnightly suppers 'for select parties of friends', at which there would be 'a plentiful supply of tripe', and no doubt musical entertainment. The first snow came in mid-October, and Harry, relieved of his duties at the Derby Castle, began to organise a number of 'bijou' bands to play at local musical events. On 28th December, the *Mona's Herald* announced that Oliver Gaggs would be re-appointed for the 1888 summer season at the Falcon Cliff. This news no doubt set Harry wondering where he, too, might be engaged for the following summer.

At home Sabra Wood applied for and was granted the licence for the Black Lion for another year. It seems unlikely that the hotel can have been a very profitable establishment, and Harry may have been in effect the principal bread-winner for the family. The fourteen-year-old Daniel continued to help out occasionally in the bar, but Harry's much younger sisters Elise and Adeline, aged eight and six respectively, and his five year old brother Haydn, were too young to have contributed much to the running of a licensed establishment.

'Fifty years ago, in 1888 . . .'

Thus read the opening words of Harry's *Cavalcade*, his personal year-by-year record of the artists who appeared in Douglas, the most popular music, and the main events of his career as a musical director, begun in 1937 and completed in 1938, the year of his death. He reveals that: 'The most popular tune in Douglas was the Hi! Kelly Polka'. Second in popularity was the *Pas de Quatre* from the burlesque *Faust Up To Date*, composed by Meyer Lutz,[20] '. . . it was played and whistled all over Douglas'. This engaging piece - a saucy 'Skirt Dance' for four young ladies in skimpy costumes - became immensely popular because its catchy tune perfectly fitted the steps of the current dance import from America, the Barn Dance. The most popular variety artist at the Falcon Cliff that season was the

Lancashire comedian Lester Barrett, famous for his song *Delaney's Chicken* with its Flanders and Swann-esque refrain:

> All the shots that were fired, on the field of Waterloo,
> Couldn't penetrate or dislocate, that elongated, armour-plated,
> Double-breasted, iron-chested, Cock-a-Doodle-do.

Barrett would appear in Douglas for many seasons and was a firm favourite. He wrote the words and music for most of his own songs, building on his persona of a north-country comedian with 'homely jokes for homely folks' as he put it. A character on and off stage, he had a reputation as a 'backer of horses' according to his brother, the composer Leslie Stuart.[21]

~

Harry stated in *Cavalcade* that he was engaged as repetiteur violinist at the Derby Castle under the musical directorship of Charles Reynolds in 1888. However, writing fifty years after the events, his memory was occasionally fallible. An undated contract letter – couched in somewhat eccentric English - from the conductor Edward de Jong clarifies the situation:

> South Shore, Blackpool
> To Mr Harry Wood
> Dear Sir
> I beg to offer you an engagement as first violin at DERBY CASTLE, DOUGLAS commencing on 21st May, and terminating on 22nd September, 1888.
> You will be required to play at an Afternoon Concert daily, and Music for Dancing each evening, and you are to be in proper Morning Dress (consisting of black coat etc) at the Afternoon Concert, and Evening Dress at night.
> I reserve to myself the right to terminate this engagement at any time in case you do not fulfil your duty.
> I remain
> Yours truly
> EDWARD de JONG

Although Harry's duties are clearly outlined, the financial terms of the engagement are not stated.

~

SOUTH SHORE,

BLACKPOOL.

To Mr. Harry Wood

Dear Sir,

I beg to offer you an Engagement as First violin ~~for a period of~~ ~~weeks~~ at DERBY CASTLE, DOUGLAS, Isle of Man, commencing on the 21st of May and terminating on the 15th or the 22 of September 1888

TERMS £ : Per Week.

You will be required to play at an Afternoon Concert daily, and Music for Dancing each evening, and you are to be in proper Morning Dress (consisting of black coat, etc.) at the Afternoon Concerts, and Evening Dress at night.

I reserve to myself the right of terminating this engagement at any time in case you do not fulfil your duty.

I remain,

Yours truly,

EDWARD DE JONG.

Please sign annexed Form in case you accept.

Harry's contract with the Derby Castle orchestra.

That year the first of two seemingly minor events occurred that Harry probably considered too insignificant to mention in *Cavalcade* in the light of his subsequent career.

Mona's Herald, 21st March:
Glen Helen
GOOD FRIDAY
30th March, 1888
An efficient band, Under the conductorship of Mr Harry Wood, will play choice selections during the day
ADMISSION TO GROUNDS 6d. Children Half-Price.

This seemingly mundane advertisement is in all likelihood the first

Edward de Jong.

time that Harry's name appears in a local newspaper as a conductor, rather than as a violin soloist or orchestra leader. Although the anticipated fine weather failed to arrive, many early visitors made Peel and Glen Helen their resorts of choice. ' . . . a goodly number were gathered to dance to the strains of Harry Wood's band, (but) a still larger number gathered under the eaves of the restaurant to get out of the way of the rain, which would persist in falling'.

'A local celebrity in the music profession . . .'

Edward de Jong's reputation as a virtuoso flute and piccolo player was very high, and his Saturday Popular Concerts in Manchester's Free Trade Hall with his sixty-strong orchestra were famous. He was also a well-loved and respected conductor in Buxton, Liverpool, Morecambe and elsewhere, with a commanding stage presence. Harry would learn much from him. The Derby Castle orchestra was variously described as numbering from twenty to twenty-eight players, but on special occasions, such as de Jong's

Grand Benefit Concert in September, was augmented to forty musicians. It was customary for the band at the beginning and tail-end of the season, when audiences were smaller, to be reduced to around sixteen players including an accompanist, Mr R. Johnson, an experienced musician and veteran of de Jong's Free Trade Hall concerts, who as the deputy conductor, directed the orchestra for the evening dance programmes when de Jong was absent from the Island.

A second detail omitted from *Cavalcade* but found hidden away in newspaper reviews, was the fact that by the height of the season in August, the numbers of those wishing to dance at the Derby Castle became so large that an open-air, illuminated 'al fresco' platform was constructed to take the overflow. A portion of the orchestra was detailed to play for these dancers with Harry designated as the conductor. In effect, Harry became the unofficial deputy to the deputy conductor, and once again the Derby Castle could boast that two bands would be playing for the dancing nightly. As one enthusiastic journalist who seemed to have swallowed a volume of Walter Pater's essays wrote: 'the pavilion was crowded with votaries of Terpsichore who have footed it merrily to the excellent music provided by the band'. Harry's name does not appear in the Derby Castle advertisements at this time, but within a few short seasons his name would rarely be absent from the entertainment pages.

~

The Derby Castle had begun to change its afternoon concert programmes more frequently from 1887, and although a new programme was promised each day, this may have been more of an aspiration than a reality, and is not reflected in the newspaper reviews of the period. More concert artistes were engaged than in previous seasons, including some new to Douglas along with others who were established favourites such as the contralto Miss Elizabeth Dews, who brought the house to tears in August with her pathos-filled singing of the soulful Irish ballad, *Terence's Farewell to Kathleen*.

The most eminent singer to appear that season was the great Irish tenor, Barton McGuckin, whose six-day engagement attracted large and enthusiastic audiences. His powerful rendering of Sullivan's ballad of a burial at sea, *The Sailor's Grave* and Braham's song of parting, *The Anchor's Weigh'd* were especially well-received, and testify to the enormous popularity of ballads with a nautical flavour. Barton McGuckin was a hard act to follow, but in August a warm Manx welcome was given

Derby Castle hotel and ballroom.

to a local baritone, a Mr Bridson, 'a fairly good vocalist with a commanding voice' who brought 'vigour and expression to his songs', particularly Sullivan's ballad in memory of his father, *Thou'rt Passing Hence, My Brother*, and Paolo Tosti's *Forever and Forever*. His singing of Stephen Adam's *A Warrior Bold*, received an ovation.[22]

The newest popular dance at the Derby Castle that season was de Jong's splendid *Ben-my-Cree*, a substantial waltz sequence consisting of an expansive introduction, followed by three waltzes and a grand coda. The colourful cover of the printed edition shows a young girl in a bob-cap setting off to row across Douglas Bay, with the Tower of Refuge in the background. Each evening the joint masters of ceremonies, Messrs R. Clucas and E. Woodcock, introduced the dances and the variety acts that followed. These included the Japanese equilibrist (tight-rope walker) M. P. Tarro, who displayed 'an amount of dexterity which it would be almost impossible to excel', the infant cyclists Lotto, Lilo and Otto, and Miss Lane, a celebrated natationist (a novelty swimmer) who performed one of her aquatic feats in a concrete basin near the engine-house which housed the electric light engine for the complex.

~

Whit-week 1888 was the busiest in living memory, with perfect weather and healthy competition between the steamship companies ensuring high visitor numbers. The Falcon Cliff also enjoyed a successful season with the final weeks seeing the largest number of visitors on record going through the turnstiles. Oliver Gaggs's benefit concert on 7th September drew a large and appreciative audience, and at the end he addressed the audience, assuring them that if he returned in 1889, he 'would leave no stone unturned . . . to give you the utmost satisfaction and pleasure'. By December, though, the *Mona's Herald* added to a rumour that Gaggs 'would be going over to the enemy next season . . . and taking his friend, the comedian G. W. Nicholson, with him'. And so it proved to be, for on 26th December, the *Herald* reported that Gaggs' appointment as musical director at the Derby Castle for the 1889 season had been confirmed. It was 'all change' at the Douglas entertainment venues, and a potential blow for the fortunes of the Falcon Cliff.

'Harry gives me a lessons'.

In February 1889, the Wood family moved out of the Black Lion Hotel, and took up residence at number 17, Albert Street, on the site of today's Courts of Law. With Clement Wood gone, Sabra, who at the age of fifty-three had once again successfully applied for the licence for the Black Lion, must have found the running of the hotel and public house, and bringing up the family - Sophia, Adeline, Elize, Daniel and Haydn - exhausting, and after the move to Albert Street she retired from the hotel trade.

On 1st June, the *Isle of Man Times* carried the following advertisement:

> LESSONS on the VIOLIN
> HARRY WOOD
> Cert. RAM and TC
> (Late First Violin De Jong's Orchestra)
> OPEN TO GIVE LESSONS
> Terms on application, 17 Albert Street, Douglas
> Concerts attended and can supply Bands for Balls etc

This may have been the year that Harry first began to give his younger brother Haydn, now aged seven, his first violin lessons, and take charge of his general musical education. Young Haydn was initially a reluctant virtuoso-in-the-making, and later recalled that he went in fear

17, Albert Street, Douglas.

and trepidation of returning home from school and being called upon to play his party pieces in front of his mother's friends or at various local events. A music manuscript book from this period belonging to the young Haydn survives, and contains some sketches for his earliest compositions, such as the *Evia Valse*.

A brief letter, dated May 4th, but year uncertain, from young Haydn to his elder brother John and sister Mary Hannah in Slaithwaite, refers to his violin lessons:

> Dear Sister and Brother
> I am very glad to tell you that Harry gives me a lessons on the violin and I practice every day. Adeline and Maud Quayle has lessons too.

Little is known about the general schooling for the younger Wood children, except that Haydn was a pupil at the Misses Greens' private school in Derby Square, Douglas, and later attended Tynwald Street School and Douglas Grammar School. Recalling his time at the Misses Green's school, Haydn recalled that:

> During the first term I played truant for three months before I was found out . . . no-one was more surprised than my dear mother because I turned up regularly for my mid-day meal during that period. I used to spend most of my time in a fruit garden on the fringe of town, but later became bolder and ventured into town.

~

In the meantime, as he waited for the start of the new entertainment season, Harry continued to accept local engagements and provide musicians for a number of local musical events, many of which were organised to raise money for local charities, and some, such as the St. Matthew's Church Parochial Teas and the St. Thomas's Bazaars, becoming regular fixtures. He was now firmly established in Douglas as a well-known figure in musical circles both professional and amateur, a reliable player and soloist, a 'fixer' or organiser of bands for all occasions and a violin teacher. Even without the summer engagements at the Falcon Cliff or the Derby Castle, he was probably able to make a modest living as well as contributing to the family exchequer.

'The long, hot summer of 1889 . . . '[23]

The most significant event for the entertainment industry in 1889 was the opening of the Castle Mona Palace and Pleasure Grounds, variously advertised as The Palace, Castle Mona and later and more commonly as The Palace Ballroom, erected in the grounds of the Castle Mona Hotel, and the last of the monster entertainment venues to be built in Douglas. Although there were doubts expressed as to whether Douglas could support three large pleasure resorts, the 1889 season opened with Charles Reynolds at the Falcon Cliff, Oliver Gaggs at the Derby Castle, and Fred Vetter,[24] a new musical personality on the Island, at the new Palace Ballroom, with Harry Wood as his repetiteur violinist.

Harry's letter of engagement for the summer season outlined his duties as follows: The season would commence on either 1st or 6th July and terminate on 28th September; his salary would be £2 7s 6d per week; there would be an afternoon concert each day lasting approximately two hours, and dancing each evening from 7.30 until 11.00, with a fifteen-minute break; there would be Sacred Concerts on Sunday evenings at 8.00 pm during August and September, for which an extra six shillings would be paid; morning dress would be worn for the afternoon concerts and full evening dress (white tie) for the evening dancing; all rehearsals must be

1 Cecil Street,
Greenheys, Manchester,
May 8 1889

Dear Sir,

I beg to offer you a 12 weeks' engagement as 1st Violin at the New Castle Mona Pavilion, at Douglas, Isle of Man, commencing Saturday, July 6th (probably Monday, the 1st), and terminating Saturday, September 28th, at a salary per week of £[redacted] the duties of which are to play at a Concert in the afternoon of each day, for about two hours, and for Dancing in the evening, from 7-30, or thereabouts, till 11-0, with an Interval of 15 minutes.

I reserve the right of extending your engagement a few weeks longer, and also the right of claiming your services at a contemplated series of six Sunday Sacred Concerts, which, if given, will take place in the months of August and September, and commencing each Sunday evening at 8 o'clock, and for which you will receive an extra remuneration of 6/-

Morning Dress (Black Coat) for the afternoon performances, and Full Evening Dress (White Tie) at night.

All Rehearsals which are required during the season must be attended by you.

Yours truly,
Fr: Vetter

Mr. H. Wood

if satisfied the salary to be increased.

Harry's contract letter of 1889.

attended. A further note in Vetter's hand was scribbled in the margin: 'if satisfied the salary to be increased'. It was suggested in one of the season previews that Harry's engagement came 'on the strong recommendation of several local gentlemen . . . a decision that will be viewed with the greatest satisfaction by many people in Douglas, who have had a long experience of the excellence of Mr Wood's playing'.

~

Fred Vetter's orchestra, probably the finest that had appeared in Douglas up to that time, was carefully selected, with many of the players being accomplished soloists in their own right. It was well funded, and boasted twenty-five musicians according to an end-of-season review in the *Isle of Man Times*. Fred Vetter directed his orchestra from the front, violin in hand which ensured the excellent, precise ensemble and tuning so often referred to in reviews. His reputation as a conductor was very high, as was his reputation as an 'English' concertina virtuoso. Audiences at the afternoon concerts began to look forward to the novelty of Vetter's concertina solos.

The orchestra's leader was Edward Flexney, a one-time principal violinist with the Hallé orchestra, with whom Harry shared the front violin desk. Little wonder that reviewers acknowledged that 'the fine orchestra, under Mr Fred Vetter . . . more than anything else, contributed to the huge success which has attended the Palace this season'.

~

The season proper began on July 6th, but the official opening of the Palace Ballroom was delayed when it was realised that the enormous project would need more time to complete. As a consequence, the first orchestral rehearsals took place at the Castle Mona Hotel, later moving to the Star Hotel on Prospect Hill for a further week. Extra rehearsals were scheduled until the Palace was ready for the official opening - now scheduled for Monday 29th July – but by mid-June the roof was still not in place, and a further delay was caused when a poorly-secured eighty-foot main supporting structure collapsed. Nevertheless, the directors were 'still sanguine that the Palace will be open by the end of July' as the entrance gates and 'general fittings' were apparently 'well in hand'. In the event, the Palace did not open until Saturday 3rd August.

In the meantime, the grounds were opened to the public for the performance of open-air Pastoral Plays and concerts from a specially erected wooden platform, with the backdrop of the cliff and over-hanging trees providing a suitable natural amphitheatre. The orchestra was mainly occupied with providing the incidental music for the plays - including that by Mendelssohn for Shakespeare's *A Midsummer Night's Dream* - and selections for the evening *al fresco* concerts. The weather was mixed; umbrellas were often required and audiences were smaller than the concerts deserved.

'One of the finest and handsomest buildings of its class in the UK'

The vast size of the new Palace Ballroom dominated the Douglas promenade. The statistics were impressive: two hundred feet long, one hundred and four feet wide and a central dome one hundred and twenty feet above the dance floor, which was made of polished oak and was larger than the floor space of London's Royal Albert Hall. There was an eighteen-

CASTLE MONA

"THE PALACE" AND PLEASURE GROUNDS
ERECTED 1888 - 1889
Opened Saturday, August 3rd. 1889

I WATCHED THE ERECTION OF THIS BALLROOM FROM THE FOUNDATION TO THE ROOF. I SAW THE WOODEN PRINCIPALS HOISTED TO THEIR POSITIONS AFTER MUCH DIFFICULTY. I WAS REPETITEUR VIOLIN IN THE ORCHESTRA WHICH WAS CONDUCTED BY MR. FRED VETTER.

The Palace Ballroom with notes typed by Harry.

foot-wide gallery running round the inside of the hall, and a twelve-foot-wide promenade down the east, sea-facing, side. The proscenium and stage were reportedly 'second to none in the Kingdom', and were bounded on each side by two large alcoves, each housing a statue of a female figure 'of heroic size' representing one of the muses of music and dance. The back-stage facilities were generous and included a band room and artistes' dressing rooms. Both the interior and the grounds were brilliantly lit by electricity, powered by two generators, described as 'engines', from the Manchester Edison-Swan Company. They powered twenty arc lamps with a three thousand candlepower output for the interior, and six hundred incandescent lamps placed strategically in the well-wooded grounds.

One Manxman left his impressions of the interior of the ballroom, the crowds and the atmosphere on two quite different occasions in the *Isle of Man Times*. The first was from one of the *Messiah* performances during the Sunday Sacred Concert series:

> ... what a sight met my eyes. Such a hall! Such a crowd of earnest, orderly people! Such a blaze of electric light! I was simply amazed! And I must add, what a concert!

The following day, he and a friend went to the Palace Ballroom for the evening:

> ... if we were surprised by the spectacle before, we were doubly so on this occasion. My friend, a visitor, exclaimed 'are we in the Isle of Man! Or is this Paris? ... I have just returned from Paris, and saw no such sight there'. Such dresses! Such delight! Such good behaviour! And what a mass of people. There could not have been less than 6000.

The gentleman also proffered a few words of advice to the management: 'Stick to your guns. Don't have a licence (alcohol) even if it is offered to you ... without it, you will have greater success, order and respectability'. The directors were also encouraged to ignore '... your carping enemies, who, as usually is the case at this stage in the development of any plucky enterprise in the Island, are numerous and noisy, and in the majority, nonentities'. Because of its central position on the promenade the Palace Ballroom soon became the premier entertainment venue in Douglas, and, as the advertising posters reminded visitors: 'no climbing' was required when visiting, unlike the Falcon Cliff, which, despite the excellent tram-car lift, was perched on a ridge above Douglas Bay.

An embarrassment of riches.

At the Falcon Cliff, Charles Reynolds' new dances for the season included the waltz *Douglas, Queen of the West* with its breezy vocal refrain, customarily sung by the dancers, and supported by those musicians not actually playing:

> Far, far over the bright sparkling waters, hope and joy fill the heart all the day,
> Winds blow gently on fair Mona's daughters, gladly we welcome them out on the Bay.

The Jolly Visitors vocal polka incorporated a vocal refrain typical of the kind characteristic of the Falcon Cliff and Derby Castle under Gaggs and Reynolds:

> Ha! Ha! Ha! Ha! Ha! Ha! Ha! Ha!
> Come and join the laugh, and the rosy quaff, to the Cliff, for the merry little dance, Ha! Ha!
> With a cheerful song, in a lively throng, you'll ne'er have another better chance, Ha! Ha!

Reynold's 'humorous and descriptive' fantasy for orchestra, *A Day in Douglas*, depicted the crush of visitors boarding a steamer at the Prince's Landing Stage in Liverpool, and a day in Douglas at the height of the season.

~

At the Derby Castle, Oliver Gaggs enhanced his reputation for capturing the public imagination with attractive dances with a topical flavour such as the vocal waltz *Mona Bouquet*, (the *Scent Waltz*, named after Greenhill's 'Mona Bouquet', a fashionable fragrance since 1852.) the *Mermaid Waltz* and *King Orry*, an arrangement of Manx airs, which it was hoped would rival the previous season's *Hi! Kelly* and *Sweet Mona Waltz* in popularity. The humorous vocal polka Kippers soon proved to be one of the most popular 'catches' of the season:

> 'Kippers, kippers, kippers, quick, a box, for me,
> the bell has rung, the boat soon goes, the wind is blowing free'.

Gaggs' other novelty pieces included a potpourri, *Ten Minutes with the Minstrels* - 'a humorous musical melange of quaint negro ditties, an Old Southern Darkies Dance, a clog dance and sand jig' – and a particular season favourite, an orchestral selection entitled *The Rooster's Festival.*

Fred Vetter at the Palace was not such a prolific composer as his rivals at the Falcon Cliff and Derby Castle; his reputation was founded rather on the excellence of his orchestra. Harry noted the titles of the most popular dances that season in *Cavalcade*: Waldteufel's Valse Militaire *The Grenadiers*, with arresting trumpet fanfares in the introduction, Strauss's *Tales from the Vienna Woods*, Bucalossi's *My Queen* and F. C. Poulter's *Ebb and Flow* among the waltzes; an arrangement of George Grossmith's *You Should See Me Dance the Polka*, Schottisches, such as Warwick Williams' *Song and Dance*, quadrilles and lancers such as *Don't Tease* and *The Royal Corinthian*. Special requests were always welcomed.

Harry also mentions in *Cavalcade* some of the most popular light orchestral pieces performed at the afternoon concerts during the 1889 season. The first march to be played at the Palace came from Suppe's sparkling operetta *Boccaccio* based on the erotic novellas of the 14th century Florentine, Giovanni Boccaccio, and the most popular selection of the season was taken from Lecocq's *La Fille de Madame Angot*, which recounts the racy adventures of Clariette, a sweet girl, but the daughter of a fishwife, who acquires a fortune but not the airs and graces to go with it.

'All was perfection' . . . The Sunday Sacred Concerts.

A musical event of great significance was the inaugural concert of the Sunday Sacred Concert series at the Palace, which took place on 4th August, 1889, when Handel's *Messiah* was given by a choir and orchestra of one hundred performers under the direction of Fred Vetter. The choir consisted of the sixty-strong Huddersfield Glee and Madrigal Society, whose musical director, John North, was a friend of Harry's from Slaithwaite, with soloists Lori Rescoschewitz, mezzo-soprano, Elizabeth Dews, contralto, John Leyland, tenor and Edward Grimes, bass.

Messiah attracted one of the largest, if not the largest audience that ever attended a concert on the Island up to that time, estimated at between three and four thousand people. The *Mona's Herald* reporter felt it necessary to remind readers that had:

> . . . too often expressed our disapproval of Sunday amusements or trading, both on moral grounds and as being detrimental to the welfare of the Island, to feel it necessary to do more than to assure our readers that late events are confirming us more and more in our opinion, that one day out of the seven should be a day of rest for man and beast.

However, in a less puritanical tone he went on to say:

> . . . we are happy to be able to report that never was a musical entertainment given in this Island of greater artistic excellence or conducted in a more orderly manner than the one on Sunday, and we hope that the directors may see their way to repeat this self-same Oratorio on a week day to give those persons (and there are many) who conscientiously abstain from Sunday entertainments, an opportunity of enjoying a musical treat that possibly they have not yet had within their reach.

A number of the choruses in *Messiah* were encored, and as is traditional the audience 'stood up and uncovered' during the *Hallelujah* chorus. The soloists 'gave complete satisfaction', and Miss Dews was prevailed upon to repeat *He was despised*.

Concert reviews at this period were unusually lengthy but predominately consisted of reiterating details of the pieces performed and the artists involved. There was little in-depth criticism of the actual performances except in very broad terms: Miss so-and-so 'gave great pleasure'; Mr so-and-so's performance of this-or-that ballad 'was a very fine rendering', or Madame so-and-so sang this-or-that aria 'in superb style' or 'with excellent effect'. Nevertheless, one gets a powerful sense of just how ground-breaking, awe-inspiring and well-conceived the first Sacred Concerts were, and what an overwhelming experience they must have been for the audiences with choral singing of a far higher standard than was usually heard on the Island. It is unlikely that *Messiah* was given in anything like a complete version, nor was it likely that Haydn's *Creation* the following Sunday was performed uncut.

~

By the time of the third Sacred Concert on 18th August, which featured selections from Mendelssohn's *Elijah*, the series was being lauded as '. . . the rage in Douglas'. Indeed, this may have the first time that a substantial portion of *Elijah* was performed on the Island as opposed to merely the favourite arias, and the Palace was full to capacity, with many having to stand. The following Sunday witnessed the Isle of Man premier of Rossini's *Stabat Mater*, and for the Sacred Concert on 1st September the Huddersfield Glee and Madrigal Society returned to the Island for a repeat performance of *Messiah*, which again attracted a large audience. Even this occasion was trumped on 8th September by 'Gems of Oratorio', which featured no less than twenty artists directed by Fred Vetter, who directed the overture, closing march and other orchestral pieces, and guest conductor Josef Cantor, who directed his Liverpool Concert Company, the chorus and soloists. Around three thousand people heard excerpts from *Messiah*, *The Creation* and *Elijah*, Spohr's *Calvary*, Costa's *Naaman* and Sullivan's *The Light of the World*. Haydn's chorus *The Heaven's Are Telling* and Spohr's aria *As Pants the Hart* were considered the 'gems of the evening'.

So popular did these events prove to be that it was decided to present two further Sacred Concerts on 15th and 22nd September; the ninth and last Sacred Concert of the season took place a week later during a spell of poor weather and before an end-of-season audience of some two thousand people.

'No dearth of amusements . . . there's life in the old town yet'.

The 1889 season at the Palace ended on Friday 27th September. Elsewhere in Douglas many shows had extended runs to the end of the month to entertain an increasing number of visitors taking holidays late in the season. To encourage such visitors many boarding-houses reduced their prices by as much as 50%.

The opening of the Palace had initiated an intense rivalry between the three principal resort venues. The Derby Castle commenced a series of improvements both inside the complex and in the grounds: the pavilion dance floor was newly waxed and polished and the lighting was enhanced; a road widening scheme from the tram terminus, as well as a new sea wall, made access to the venue both easier and grander; the gardens were substantially up-graded and featured new rustic seats and arbours, and the familiar castellated hotel facade was 'newly whitened'.

Further afield, the talented Holden family 'orchestra' of seven musicians entertained visitors at the seven hundred acre Injebreck pleasure grounds; another favourite excursion from Douglas, and Belle Vue Gardens, a twenty acre pleasure ground incorporating an athletic track, lake, ornamental pagoda, a small zoo and circus, switchback railway, bowls, tennis and archery also attracted a large number of holiday makers.[25] The smaller rural resorts of Tholt-e-Will, Glen Helen, Dhoon

Belle Vue pleasure grounds.

Glen and Laxey Glen all welcomed large numbers of visitors to their pleasure grounds.

For those who wished to stay in Douglas, a genteel hour-or-two could be idled away at the Free Library or Webb's Public Lounge, where not only refreshments were available, but writing galleries with pen and paper provided for those who wished to write home, or perhaps to record their impressions of the Island, with music provided by an orchestrion.[26] The Egyptian Hall, Loch Parade, offered conjuring acts and spiritualistic séances, and 'Professor' T. R. Wood's Phrenological Expositions again sought to mystify visitors with enquiring minds. For the more energetic or fastidious, the Victoria Swimming Baths, incorporating a public baths, were open daily, and the Manx Fair at Pulrose on the outskirts of Douglas offered entertainments every day. As one end of season reviewer declared: 'We have been favoured this year with everything the mind could desire'.

The variety artists at the larger venues had been a huge draw. The northern comedian G. W. Nicholson at the Derby Castle, and Lester Barrett, at the Falcon Cliff, whose comic songs *One More Polka* and *Saved it for the Lodger* were noted for being refreshingly 'free from vulgarity'. As popular as these entertainers were, though, it is fair to say that until 1892, when Marie Lloyd, Little Tich and R. G. Knowles appeared in Douglas for the first time, no really famous variety artists had appeared on the Isle of Man. Thereafter, all the biggest music hall and variety stars flocked to the Island, and the era of Douglas becoming established as the 'home of popular song', began in earnest.

'Douglas, the Empress of Watering Places'.

One visitor from Southport communicated his impressions of Douglas to the *Isle of Man Times*:

> Southport should take a leaf out of Douglas's book! So much more amusement of a lively nature is to be found on the Island. I was amazed to find that not only the new Palace Ballroom was full, but also Falcon Cliff and the Derby Castle were thriving! Douglas was crammed full in late August.

Yet another visitor was amazed that: 'On Saturday evening a complete blaze of electricity illuminated the regions of Castle Mona, Falcon Cliff and Derby Castle'.

A correspondent from the *Galloway Advertiser and Wigtownshire Free Press* expressed his enthusiasm for the Island and his enjoyment of his summer holiday in a piece entitled A Trip to the Wonderful Isle of Man:

> . . . a compact little country . . . there are no murders in Man, no poisoning cases, no forgeries, no assaults. Several hundred local people came down to the pier to watch the Scots folk landing. We were captivated by the tall spires and palatial buildings round the beautiful bay and impressed by the magnitude and magnificence of the tall boarding houses along Loch Promenade, whose long dining rooms face the sea . . . from which a delightful aroma flowed forth.

He was also charmed by the sight of a young holiday-maker offering to 'turn the handle' for a tired, 'fair and dreamy-eyed' young female Italian organ grinder, 'a gallant action which brought good-natured smiles to everyone's faces'. Not everyone it seems was dismayed at the proliferation of street musicians in Douglas.

A visitor from Sheffield alluded to the importance of the recently extended Victoria Pier in making it possible to safely and efficiently land large numbers of visitors, and compared it favourably to those at Llandudno. Brighton, he concluded, might be the 'Queen of Watering Places', but was a resort where no steamer can dock. Douglas therefore justifiably earned the title of the 'Empress of Watering Places'.

As the season tailed off and the last visitors left the Island, the more thoughtful newspaper columnists began to anticipate the long winter months ahead, characterised in Douglas by forlorn boarding houses effectively closed for up to eight months, and the rest of the Island lapsing into what many regarded as a state of lethargy. A number of them proposed that strong working committees of leading businessmen, tradesmen, owners of hotel, guest house and private boarding houses, the Steam Packet and other ferry companies should organise public meetings and formulate plans to extend the visitor season in the years to come. Although it was agreed that there was no real reason to be apprehensive, it was suggested that there was 'NO TIME to be LOST!' Douglas would not maintain its position among the 'places of resort' unless it could be popularised as both a summer and winter resort.

Expanding influence.

Harry remained at the Palace as the repetiteur violinist in an orchestra of thirty players throughout the 1890 season; Oliver Gaggs continued as musical director at the Derby Castle, 'Mona's Elysium Palace' and J. H. Greenwood took over from Charles Reynolds at the Falcon Cliff in the dual roles of conductor and entertainer, introducing a comic interlude entitled Mirth and Mimicry during the intervals in the afternoon concerts.

In January he supplied a band to play at a convivial Stanley Club Ball and smoking concert at the Masonic Hall, Douglas. Among the quadrilles, schottisches, waltzes, polkas and lancers, was Poulter's popular *Ebb and Flow* waltz from the previous season,[27] and Harry's waltz, *Seraglio*. *The Isle of Man Times* mentioned Harry's waltz in their report of the occasion, one of the earliest references in the local newspapers to one of his compositions.

The Grand Concert in the Grand Theatre at the end of January was not as successful as the organisers had hoped. The venture, thought to be highly speculative in winter, was seriously affected by cold and raw weather, and according to the the *Isle of Man Times*, the 'house was thin', and the programme 'too classical', lacking the selections from popular operas and operettas that audiences expected. Harry, Daniel Wood, F. C. Poulter and the contralto Elizabeth Dews, gave of their best, but many of the songs and instrumental pieces were spoilt because the restless audience made a great deal of noise turning the pages of their programmes.

As the Island waited for Whit-week to arrive, Harry busied himself fulfilling a number of engagements and expanding his private teaching. The annual entertainment for New Year's Day organised by F. C. Poulter and Harry Johnson, a well-known local entertainer and singer, took the form of a diorama presentation entitled 'A Visit to the Paris Exhibition', consisting of sixty 'beautifully coloured views, many of them with mechanical effects, shown through one of the finest lanterns ever seen on the Island'.[28]

The Inaugural Students' Orchestral Concert.

The first of Harry's ground-breaking students' concerts took place at the Douglas Gymnasium on Thursday, 17th April, 1890. Just one year after his first advertisement as a violin teacher, some of his pupils had reached a sufficiently high standard to be able to benefit from orchestral experience. No doubt he recalled his own first exciting taste of orchestral playing in his teacher George Haddock's annual students' concerts in Yorkshire in 1882.

The orchestra consisted overwhelmingly of young violinists including twelve first violins led by Miss Laura Clinch,[29] and thirteen second violins, one of whom may have been a viola player, supported by two experienced local adult violinists, F. Farrell and J. E. Quayle.[30] There do not appear to have been any 'cellists, but the two double bass players were Harry's colleague F. C. Poulter - who also acted as the piano accompanist in one piece - and P. Wright. Harry's brother Daniel, on the threshold of his studies at the Royal College of Music in London, played the flute and piccolo; the piano accompanist was Miss Eveleen Wood (no relation), and the organ accompanist was Miss Amy Mew.[31] Daniel Wood, Miss Clinch and Miss Etta Wood (again, no relation), performed instrumental solos and duets, and Harry himself played a duet with Amy Mew and conducted the entire concert. Four local singers also gave their services: Nellie Broadbent – who also played in the first violins - Miss Sissie Rowe,[32] Mr T. Brockbank and Charles Bamber. The piano was generously loaned by the directors of the Castle Mona Palace; ticket prices were one shilling for front seats and two shillings for rear or 'second' seats, and the net proceeds of £13 0s 6d were donated to the Isle of Man Industrial Home for Destitute Children.[33]

The 'very varied' programme began with Rossini's overture *Tancredi* and concluded with Mendelssohn's *War March of the Priests* and ended at 10.30pm after the singing of the National Anthem. According to the *Isle of Man Times*:

> The audience . . . in the anticipation of enjoying a musical treat were in no way disappointed, for Mr Harry Wood's well-selected programme was admirably executed by his clever and well-trained students. They were listened to with rapt attention, and were heartily applauded at the close of each piece. All the pieces were rendered with a precision, smoothness and expressive animation that would have done credit to a band of experienced professionals.

The purpose behind the concerts was of course to provide a showcase for his most able and talented pupils, some of whom went on to enjoy long and distinguished careers in music, most notably his younger brother Haydn; his nephew Hilton Cullerne;[34] Samuel Robinson, known as Orry Corjeag,[35] the first Baume Scholar in 1904;[36] Cecil Corlett, the Baume Scholar in 1915, and Kathleen Rydings,[37] who won a scholarship to the Royal College of Music in 1903, and later returned to the Island to become a highly respected violin teacher and conductor.

'Douglas lay before us, ablaze with light'.

Whit-Saturday, 24th May - coincidently, Queen Victoria's birthday - brought with it 'genuine Queen's weather', and all was spick-and-span and alive with flags at the pier when the first steamer, the Prince of Wales, arrived in the early afternoon after a remarkably swift passage of three-

and-a-half-hours. Her departure from Liverpool had been 'flashed along the electric wire', and the fast beat of the paddles of this fastest vessel in the Steam Packet Company fleet could be heard a full 15 minutes before she appeared from behind the breakwater by huge crowds waiting to greet her. The opening of the 1890 season was thus heralded by several blasts on the ship's foghorn which apparently could be heard some miles inland. Four gangways were run out, some sixteen hundred passengers disembarked in just twenty minutes, and were immediately accosted by white-jacketed 'hobblers', or porters, and carriage and waggonette drivers touting for business. Other visitors were already transferring to the black-smoke-belching cross-harbour ferries. All was hustle, bustle and confusion.

One of the last steamers of the day, the *Ben-my-Cree* with one thousand passengers, arrived just after 9.00pm as the sun was setting. The visitors were momentarily awe-struck by the beautiful scene before them, particularly the contrast between the blaze of gas and electric light from the Derby Castle two miles away across the bay, and the rest of Douglas in comparative darkness. After a few moments of silence one holiday-maker reputedly turned to his Manx companion and remarked: 'I thought you told us they burnt nothing but candles here? Why, I've travelled the world - the Indian Pacific, the Mediterranean, the Indian Ocean - and never saw anything to equal this'.

~

The Palace closed as usual after Whit-week and re-opened early in July with an important innovation, the introduction of morning concerts between 11.00am and 1.00pm, which quickly 'proved a source of delight and enjoyment' and drew enthusiastic if not always large audiences. The afternoon concerts at the open-air band stand were generally more successful, and Vetter's band received much praise in the local newspapers, with most commentators drawing attention to the improvement in the band since the previous season. By the height of the season the morning orchestral concerts at the Palace had become 'the most fashionable in Douglas', and for those wishing to while away a couple of hours in charming surroundings before lunch 'to the sounds of an excellent band discoursing sweet music', little more could be desired. The evening dance assemblies in the ballroom were also growing in reputation, with four thousand people often attending.

Bucalossi's waltz *My Queen*, and a selection from Lecocq's *La Fille de Madame Angot* were the 'hits' of the 1890 season at the Palace, as they had

A Sunday sacred concert at the Palace.

been in 1889. At the Derby Castle, Oliver Gaggs' new medley of minstrel songs, the *Minnehaha Lancers*,[38] and the *Mermaid Waltz*, with references

Charles Blondin.

to Mona's Isle in the vocal refrain, were frequently requested. All three orchestras from the Palace, Derby Castle and Falcon Cliff took it in turns to provide the musical entertainment for the formal opening of the newly extended Queen's Promenade on 8th July,[39] an event that also witnessed a performance in the Palace grounds of one of the greatest entertainers of the era, Charles Blondin,[40] the famous tightrope walker, the 'Hero of Niagara'. Although only fifty-five feet above the ground, suspended between two masts two hundred feet apart, and hidden behind a screen to prevent people getting a free view, the great funambulist still managed to execute some of his best-known feats on the rope: riding a bicycle, sitting on a chair and cooking - and presumably eating - an omelette. In an interview, he said that his first performance on the rope had been at the age of four, and although he was now sixty-six, he never felt nervous. He confirmed that he was, indeed, French, but contrary to speculation, his long career was not due to being teetotal, as he occasionally 'enjoyed a glass'.

There were fourteen Sunday Sacred Concerts at the Palace during the 1890 season. Most contained popular arias and choruses from the sacred music of Handel, Haydn, Mendelssohn, Rossini, Gounod and Sullivan.

Joseph Cantor's 'Gems of the Oratorios' Concert Party appeared on four occasions; *Messiah* was performed twice and *Elijah* just once. One of the most spectacular sacred concerts was given on 7th September by the Huddersfield Festival Choir and the Palace Orchestra - a total of one hundred performers – which attracted an audience of four thousand. Following the sacred concert on 10th August at the Grand Theatre the *Isle of Man Times* reviewer wrote: 'The magnetic power of these concerts . . . can only be likened to that of a popular preacher of the first rank, who can always rely on a large congregation . . .'

~

The variety entertainments that season included the Cee Mee Troupe of 'beautiful areolites', or trapeze artists, the climax of whose act was a twenty-five foot 'Alpine Leap' from forty feet above the ground through a fire balloon to a stationary trapeze. Their long and successful run was however trumped in early August by the

> . . . tastefully attired' Sisters Ongar, whose 'unsurpassed trapeze entertainment . . . and marvellous and daring evolutions in mid-air . . . cannot be described, but must be seen. It may be stated without fear of denial, that there has been nothing cleverer of the kind in the Isle of Man, which is saying a good deal.

The 'versatile and funny comedian' Charles Cookson, whose 'first rate voice and dry humour invoked not a little hilarity' continued to provide light relief during intervals in the dance programmes; the Brothers Horne were adjudged 'exceedingly clever and entertaining in their novel musical performance', and Ottoway and Pepper kept the audiences amused with their particular brand of zaniness. One of the high-points each evening was the appearance of a pipe band in full Highland dress.

Fred Vetter's benefit concert took place on 2nd September in the presence of His Excellency the Lt. Governor, Spencer Walpole. Three of the most popular vocal soloists of the season took part and there were instrumental solos from some of the band's principal players, and selections from Bizet's *Carmen* and Wallace's *Maritana*. The variety artists were represented by the Sisters Ongar and the Eclipse Trio. To mark the occasion, on entering the Palace each lady was presented with a bottle of Mr E. J. Bowman's new perfume, 'Heather Bloom': an agreeable souvenir of an undoubtedly enjoyable evening.

~

The sisters Ongar.

The Palace band contracts were terminated at the end of the season as was customary, and the musicians returned to their regular winter engagements in Manchester, Liverpool or London. Harry saw out the year by participating in a number of local musical events, the last recorded of which was a concert at the Loch Promenade Schoolroom.

One local event Harry was surely present at in October was the foundation-stone-laying ceremony for one of the most ambitious projects ever planned for the Island: the Douglas North Quay Tower and Bridge, dubbed the Douglas 'Eiffel Tower'. When completed, the immense structure was to have been just over four hundred feet in height, incorporating six floors accessed by a lift and spiral stairway, and including a ballroom, a grand concert hall – some reports suggested a skating rink - a bazaar, restaurant and a large summit observation saloon. The tower, which could have opened three years-or-so before Blackpool's famous Eiffel–inspired tower, would have presented a spectacular and awe-inspiring sight from the decks of the steamers crammed with visitors as they approached Douglas harbour, particularly at night, lit up with 'electric light of great power'. It could have constituted an immense added draw for those seeking pleasure and entertainment on the Island during those late Victorian summers, but it was not to be. The project foundered and the tower was never built.[41]

As the year drew to a close, at the Wood family home there was one less mouth to feed, for Daniel Wood had commenced his studies at the Royal College of Music in London. Although he visited the Island on a number of occasions throughout his life, and for a few more years continued to take part in both Derby Castle and Palace concerts under Harry's baton, he was never again to be a permanent resident, his remarkable talent as a flautist taking him to the peak of his profession in London and elsewhere.

Great preparations 'at our principal pleasure resorts . . .'

Harry Wood was twenty-three-years-old in 1891, and this was the year his career took the decisive turn away from a comfortable existence as a repetiteur violinist, orchestral soloist and relief assistant conductor, towards his first official appointment as orchestral leader and deputy conductor at one of Douglas's prestigious entertainment venues.

After 'a long and monotonous winter' it was all change at the Palace, the Derby Castle and the Falcon Cliff in 1891. Fred Vetter disappeared from the scene to be replaced by 'able, genial and courteous' Oliver Gaggs at the Castle Mona Palace, with his youngest son, Joseph Woof Gaggs, as leader, and his eldest son, Thomas Harold Gaggs, as the accompanist. The Palace Sacred Concerts would continue to flourish under his baton, and his new compositions, the waltz *Sweet Isle of the Sea*, his amusing orchestral novelty *A Trip to Manxland*, and 'the thrilling and realistic Galop' *The Lifeboat Resue*, featuring Douglas Lifeboat Crew in full costume, would be among the novelties of the season.

J. H. Greenwood retained his position as musical director at the Falcon Cliff, with his son J. H. Greenwood Jnr, as band leader, together with the added attraction of his popular short entertainment 'Mirth and Mimicry' during the afternoon concerts. He was supported again by resident comedian Lester Barrett and 'Professor' Grant, 'the inimitable ventriloquist'. His new dance compositions for the season included the *Cliff Lancers* and the *Falcon Waltz*.

At the Derby Castle, 'the Romantic Resort of Douglas', the

comparatively young Bradford composer and conductor Stocks Hammond[42] was appointed musical director, with Harry Wood as leader of the orchestra and deputy conductor. Like the musical directors at the other two venues, Hammond was not backward in introducing his own topical new dances, the *Derby Castle Lancers*, the waltz *Down by the Sea* and *As Pretty as a Pink* - described by Harry Wood in *Cavalcade* as 'that very popular Schottische' - during a vibrant season. The afternoon concerts at the Derby Castle were expected to attract large crowds, but there were no morning or sacred concerts that season.

In the months leading up to the start of the summer season, though, the most urgent and pressing of Harry's forthcoming musical events was the organising of his second annual students' orchestral concert, which took place in front of a capacity audience at the Grand Theatre on 16th April, and was adjudged 'one of the most enjoyable and popular of the season'. The format was identical to the previous year and the orchestra of thirty-five players was again led by Laura Clinch who also contributed a selection of violin solos. Daniel Wood played Paggi's *Neapolitan Airs* on the flute, and Demare's delightful evocation of bird song, *Les Echoes des Bois*, on the piccolo, whilst Frank Heslop entertained the audience with some 'comical twanging' on the banjo.

Harry takes the helm

Stocks Hammond's band at the Derby Castle had a complement of twenty-five players at the start of the season, rising to thirty-five in August and early September. Until early July Harry was in charge of both the afternoon concerts and evening dance programmes; as one reviewer prophetically wrote: 'doubtless this gentleman before long will blossom forth as a conductor himself'. Stocks Hammond arrived in Douglas during the first week of July and as the *Manx Sun* noted 'would be in personal command of his magnificent orchestra'. He was briefly away from the Derby Castle again during the last week of that month, but was in full charge of the band throughout August. However, following his benefit concert in September, he left Harry in sole charge of the afternoon concerts, whilst he continued to conduct only the evening dance programmes.

For the first time in his career Harry, 'our able and gifted townsman', had sole charge of one of the finest orchestras in Douglas, 'and discharged his duties carefully and well'. One particular afternoon concert delighted the *Isle of Man Times* reviewer, who wrote:

Harry Wood as depicted in a magazine of the 1890s.

> On Thursday afternoon there was a capital programme, and the various items entrusted to the band were executed with refinement and true artistic skill. Mr Harry Wood's conducting of the musical numbers was done with superlative excellence.

The local newspapers continued to publish complimentary reviews about the excellence of the Derby Castle band under Harry's direction:

> On Tuesday afternoon there was an excellent programme musically, and the splendid little band under Mr Harry Wood's conductorship

> fairly excelled itself, the various items being highly appreciated. The grand selection 'Kenilworth' was undoubtedly the gem of the afternoon, and showed off the capital tone and quality of the able orchestra.

Such positive concert notices as these will have given Harry immense pleasure, and he must have suspected that he might be 'on trial' as a possible successor to one of the principal music directors in a future season.

At such crucial times in Harry's career, one especially regrets that no correspondence or further engagement diaries have survived. The bald, factual statements in *Cavalcade* that head the year 1891 offer no clues as to Harry's personal feelings about the progress of his career:

> Derby Castle. Stocks Hammond. Conductor of the orchestra. I was his leader and deputy conductor.

One longs to know what his impressions were of the 1891 summer season when he stood on the brink of one of the most influential careers in the story of music-making on the Isle of Man, and began to flex his musical muscles and put into practice those valuable, practical lessons and experiences that he had absorbed as a young professional musician playing in the Huddersfield Theatre orchestra.

~

The variety artists at the start of the season included La Belle Maude, 'The Queen of the Air', 'whose dexterous and graceful aerial flights are such as to call forth amazement', and the Irish comedy dance duo and knock-abouts, the Two Armstrongs, whose 'sketches, songs and excruciating antics kept the house in a constant state of uproar'. Les Petites Jolies Quartette,[43] a concert party of graceful and pretty young ladies who sang and danced gave 'the most charming performance ever seen in Douglas'. Their act included a skipping rope dance and Lutz's saucy *Pas de Quatre*, which 'brought forth deafening applause'.

La Belle Maude and Les Jolies Petites Quartette were still topping the bill in early July, when they were joined by the The Dezmonitis in their first appearance on the Island with 'a classical and grotesque horizontal bar act', and The Beautiful Geraldine, billed as 'England's Greatest Lady Gymnast - 'the bright particular star of the evening' - who thrilled the audiences with her daring gymnastic feats on the high trapeze. Harry Freeman,[44] 'Prince of Vocal Comedians', entertained each evening with his famous song *Can't Stop, They're after Me*, and 'was persistently recalled'.

His constantly re-vitalised thirty minute act of 'rollicking joviality' proved to be 'very contagious' and he was re-engaged for a further fortnight.

The engagement of Miss Elsa Joel in July, 'without parallel on the variety stage' and 'the finest lady vocalist ever heard in Douglas', aroused great expectations. Today she would be styled a 'cross-over' artiste, appealing to both the genteel afternoon promenade audiences and the livelier evening dance crowd. She introduced a varied repertoire of songs including *Killarney* and *The Song That Reached My Heart*, a ballad by American composer Julian Jordan, which incorporated the refrain of *Home, Sweet Home*.

'Shadows of evening are falling'

The dance programmes commenced at 7.30 each evening and included many of Stocks Hammond's new pieces for the season, principally the schottische *As Pretty as Pink*, the polka *The Harvest Hornpipe*, the American Polka *Brother Jonathan*, the waltz sensation of the season *Dolorosa*, *The Old Stagecoach Galop*, the *Derby Galop* and the *Derby Castle Lancers*. Three dances - *As Pretty as Pink*, *Dolorosa* and the vocal waltz *Stageland* - were demanded every evening, and at the end of August he introduced his new waltz, *Dreaming of Thee*. Throughout September there was 'the special attraction' of two bands playing each evening: Stocks Hammond in the Pavilion, and Harry Wood with a smaller band on the open-air platform.

The repertoire of the afternoon concerts continued to consist of well-tried, light, tuneful overtures, selections from popular operas and operettas, marches, short descriptive concert pieces, instrumental solos, ballads, songs and arias. Dances often featured in the promenade concert programmes, although for listening to rather than for dancing. Among the most popular that season were Stock Hammond's new gavotte *Ima*, Theo. Bonheur's *Les danse des Dwarfs* and the gavotte *Old and New*,[45] Waldteufels waltz *Sentiers Fleuris* and Gungl's waltz *Immortellen*. Instrumental solos were always popular and the 1891 season featured the orchestra's principal cornet, clarinet and flute players in a variety of popular pieces including a morceau entitled *Lion Noir* for piccolo, composed by Harry himself, and perhaps named after the Black Lion Hotel on North Quay. The concerts invariably concluded with a rousing march.

~

Each entertainment venue introduced new novelty dances that season.

At the Palace, Oliver Gaggs led the field with the innovative and spectacular Shadow Dances at 10pm each evening. An enchanting fairy scene was created with special lighting effects which lit the dance floor with a blaze of colour combinations. As the dancers glided around the floor, they sang the following evocative lines:

> 'Shadows of evening are falling, the old village clock chimes nine;
> From the porch dear mother is calling – "To rest, dear children of mine".
> Shadows darken the distant green, moonlight gilds with silvery sheen;
> Shadows everywhere are seen, shadows, fleeting shadows'.

Stocks Hammond at the Derby Castle responded to the challenge with his vocal waltz *Sundown Shadows*. Later in the season, the Palace presented a Japanese Fan Night, when every lady through the turnstiles received a Japanese fan, and a lithograph of the ballroom.

In *Cavalcade* Harry briefly mentions *The Infernal Polka* by Bonniseau which was accompanied by a mock storm with lightning effects, 'much to the enjoyment of the merry-makers'. At the Falcon Cliff, J. H. Greenwood, 'very popular with Yorkshire and Lancashire folk', interpolated a 'laughter-provoking sketch' entitled *A Visit to the Isle of Man*, and the vocal polka, *The Rollocking Polka*, into the evening's entertainment. As well as novelty dances, novelty nights at the Derby Castle such as the Grand Nautical Night, the Grand Comic Carnival and the Popular and Original Carnival of Flowers all drew substantial crowds.

By mid-September the season was flagging, and the Falcon Cliff, the Castle Mona Palace and the Derby Castle all made final strenuous efforts to attract the patronage of the last few visitors still on the Island. The afternoon concerts at the Derby Castle continued to attract good audiences; Daniel Wood appeared again as the piccolo soloist in J. Harrington Young's *Danse des Sabots*, and Allan Macbeth's little intermezzo for strings, *Forget-me-not*, delighted one *Isle of Man Times* reviewer so much that he wrote:

> . . . one of the prettiest pieces of music one could wish to hear, a beautiful recurrent melody running through it, now seeming close at hand, and the next instant sounding like sweet music being wafted across a broad lake. This piece was exquisitely performed, and the audience was not slow to appreciate it, but to demand an encore, which being granted, again evoked loud applause.

'At Home' with the Stanleyites

In October 1891 Harry was appointed the conductor of the Douglas Musical Society just prior to the commencement of the winter rehearsal schedule. The *Isle of Man Times* greeted the news with approval: 'The society has plenty of energy and ability and its public appearances may be awaited with interest. With Mr Wood at the helm we may be sure the technical work will be thoroughly well looked after'.

At the end of October Harry took part in one of a series of Monday evening entertainments aimed at promoting the cause of Temperance at the St. George's Mission Hall, Douglas, during which he performed in a trio with two other Woods, Miss Ella and Miss Eveleen, who organised the concert, but who were not members of his family. Other events for which Harry provided musical refreshment included the Douglas and Isle of Man Chrysanthemum Show - the report of which was afforded no less than two columns in the *Mona's Herald* - during which he and his accompanist performed 'very choice selections on the violin and pianoforte'. A larger band was required for the musical entertainments at the Annual Guild Exhibition at the Palace in early December, at which a large number of paintings and drawings in all categories, and various crafts, were exhibited. Harry's ensemble provided background music twice each afternoon and on the Wednesday, Friday and Saturday evenings.

The 'At Home' or bachelor's fete with refreshments and dancing for members of the Stanley Club and their friends, was held at Windermere House on Douglas promenade in mid-December, and Harry, described as a 'confrere' of the club, provided the band and arranged the dance music for the ball in the grand dining room. 'The young and the gay' thoroughly entered into the spirit of Harry's selections 'from all that was most popular' and responded to the 'unerring knack in his direction'.

~

On 12th December, the *Manx Sun* published a list of forthcoming events for the New Year. The final entry, dated 22nd April, 1892, read: 'Grand Theatre. Harry Wood's Orchestral and Operatic Concert'.

As he cast his eye over the musical events for the first part of 1892, he was, I am sure, already aware that long before he would lift his baton that April evening and start the opening chorus of his third annual students' concert, he would have secured for himself one of the most prestigious musical posts in Douglas. For an announcement of his appointment as musical director of the Derby Castle band appeared in the gossip column of the *Manx Sun* on New Year's Day:

> At the Derby Castle, during the ensuing summer, we are to have 'Sir' Harry Wood to conduct the orchestra. He will be met with a hearty welcome from all . . .

What he may not have envisaged, though, was that he would hold that post, and others, with distinction and honour for the next forty-six years.

Chapter 3

Harry Wood at the Derby Castle

1892-1901

This was the decade when the Isle of Man tourist and entertainment industry got fully into its stride; the decade that witnessed the opening of the Queen's Promenade[1] and saw significant improvements to the Harris and Central Promenades, and to two of Douglas's premier entertainment venues, the Derby Castle and the Palace, both of which acquired variety theatres in 1893. It also witnessed the rise and demise of a new venue, the Marina Pavilion or Pavilion Variety Theatre as it became known, and the disappearance of two much-loved landmarks: the Falcon Cliff Pavilion and the Old Iron Pier, the latter referred to at a meeting of the Douglas Town Commissioners as 'an eyesore and a nuisance . . . a hideous object, which spoils and cuts the views of the bay in two from all directions'.[2]

Public transport in and around Douglas was much improved during this period, including the extension of the electric railway to Ramsey via the small resort of Groudle Glen, the industrial village of Laxey and an important extension to the top of Snaefell mountain.[3] In 1897 the newly formed Isle of Man Tramways and Electric Power Company acquired the rights to develop tram routes in Douglas; the Douglas Head tramway opened in 1896, and in the following year the first charabancs appeared on the streets for the summer season. The Douglas Bus Company began operating in 1899 and, in July that year, a motor car appeared on the Island for the first time.

Away from the promenades, beaches and bathing machines, yet within walking distance from the centre of the town, Douglas Head offered pleasure seekers incomparable views both landward and seaward, a popular hotel for refreshments and music, and nearing completion, the dramatic development of the Marine Drive. Officially opened on 25th July, 1892, this magnificent coastal drive led to Port Soderick, where a hotel, refreshment rooms and a 'smuggler's cave' could be found. The Belle Vue Pleasure Ground, just a mile from the centre of Douglas, offered a good race track for athletes and cyclists, a monkey house, a bear pit - although one of the bears had recently died after attempting to eat a football - a switchback railway, refreshments, a band and variety entertainments throughout the day.

Before long other towns and villages were attempting to emulate Douglas. Ramsey, the 'Queen of the North', with its recently developed Mooragh Park which had a regular band engaged for the summer season, began to benefit from the extension of the electric tram line from Laxey, as well as steamers from Liverpool, Fleetwood and Barrow calling at the Queen's Pier. Peel, a fishing community still, with its ancient castle on St. Patrick's Isle, boasted excellent beaches, an outdoor bathing pool and a fine hotel, the Fenella, named from a heroine in Sir Walter Scott's *Peveril of the Peak*. Castletown, the Island's ancient capital, had a wonderfully preserved medieval castle as well as nearby Rushen Abbey pleasure gardens. Gradually even the smaller centres of Port St. Mary and Port Erin improved their facilities and attractions and, by the end of the century, each had developed its own distinctive style to attract a particular type of clientele.

In May 1897 the Island reeled from the shock of the mining disaster at the Snaefell Lead Mine when nineteen men lost their lives as a result of carbon monoxide poisoning. In October that year the Manx people bade farewell to their national poet, Thomas Edward Brown, who had returned to live in Ramsey in 1892 after a distinguished academic career both on the Island and in Clifton, Bristol. His richly descriptive lyrical poetry is redolent of the Island, its people and its language. On a happier note, the Island celebrated the Diamond Jubilee of Queen Victoria in 1897 with a huge parade through the town, including some four thousand children representing the Douglas churches and schools led by two brass bands. The Queen's death was mourned on 22nd January 1901 with a Day of General Mourning followed by a memorial service at St. George's Church two days later.

A cavalcade of talent

It was during the 1890s that the Isle of Man, and Douglas in particular, became established as one of the finest entertainment resorts in the British Isles. Of course Douglas could never compete with its big brother Blackpool across the water for sheer numbers of visitors passing through the turnstiles, but in terms of the quality of both the variety entertainers and concert artistes - many of whom returned for many seasons - and the diversity of the nightly dance programmes and the afternoon and Sunday Sacred Concerts, the Island punched well above its weight. In the high-season month of August 1894, for example, a host of famous names all appeared on the same bill at the Derby Castle: Cinquevalli, 'the most

The Derby Castle.

famous juggler who ever juggled'; Marie Lloyd, 'piquante comedienne'; Ida Heath, 'an exotic and clever dancer', and a Douglas favourite, the comedian Harry Randall. Visitors to the Island in August 1896 could have seen Marie Lloyd at the Pavilion Variety Theatre, and Vesta Tilley and Valoni the juggler at the Derby Castle. As the *Manx Sun* observed: 'Such a galaxy of talent has rarely been seen on the same programme'. The following year the prima donna Emma Albani, the great contralto Clara Butt and the Welsh baritone David Ffrancon-Davies all appeared at the Palace Sunday concerts.

Variety artistes such as Vesta Tilley, Dan Leno, Gus Elen and Harry Randall were at their peak when they first appeared in Douglas. Others, such as Marie Lloyd and Wilkie Bard were on the threshold of spectacular careers, and others such as the male impersonator Hetty King, Harry Lauder and the great chorus singer Florrie Forde, were virtually unknown when they first walked onto the stages of the Falcon Cliff and Derby Castle. Today we look back at the music hall era and the great stars who dominated it through a rosy glow of nostalgia for an age no-one alive today witnessed. Scraps of film and recordings of variable quality - many of them deriving from last years in the artiste's careers - give little idea of the way stars like Marie Lloyd, Vesta Tilley or Little Tich 'worked' their audiences, or of the colour, vibrancy, excitement and unique interaction between performer and audience that was the essence of music hall.

~

The entry in *Cavalcade* for the year 1892 names twenty-three variety artistes who appeared in Douglas over the following two decades and many of the songs they performed. Marie Lloyd, the Queen of the Halls, first appeared at the Derby Castle in June that year. Her reputation preceded her, and calls of 'Bravo Marie' greeted her as she stepped onto the stage: '. . . the applause bestowed was loud and frequent, and every evening she has been persistently recalled'.

She sang four songs in an act that probably lasted forty minutes, laced with the saucy 'patter' or 'schtick' for which she was becoming known. Songs such as *Twiggy Voo* and *When you Wink the other Eye* were

Marie Lloyd (left) and Vesta Tilley.

The Derby Castle Ballroom.

characterised by a 'Carry On' style innuendo, and were delivered with the knowing winks and other highly suggestive gestures that typified her act. Her other Derby Castle songs included *Wacky, Whacky Whack* and *Oh! Mr Porter,* and she was a sensation, returning in 1893 and 1894. Her last appearance was at the Pavilion Variety Theatre where she was engaged for a second week and broke all box-office records in 1896.

The supreme male impersonator Vesta Tilley - 'No artiste a greater favourite on the Isle of Man' - was engaged at the Derby Castle on five occasions between 1892 and 1899. Billed as 'The Great London Idol', the hall was so crowded for her first appearance that not everyone could see or hear her, and those at the sides had to 'make do with a pantomime'. Her songs were described as 'tricky and catchy' and 'elevating and touching' and of 'that class that could offend nobody'; the infectious choruses were 'quickly taken up by the audiences with gusto nightly'. In her roles as a 'masher', a Tommy, a policeman or a sailor, she was perfect and exuded immense vitality and boyish charm, 'the quintessence of seaside dandyism'. In female attire she was bewitching and sprightly, and audiences found her adorable. Reporting on her appearances at the Derby

Castle in August 1896, the *Isle of Man Examiner* had this to say:

> Tilley is indeed a marvel. It is the artist that achieves success, for she disdains to resort to such adventitious aids as suggestion, double entendre, or anything else that savours in the slightest degree of impropriety.

In 1897 Tilley's most popular song at the Derby Castle was *Sweetheart May*, which she sang with such yearning that every young man would 'fumble for his sweetheart's hand and swear by the last instalment on his push-bike that he would gladly die for her'. At her final appearance at the end of the 1897 season, Harry presented her with two handsome bouquets on behalf of her Douglas admirers. In 1899 she sang her new 'Isle of Man song', *The Giddy Little Isle of Man*, and the reviews record that she was invariably recalled to the stage repeatedly and was generous with encores.

Charles Coborn.

Charles Coborn, the 'Society Comedian', appeared at the Derby Castle in August 1892, sporting tails, monocle, cigarette and a top hat set at a rakish angle, with a drunken man persona and his best-known songs *Two Lovely Black Eyes* and the 'swell' song *The Man Who Broke the Bank of Monte Carlo*. Harry Randall, the self-styled 'Old Time Comedian', appeared at the Derby Castle for nine seasons between 1893 and 1902, at the Falcon Cliff in 1895, and in 1896 at the Pavilion Variety Theatre. Harry Wood notes in *Cavalcade* that 'he is a great favourite at the Castle' and that he introduced his popular song *I'm Little Teddy Brawn from Douglas* into his act that first season. Apparently the comedian adapted this song to be topical wherever he was appearing: in London he would sing I'm Little Teddy Brown from London, and in Margate, he would sing I'm Little Teddy Brown from Margitt.

One of the few anecdotes about variety entertainers noted by Harry in *Cavalcade* concerns the Canadian comedian R. G. Knowles during his only engagement at the Derby Castle in July 1894. Knowles' appearance had a Dickensian seediness about it as he strode around the stage in a red

R. G. Knowles

wig and battered old opera hat, long frock coat and baggy white trousers, bombarding his audiences with a series of quick-fire stories on the subject of love, marriage and divorce leaving them breathless and bewildered. Harry takes up the story:

> I remember a very amusing incident shewing the quick-wittedness of this comedian. I was conducting his show, and during his performance said to my young brother Haydn, who was sitting near me, 'immediately Knowles begins to leave the stage, take my place'. Haydn did so. Knowles was back on stage in a moment, and, looking down at the orchestra said, 'good gracious Mr Wood. How you've shrunk'. (I am portly, and my brother was a thin little lad).

Harry made a special point of referring to Knowles' songs *All the Girls are Lov-er-ly Ov-er-ly* and his current 'hit' *Brighton*. I wonder if he altered the words of the chorus of *To Brighton! To Brighton!* to give the song a topical and local feel:

> To Douglas! To Douglas!
> Where they do such things
> And they say such things
> In Douglas! In Douglas!
> I'll never go there anymore.

If Marie Lloyd was arguably the greatest female music hall entertainer, then Dan Leno, a half-pathetic figure dressed in outlandish shabby clothes, with the face of a grown up child, was the most unforgettable male star. He appeared at the Falcon Cliff in 1893, and at the Derby Castle in 1894 and 1897 with some of his most memorable sketches: *The Jap, The Waiter* and *The Recruiting Sergean*t, and as an encore his famous clog dance which reduced the audiences to 'roars of laughter'. When interviewed by *The Manxman* in 1897, he confessed that the Island air suited him and he relished his appearances at the Derby Castle:

> It is unique . . . unlike London places of amusement in that the

Dan Leno and George Robey.

audience are close up and standing around the artist. I like the mixed crowd you get in Douglas; everybody so orderly and well-behaved!

Time cannot wither, nor custom stale their infinite variety.

George Robey's was one of the most instantly recognisable stage personalities in the world of variety entertainment. Dressed in sober black clerical garb, a flat pork pie hat, collarless coat, outrageous eyebrows, Chaplinesque knobbly cane, with a cultured voice, quiet delivery and the cherubic countenance of a bishop, the self-styled 'Prime Minister of Mirth' was the antithesis of the loud, larger-than-life Cockney or Costermonger comedians who were his contemporaries. He had enjoyed early success with songs like *Where Did You Get That Hat* but soon developed a range of songs with memorable punch-lines such as 'Bang went the chance of a lifetime'. Character-actor, singer, artist, scholar, athlete, musician and violin maker with his catch-phrase, a pained 'I haven't come here to be laughed at', this archetypal music hall artiste wasn't archetypal at all.

Little Tich.

At just 4' 6" tall, Little Tich, 'the drollest comedian in the entire world', was greeted with such a tremendous ovation when he first appeared at the Castle in 1894, that it was several minutes before the audience allowed him to proceed. He sang *That was Close* and *I'm an Inspector*, did an impersonation of a serpentine dancer and finished with his famous 'Big Boot' dance, during which he stood on tiptoe in boots half as long as he was tall.

Lester Barrett's star shone less brightly than Little Tich's and George Robey's but he continued to be one of the most popular comedians ever to appear in Douglas, a huge draw for Lancashire visitors, and a regular summer resident entertainer at the Falcon Cliff, the Palace and the Derby Castle for many seasons. During Whit-week at the Palace in 1899 he sang a new song *Take her to the Isle of Man, boys.*

In August 1893 Gus Elen, one of the best-loved 'coster comedians' (Costermongers were colourful street traders and one of the most enduring music hall stereotypes), appeared at the Falcon Cliff and sang two of his most famous songs: *Never introduce your donah to a pal* and *'E don't know where 'e ar'.* In the quaint accent of Dickens' Sam Weller in phrases like 'Oh it really is a wery pretty gardin', he sang of the hard lives

Gus Elen.

many in his audiences knew well and thereby made their lives more bearable.

Some artistes adopted stage personas and sang songs that would be totally unacceptable today. The actor, singer and dancer, George H. Chirgwin, 'The White-eyed Musical Kafir', enjoyed a forty year career as a 'black face' entertainer, delivering his affecting song *The Blind Boy* in a strange, wavering falsetto voice every time he appeared. Eugene Stratton, 'The Whistling and Dandy - coloured Coon', appeared at the Falcon Cliff in 1894, and became a 'superstar' after he met the composer Leslie Stuart who wrote *The Lily of Laguna* for him, one of the finest of all love songs. Many of Stratton's songs could not be performed today: *All Coon's Look Alike to Me, Black's de Colour and The Coon Drum Major* to name just three. Many considered him to be a better actor than a singer and he certainly wrung a good deal of emotion out of songs such as *Little Dolly Daydream* and *I May Be Crazy, but I Love You.*

One-song wonders

The other Vesta, Vesta Victoria, appeared at the Palace Opera House in 1897 with the silliest of songs, Joseph Tabrar's *Daddy Wouldn't Buy Me a Bow-Wow,* a 'little girl' song that despite her coy delivery, was a thinly disguised lament of a young women kept by a sugar-Daddy. One of the most famous of all music hall songs, *Daisy Bell* or *A Bicycle Made for Two,* written by Manx-born composer Harry Dacre was sung by Katie Lawrence on her only visit to Douglas at the Palace Opera House in 1893. Her fame was short-lived and *Daisy Bell* her only big hit; she died in poverty and obscurity meriting only a one line obituary in *The Stage* magazine.

Another artiste remembered mainly for one song was 'the coster genius' Bessie Bellwood, the pugnacious Queen of low comedy who appeared at the Falcon Cliff in 1893 when her song *Molly, and I, and the Baby* was encored five times! Dressed up to the nines in the multi-coloured

Lottie Collins and Bessie Bellwood.

skirts of a factory girl on a night out, her best-known song, *Wotcher 'Ria!*, captured the spirit of music hall's rumbustious heyday:

Wotcher 'Ria? 'Ria's on the job
Wotcher 'Ria? Did you speculate a bob?
Oh, 'Ria she's a toff
And she looks immensikoff,
And they all shouted, Wotcher 'Ria?

The riotous *Ta-ra-ra-boom de-ay* lifted Lottie Collins from obscurity among the sand dancers to the highest notoriety. In an interview with The Manxman during her only visit to the Derby Castle in September 1897, she described it as 'a wonderful song, so difficult to render, but tremendously effective', and recalled that she often exhausted herself four or five times an evening in different music halls. She thought the Castle audiences were 'kind and appreciative' and warmed to the '. . unique way the audience stands *en masse* before you, crowding up to the footlights, all in their holiday attire, looking merry and cheerful . . .'

The young girl who would become Vesta Tilley's greatest rival first

Florrie Forde. HANA, PHOTO LONDON

appeared in Douglas at the Derby Castle in 1897 aged 14. Hetty King, fresh from pantomime, was billed as 'The ideal boy' and 'A novel mimic and graceful dancer'.

'. . . and now we shall go and hear Florrie Forde'.

The twenty-five-year-old chanteuse, formerlly known as the 'Australian Marie Lloyd' and eventually as 'The World's Greatest Chorus Singer', arrived in Britain in 1897, and first appeared in Douglas at the Derby Castle for a two-week engagement during the second week of September 1900. The Manx would soon take her to their hearts, Derby Castle would become her 'official' Douglas home and she would appear there almost every summer until 1939. Her first appearance was voted a 'popular triumph' by the *Isle of Man Times* and Florrie herself was described as '. . . a really clever burlesque artiste (who) sings catchy songs in picturesque costumes . . .' So it seems that early in her career she developed her familiar stage persona, imposing, like '. . . a feathered Valkyrie . . . adorned in luxurious clothes and accessories'. Florrie returned

Marie Loftus.

in July 1901, appearing at both the Palace and the Derby Castle with new songs and new dresses, including in all probability *All Aboard for Douglas* (adapted from *All Aboard for Margate*) and *What-Ho, She Bumps.* The key to her success soon became clear: it was her ability to get audiences joining in with the choruses of her songs, and in this respect, she was without peer.

Charlie Chaplin never visited the Isle of Man, but his father Charles Chaplin senior appeared at the Falcon Cliff at the height of his short-lived fame in 1895. He was billed as a 'Star Actor, Vocalist and Comedian' and made some impression with *How he Wins and Loses* and his great dramatic song *Duty Calls.* He specialised in songs about everyday life peopled with nagging wives, mothers-in-law and crying babies such as *The Girl was Young and Pretty,* the front cover of which shows him dressed as a smart 'toff'.

Marie Loftus, actress, singer, pantomime and burlesque star appeared at Falcon Cliff and the Derby Castle during the 1890s. According to the *Manxman* it was at the Derby Castle in 1897 that she introduced a song specially written for the Isle of Man: *A Trip to the Isle of Man,* from which the following lines are taken:

She went on a cheap excursion, seven-and-six return . . .
She sold her return, for she found she could learn
A bit on the Isle of Man.

Novelty and Speciality Acts

These artistes, many of them little-known, forgotten today and very much 'Down among the wines and spirits', encompassed the awe-inspiring and remarkable, the weird and wonderful and the bizarre and tasteless. They included acrobats, trapeze and high wire artistes and other aerial acts, one-legged dancers, jugglers, trick cyclists, acts involving electricity, animals and birds, illusionists, ventriloquists, puppeteers, slapstick artistes,

Zaeo.

but mercifully not, as far as I am aware, the most tasteless of all, the 'spouters' or fartistes, who could spout water and even blow out candles from their rear orifices. Nor did human 'freaks' or 'curiosities' of any sort appear in Douglas unless we count child stars and Dwarf Quaker dancers among the 'freaks' and oddities.

Zaeo, 'The Immortal Zaeo', the 'Diva del Aria' whose buxom, hourglass figure epitomized 'The New Woman', held a strange fascination for Victorian audiences who were thrilled and titillated by her alluring sexual glamour, daring stunts of female athleticism and gyrations on the high trapeze. The 'Star of Stars of Aerial Performers' appeared in her weird aerial creation specially designed for the August Bank Holiday 1893: *Mephisto, the Prince of Darkness*, during which she appeared scantily dressed 'with sparkles and spangles', and amazed audiences with her remarkable wire walking act during which she balanced in the middle of the wire and sang a sentimental love song! Some damned her act as a 'most gross and wanton insult to the delicacy of moral feeling', but no feathers were ruffled in Douglas save those worn by Zaeo herself.

Cinquevalli, described as 'the greatest juggler who ever juggled', was so famous that his name appeared even above Marie Lloyd's on play bills. He appeared at the Palace and Derby Castle on a number of occasions between 1895 and 1906 and juggled with everything: cannon balls, billiard balls, barrels, cutlery and other domestic items.

All Creatures Great and Small and other novelties

Animal and bird acts were amazingly popular, although in many cases it is difficult to envisage what form these performances took as reviews seldom described the acts in any detail: Galetti's Monkeys, a 'side-splitting performance'; Lieutenant Chard and his talking dog; Fillis's Dogs, a pretty animal show 'approaching the incredible'; Apasinorum, a donkey and baboon act; and Herr Grais, 'the great German eccentric chef and his juggling and animal act'. However, all pale into insignificance when

Cinquevalli.

Vasco the Mad Musician.

compared to the sheer extravagance of Leoni Clarke and his 170 cats, mice, rats, rabbits, canaries and cockatoos, billed as 'The Greatest and Most Marvellous Show in the Universe!'

Sadly, Harry left us no personal impressions of the many novelty musical acts he witnessed at the Palace and Derby Castle. The Seven Savonas were billed as 'musical marvels' and said to be the first stage saxophone band, playing fifty instruments between them; Vasco the Mad Musician, 'a multi-instrumentalist of genius' played twenty-five 'instruments' among which were 'the unlikeliest receptacles for musical sound imaginable'; Bi-Bo-Bi, 'The Sousa of the Bells'; Angyal Trepp, the sleigh-bell virtuoso; Werner and Rieder, the sensational Styrian yodellers and nightingale imitators; and Madame Burelli, the renowned 'siffleur' or whistler. We may wonder today what level of skill was displayed by these performers; were they in fact 'musical marvels', or were their antics thoroughly risible?

Mr Victor Andre, 'Conjuror, Illusionist, Ventriloquist and Mimic' delighted audiences with an act during which he transformed himself from a Red Skin into a Beautiful Girl; Jean Seul revealed the secret magical illusions and practises of the Mad Mullahs of the Indian Frontier whilst Talma, 'Queen of Coins', amazed those who witnessed her performances by the 'Mysterious Manipulation of Various Coins'. The 'Master Calculator' Jacques Inaudi achieved calculations in his head 'larger than the mind of man can conceive' and Lieutenant Albini, 'the most marvellous illusionist and prestidigitateur of modern times', entertained with amazing conjuring feats and by making his assistant, Miss Gautier, vanish into thin air.

Illusions of a different kind were supplied by Edison's Kinematograph at the Derby Castle and Animatograph at the Palace which showed short films with titles like *Boxing Cats*, *The Fire Brigade*, *The Awkward Boatman*, *The Final Cup-tie* and *A Duel*. Hubner's Cinematograph was a popular feature of entertainments at the Palace in 1896 and 1898 along with the American Bioscope, which reputedly showed 'the steadiest pictures yet'. Primitive though these 'films' were, they attracted large crowds.

Another familiar figure in Douglas was Professor Wood, phrenologist, 'The Greatest of Character Readers', whose Sunday Sacred Concerts and Pictorial Recitals attracted large audiences including many who desired to have their 'bumps' read, and their destiny's foretold. The professor was an impressive bearded, picturesque figure often seen driving around Douglas in a pony and trap.

The figure of Harry Wood hovers barely perceived in the background of many of the variety acts described above, and we would like to know more of his professional relationships with stars like Marie Lloyd and Vesta Tilley. His orchestra accompanied their songs, provided appropriate dance and mood music - Romantic, Eastern, mystical or stormy as required - for the transformation and exotic serpentine dancers, contortionists and 'leg mania' artistes, stage entrance and exit music and occasional drum rolls, cymbal clashes and other percussion effects for the magicians and acrobats. Monday mornings will have been hectic with Harry presiding over the orchestra, and if a new artiste with new songs was opening that evening, the rehearsals would be 'closed' so that no details of the evening's entertainment would leak out. At the Derby Castle, every Monday night was a 'first night'.

'The luck to be talented, and the talent to be lucky'.[4]

Harry's first years as musical director of the Derby Castle Orchestra were some of the most active and fulfilling of his entire career. During

The young musical director.

this period he would play a major role in some of the Isle of Man's most prestigious musical events, beginning in 1892 with the inauguration of the Manx Music Festival. The growing prestige of his annual students' concerts, his first Sunday Sacred Concert series at the Marina Pavilion, the Grand Operatic and Instrumental Concerts, and in 1897, his significant role in presenting the first concert of Manx National Music - one of the most spectacular and ground-breaking musical events ever staged on the Island - resulted in a meteoric rise to prominence.

The reason for his success was that Harry was seen and heard everywhere. No engagement was too insignificant, and he would help in any way within his power at even the most parochial and modest of local of events where music was required. He was just as happy to appear as a guest violin soloist, the leader of a small ensemble of two or four players performing light selections, as the organiser and conductor of a small orchestra of up to a dozen players providing dance music at a wide variety of charity events, balls, bazaars, tea festivals, harvest homes and Easter and Christmas services.

Furthermore, his genial disposition and rotund, jolly figure endeared

A minstrel show on Ramsey beach.

him to all who met him. As W. H. Smith, a director of the Palace & Derby Castle Company from Manchester, said during a shareholder's meeting in 1901: '. . . it is always a pleasure to come into the Derby Castle and see the beaming countenance of Harry Wood'.

Newspaper reviews frequently attest to what were the most important elements of Harry's popularity in Douglas. Following his Grand Miscellaneous Concert at the Grand Theatre in March 1896 the reviewer had this to say:

> Harry Wood is certainly the most popular of the musical people of Douglas who provide amusement during the long winter months. He certainly knows how to hit the popular taste, while never lowering the standard of his concerts . . . (and) employs only the best local talent.

The extent of his personal popularity may be gauged by the opening address to the audience at the Douglas Amateur Minstrel show at the Grand Theatre in January, 1896, in what today would be regarded as a highly offensive piece of doggerel:

Our show this year of merry niggers, we hope will cause a heap of sniggers.
Our farce alone will do you good, as you will the smiling face of Wood,
You all know him, his name ensures that when,
you've seen us once, you'll want to come again.

Perhaps the highest tribute bestowed upon him came in a review in the *Isle of Man Times* from 1897:

> Mr Harry Wood, though not a native of Douglas is probably one of the most popular men in the town, and he always manages to hit the popular taste in musical matters in a way that could not be improved on were he Manx born and Manx bred.

'The Equal to any heard in Douglas'

By the end of January, 1892, the news of Harry's new appointment featured in all the main newspapers:

> The many friends of Mr Harry Wood will be delighted to hear that he has scored another honour. At a meeting of the directors of Derby Castle, held in Manchester on the 19th inst. Mr Harry Wood was appointed musical conductor for the next season at the Castle.

The choice of Harry as the new musical director of the Derby Castle band was a popular one, and reflected credit not only on the 'Hall by the Sea', but on the 'able Douglas musician'.

The *Mona's Herald* echoed the above sentiments in their short report the same day:

> We are happy to congratulate Mr Harry Wood on his appointment as musical director of Derby Castle during the coming season. His ability has already been sounded loudly abroad by those who have heard him last year, when he took Mr Stocks Hammond's place during that gentleman's enforced absence. The directors have taken a sensible step in making the appointment, which is complimentary both to their judgment and to Mr Wood's talent.

Finally, on 30th January, the *Manx Sun* chipped in with its own brief notice in the local gossip column, clearly derived from the same source as those in the *Isle of Man Times* and the *Mona's Herald*:

> Mr Harry Wood's appointment to the musical conductorship at Derby Castle is well deserved, and it is sure to be a popular step with all his Douglas friends. Mr Wood did a great deal of work last season, and did it very well indeed, so that his promotion does not come as a surprise, to me at any rate.

As Whit-weekend and the start of the season approached, the local newspapers devoted several columns to the entertainments on offer at all venues and their musical directors. The *Manx Sun* was at pains to remind its readers that:

> Last year, Mr Stocks Hammond had charge of the band, though Mr Harry Wood, our talented young townsman, so frequently wielded the baton as to entitle him to be styled the conductor. This year Mr Harry Wood will have the whole and sole control of the orchestra, and certainly the directorate could not have made a wiser or more popular selection. He is a native, is known to most people, is a born musician, knows his business, and does it thoroughly . . . . We may depend upon it that during the season the musical programmes will be of the choicest.

The above comments contain a curious yet telling endorsement of Harry's position in the Island's musical life. A born musician he certainly was, but not a native Manxman. For a time some reviewers would point out that even though Harry was not a Manxman, he was nevertheless an influential musical personality 'in tune' with local musical tastes, and an efficient musical director. Before long the majority of his supporters quickly forgot, or were not aware, that he was a Yorkshireman born and bred and had been resident on the Island for less than ten years. As he became more established he was increasingly referred to as a 'Manxman'; this acceptance will have given him much quiet satisfaction, for although he never forgot his roots in Slaithwaite, he came to regard the Isle of Man as his home.

By 1898 Harry's position at the Derby Castle was unassailable, as the *Manxman* reported at the beginning of the season:

> Mr Harry Wood's orchestra is as well-known in most parts of Lancashire and Yorkshire as here. Mr Wood's reputation is made and that is a guarantee that the music will be of the very best quality.

The *Ramsey Weekly News* concurred, describing Harry as:

> . . . the accomplished young musical director, who controls as smart

a set of instrumentalists as was ever got together in the Isle . . . In other words, once Mr Wood and his merry men strike up, the hearers must, willy nilly, dance.

By common consent, Harry was possessed of a rare combination of virtues: highly-skilled, energetic, reliable, sociable and obliging. In modern parlance, Harry had quickly established himself as the 'Go-To' man in Douglas musical circles.

'A Capital Band'

The young Haydn Wood.

Harry's most pressing task before the opening of the Derby Castle for the Whitsun holiday entertainments was the engagement of his orchestra. How good that must have felt! His orchestra. No longer Stocks Hammond's, Oliver Gaggs's or Fred Vetter's orchestras, but Harry Wood's 'Popular', 'Splendid', 'Famous', 'Celebrated', 'Incomparable', 'Pre-eminent', 'Magnificent' or 'Grand' orchestra.

The players he sought to engage for his new Derby Castle orchestra were well known to him, some of them inherited from Stocks Hammond's band and Vetter's Palace band, many of whom came from Liverpool or had been associated with de Jong's orchestra or the Hallé Orchestra in Manchester. A handful came from further afield, Glasgow or London, and some of the most experienced had connections with opera companies such as the Carl Rosa Company.

At the start of the 1892 season Harry's band consisted of twelve to fifteen players, but at the height of the season in July and August, the numbers increased to thirty or sometimes thirty-five. The smaller band required at the beginning and end of the season was often billed as 'Mr Harry Wood's Bijou Orchestra', and as musical director, he engaged additional players such as his younger brothers and experienced local amateurs to make up numbers as necessary. Harry included the following note in *Cavalcade* for the year 1892:

'I have a photograph of the orchestra taken this year, in which my young brother, Haydn, is included. He is in his ninth year'.

The photograph is no longer extant, but in later years Haydn recalled that he played regularly with the Derby Castle orchestra 'for an hour or so each evening or afternoon', until he left the Island to study at the Royal College of Music.

The Palace, Derby Castle, Falcon Cliff and short-lived Marina Pavilion orchestras were essentially theatre bands rather than military-style bands, and therefore included strings, woodwind and brass instruments, a timpanist or general percussionist and a keyboard accompanist, often a local pianist. A modest number of stringed instruments – even as few as six players – would be adequate to do justice to the evening dance programmes, but would have sounded undernourished when performing the light classical pieces that were the mainstay of the afternoon ballad concerts or accompanying the arias and choruses during the Sunday Sacred concerts. Many reviews, however, refer to the good balance achieved by the Derby Castle band, often referred to as 'a capital band' and 'the premier orchestra for dance music'.

~

There are few descriptions of Harry's conducting style extant, but one or two cartoons of him baton in hand offer some clues. I imagine that he adopted the economical style of directing used by many of his contemporaries: short, precise 'military' style baton movements for orchestral and dance music, and an absence of extravagant gestures from the orchestra pit when directing shows and pantomimes. There is just one brief report that suggests Harry sometimes directed the dance music from the violin, in the manner of the great Willi Boskovsky at the New Year's Day Concerts from Vienna: 'Harry Wood wields his baton – no, his fiddle, when he is not playing it – with a charm all his own'. There are many references to his always maintaining the perfect steady tempi for dancing. 'Just listen to that waltz', wrote one reviewer, 'and note with what magnificent and emphatic precision the first note of every bar comes out'.

Anatomy of an Orchestra

The surviving engagement books, cash books, ledgers and sundry contracts of the Palace, the Derby Castle and the Falcon Cliff contain a great deal of fascinating information about the engagement of artistes and their fees, both variety and concert artistes and the cost of the various orchestras and the numbers of players engaged. They don't, however, reveal how much individual orchestral players received - apart from the fees paid to extra players engaged for short periods - but rather give weekly costs for an entire band. Until the Amalgamated Musicians' Union[5] took an influential role in negotiating theatre musicians' wages, the situation was confusing with individual theatres and theatre companies fixing their own rates of pay for musicians. The conductor's personal remuneration was negotiated separately, and took into consideration a projected amount likely to be derived from the annual benefit concert.

As the musical director, Harry was allotted a sum of money for his orchestra and negotiated individual fees directly with his players.[6] The leader of the orchestra would have received the largest amount, the repetiteur violinist slightly less and the rank-and-file string players the lowest weekly wage. Principal players, such as a principal flute or cornet player received slightly more than the second desk players, but players of unusual instruments such as the harp, or a much-needed and experienced double bass player or percussionist, were often able to negotiate their own fees. Musicians were engaged for the summer season only, and some players only from the height of the season. Locally hired musicians were paid less than English professional players.

The receipts from the annual benefit concerts constituted an important element in the musical director's financial package. Benefit nights took place in early September when some of the best-known variety and concert artistes were still appearing, and when there were still good numbers of visitors in Douglas. Not everyone approved. 'The Benefit Boom is on us again, much to many people's disgust', heralded the *Manx Sun* in September 1893:

> It is grown into a habit at all, or nearly all, of our places of amusement, that every man about the establishment - secretary, manager, conductor, bill-distributor, bill-sticker, floor-sweeper, gas-lighter etc etc - should have a benefit to compensate them for the wear and tear of three months' work at good wages.

Benefit nights were nevertheless popular with audiences, and for Harry's first benefit night on 8th September, 1892, a Monstre Programme was promised both afternoon and evening. Charles Coborn topped the bill supported by a trapeze artiste, a child dance troupe, Elsa Joel, soprano, James Taylor, the solo cornet player from the orchestra and the 'cellist

Walter Hatton. With both Daniel and Haydn Wood taking part, it was also something of a family affair, and Harry introduced his new *Minstrel Lancers* for that night only.

The report of Harry's fifth benefit night in 1896 indicated that his benefit concerts were among the most popular of each season:

> On Monday Mr Harry Wood expects to see all his friends and enemies (if he has any) at the Derby Castle . . . a capital programme has been arranged, which will be considerably augmented in the evening with teams from the other show places . . . (he) has never yet been disappointed with his house.

Managers of the larger venues also enjoyed benefit nights, as did the Masters of Ceremonies and occasionally the working staff. In 1893 Lester Barrett was also awarded a benefit night in recognition of his long association with Douglas. The directors of the various companies grudgingly recognised that benefit nights could be lucrative for everybody; an equitable profit-sharing plan was eventually agreed upon, which acknowledged that such events benefitted the management and the company because the friends and supporters of the beneficiary generally ensured a healthy audience, and receipts were often doubled.[7]

~

Harry's relationship with his players was cordial and professional at all times; many of them were familiar colleagues and close friends, and when necessary Harry willingly interceded on their behalf in disputes with the management as a letter dated August 1920 from the Palace & Derby Castle orchestras illustrates. The letter advised Harry of the circumstances surrounding the flautist John McIvor, who was ill, and whose salary had been suspended by the Company. The players had asked for a meeting with the management, and 'have resolved not to resume business until settlement in full is made'. McIvor wrote to Harry to clarify his predicament and confirmed that regretfully he was unable to play because of 'a severe attack of lumbago'. He promised to make every effort to get to the theatre the next day 'even at the expense of a pair of crutches, and will do my best if the programme is not too heavy'. However, he did not appear at the Palace the following day as the effort proved too much for him despite spending 15 shillings on cabs in an effort 'to see the concerts through'. He concluded by reminding Harry that this was the first time in his career that he has had 'to cry off', and asks that Harry will 'do his best for one who always does his'. Harry received a letter the following day in a doctor's almost indecipherable scrawl confirming that he was satisfied that 'John McIvor is suffering from (unreadable) and is unable to leave his bed'. The matter was satisfactorily resolved and John McIvor became one of Harry's most reliable soloists for many more seasons.

The plight of another musician was not amicably resolved, although with only a short letter surviving we are left with few clues as to the issues involved. Letter dated 19th January, 1921, from H. Schofield of Manchester:

> Dear Mr Wood
> Thanks for letter of the 15th you however omit to state any reason. I think you will agree (after having 9 seasons with the Palace Co) I am at least entitled to some explanation why you cannot offer me re-engagement.
> Yours faithfully,

Harry noted at the foot of the letter: 'No reasons are necessary except your services are not required next season'.

Perhaps the most bizarre affair associated with one of Harry's players concerned Mr Robert Lewin, a clerk in the Isle of Man Steam Packet offices in Douglas, and a piccolo player in the Derby Castle orchestra from time to time, who left his home one evening in October 1899 for the Castle, failed to return home, and was not heard of again. Mr Lewin's strange disappearance remains a mystery as no further mention of him appears in the local newspapers. It was the kind of mystery that might have appealed to Sherlock Holmes: 'The Affair of the Vanishing Musician', perhaps one of the 'lost' cases that Dr Watson did not feel 'was appropriate to place before the public' at the time.

At the season's end Harry invariably gave a dinner in honour of his orchestra at a local hotel, and on one occasion in 1893 J. P. Callow, manager of the Derby Castle, treated the staff to 'a substantial spread followed by toasts' at Hampson's Restaurant, Douglas. In early September 1899 Harry hosted a dinner at the Nursery Hotel, Onchan, for the members of the Castle band, and at the end of the season, Charles Fox, manager and secretary of the Palace and Derby Castle Company, hosted a dinner whose guests included Harry, George Eyton and Lester Barrett. A 'very convivial evening' ended a little before 2.00am.

The resort orchestras in Douglas were a major attraction for holiday makers and the most popular conductors, Oliver Gaggs, George Eyton and Harry himself, were well-known personalities, their annual topical waltzes, polkas and lancers essential ingredients in establishing loyalty in the hearts of the visitors.

Concerts great and small

One of most unusual small-scale local events that Harry played a part in occurred in March 1896. Advertised as The Times Newsboys' Treat, one hundred and fifty *Isle of Man Times* delivery boys from the Douglas area - described in almost Dickensian terms, as 'Street Boys' from poor families who led 'dark and cheerless' lives - attended a tea and concert during which they were addressed by a chairman who extolled the virtues of 'perseverance, honesty and sobriety', entertained by Harry playing 'an extravaganza of popular songs' on the violin, with everyone joining in. Each boy received a parting gift of an orange at the close of the evening.

Some annual concerts were on an altogether grander scale, such as the Misses Cannell's Concerts and the Douglas Musical Society concerts. The Douglas Musical Society Grand Sacred and Secular Concert at the Grand Theatre in March 1892, for example, featured an orchestra and chorus of no less than seventy local performers conducted by Harry, who also played a selection of violin solos. Excerpts from the sacred works of Rossini, Handel and Haydn rubbed shoulders with songs, glees and popular arias.

The Misses Cannell's concerts were organised by the three prominent Cannell sisters: Miss M. Cannell, a teacher of singing and voice production, Miss Emmie Cannell, a vocalist and Miss Lizzie Cannell, a well-known Douglas piano teacher. Their concert in the Grand Theatre in February 1893, in aid of the Isle of Man Industrial Home for Orphan and Destitute Children, was a splendid event with a choir of forty and a small ensemble led by Harry, and raised the princely sum of £37 12s 4d.

One of the grandest events of the decade took place in December 1899 at the Palace Ballroom: the Manx (South African) War Fund Parade and Grand Tableaux. A bank holiday had been declared and the hotel and boarding houses on the promenades were brilliantly illuminated. At the Palace, a special stage was erected to accommodate a cast of 1,100 in a series of colourful displays, cutlass and physical drills, gymnastic disciplines and recitations. Harry's orchestra together with the Douglas Volunteer and Town Bands performed the popular march-medley Turkish Patrol, and the day ended with a parade and the singing of the *National Anthem* and *Soldiers of the Queen* with choir, orchestra and eight bands.

The Douglas Philharmonic Society

This choir was formed following a meeting of interested parties at the Masonic Hall, Douglas, in December 1892 with the principal object of giving concerts at the Palace during the summer season, after which Harry was appointed as musical director and the violinist E. B. Bennett as secretary. The directors of the Palace further confirmed that they would engage the Society for the Sunday Sacred Concerts during 1893. The choir was never Harry's personal choir, but was trained by him, and was available to take part in both his own operatic and ballad concerts, his annual students' concerts and later the short-lived Sunday Sacred Concert series at the Marina Pavilion. It was agreed that the members of the new choir would not permit their commitment to their local churches or chapel choirs to be compromised, and in return it was hoped that ministers conducting their regular Sunday services would finish in good time so that Philharmonic Society members could be in their seats in time for the start of the Sacred Concerts.

The choir's first appearance was on 26th January, 1893, at Harry's Students' Orchestral and Operatic Concert in aid of Noble's Hospital at the Grand Theatre, when, together with seven local vocal soloists, Harry presented a programme of substantial excerpts from popular operas and operettas including Gounod's *Faust*, Verdi's *Il Trovatore*, Wallace's *Maritana*, Benedict's *Lily of Killarney* and Gilbert and Sullivan's *Mikado*, *Yeoman of the Guard* and *The Gondoliers*.[8] In all, some seventy-five performers took part and the new choir was highly praised. The only caveat was that although the performance of the *Anvil Chorus* was adjudged to be perfect, the anvils were said to be underwhelming.

The *Isle of Man Times* critic considered that the choir was 'well-balanced and thoroughly harmonious', and that 'every arrangement about the concert was perfect . . . the audience dispersed shortly after ten o'clock, thoroughly delighted with the affair'. The *Mona's Herald* thought that the chorus 'lacked volume' in certain pieces, but made up for this by 'a rich sweetness'. Furthermore, ' . . . there was something about his (Harry's) manner of conducting which was not without interest'. A curious comment, but perhaps reflecting the fact that Douglas audiences were as yet unaccustomed to their young musical director appearing in a new guise as a choral conductor.

Douglas Philharmonic Society appeared many times during the decade and quickly became an important feature of the most significant musical events that Harry organised and directed, notably his Grand Operatic Concerts which began in January 1894, and the Sunday Sacred Concerts for which normally assembled a choir of around sixty and an orchestra of twenty players. The *Isle of Man Times* paid tribute to his initiatives at the time of year 'when many people do not care to attend concerts' Harry had again managed to provide something of high artistic worth, high entertainment value and most of all, novelty, to brighten even the dreariest winter months:

> . . . the most popular of the musical people who provide amusement during the long winter months . . . he evidently knows how to hit the popular taste . . . never lowering the standard of his concerts . . employs the best (local) talent available . . . avoids the fault of 'ultra-classicism' in the style of music he sets before his patrons.

Elijah: 'A really good classical work before a Manx audience'.

The second important musical event of that year was Harry's Jubilee performance of Mendelssohn's *Elijah* at the Grand Theatre on 30th April. As far as anyone could remember Mendelssohn's masterpiece had not been performed uncut or in anything like its complete form for a quarter of a century or more, and no expense was spared to ensure that the performance would be an unprecedented success.

The soloists were naturally nervous and in varying degrees over-awed by the occasion. The *Isle of Man Examiner* reviewer praised Alister Proctor in the demanding title role noting that 'he rose to a height of dramatic force that fairly thrilled the house', even if he ran out of steam towards the end of the evening. Winefred Adams' light soprano was not heard to its best advantage in the genre, and although Mrs Nicholls' *O Rest in the Lord* received a 'sympathetic rendering', her performance was marred by a tendency to run out of breath during long sustained passages. Mr G. James of J. W. Turner's Opera Company was 'in fine voice', but was frequently out of tune, and the tenor J. E. Kelly, whose first aria, *If With All Your Hearts*, is one of the most beautiful in all Mendelssohn, failed to impress as his voice was recessed and unfocussed in anything but the quietest passages. The trio of local soloists, Miss Garrett, Miss Kneale and Mrs Corlett, gave one of the most secure performances of the evening in the Terzetto *Lift Thine Eyes*.

The choir, The Douglas Choral Union[9] on its debut appearance, had been re-organised and enlarged by Harry from members of the

The Marina Pavilion, ballroom and theatre.

Philharmonic Society, Douglas Cantata Choir and probably members of the Misses Cannell's Choir, to form a body of around one hundred singers. The large-scale choruses *Thanks Be to God* and *Be Not Afraid* were delivered 'without the slightest raggedness or faltering', according to the Examiner critic, and with a 'power, precision and expression which would be hard to match'. The scene in Part I where the Prophet taunts the Priests of Baal was thrilling. The sopranos and altos were judged 'very good'; the tenors, 'a very mixed lot' and the bass section disrupted because one singer audibly persisted in commencing every entry ahead of the beat.

As the concert took place during the off-season months, Harry did not have his Derby Castle players to call upon to swell the ranks of local musicians and students. Nevertheless, he managed to engage an orchestra of nineteen, plus a piano and an organ to fill in the missing instrumental parts and boost the sound of the massive choruses. Bizarrely, the *Isle of Man Times* thought that the orchestra was too loud, and sometimes drowned the choir and soloists.

Harry had taken a calculated risk in attempting to perform a well-loved and large-scale choral masterpiece with predominately local amateur singers and instrumentalists, but the gamble paid off, and the performance exceeded all expectations. The critics were unanimous in their view that the objective was laudable and the choir was rapidly establishing itself as a national asset.

'Devotional and elevating': The Pavilion Sunday Sacred Concerts

The Sunday Sacred Concerts at the Palace were well-established by 1896, but no such series had been inaugurated at the Derby Castle. The short-lived Sunday Sacred Concert series at the Pavilion Variety Theatre, formally the Marina, however, gave Harry a unique opportunity to further establish his credentials as a choral conductor in his own series of sacred concerts with a specially selected choir, many from the Douglas Philharmonic Society, and invariably billed as Harry Wood's Choir, Harry Wood's Select Choir or Harry Wood's Special Choir. Previewing this new venture in July, the *Manx Sun* suggested that hitherto:

> sacred concerts held elsewhere have a tendency to secularism, and this tendency they wish to combat by providing music which will not offend the tastes of those who really desire sacred music to be performed on a Sunday. Mr Harry Wood will be the musical conductor, and this gentleman's knowledge of his art will undoubtedly enable him to choose only that class of music which will keep these concerts from the reproach of secularism.

The first of this series of sacred concerts at the 'Pavilion on the Promenade' took place on Sunday 19th July, 1896, and there were five further sacred concerts in August. Although they had been an artistic success, as the season wore on it became apparent that the series could not compete with the well-established Sunday Concerts at the Palace under George Eyton. Even the engagement of the baritone, raconteur and teller of incredible tales, G. H. Snazelle, presenting his one-man 'Sacred Recital of Music, Song, Story and Travel' on three consecutive Sundays in September, could not disguise the fact that the concerts were not attracting large enough audiences.

Harry will have been disappointed but, if I have judged his character correctly, not disheartened, and had he but known it, in just a few short years, he would be the musical director of the amalgamated Palace &

Madame Albani.

Derby Castle Company Limited, and conductor of the most renowned Sunday Sacred Concerts in the Island's musical story.

The concert artistes

The Canadian-born operatic soprano Madame Emma Albani[10] was the prima donna Douglas audiences truly took to their hearts. Furthermore she was destined to play an important role in the careers of both Daniel and Haydn Wood, who appeared with her in Douglas and toured extensively with her concert party. The favourite singer of Queen Victoria, she first appeared in Douglas at a Sunday Sacred Concert at the Palace in July 1897, and again in 1898, under the baton of George Eyton, one year after her final appearance at Covent Garden and retirement from the operatic stage. She was billed as 'one of the greatest singers the world has ever heard' and possessed a voice that everyone who heard her agreed was of exceptional beauty. She sang arias by Verdi and Handel and the favourite ballad of the age, *Home, Sweet Home*, leaving 'not a dry eye in

Clara Butt and her husband Bertie Kennerly-Rumford.

the house'. Always gracious in responding to the many calls for encores, Albani was that rare phenomenon: a prima donna loved for her personality as well as her voice.

It could be argued that today's obsession with celebrity began with the great contralto Clara Butt, 'the simple Bristol girl with a lovely voice', who at 6' 2" tall had an imposing and statuesque stage presence. She rarely appeared on the operatic stage (she would have towered over most of her leading men), and together with a taste for flamboyant dresses second only to Florrie Forde's, her enormous reputation rested solely on her concert hall, recital room and festival appearances. Her stentorian contralto voice[11] was heard to its best advantage in well-loved, slower-paced arias from popular operas, oratorios and in 'respectable' well-loved ballads, and in a ballad-obsessed age, her following amounted to adulation and her performances of popular scared songs were considered by many to be akin to sermons in themselves. Her recitals were often built around her favourite arias: Handel's *Ombra mai fu* and Mendelssohn's *O Rest in the Lord*, and encores such as the hymn *Abide With Me*. 'Claramania' had arrived in Douglas.

Charles Santley and David Ffrancon-Davies.

Three famous tenors in particular appeared in Douglas during this period. John Sims Reeves, the doyen of English tenors in the Victorian age, appeared at a Sunday Sacred Concert in 1895, although at seventy years of age he was sadly past his prime. Edward Lloyd, the great tenor of the late Victorian age and said to be unsurpassable in Bach and Handel, passed the mantle of Reeves on to the Welshman Ben Davies, whose clear, resonant and penetrating voice was heard in many English music festivals.

The bravura-baritone Charles Santley, arguably the greatest Victorian English baritone, appeared in 1894 aged sixty-two. He brought with him a huge reputation and a voice of great beauty of timbre, power and range.[12] The Irish bass Signor Foli[13] appeared in Douglas that year. He possessed a large repertoire of operatic and sacred roles, but died suddenly just five years after his Isle of Man debut. The Welsh operatic bass-baritone David Ffrancon-Davies, a notable Elijah, appeared in 1896 and 1897, and was considered by Sims Reeves to be the purest baritone he had ever heard.

'A rale Manx Concert'.

In February, 1892 Harry and F. C. Poulter took part in a Scottish Concert at the Grand Theatre under the auspices of the Isle of Man Caledonian Society together with 'a splendid array of talent from the Glasgow City Hall concerts'. The following week, the *Mona's Herald* published a letter, signed 'Mannin-dy-Bragh', proposing a Manx National Concert that Easter, organised along the lines of the Scottish Concert. The writer suggested that A. W. Moore[14] be engaged to select well-known Manx songs, and be encouraged to unearth further examples of 'Manx Minstrelsy'. Popular traditional songs such as *Hunt the Wren* could be performed in traditional Manx costume, and Oliver Gaggs should be invited to be the overall musical director. Nothing came of this at the time, but four years later, some of the ideas outlined in the letter found their way into a far grander plan for a ground-breaking and spectacular Manx musical event.

We next hear of a concert of Manx National Music in a letter from W. H. Gill to Harry Wood dated 3rd September, 1896:

> Dear Mr Wood
> Our book of Manx Songs is on the eve of publication. I think today was the day fixed, but I have an advance copy.
> We have in contemplation a concert of Manx Music this Winter and can I think make a very attractive programme if it can be carried out as we would wish. I should like to consult you as to details. If you could spare me an hour or so of your time on Saturday next or any time after noon tomorrow . . .
> Yours faithfully

W. H. Gill (above) and Dr John Clague.

The book of Manx Songs referred to was *Manx National Songs*, published by Boosey & Co. in their Royal Edition,[15] a long-awaited collection, and although the following report in the *Isle of Man Times* over-romanticised the enterprise behind the collection, many will have agreed with the sentiments expressed:

> They discovered the melodies locked in the hearts and minds of a dozen or so of the oldest men and women, unlettered, unskilled in music, and all belonging to the peasant class, toilers by land and sea. They dwelt in little cottages of rough-hewn stone, which looked as though they had built themselves.

Few would have disagreed with the following summation in the same newspaper:

> Such a service to the Manx nation cannot be measured . . . a tribute to Deemster Gill, Mr W H Gill and Dr Clague.

~

Planning for the concert was well under way by early November, as the following letter to prospective choir members signifies:

> MANX CONCERT. The Deemster Gill is interested in a concert of Manx Music to be given in the Grand Theatre, Douglas, on Thursday, 7th January next (proceeds for the Hospital). May he count on your help in the chorus, and if so, will you kindly attend the first meeting for practice, and for arranging details, at the Central Hall (foot of Broadway), on Tuesday, 10th November, at 8 p.m.
>
> Anfield Hey
> 2nd November, 1896.

The Gill brothers and Dr Clague took enormous pains over the selection of Manx melodies from their new publication and particularly over the way they should be arranged and presented on stage. In the meantime, a concert advertisement appeared in the *Ramsey Courier* for an evening of vocal and instrumental music featuring *Manx National Songs* at the Wesleyan School, Ramsey, on Thursday 3rd December. Was this the first public concert to feature Manx traditional songs from the new publication? It must certainly have been amongst the earliest.

Harry Wood, too, was busy during the last weeks of the year, too busy, in fact, to present himself for jury service on 15th December. When he explained that attendance would interfere with his violin teaching and other musical activities, he was excused jury service in perpetuity.

The *Manx Sun* included the following advertisement on 19th December:

Preliminary
FIRST GRAND CONCERT
Of Manx National Music
(Selected from Mr W H Gill's Collection of Manx
National Songs – Royal Edition)
THURSDAY JANUARY 7th
1897 in the
GRAND THEATRE
Manx Songs! Manx Dances! Manx Choruses!
Manx Scenes in National Costume by the
MANX NATIONAL CHOIR
Harry Wood's Grand Orchestra
Net proceeds to the Hospital

'There was a great crush to be present'.

Apart from the previews and reviews published in the local newspapers, a far more entertaining and colourful commentary about the concert comes in the form of a satirico-humorous letter published in the *Mona's Herald* on 13th January. The letter begins 'Dear Misther Editor' and is signed 'Tommy the Wren, Balldin, 1897', and is written entirely in the Anglo-Manx dialect. It is clear from the tone that the writer did not altogether approve of the way traditional Manx songs had been 'Englishfied' in *Manx National Songs* and presented on stage for the Manx National Concert.[16] Nevertheless, the letter does give some idea of what the spectacle was actually like, and I have quoted from it freely below.

Once again, the *Isle of Man Times* caught the mood in the days before the concert:

> . . . for the first time we were to have an entertainment the programme of which was made up of Manx airs, choruses, quaint old Manx customs, all given by local people, in appropriate costumes and scenery. Who would have thought that our proud little Manx nation possesses such soul-stirring melodies and choruses . . .

The Lieutenant Governor, the Lord Henniker, was naturally invited to attend, but was indisposed, and was represented by his daughters, the Hon. Ethel Henniker and the Hon. Cicely Henniker, both great supporters of music on the Island. Naturally, Deemster Gill, his brother W. H. Gill and Dr Clague were present.

The Grand Theatre opened its doors at 7.00pm, and by 7.15pm there was hardly a seat to be had in the house. Predictably, perhaps, tickets were over-sold and even as the concert was about to begin, Victoria Street was still blocked with disappointed and disgruntled ticket-holders:

> Well . . . I was theer at seven o'clock, but, lor bless ye, the crowd that was at the door was dhreadful . . . so after pushin' and shuvin' I managed to get in, and got a good sate too. Well, the theatre was jammed altogathet. The people outside were complaining it were cowl morthal, but deed it was hot morthal inside.

During the interval Deemster Gill announced that, in view of the great demand for tickets, the concert would be repeated the following week.

'Too many oilskins, but the effect was splendid'.

Despite the fact that 'all the arrangements' were said to be by W. H. Gill, it seems more likely that Harry, as overall musical director, undertook the actual orchestrations of the Manx songs after consultation with the Gill brothers. He had an orchestra of twenty-one players at his disposal, led by his reliable and experienced colleague, J. E. Quayle, with Miss Eveleen Wood as the accompanist: 'The orchestra was well-balanced, although we would like to have seen the wind instruments supplemented'.

The wind section of the orchestra was indeed small - just one of each of flute, clarinet, cornet and trombone – reflecting the dearth of good local wind players on the Island at this period. The chorus was named The Manx National Choir for the occasion, and included members of the Douglas Philharmonic Society and the Douglas Choral Union. There were fourteen sopranos, nine altos, nine tenors and ten basses, and each member made their own costume.

Whilst a piece-by-piece description of what was a very long concert is beyond the scope of this book,[17] some comments from Tommy the Wren's letter and extracts from newspaper reports give a unique contemporary glimpse of the spectacle that greeted the audience that January evening.

Part I opened with a scene representing Ramsey Bay, with boats drawn up onto the beach, lobster pots, creels, mollags[18] and nets. Groups of fishermen, old men and women, children, Manx girls in the fields at harvest time, 'hobblers', or horse keepers, and smugglers, with 'almost every branch of Manx life represented'. In the background, an inn, The King Orry Arms, with a jolly landlord at the door and 'a comical depiction of an old Manx farmer in a straw hat', no doubt waiting for his pint. The choir burst forth with *Ramsey Town*, the verses lustily sung by the men, the chorus by the entire company.

This opening chorus was followed by *The Wreck of the Herring Fleet*, with Harry Wood's fine stormy orchestral introduction; Mr T. Brockbank's declamatory style pleased even Tommy the Wren:

> He is worth going to hear, is Misther Brockbank . . . he were in grand voice.

The lovely Manx song *The Sheep Under the Snow* was sung by Miss Phoebe Jull:

> . . . in English of coorse. Well, the song was rite enough, only she was'nt Manx enough herself over it. She was too Englishfied.

Hunt the Wren was performed by the chorus and a semi-chorus of six boys, each holding a bush and a net, according to the old Manx St. Stephen's Day custom:

> Aw, theer was a lump of a bhoy came in, with a net over him and a pole with a leak tied at the top of it, followed by several other bhoys, and my gough, what fun we had. Aw, the ould people laughed tremenjus.

Miss A. A. Turner, a popular local soprano, replacing Miss M. L. Wood who was indisposed, sang *The Parting Hour*:

> Well, man, Miss Turner came on – aw, a nice lump of a gel about 16, with a foine sun bonnet and golden curls over her shoulther; and, dear me, with her nice blue dress and red apron, she looked that purty and innercent.

Alister Proctor, baritone, then gave *The Manx Wedding* which turned out to be the 'hit' of the first half of the evening. 'From the humorous point of view this song is the best in the collection . . . it was the most successful item in the programme . . . the audience would have kept Mr Proctor repeating it all night'. Tommy the Wren enjoyed this performance too:

> I heard bells ringin' and young Proctor came out, and he sang the "Manx Wedding" – about a wedding at Lezayre – my gough, and he sang it well, too. When he sang of the herrin's and the spuds, aw, he was Manx propar.

Part II of the concert opened with the orchestra playing two Manx songs arranged either by Harry or W. H. Gill. Tommy the Wren was lukewarm about Miss Turner's singing of *Oh Hush Thee, My Babe*, which he refused to acknowledge was a Manx song at all, and Alister Proctor's rendering of *The Two Lovers*, performed in oilskins and sou'wester, he judged to be too slow. However, another old Manx custom represented in song, Hop-tu-naa, did meet with his approval:

> . . . well, man, it was good, an' they had three good lusty Manx voices. "That's the thing I like", says I, "Why dont they give us more of that".

The grand finale once again featured the beach scene from the opening of the show, with a crowd of villagers greeting the fisherman as they came ashore with the night's catch. *The Herring is King of the Sea* was sung by Alister Proctor and the full chorus, '. . . an' a gran' song it was', followed by the Manx fishermen's evening hymn, *The Harvest of the Sea*:

> An' then, man, we had the closin' hymn, an' aw man it was beautiful. Eh, man, I felt quite raised. An' we all stood up just the same as in chapel, an' to hear the gels an' the fellars sing this, aw, it was beautiful.

Tommy the Wrens' final comment after the singing of the *Manx National Anthem* was rather dismissive:

> Well, I'd often heard this before, an' so this was northin' new to me.

Following *God Save the Queen* there was special thanks and praise for Harry, the resourceful stage manager Fred D. Johnson and his assistant J. L. Killip. As Deemster Gill promised, the Manx National Concert was repeated on 14th January, in the presence of the Lieutenant Governor, the Lord Bishop, the Archdeacon, the Mayor and other dignitaries, and during the interval the Mayor of Douglas addressed the audience from the dress circle:

> . . . (I am) sure that . . . those present would allow (me) to say a few words of thanks to the authors of the beautiful music to which we have listened . . . (I) consider this to be an important epoch in the history of the Island, as for the first time its national music, which has been floating about unrecorded, and handed down by tradition only, (has) now (been) crystallised into written notes . . .

~

The publication of *Manx National Songs* at the end of 1896 had been the inspiration for the Manx Concert, and like the concert, was greeted with enthusiasm and adverse criticism in roughly equal proportions. Traditionalists were unimpressed by the old traditional Manx melodies in their new up-to-date orchestral and choral clothing, but the audiences generally disagreed with the purists and enjoyed the colourful and entertaining spectacle.

Although neither Harry nor Haydn Wood were pioneering field collectors of traditional Manx music, both played significant roles in the popularisation of Manx traditional melodies.[19] Harry continued to be involved in large-scale concerts of Manx music throughout his life - breathing new life into the lovely old tunes - and introduced the most popular Manx songs into his Derby Castle dances from time to time, such as his *Manx Lancers* of 1897. He was always ready to enter into the spirit of every occasion and share a musical joke, as he did in 1898 and 1901, by arranging some 'catchy Manx melodies' as waltzes, schottisches and polkas, and by giving some popular German waltzes tongue-in-cheek Manx titles for the traditional end-of-season Mhelliahs[20] at the Derby Castle. The special dance programme he arranged for the 1898 Mhelliah consisted of seven waltzes, three lancers, a post dance and a pas de quatre, each given the name of a traditional Manx melody: *Vannin Veg Veen*, *The Lonely Flitter*, *Kirree fo Niaghtey*, the *Lively Govag* and the *Wobbly Mollag* and so forth. At the conclusion, the large assembly of managers, directors, shareholders and the general public formed a circle and with linked arms heartily sang *Auld Lang Syne* and *God Save the Queen*.

In due course Haydn Wood's fine orchestral works based on Manx melodies, *A Manx Rhapsody*, *Mannin Veen* and *King Orry*, would established themselves amongst his best-known compositions, and Manx-born composers, such as J. E. Quayle, would introduce traditional Manx melodies very evocatively into their orchestral works.

Brother Harry Wood

On 16th November 1892 Harry became installed as a Freemason. There are many references in the local newspapers attesting to his attendance at many Masonic concerts and other events. Earlier that month he had taken part in the fourth annual grand concert promoted by the Tynwald Lodge in aid of local Masonic charities, and was listed as plain Harry Wood. The following year, though, he was named as 'Bro (ther) H. Wood, St. Trinian's Lodge no. 2050', among the musicians who took part in a supper and concert at the Granville Hotel, Douglas, together with other musical colleagues who were also Freemasons: the 'cellist Walter Hatton, Brother Taylor, a cornet player, Brother Richardson, a clarinettist and his close associate Brother F. C. Poulter. It is possible that Harry was proposed for membership of the St. Trinian's Lodge by C. P Callow, the manager of the Derby Castle, who is known to have been a member in 1890. In May 1894, 'Brother H. Wood' conducted the seventy-strong Douglas Philharmonic Society at the Fifth Annual Grand Concert of the Tynwald Lodge. The Brethren, who included some players from the previous year's grand concert, were requested to appear in 'Masonic Clothing and Jewels'.

On 24th November 1894 he had the pleasure of witnessing the installation of his younger brother Daniel to the St. Trinian's Lodge. Daniel is listed among the members until 1898, when he left the Island to pursue his career as a professional flautist. In 1901 Harry appeared with a small band at the annual Ladies' Night of the Spencer Walpole Temperance Lodge, when the designation SW (Senior Warden) appeared after his name, indicating that he passed swiftly through the first three degrees of Freemasonry. Harry's obituary confirms that he was a Past Master of his lodge, with the rank of Past Provincial Grand Senior Deacon (PPGSD).

We need not follow Harry's association with Freemasonry any further here. Suffice it to say, he remained a committed member of the St. Trinian's Lodge all his life. A few days after his death, the secretary of the lodge wrote to his sister Adeline in Yorkshire:

> Dec 28th, Freemasons' Hall, Woodbourne Rd, Douglas
> After knowing him for so many years, it is hardly necessary for me to say that he was a highly esteemed Past Master of our Lodge, and will long be remembered by his many friends.
> Signed J. Norman Cowley, Secretary.

Concurrent with his commitment to Freemasonry, was his dedication to the church, for at Easter 1901, he was elected a church warden at St Matthew's Church, Douglas, in recognition of his services to the church's music. He was also a Rotarian.

~

In January 1897 the Wood family moved from the comparatively modest terraced house in Albert Street to a much more impressive residence at number 1, Marathon Terrace, Queen's Promenade. The house was the first of five residential properties situated between Palace Terrace

Daniel Wood in livery.

and Athol Terrace, thereby placing Harry at the centre of his musical world midway between the Palace and the Derby Castle with the Falcon Cliff Hotel towering above. Sabra Wood, now fifty-six years of age, had retired from the arduous life of a publican, and within a few short years Harry's two talented younger brothers, Daniel and Haydn, would leave the Island to pursue their studies in London. Daniel, a future flute virtuoso, attended the Royal College of Music from 1890, and Haydn, the young violin virtuoso and future composer, began six years of study at the Royal College of Music in 1897. Neither of the brothers resided in the Isle of Man again, but both returned frequently during their years of study to play under Harry's baton in the Derby Castle orchestra and as guest soloists.

Marathon Terrace on Queen's Promenade.

Operettas and Pantomimes

Throughout the decade that Daniel and Haydn often played in the Derby Castle Orchestra under Harry's baton, two of his talented younger sisters, Eliza and Adeline, also began to appear in public, often singing and dancing in children's operettas, pantomimes and church concerts. Adeline, the extrovert in the family, sang a character song, *The Gypsy*, at a Free Dinners Fund Juvenile Concert in February 1892, and in October that year both sisters were part of a group of 'daintily and chastely-attired children' who took part in a Maypole Dance '. . . a distinct novelty reviving memories of bye-gone days' at a bazaar at Kirk Braddan Church to raise funds for the organ.

In February 1897 Harry and Mr H. Fielding, the Head Master of a local boys' school, arranged the music for a children's operetta entitled *Bold Robin and the Babes*; Harry led the orchestra and his sisters trod the boards in a 'pretty Gavotte'. *Robinson Crusoe* followed in February 1898, with some two hundred children taking part, and in February 1899, *The King of Carribee*, for which Harry wrote some of the music and led the band. In December 1900, Adeline took part in a comic sketch, *Juliette*, at a St. George's Church sale of work, and the following year assumed the role of Topsy 'to great advantage' in *The British Empire*, a children's operetta set in South Africa during the Boer War. The music for this operetta, which is lost, was wholly composed and arranged by Harry.

Adeline was destined to play an increasingly vital and significant role in Harry's life on the Island and by all accounts had a vivacious and engaging personality. In due course she would take small roles, choreograph the dances and design some of the costumes for his pantomimes *King Gob-ne-Geay* (1902) and *The Babes in the Wood* (1904), and, more importantly, after the move to Osborne Terrace in 1911, would help organise his huge music library, act as his secretary, copyist, greatest supporter and general *factotum*.

In addition to amateur theatrical productions, Harry was often engaged to direct the orchestra for the pantomimes at the Grand Theatre, Douglas. Did he perhaps recall a ten-week pantomime season back in 1884-5 at the Leeds Grand Theatre, when Alfred Hemmings, the current lessee and managing director of the Grand Theatre, appeared as 'The Dame' in *Bo-Peep, Red Riding Hood, Cinderella* and *Robinson Crusoe*. Planquette's *Les Cloches de Corneville* was given in the winter of 1899-1900, with the Douglas Choral Union conducted by F. C. Poulter, with Harry once again in his old role as the leader of the orchestra. What memories those occasions must have brought back!

The Douglas Amateur Minstrels

In November 1892 the *Manx Sun* announced that Harry and a colleague, Harry Rushworth,[21] were organising a series of concerts with the Douglas Amateur Minstrels in aid of the Douglas Gymnasium Reading Room, although the first official concert took place in February 1893, with the proceeds donated to the Ladies' Soup Dispensary and Coal Fund.

The enormous enthusiasm for minstrel shows would raise an eyebrow today. Known as 'Black Face' or 'Burnt Cork' entertainments, but often referred to as 'Coon'[22] shows, or merely the 'Niggers', Minstrel shows had been popular in Victorian England from the time that the Christy Minstrels undertook their first tour in 1857.[23] Unlike other forms of clowning in music halls, pantomimes and circuses, minstrel entertainments were essentially comic impersonations of black people by white people. Two broad stereotypes quickly evolved from these crude characterisations of 'negroes': simple, God-fearing, superstitious and childlike; or stupid, vain, lazy and criminal.

While we find the whole concept distasteful and unacceptable today, it should be remembered that, in Victorian Britain, taking the family to

Eugene Stratton (above) and George H. Chirgwin.

gawk at Joseph Merrick, the Elephant Man, Jo-Jo the Dog-faced boy, Sophia Schultz the Dwarf Fat Lady or any of the numerous carnival and circus shows advertising 'human curiosities' and 'freaks', was considered to be a perfectly acceptable form of popular entertainment. Nobody in Douglas would have been offended by a 'Nigger' Farce entitled Black Justice given at the Grand Theatre by the Douglas Amateur Minstrels in February 1893, nor the song *The Coon on the Moon*, performed at a similar event in 1896.

Minstrelsy also found its way onto the operetta stage. When drafting the libretto of *Utopia Limited* in 1893, W. S. Gilbert wrote the following note to Sullivan:

> Don't you think that a nigger prelude with bones, tambourine, banjo etc, would introduce the king's song very well?[24]

Minstrel entertainments were received with great amusement, not embarrassed gasps, and our present-day aversion to these shows has blinded us to their place in the history of entertainment. Black-face shows popularised black American culture in Europe and injected the typically slightly seedy music hall world with a refreshing touch of the colourful and exotic, with new songs, new jokes and a range of new comic characters.

Many famous variety stars began their careers as black-faced entertainers, and some of the finest appeared in Douglas: Harry Campion, Little Tich, Dan Leno and Gus Elen - whilst others - Eugene Stratton, George H. Chirgwin, 'The White-Eyed Kaffir' and G. H. Elliott, 'The Chocolate-Coloured Coon' - maintained a black-faced persona their entire careers.

Harry's role in the Douglas Amateur Minstrels was principally that of director of the band, but one newspaper review suggests that from time to time he sang comic songs. Local minstrel shows followed the traditional format adapted to suit local conditions, during which the pompous and verbose Mr Interlocutor engaged in cross-talking banter with the tambourine playing, down to earth, simple and unworldly Tambo and the wisecracking, street-wise, smartly dressed, permanently broke dandy, Bones. The highlight of the entertainment was the 'stump speech', a subversive, over-the-top parody of the political stump speech accompanied by wild gestures and peppered with malapropisms, puns and other contortions of the English language. The evening invariably ended with a burlesque incorporating further comic songs and dances.

Amateur minstrel troupes flourished on the Island. King William's College formed its own Christy Minstrel Troupe, and even the small, rural Jurby Parochial School had a 'Nigger' Troupe who appeared at a Patriotic Concert on behalf of the Belgian people as late as December 1914. The public's taste for minstrel shows eventually waned, and they were superseded by the Pierrot Troupes familiar to visitors to Douglas Head and Frederick Buxton's Operatic Pierrots at the old bandstand on Harris Promenade.

Teaching, Annual Students' Concerts and the Manx Music Festival

In addition to his private pupils, some of whom went on to enjoy successful careers, Harry also taught the violin in some of the Island's private schools such as Miss Oldham's High Class School of Girls and Little Boys in Hutchinson Square, Douglas, from 1895, and at Victoria College, Douglas, from 1899. He was joined on the music staff of these establishments by other well-known local musical educators, Miss M. L. Wood (class singing) and the Misses Cannell (music theory and piano). These schools prided themselves on thoroughly preparing their charges for 'the professions and for commercial pursuits', and with a solid grounding in English, Latin, French, German, Maths, drawing, painting, dancing and gymnastics. He also taught violin at King William's College, Castletown, from 1895 until 1917.

Kathleen Rydings.

In 1898 the Hon. Miss Henniker, daughter of the Lieutenant Governor, an excellent amateur singer and enthusiastic supporter of music on the Island, produced her 'Assessment of the State of Manx Music and Musical Education' which appeared in the *Manxman* on 22nd January. She paid tribute to Harry 'for inspiring a love for orchestral music', F. C. Poulter 'likewise for brass band music', and the Misses Cannell and Miss M. L. Wood for their pioneering work and influence on musical education in general and choral singing in particular. In conclusion Miss Henniker wrote that it was very gratifying to see so many young Manx musicians applying to enter the London colleges of music.

~

The annual students' concerts continued to flourish throughout the decade, and although not always advertised as such, the presence of Harry's pupils among the violins is often attested to by the title 'Harry Wood's Special Orchestra'. There were annual students' concerts in the years 1892-5, 1897-8, 1900 and 1901. There was no official students' concert in 1896, but Harry's most experienced pupils probably took part in the first Sunday Sacred Concert at the Marina Pavilion in July.

The year 1897 was one of the busiest for the young musicians. The seventh students' concert took place in March that year at the Grand Theatre with an orchestra of thirty players, of which twenty were Harry's pupils, led by his colleague J. E. Quayle. The concert also marked the first important appearance of one of his most promising pupils, Kathleen Rydings of Laxey,[25] whose performance so surprised and delighted the audience that the request not to insist on encores was ignored. Harry must have been especially delighted to welcome Edwin Stead of the Grenadier Guards to perform two trombone solos, as some years before he had been one of his promising young violin pupils in Slaithwaite. The fourth students' concert in 1893 finally concluded at 11.00 pm, mainly due to the number of encores insisted upon by an audience who showed no sign of weariness.

Harry's Grand Concert at the Palace Opera House on 19th April 1900 featured an augmented orchestra of twenty-four players made up of his students and experienced local amateurs, and prize-winning singers from the recent Manx Music Festival. Haydn Wood played a duet with Kathleen Rydings which was adjudged the sensation of the evening.

The annual students' concerts followed the 'choice and select' pattern established by the first such event in 1890: tuneful light overtures, orchestral selections from popular operas and operettas, short descriptive pieces, concert waltzes and instrumental solos, choruses, arias and ballads from the operas of Verdi, Donizetti, Bizet and Gounod, and the operettas of Sullivan, Wallace, Balfe and Benedict, often supported by the Douglas Philharmonic Society and featuring local singers.

The local newspapers were generally kind and supportive to Harry and his young musicians in their reviews, with rarely a negative tone evident. The *Manx Sun*'s report of the 1892 students' concert was typical:

> Harry Wood's student's and orchestral concert on Thursday was a great, even a brilliant, success, and must have been gratifying to the talented and deserving musical connoisseur, and all who were associated with him. Everything went off splendidly. Almost everybody was there and every seat in the dress circle was taken by a large and fashionable audience . . . it was a capital opportunity for rubbing noses together.

'A hearty and healthy rivalry'.

On 5th December 1892 the fifth Annual Exhibition of the Isle of Man Fine Arts and Industrial Guild,[26] founded in 1888 'to stimulate and foster fine arts and industry on the Island', included music for the first time, and what would become known as the Manx Music Festival, or 'The Guild' as it is still affectionately known, took place on Thursday 8th December at the Palace.

The choir competitions were the inspiration of Miss M. L. Wood and were designed to make the event more attractive and interesting. Her principal aim was to cultivate an interest in good music and to encourage excellent choral singing, and she would probably have agreed with Dr James Kay, Secretary of the Privy Council's Education Committee, that choral singing was 'an important means of forming an industrious, bright,

Miss M. L. Wood, 'the Mother of Manx Music'.

loyal and religious people'. A 'hearty and healthy rivalry' between local choirs, apparent even at the first competition, became 'one of the most pleasing features of the Guild'.

From 1893 Miss Wood was ably supported by an energetic and sympathetic secretary, Mrs Florence H. Laughton, the wife of A. N. Laughton, High-Bailiff of Peel. It was her great organising ability, patience, tact and perseverance from the beginning of the venture that won over discouraging voices – the 'carping critics' who attempted to pour cold water on any new idea - and oiled the wheels of the fledgling music festival; by all accounts Mrs Laughton was a charming hostess who brought grace and goodwill to bear on all she undertook.

The early festivals lasted just one day and consisted of classes for

Mrs Florence H. Laughton.

choirs, children's choirs, sight-singing and composing a hymn tune. The first solo vocal classes were introduced in 1894, and the following year the competitive musical section of the annual exhibition moved forward to spring time in order to avoid the crush of musical activities for church choirs at Christmas, and to allow individual contestants more time to learn their festival pieces once the summer season was over. In 1897 the festival was extended to two days and, from the outset, the adjudicators were surprised and delighted by the standard of choral singing on the Island. Mr F. Maskell of Edgehill Training College, the adjudicator at the first competition, said in his remarks: 'I never heard such splendid part singing as that by the Douglas Cantata Society', who were the winners that inaugural year. The Manx language and traditional music appeared in the syllabus for the first time in 1899 with classes for Manx Bible reading and songs in the Manx language.

~

Harry's role during the early years was two-fold: to provide a small band to play selections during afternoons and evenings on the three exhibition days, and to direct the orchestra and provide instrumental and orchestral interludes at the festival gala concert. There is no evidence that he actually conducted the small band at the first music festival; more likely, he directed the ensemble, which included a piano and possibly only one other violin, from the leader's seat.

The following year, 1893, the 'band' had grown to fifteen players including his most experienced students and local adult amateur musicians, J. E. Quayle, Nella Mew and Haydn Wood, violins, plus one flute, one clarinet, a cornet player and a percussionist. They played an altogether more significant part in the festival concert by contributing a selection of appealing light classical pieces. Joseph Barnby's sacred idyll *Rebekah* (1870), for soprano, tenor and bass soloists and mixed choir was the chosen cantata for the combined choirs' performance, accompanied by one or two pianos.

By 1896 the orchestra had acquired an even greater role and Harry's 'Special Orchestra' featured in the opening hymn, a Rossini overture, a concluding march and the national anthem. There was no orchestra engaged in 1895 and Miss M. L. Wood, 'the axis on which the musical world of the Island revolves', conducted the combined choirs in a new cantata, *The Silver Penny* by Joseph Roeckel. Harry's orchestra was engaged again in 1897, and in 1898 and 1899 performed a selection of Manx melodies arranged by himself.[27] The eighth Music Festival in 1900 attracted one hundred and twenty individual entrants and twenty-eight choirs. The Gala Concert was a large-scale event featuring the combined choirs of two hundred and twenty voices supported by Harry's orchestra numbering twenty-four players. Harry himself was described as 'one of the most eminent professors on the Island' in the *Musical Times* and the reviewer went on to report that 'on the whole, the proceeding showed that there is considerable musical ability and activity in the isolated community'.

Harry was associated with the Manx Music Festival throughout his long career on the Island, but intensively from 1892 until the competition was suspended during World War I. Thereafter, J. E. Quayle and the Douglas Amateur Orchestral Society[28] were engaged, and when that orchestra dissolved in 1930, Kathleen Rydings and the Manx Amateur Orchestral Society kept the association alive. It is sad to reflect that since the end of World War II, no orchestra, local or otherwise, has taken part in the festival concert.

'Always Bright! Always Jolly! Always a Good Show!

No doubt each visitor had their own favourite entertainment venue, but the following conversation between a young lady and her companions overheard on a tram would have given J. P. Callow and Harry much satisfaction had they been eavesdropping:

> I love Derby Castle. It is my favourite place – so homely and cosy – and I shall always go there.

As would this comment from a Lancashire correspondent of the Manxman from the height of the 1896 season:

> Musically, no dance music I heard delighted me so much as Harry Wood's 1896 Lancers.

For others, the Palace was the place to be seen, as the following visitor's view from Belfast, via the *Belfast Evening Telegraph* in the *Isle of Man Times* 19th September, 1892 shows:

> In the matter of evening attractions, the Palace still holds the field. It possesses the largest floor, and has the best music. A reverie and chat are very refreshing . . .

The Falcon Cliff, however, trumped its competitors with a song praising its many virtues. Entitled *Falcon Cliff is the Place for Me,* with words by J. H. Wicklow and music by A. Wilson Seymour, and written sometime during the 1890s, the chorus declared that:

> Falcon Cliff is the place for me,
> Beautiful girls each night you will see.
> Come and enjoy yourselves with me,
> And dance at the Falcon Cliff

~

There is no doubt that the vast majority of visitors thoroughly enjoyed their holiday on the Island. Perhaps they would have enjoyed it a little less had they been aware that the welcome that awaited them in Douglas had a negative undercurrent. A more grasping attitude of some Manx towards their visitors was portrayed in a 'New Sketch of Life in Douglas', a 'mirth-provoking burlesque of the masher'.[29] Entitled *Fun on the Sands* and produced at the Palace Opera House during its opening season of 1893, it charted the escapades of a certain Mr Strangeways of Leeds. The opening chorus of landladies, cab drivers and bathing women begins:

Bring in the golden shekels, roll in the golden shekels,
The shekels that will pay us for our toil;
We're waiting and we're yearning, your money to be earning –
Roll in the coin, and let us share the spoil!
Roll it in! Roll it in!

'The music was charming, no music was ever so sweet'.[30]

The repertoire of the Derby Castle orchestra for the afternoon concerts under Harry's direction continued to feature the popular light classical musical fare of previous seasons: tuneful overtures and intermezzos, selections, marches, ballet suites, instrumental solos and short descriptive pieces complemented by arias and ballads from well-loved operas and operettas. Novelty descriptive pieces were always welcome and Oliver Gaggs, the musical director at the Palace in 1891-92, rarely disappointed his audiences. His serio-comic fantasia *A Trip to Manxland* was the highlight of the 1892 season with its depictions of the embarkation at Liverpool and the landing in Douglas, a tram journey to the Palace to hear an afternoon concert and even a German band on the promenade.

As popular as the afternoon concerts were, many more visitors looked forward to the new dances each summer, and between 1892-97 John P. Callow, the manager of the Derby Castle and the skilful composer of catchy polkas and topical vocal waltzes, introduced a number of his own compositions into the evening dance programmes. The waltz sensation of 1895, *We Two,* contained the following sentimental vocal refrain:

We two together, whate'er may betide
Whate'er be the weather, we'll roam side by side.
The frowns and the smiles of Dame Fortune we'll share,
With your hand in mine, love, the future we'll dare.

~

It was during this decade that Harry himself emerged as the composer of attractive, topical dances, many of them with a Manx theme. The *Derby Castle Lancers* of 1892 celebrating his appointment as conductor there, and the *Minstrel Lancers* dedicated to the Douglas Amateur Minstrels performed at his benefit night in September that year, may be his first important dance sequences performed on the Island.

Harry composed a new set of lancers every summer during this period. Often entitled Harry Wood's *Up-to-Date Lancers*, with the appropriate year included in the title, he seems to have found the perfect genre for his talents, as comments in the newspapers confirm: 'played every evening . . . very tuneful and enjoyable . . . comprising all the rollicking comic songs of the day . . . contains all the music of all the most popular songs'. A set of lancers was essentially a medley of 'all the latest and liveliest tunes of the day' and some of Harry's contained up to twenty different tunes. The 1893 lancers are typical of the genre and included Leslie Stuart's new song *The Soldiers of the Queen*. The audience unsurprisingly 'hollered for more'.

There were several new Derby Castle waltzes from Harry's pen, notably *Sweetheart May* in 1895, *Two Little Girls in Blue* based on the song by Charles Graham in 1894 and *Her Golden Hair* the following year. Harry was doubtless gratified to learn that his waltz *Bells of Dawn* was a great favourite of Mary, the future Queen Consort, who requested that it should be played at the Christmas Balls at Balmoral. One of the few novelty dances that did not 'take' was his 1898 *Washington Post* dance, *The Dandy Fifth*; by the end of the season the *Manxman* observed that 'men don't like it', and refused to take to the floor as it was 'the silliest dance ever introduced at the ballroom'.

The evenings drew to a close with special dance sequences such as the *Rainbow Dances* of 1893 and the *Kaleidoscopic Dances* of 1894. Especially popular with the visitors was the *Snowflake Dance* conceived by Harry for the Castle in 1896 as the successor to the once-popular *Shadow Dances*. The lights were dimmed, and as the orchestra softly began Waldteufel's *Les Patineurs* waltz (*The Skater's Waltz*), thousands of pieces of white paper drifted down from the roof, and the musicians would softly sing:

> Softly the Snow, falls in the night,
> Covering the World in a mantle of light.

Harry wrote in *Cavalcade*:

> The psychological effect of the 'crooning' number was wonderful – you could almost hear the poor dears getting cooler even in their high-necked dresses with puffed sleeves.

The dancers were enthralled as one enchanted visitor wrote:

> .. and crowds stand by admiring the fair ones whose graceful forms arrayed in flowing robes whirl through the maze of the joyous dance aided and impelled by the lively strains of Mr Wood's band.

'The summer season in Douglas tends to evil'.[31]

As Whit-week 1894 approached, Douglas became once again embroiled in hectic preparations for what was expected to be another 'bumper' summer season. The Derby Castle, the Falcon Cliff and the Palace vied with each other to introduce ever more spectacular improvements to their ballrooms and grounds and engage the most sought-after variety and concert artistes. All tastes were catered for. During September 1895, the Grand Theatre presented Gounod's *Faust* one week and Caryll and Monckton's *The Shop Girl* the next. 'Rumpy' of the *Manxman*'s Mews and Musings column wickedly observed: 'Last week stuffed turkey, this week tripe and onions'.

The exciting growth and expansion of entertainment that characterised the decade was not universally welcomed. The church often expressed views which were more in tune with Victorian sensibilities than with ours. The most virulent attack on Douglas came in 1893-4 from the pen of Rev Thomas Rippon, a Wesleyan minister on the Douglas circuit, in two addresses entitled *The Morals of Douglas, What is the Remedy?* These sermons were thought to have done Douglas and the Isle of Man incalculable harm for a quarter of a century and enraged all shades of local public opinion. The Reverend Rippon also detested the dance halls and 'certain houses of entertainment', whose promoters were 'men whose god was gold'. Douglas, he claimed, had earned an unenviable notoriety by 'serving the devil in summer, and the pious in winter'. Dancing or 'promiscuous immodest gymnastic movement' was the main target for his attack. That men and women of all ages should wish 'to spend the whole night, and night after night, in a mazy whirl', was a sign of evil, and when drinking and dancing were combined, then 'there is the gravest moral peril'.

The promenades were singled out as being rife with blasphemy, obscene language and gross immorality. His final verdict on the dance halls of Douglas:

> . . . having carefully weighed all the evidence put before me, I affirm with all solemnity and earnestness, that the dancing halls of Douglas are demoralizing in their tendency, that they are the rendezvous of persons bent on immorality, and that they are neither more or less than Public Marts for Prostitution.

The Reverend Rippon's remedy was strangely prophetic, for although his suggestion that all the main entertainment venues 'should be closed and never open their doors again' was ignored, his view that four ballrooms was too many was shared by their managers, particularly Charles Fox at the Derby Castle. The entertainment venues eventually regulated themselves as a result of the Great Amalgamation in 1898, one year after the minister's three-year appointment on the Island expired.

On a lighter note, the final word on the subject of the ballrooms in Douglas for the time being should go to 'Owd Jerry' in the *Manchester Evening Mail* in 1901. His adventures in Manxland were related in a cringe-worthy article written entirely in what one supposes to be a representation of the Mancunian accent. His enthusiastic but eccentric views of the Island, its natural beauties and its entertainments are tedious to read, but the following extract is an example of the general style and tenor of the piece:

> They say as marriages is med i' heaven, but at th' Isle o' Man aw should think th' mooast on 'ems med i' grounds at Th' Palace an' Derby Castle, an' sich like places.

Visitors' voices

As each season ran its course, visitor numbers were monitored and analysed with great interest. The 1892 season was a case in point, for as it progressed there seemed to be a worrying falling off in visitor numbers. The effects of the twenty-week Oldham Cotton Strike, symptomatic of the depressed state of the cotton industry, 'which affords the bulk of our visitors', had come to an end in April, but led many boarding house keepers to declare that 1892 was the worst season for years. By the end of the season, though, it was clear that there was no strong evidence suggesting that holiday-makers were economising and demonstrating a preference for the more accessible resorts of Blackpool or Llandudno.

The professional commentators were not concerned with such matters, as 'Bayard' in the *Manchester Sunday Chronicle* wrote:

> Delightful Douglas, with its superb promenades, beautiful bays, charming headlands and countless attractions (is) the Star Chamber that leads to delight . . . mountainous heights, sylvan scenery, bewitching glens, rugged rocks, swirling seas and pastoral plains . . . all could be found within the Isle of Man's ravishing specimens of sweetest nature. The Isle of Pleasure . . . jump on a passing tram. It will take you to the doors of the Derby Castle, and when you have sauntered along the neatly gardened grounds, you enter the ballroom, and a wonderful sight greets your eyes. To the dreamy

> music of a melting waltz you will see hundreds of couples floating with rippling motion across the polished parquet floor. At intervals variety artists of uncommon ability occupy the spacious stage, the orchestra giving place to the gymnast, the comic singer, the ballad warbler, or the knockabout comedians ...

The visitors, too, were unequivocal about the Island, as one satisfied holiday maker from Birmingham wrote:

> There is no other place in Britain where there is so much freedom .. . as will be found in Douglas. People who come here seem to live in another world, care is left behind and gladness is expressed in every face you meet'. From Victoria Pier to Derby Castle, Douglas Bay has never looked more beautiful than it does now.

For many coming from the northern industrial towns, the overriding purpose of the annual holiday was to seek enjoyment and escape from their hard-working lives. Douglas represented nothing less than 'the joy of living':

> The breath of life in its youthful vigour pervades the place, and the sea breeze ... seems an echo of the feeling. In place of dull grimy streets, a wide expanse of water, rivalling the sky in its blueness ... stretches away to an illimitable distance. One feels that here indeed is space to move and breathe. The beauty of the morning and the scene appear to re-act on the crowd lazily strolling along the promenade, or gathered in groups at the steps of the (boarding) houses, or lounging at the sea wall. As compared with the Manchester street, the gay scene resembles a picture out of a fairy tale.

For those who had never set foot outside of Britain, Douglas was the nearest to a continental watering place they would ever experience; a 'realm of youth and high spirits'. For those who frequented the 'Dancing Palaces', the spectacle of four or five thousand young men and women – 'the men in tennis flannels and coloured scarves, the young women in light muslins and straw hats' – was an extraordinary, almost indescribable scene.

The Isle of Man certainly punched above its weight in terms of natural beauty, and for many visitors offered much of the sense of freedom associated with the far more extensive wild open spaces of Derbyshire and Cumberland. By the end of the decade, though, advertisements for some of the glens undermined this perception by ludicrously exaggerating their beauties: Groudle Glen was announced as 'a canyon!' and Glen Helen was described as the 'Riviera of Manxland'. A letter in the *Isle of Man Examiner* from July, 1899, originally published in the *Manchester City News* warned that many of the Island's beauty spots, specifically Port Soderick, Belle Vue, Kirk Braddan Valley, Douglas Head and the area behind the Derby Castle, were sadly defaced by the creeping development and erection of 'shanties and advertising hoardings':

> Inhabitants are simply killing the goose that lays the golden egg. When all the best bits of the Island are choked with dancing and drinking saloons, cheap shows, niggers and circuses, the authorities will perhaps waken up and find they have made a mistake in allowing it to thus become a paradise for hordes of visitors and rowdy playground exploiters.

The menace of touting.

The activities of touts on the Douglas promenades continued to be of concern, and by the end of the decade could be fairly described as a public nuisance which threatened to spoil the experience for visitors. 'GR' of the *Manchester City News* noted that numerous advance agents for Douglas boarding houses and hotels were on board the steamers and pestering holiday-makers almost immediately after they embarked from Liverpool. Immediately they disembarked visitors were frequently mobbed by vendors of all sorts, and that after three or four days of running the gauntlet the conclusion was:

> One cannot sit or walk anywhere for five minutes without having to contend with a small tribe wishing to sell something or other. They are around visitors like flies round a honey pot. There is no escape!

One visitor of a literary frame of mind was moved to put pen to paper in 'A Visitor's Complaint', being a poem by 'B':

> 'They've sent me here for quiet, for change of air and rest:
> But oh! what racking riot awaits this sorrowing guest!'

There followed descriptions of the crush at the pier, and the cries of street vendors, newspaper sellers, match sellers, boot cleaners and delivery men shouting 'coal' and 'herrings'. For some the Isle of Man had become 'The Isle of Noise', and the *Manx Sun* in June 1894 agreed:

> . . . no place in the British Isles has greater natural advantages in making a good first impression. As in the Lancashire watering

> places, the touting system prevails in full force. Worthy but excitable lodging and boarding house keepers would fight with muscular enthusiasm for the visitor like so many Manx cats if the authorities did not step in for his protection to prevent his luggage being torn from him.

Although the authorities eventually regulated the bands and other groups of itinerant entertainers on the promenades, little seems to have been done to discourage even the most aggressive tactics of touts despite many references to their intimidating methods in the local newspapers over many years.

Douglas versus Blackpool.

For first time Douglas and Blackpool began to be compared in holiday reviews. After visiting the Island in September 1898 the advertising secretary for the Blackpool Corporation expressed in the *Manxman* his view that 'it is advertising that has made Blackpool the popular visiting resort it is'. Even taking into consideration the Island's natural beauties and attractions, his opinion was that 'we are asleep' in not attracting thousands more visitors. He further commented that 'Douglas's amusement resorts do not give as much for a shilling as those in Blackpool

Douglas Promenade in high season.

give for sixpence', and that the town's policy was to put the needs of the visitors first during the season by adopting prices that scared the locals away. His solution was to open the places of amusement for 6d, and 'give twice as much in the way of talent and other attractions as are now given for one shilling', generating a greater turnover and bigger dividends for the shareholders. 'What', the *Manxman* wondered, 'will the directors of the Palace & Derby Castle Company say to that?'

In fact Charles Fox, managing director and later chairman of the Palace & Derby Castle Company, had a good deal to say concerning the relative merits of Douglas and Blackpool, as he later revealed in a paper delivered to the Dilettante Debating Society. After stating the obvious: that Blackpool had many more theatres, ballrooms, cinemas and piers than Douglas and attracted as many visitors in one bank holiday weekend as Douglas attracted in an entire season, Fox recalled that matinees and indoor entertainments were generally unavailable in Douglas except on wet days, whereas in Blackpool indoor attractions were open and well patronised throughout the day come rain or shine.

Glasgow Week or 'Scotch week' was traditionally always lively, and in 1894 two thousand visitors from Scotland 'on pleasure bent . . . have thrown some life into the season'. They behaved in 'an orderly yet decorous fashion' and were often encountered at the Palace, Derby Castle or Falcon Cliff, where 'Scotch music' and dancing was on the menu:

> Mr Harry Wood, who has the knack of doing the right thing at the right time, has taken care that the dance music nightly played by his splendid band has had a decidedly Caledonian flavour.

In 1901, to ensure that the visitors from 'the land o'cakes' felt thoroughly at home,[32] the Derby Castle specially engaged the Scottish comedian W. F. Frame, billed as 'the man you know', to appear every evening.

For many visitors the following brief lines encapsulate the essence their experience of a night at the Derby Castle in 1901:

> Lancashire lads and lassies; Yorkshire tykes and their sweethearts; young men, old men, women from 16 to 60 with every type of garment and type of face – young and pretty, some even beautiful . . . they had come to the Derby Castle to enjoy themselves . . . knowing that every facility for doing so as afforded them there by the management . . . when the orchestra struck up, the Derby Castle was a pretty picture.

However, the Island could not afford to lapse into a comfortable complacency and, throughout the nineties, vigorous attempts were made to extend the holiday season, beginning with the commencement of dancing at the Derby Castle at Easter, keeping at least one of the resorts open during the slack period between Whit-week and early July when the summer season proper began, and by extending the season to the end of September. The Derby Castle stayed open throughout May and June in response to an appeal from hotel and boarding House keepers, but in 1899 the *Manxman* reported that both the Derby Castle and the Grand Theatre were often thinly patronised.

Most visitors still enjoyed the popular dance tunes from the 1880s, particularly the *Hi! Kelly* polka, and the popular local 'view halloo' of 'Hi! Kelly' was noted in the *Manxman* in 1900 in the published holiday recollections of one Timothy Rigg of Leeds:

> Crossed by Barrow . . . Some people on Walney Island shouted 'Hi Kelly!' at us; we replied 'Hi Fatheads!'

And so it was that shop assistants, clerks, school teachers, would-be 'mashers' and textile mill workers and their families began to flock to the Isle of Man during the summer seasons in ever increasing numbers, and W. S. Gilbert's 'steady-and-stolid-y, jolly-Bank-Holiday, everyday young man'[33] would continue to enjoy the Island's lovely scenery and secret places, the excursions by electric tram, the hustle and bustle of the crowded promenades, the dancing in the ballrooms and the afternoon concerts for many decades to come.

The Great Amalgamation.

The *Isle of Man Examiner* under the headline 'Pleasure Resorts Amalgamation' announced that a scheme to combine the four entertainment venues - the Palace, the Derby Castle, the Falcon Cliff and the Pavilion Variety Theatre, originally known as The Marina - under one management would be placed before the shareholders at a series of extraordinary shareholders' meetings to be held in March. The radical scheme was unanimously accepted, and a new company, The Palace & Derby Castle Limited, was formed, with a provisional prospectus promised for the following week. The four old companies went into liquidation but existing shareholders enjoyed the privilege of a priority allotment of shares in the new company. The directors of the Palace Company became the directors of the new company with John A. Brown - 'the father of amusement enterprise in Douglas' in the opinion of many - as secretary and Charles Fox as manager.

The principle objective of the amalgamation as reported in the *Mona's Herald* was 'to prevent the competition of the past', and there is no doubt that by the late 1890s the entertainment scene in Douglas had become very congested. A week later the newspaper elaborated on the theme:

> . . . it is expected that the enormously lavish outlays for artistes, working staff etc will be to a great extent abolished . . . it is proposed by amalgamation to 'tap' this expenditure, and to save for dividend what has hitherto run waste, caused by previous keen rivalry and undue competition.

~

The amalgamation plans revealed the true state of affairs. The Palace and the Derby Castle Company showed healthy figures; the Falcon Cliff and the Pavilion Variety Theatre did far less well. The share prospectus of the new company painted an attractive picture of the four venues with much being made of the entertainments on offer: dancing, variety shows and Sacred Concerts on Sundays, 'which have become immensely popular of late years'. The prospectus concluded with the observation that 'the Palace and Derby Castle were invariably full nightly'.

The old Palace (Douglas, Isle of Man) Limited was finally wound up in May 1898. The shareholders' meeting of the new Palace & Derby Castle Company Limited held that month reported 'a satisfactory start', with some operating expenses down and some takings up. There would be no free tickets for shareholders as in the past, therefore bringing Douglas in line with the convention in Blackpool and other resorts. It was confirmed that the Derby Castle would remain open during the so-called slack weeks between Whit-week and the official start of the summer season in July, and that the management would endeavour to keep the Palace flourishing until beyond the normal close of the season. In September there was a presentation to Charles Fox by the working staff of the Palace, Derby Castle and Falcon Cliff of a large silver salver; Harry's appointment as musical director for 1899 was confirmed at the meeting, as was George Eyton's at the Palace Ballroom and Jonghman's at the Palace Opera House.

The passing of the Falcon Cliff and Marina Pavilion

Many, however, will have been dismayed at the decline of the Falcon Cliff as a pleasure resort, and more particularly the eventual disappearance of its large Pavilion, for nearly twenty years a dominant feature on the Douglas skyline, and one of the finest spots from which to enjoy the magnificent sweep of the bay. The final splendid seasons between 1893-96, when variety stars like Bessie Bellwood, Vesta Tilley, Dan Leno, Eugene Stratton and Charles Chaplin Sr appeared, gave way to leaner years as the resort limped on, 'a mere shadow of its former thriving self'. Arthur Q. Moore writing in the *Mona's Herald* more than thirty years after the event, added a personal footnote to the story of the Cliff's demise:

> Under the new name of Olympia, the Cliff later housed Mexican Joe's Circus (Wild West Show), and other entertainments, but . . . for years it remained a sort of No-Man's-Land . . .

There was a last throw of the dice in 1897, when the Falcon Cliff opened for Whit-week with a programme of entertainments, closed after the holiday, and re-opened in mid-July with concerts morning and evening and a popular dance programme given by Mr M. McDermott's Tower Orchestra from Blackpool. The Falcon Cliff Pavilion itself was demolished during the winter of 1898-99, but the precise moment when the imposing edifice finally disappeared from view does not seem to have attracted the notice of the newspapers. Harry will surely have mourned its passing as

The morning after the collapse of Dumbell's Bank.

he recalled his first visit to the Island fourteen years earlier. By June 1899, the *Manxman* expressed some regret at the loss of the once-popular entertainment venue:

> The old pavilion has gone, and its threshold, the scene of so many revels and orgies in a past generation, is also swept away . . . from rosy dividends to falling on evil days and being sold for a song. How things change!

~

The fate of the Pavilion Variety Theatre after the amalgamation was of a different order altogether. Opened in July 1893 as a new ballroom, with Oliver Gaggs as manager and musical director, and an ambitious programme of dancing, variety acts, afternoon and Sunday concerts, it was 'wallowing in a financial mire' after just one short season. The omens had not been favourable. Building work on the grand entrance was still unfinished on the opening night, and the initial optimism, dulled by 'ill-natured attempts to damage the Marina' and 'a whole artillery charged with spite, envy and hatred', did not last despite the steady increase in attendances. Gaggs' new vocal waltz, *The Marina*, was played nightly to great acclaim and the Sunday Sacred Concerts throughout July proved to be popular, but Gaggs was 'severely indisposed' at the end of July although well enough to direct his 'Pre-eminent Marine Orchestra' at a garden party at Government House early in August. His benefit night in September attracted a large crowd of well-wishers and supporters, but he was in poor health again later that month, the result of over-work.

Early in 1894 Gaggs was enticed to Blackpool to become the musical director at the Tower Ballroom, and although the Pavilion continued under new management and with new musical directors for the remainder of the season, in November, the *Manx Sun* announced: 'Marina Company in liquidation!'[34] By 1895 the management seem to have given up the idea that the Pavilion Variety Theatre could compete with the other established ballrooms. The venue was redesigned as a variety theatre, with an enlarged stage and balcony and tiered seating and in August 1896, Marie Lloyd appeared there. However, hard on the heels of the amalgamation, rumours of a new theatre on the site began to circulate, and although the Pavilion continued as the venue for bazaars and trade exhibitions for another year, the company was wound up in May 1898, and at the end of the 1899 summer season the building was demolished. It rose again, phoenix-like,

The Derby Castle hotel, ballroom and variety theatre.

in 1900, as the new Gaiety Theatre, and still stands today as the jewel in the crown of the Douglas entertainment venues.

'Black Saturday', 1900.

Today we are inured to the possibility that our well-established financial institutions could fail for one reason or another, but the collapse of Dumbell's Bank in Douglas on 3rd February 1900 on what became known as 'Black Saturday', was an almost unprecedented and unimaginable event on the Isle of Man. The effects were devastating and many individual investors and local businesses faced bankruptcy.[35]

Dumbell's had been a feature of Manx commercial life for nearly half a century, and was thought to be as solid and dependable as the Tower of Refuge in Douglas Bay. The problems facing the bank are all too familiar to us: businesses both large and small had been granted extended credit during a wave of speculative loans, and by the late 1890s the bank's affairs were in a precarious state. The danger signals had been ignored for years; the head cashier resigned and a last-minute plan to sell Dumbell's to a London bank came to nothing.

The Palace & Derby Castle Company shareholders' meeting in December 1900 was mainly concerned with the setting up of a contingency fund amounting to £4,000 to offset the losses incurred by the failure of Dumbell's Bank, bearing in mind that when the bank closed it held Company funds of just over £14,700. The 1901 shareholders' meeting continued to wrestle with the on-going effects of the bank crash and accordingly raised the contingency fund to £6,000. The amount of money required to meet the deficit caused by the bank's collapse was 'variously estimated' as the director's moods veered between pessimistic and despondent, sanguine and optimistic. The age of morally unimpeachable bankers on the Isle of Man had ended, if, indeed, it had ever existed.

All they want is dancing.

There were other consequences for the Palace & Derby Castle Company resulting from the collapse of Dumbells' Bank, some of them directly impinging on the entertainments, the performers, the orchestras and Harry himself. Loans were negotiated in order to fund the building of the theatre at the Derby Castle, but well advanced plans both for the development of the Falcon Cliff estate for building and for transforming the Falcon Cliff Hotel into a 'high class hydro' were quickly shelved. Local societies now found it harder to obtain bookings at the Palace Ballroom for their events; the size of the fees paid to variety and concert artistes were closely examined and the financial arrangements surrounding Harry's and George Eyton's potentially very lucrative benefit nights also came under scrutiny. Some of the shareholders cared little if stars of the calibre of Vesta Tilley and Dan Leno were no longer engaged for they believed that the Palace and Derby Castle would continue to flourish as visitor attractions solely on the strength of their dancing programmes. As one Company director put it: 'all they want is dancing'.

Perversely, in the manner of these things, some variety entertainers unknowingly benefitted from the Dumbell affair and its aftermath, for as we shall see in the following chapter, the absence from Douglas for a few years of some very expensive artists made room for less expensive up-and-coming talents of the future. Florrie Forde first appeared in Douglas in 1900, and Harry Lauder in 1902.

Chapter 4

The King at his Palace

1902-1913

In the decade before the First World War, visitor numbers increased every year, inexorably rising to an unequalled peak of 634, 500 in 1913. In those years:

> There was music on the promenade and music on the Head; the Palace and the Derby Castle were doing good business; visitors could be seen bathing joyfully at Port Skillion or attending Divine Service at Kirk Braddan; hundreds of carriages hurried two and fro, luggage boxes piled high, porters perspiring and tradesmen smiling. Behold, the beginning of another summer season on the Isle of Man . . . when the Island became the happy hunting ground of two of the largest and most populous counties in England – Lancashire and Yorkshire - and nothing may, nothing can, rob us of their patronage. It is their birthright – and ours!

A combination of fine weather, a quick passage on 'the finest paddle steamers in the world' and reasonable fares resulted in a Whit-week of unparalleled prosperity. Indeed, the Steam Packet Company had much to be proud of with the new fast turbine steamers *Ben-my-Chree* and *Viking* and a new twin screw steamer *Snaefell* coming into service.

As the crowds assembled to meet the steamers in glorious sunshine, the pier masters were on alert directing the berthing and departure of the vessels as the harbour ferry boats began to ply between the Victoria and Battery Piers. Inspector Coole could be observed marshalling hundreds of awaiting carriages that stretched back to the North Quay, and a vigilant control was kept on the army of licensed porters. Upon landing at Victoria Pier, visitors would be delighted to find that the tramway had been extended almost to the boat's side, resulting in great savings on portage charges and carriage fares. Those disembarking on Friday and Saturday nights would find that the promenades were thronged as crowds made their way to the various entertainment venues.

'An island just large enough to be perfect . . .'[1]

> Whit-week! It means a lot to the people of Douglas and the Isle of Man. It means the end of a long dull winter, dreary in the extreme,

> and in too many cases accompanied by want and penury . . . It means that a long period of enforced idleness gives place to a foretaste of the season's rush and bustle, when boarding-house keepers can scarce snatch a few hours of the night from the seamless round of duties . . . such is life.[2]

The Island's image of itself can be glimpsed from the 1911 season *Holiday Guide & Programme of Tours*. Statistics from the Secretary of the Meteorological Council of Great Britain indicated that the Island enjoyed 5% more sunshine than Scarborough, Blackpool and Llandudno, 1% more than inland watering places such as Bath and Tunbridge Wells and 9% more than Buxton in Derbyshire. The guide made much of the island's natural assets:

> Rocky enough to make its coastline charming; just hilly enough to healthily tax one's climbing abilities; mountains just high enough to show one England, Ireland, Scotland and Wales; glens and ravines just big enough to be bold and inspiring; waterfalls full enough to be overflowing – nothing in nature to be too much or too little.

In other words, small but perfectly formed!

~

In September 1902 a Yorkshire journalist accompanied by a number of friends took a late season holiday on the Isle of Man. The party accomplished the journey from Selby to Leeds via the Lancashire and Yorkshire Railway Company's express service to Fleetwood in three hours, in good time to board the *Mona's Queen* and make for the dining saloon for 'an excellent spread'. In just over four hours they disembarked and made for the Central Promenade in search of their lodgings and the 'excellent hospitality . . . and catering that would have done credit to a Yorkshire household'. The only cloud in the otherwise clear skies was the disturbance caused by inebriated guests returning back late after an evening at the Palace or Derby Castle, and then continuing the 'entertainment' in their rooms.

The party visited all the main sights and towns including Ramsey by electric tram, attended the Sunday outdoor services at Kirk Braddan and Douglas Head, and witnessed King Edward VII's yacht steam into Douglas Bay accompanied by a cruiser and two torpedo boats. Even the tremendous gale that passed over the Island towards the end of their holiday, with huge waves dashing against the beaches, failed to dampen their enthusiasm for the Island:

> In musical matters Manxland is well to the front. More than charmed was I with the efforts of two English prima donnas whom I heard at the Palace. In Madame Ella Russell and Miss Clara Butt we had the pick of 'home' vocalists, and their vocalisation was as unique as it was brilliant and effective.

The group attended one of the first Sunday Sacred Concerts under Harry Wood's direction and were amazed that the Palace was packed to overflowing. In conclusion the journalist wrote that the 'homely character of the Manxlanders . . . their sterling worth and friendship and hospitality' was fondly recalled after their return to Yorkshire, and predicted a 'glorious and prosperous future' for the Island, 'the land of sunshine, of pleasure and of unalloyed joy'.

'It's a braw place is Douglas'.

With so many visitors hell-bent on making the most of their holidays, many of them young men, it is hardly surprising that there were occasional contretemps as related in the *Manxman* in a report headed 'Consturbances at a boarding house on the promenade', principally pillow fights, mat scrimmages, late smoking concerts and bedroom nap parties going on until 4.00 am. 'Up went the bloomin' monkey' after the landlord, attempting in vain to stop a raucous sing-song in the smoking-room led by 'a little podgy pork butcher from Blackburn', was 'invited to commit various acts and deeds', presumably of an unsavoury and anatomically taxing nature. When a glass panel was broken, a solicitor from Birmingham who had been visiting 'thilerman' for twenty years interceded on behalf of the guests and outlined their grievances:

> the baggin' wur t'worst on th' prom; there wasn't 'an egg a-piece for breakfast, and shop 'uns at that. Worst of all 'Eawr 'armless 'armony hes bin spiled, and you've been done eaut of . . . as good a top-note as any throstle could tip of.

The guests were about to return to their rooms and pack their bags, when the landlord appeared 'thoroughly cowed and apologetic' and said 'that we might in future do as we pleased'. The late night in-house entertainments continued unabated:

Freer than the air,
More untrammelled than the wave;
You'll see the blushing fair, the bold and the bounding brave,

Douglas Coronation & Jubilee Carnival Parade, Douglas.

A-cuddling on the sleepy stair,
Or flirting on the pave.

Whether holiday makers stayed in the most economical and basic boarding houses or stretched their wallets to secure accommodation at one of the fine, well-appointed hotels, the new Steam Packet handbook would be their reliable guide and could reasonable argue that 'there is no place in the British Islands where the traveller is more cheaply and efficiently catered for than in Douglas'.

'Douglas Makes Holiday 'Twixt Joy and Sorrow'.

The announcement of the end of the second Boer War on 1st June, 1902, was greeted with great joy and thanksgiving; the streets of Douglas were thronged with thousands of people the following week to welcome home two Manx Volunteer battalions who received an enthusiastic reception.

The main civic event of 1902, however, was the Douglas Coronation & Jubilee Carnival on 25th June in celebration of the accession to the throne of Edward VII, marred only by news of his sudden illness.[3] Despite the postponement of his Coronation and the resultant curtailment of some of the events and processions, the town was lavishly decorated with arches, flags, pictures, garlands and illuminations; the Tower of Refuge in Douglas Bay was adorned with an immense crown to which were attached the letters E.R. Over 3,500 children from the churches and schools took part in a grand pageant accompanied by local bands.

During the afternoon all the processions and bands converged on the Palace for a fete followed by the massed singing of the National Anthem led by Douglas soprano Mrs Bunting, the Douglas Choral Union and other local singers. The Volunteer Band and Harry's orchestra played background selections, and there were sporting tournaments, a brass band contest, choral competitions, cricket matches, trips around the Island on the Ben my Chree, fancy-dress parades, a battle of flowers and a confetti carnival to keep the crowds entertained.

Two months later large crowds flocked to greet King Edward VII and Queen Alexandra as they came ashore in Ramsey and toured the Island on a surprise visit that made up for any dampening of the holiday atmosphere in June. Although the announcement of the Island's new Governor was made on 14th August, Lord Raglan had not taken up his duties at the time of the Royal visit and the Acting Governor, Sir James Gell, stood in for him. Raglan proved to be charming and personable, a 'sound man' and a 'good chap', and at his most effective during the early years of his tenure when all was right with the world. Cautious by nature but lacking tact and diplomacy, he ultimately refused to take Manx concerns seriously and failed to endorse the reforms in social legislation the Island desperately needed.

~

There was much for the Island to be proud of during the decade: May 1912 saw the opening of Noble's Park in Douglas with twenty-four acres of free public access to bowls, tennis, croquet, cricket, a race track, lovely coastal and mountain views, and a fine refreshment house with verandas and comfortable seating throughout. In September that year the new Noble's Hospital was opened by Lord and Lady Raglan with Harry Wood's Palace orchestra providing music during the afternoon tea. Later that month a *Titanic* memorial service was held in the Palace Ballroom attended by 6,000 people who sang a special new hymn for the occasion with words by Hall Caine. In July 1913 the new Villa Marina Kursaal opened, the first real competition for the Palace & Derby Castle Company,

The Palace Ballroom in 1904.

and in August the first purpose-built cinema, the Strand, appeared.

There was tragedy too, for on 3rd December 1909 the steam packet vessel *Ellan Vannin* sank in a storm approaching the River Mersey with the loss of twenty-one crew and fifteen passengers. Edward VII died in May 1910 and the Coronation of King George V took place on 22nd June, 1911. The Island celebrated 50 years of municipal government in Douglas with the Douglas Coronation and Jubilee Carnival which took place between 28th June and 8th July. Harry and the Palace orchestra were present on several occasions during the festivities including an evening of Manx Music and a vocal and choral competition.

Harry Wood at the Palace

> Mr Harry Wood, for many years musical director at the Derby Castle, has been appointed to the more important conductorship of the Palace Orchestra. This is an advance for Mr Wood; he is well deserving of it.

Early in the new season, following the above announcement in the *Isle of Man Examiner* in March 1902, there was a noticeable improvement in the playing of the orchestra and in the selection of music for both the afternoon concerts and evening dance programmes. The thirty-four-year-old Harry also assumed control of the Sunday Sacred Concerts, for which the orchestra was enlarged to forty players, possibly in response to one reviewer's suggestion that the Palace and Derby Castle orchestras should be combined into a truly 'Grand Orchestra' for these prestigious events. Thus, in the year that saw the publication of Beatrix Potter's *Peter Rabbit* and Conan Doyle's *The Hound of the Baskervilles*, when Dame Clara Butt sang *Land of Hope and Glory* for the first time and Scott, Shackleton and Wilson reached the southern-most point reached by man, Harry Wood at last assumed a position that fully exploited his talents.

The Derby Castle Orchestra – often referred to as the Derby Castle Bijou Orchestra - now played under another conductor, Harry's newly-appointed deputy Edwin Bogetti, sometimes known as Signor Bogetti or Professor Bogetti 'the famous London conductor'. Little is known about him beyond the fact that he was the composer of beguiling short pieces such as the *Beautiful Mona Waltz*, the gavotte, Charming and an intermezzo, *Dresdina*, which he penned under the name Carl Malenberg.[4] The *Isle of Man Times* was soon reporting that 'the new musical director has caught on' and that 'his up-to-date, sprightly music' helped to maintain the Castle's reputation. An innovation that would have pleased many visitors was that on wet mornings Bogetti's orchestra provided an hour-or-so of music in the ballroom.

'Beauty and comfort without equal in Douglas'.

On the penultimate night of Harry's first season at the Palace a fire broke out destroying part of the roof and approximately one third of the main body of the building. This may have been a blessing in disguise as the 1889 ballroom was beginning to show its age. Re-building work was urgently undertaken during autumn and winter, and the New Palace was officially opened on 4th July, 1903, the largest dance hall in Britain, without a rival - not even in Blackpool - and the finest anywhere in the world.

The new building was far handsomer, larger and more luxurious than its predecessor, with wider galleries, a new stage, spacious dressing rooms and no doubt to the delight of Harry and his musicians, improved backstage orchestra facilities. The ballroom was lit by electric arc lighting, and to keep the dancers cool and refreshed during the warmest months,

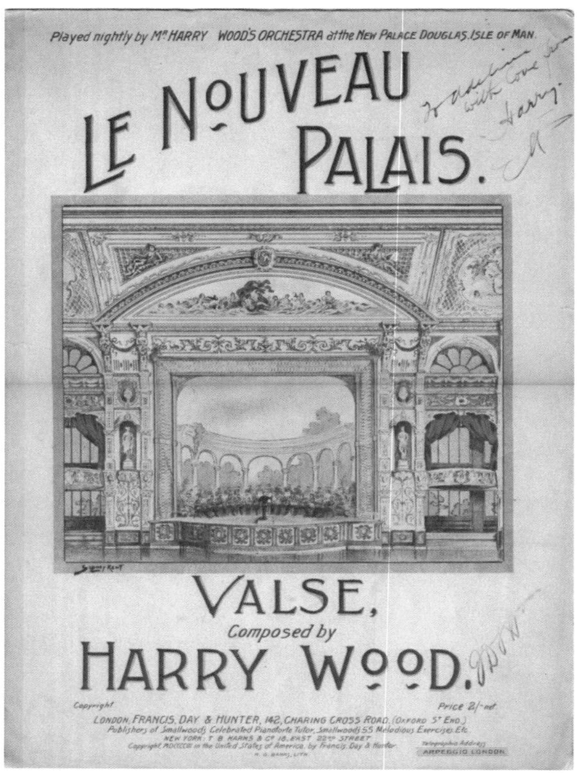

there was a large open ventilator in the centre of the ceiling. The restaurant was enlarged and a new annex was built housing two bars. The 170 x 80-foot dance floor was completely refurbished with parquetry squares of oak, walnut and pear wood at a cost of £1,000. The centrepiece of the up-graded gardens and grounds was a thirteen-foot fountain. On the opening night, the first five hundred ladies entering the ballroom to dance on the new floor received either a bouquet or spray of roses.

The Derby Castle Opera House - 'still the people's favourite; always bright; always jolly and always a good programme' - also benefitted from a substantial make-over during this period. In 1905 the old cramped interior was transformed into a fifty-foot lounge for variety entertainments panelled in crimson and gold, with four refreshment stalls and other improvements including electric lighting, courtesy of the Electric Tramway Company. In the ballroom there was dancing from 7.30pm until 10.45pm to the Castle Bijou Orchestra, no longer under the direction of Edwin Bogetti, however, but with the music selected by Harry and conducted by new appointee, A. J. Graham, who directed the band of twenty players led by Harry's brother Haydn, and according to the *Isle of Man Times*, 'acquired a perfect balance' in music 'played with confidence and sparkle'. As another correspondent wrote two days later:

> Bohemia, dead in London, has an annual revival for a short season at Derby Castle . . . an institution with excellent side shows and picture galleries, and Harry Wood's orchestra plays the newest dance music, and accompanies the mood of charm, honest recreation, simple pleasures and infectious abandon perfectly.

Furthermore, 'the mugwumps' (presumably Douglas Town Council's Licensing Committee) who being 'adverse to cakes and ale themselves would deny ginger hot in the mouth to others, still allow reasonable refreshment at Derby Castle'.

A brief note in *Cavalcade* for the year 1903 is Harry's only reference to one of the most exciting musical events of that year, the appearance of 'The American March King' and his famous band at the new Palace in July:

> Sousa and his band visited the Palace this season. I think the most popular march was 'Stars and Stripes'.

Sousa himself was a short, thick-set, energetic man who directed his famous band of fifty-two musicians with exaggerated military strokes of the baton, and in the opinion of the *Isle of Man Times* was 'the greatest band conductor who ever visited Manxland'.[5] He demanded and received 70% of the takings for his concerts and then moved on to Belfast, Newry, Dublin, Cork, Llandudno and Blackpool.

Overall musical director

Another brief note in *Cavalcade* from 1903, appended in Harry's hand almost as an afterthought after the manuscript had been typed, announced the most important appointment of his entire career, that of overall musical director of the Palace & Derby Castle Company: 'This year I had the orchestra at the Palace and D.C.'

His first two years in this role were very successful as he juggled skilfully with his various responsibilities: the Sunday Sacred Concerts, selecting the music for the evening dance programmes and the afternoon concerts, organising the rehearsals for a constant stream of concert and variety artistes – and attempting to comply with their demands and whims - and all with his customary good grace and a beaming smile.

Harry's personal prestige and popularity at this period can be

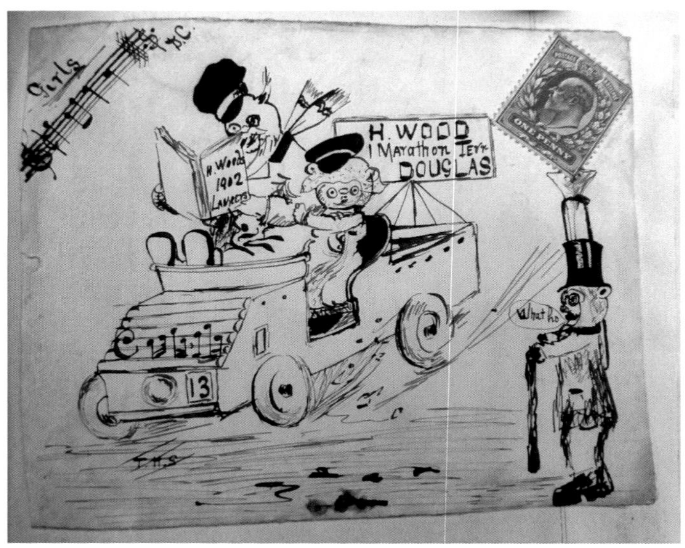

A cartoon of the 'popular music king'.

measured by the success of his benefit nights. His twelfth benefit night in September 1904, for example, was attended by 4,000 people who braved vicious gales and torrential rain to enjoy a varied programme with no less than thirteen acts on display even if the *al fresco* Pierrots and fireworks had to be cancelled. The *Mona's Herald* called him 'one of the most genial men in Douglas' and hailed him as the 'popular music king'. Perhaps this was the origin of his later title: 'Manxland's King of Music'.

Harry's library

The secret of Harry's success in his new role was his flexibility and total dedication to making things work, supported by a large number of musical contacts both on and off the Island. However, there was a secret weapon in his armoury, namely his large and ever-expanding personal music library, which from 1911 was housed in his new residence at 1, Osborne Terrace, Douglas, formerly the home of Miss M. L. Wood. In an interview with Philip Cain, the principal reporter of the *Isle of Man Times* in January 1929, Harry revealed that his library was one of the largest private collections of sets of orchestral parts and scores in Britain, and that it contained some 6,000 titles, or more than 90,000 individual sheets of music, embracing dances, marches, suites, rhapsodies, ballet extracts, short descriptive pieces, more than forty hymns to open the Sunday Sacred Concerts, overtures, concertos and even full symphonies.

Because of its immense size, and the need to be able to locate any piece of music instantly, Harry devised his own ingenious indexing and filing system maintained in a series of large manuscript books, and a card index system developed with the help of Douglas librarian John Taylor. The index cards contained the relevant details of every piece of music in the collection: the composer, the title, a brief description of each piece and the instrumentation. The sets of orchestral parts were kept in packets or folders in two large rooms, each fitted with seventy or more shelves.[6]

In a later, undated article for the *Colne Valley Guardian*, Harry revealed a little more of how he operated and maintained his library throughout each summer season when the demand for new programmes was relentless:

> Mr Wood staged a complete change of music every alternate night during the season ie he gave fifty-one different programmes plus seventeen Sunday Concert programmes.

Pieces that he considered successful or were especially popular were retained for future seasons, but any piece that failed to please or that he felt was inferior was discarded and rarely revived. Harry's sister Adeline acted as his assistant librarian, and during the winter months assisted in the vital work of repairing damaged scores, orchestral parts and folders and replacing lost or damaged parts with newly copied ones. In this way, the music in Harry's library was always fresh and up-to-date.

Roll up! Roll up! Harry in Circus-land

Hengler's circus is coming, with its freight of fun.
Don't forget to take a peep when your work is done.
Down by the Promenade, near the end of pier,
Down by the Promenade, it will soon be here.[7]

Harry Wood's connection with the circus world might appear to be a strange departure from his normal activities, but during the long winter months when the Palace and Derby Castle were closed except for local events, he naturally sought other sources of employment. We first hear of Harry Wood's association with Hengler's circus in the following brief notice in the Examiner in the autumn of 1904:

> Harry Wood accepts three months engagement as musical director at the Hippodrome, Glasgow, to be opened early in December by Mr Albert Hengler, who is well-known in Douglas.[8]

The water pantomime at Hengler's circus.

Hengler's circus had been a prominent and popular summer feature in Douglas for many seasons, but what was to be the final period associated with the Island began during the early months of 1896 when a wooden cirque was erected near the ill-fated Douglas 'Eiffel' Tower site on Parade Street, housing a circus ring and hippodrome with seating for some 3,000 people. For the next five seasons the holiday crowds enjoyed a lavish two-hour show comprising some twenty acts involving horses, ponies and dogs supported by clowns, acrobats, jugglers, cyclone riders, Indian Club swingers and much more. Hengler's speciality was the water carnival where 'entirely new, grotesque pantomimes' and 'screamingly comic spectacles' took place in the arena which could be converted into a lake up to ten feet deep and holding 50,000 gallons of water pumped in within just a few minutes, and featuring a Great Water Chute, twenty feet high and forty feet long.[9]

A circus band of between fourteen and twenty players conducted by George Clements provided traditional circus music to accompany the equestrian performances characterised by 'a preponderance of wind instruments and a good tattoo on the drum'. Military marches were especially poplar and 'every member of the orchestra was kept hard at work without intermission'. Albert Hengler was a larger-than-life character, described as 'tall, well-built, sixteen stone in the saddle', but although Harry knew him well there is no evidence to suggest that he either arranged music for or conducted the circus band in Douglas.

~

Harry was expected to be away from the Island for three months during the winter of 1904-5 during his engagement with Hengler in Glasgow. The report in the *Isle of Man Examiner* further revealed that he would be taking some of his Palace orchestra musicians with him, and would 'arrange, compose and conduct' the music for the famous water spectacles. He joined Hengler at the new Hippodrome, Sauchihall Street, Glasgow every Christmas for fourteen seasons until 1917, and apparently also in Newcastle, Sheffield, Manchester, Leicester and Liverpool. Harry's younger brother Haydn returned to the Island to take over Harry's violin teaching 'and arrangements' during the winter of 1904-5, and it is reasonable to assume that he also gave violin lessons to Harry's pupils at King William's College during this period.

By 1901 Hengler's days in Douglas were numbered, for although he was successful and personally wealthy, he struggled to cover the enormous costs of the Douglas operation, and in September announced the closure of the circus on Parade Street after the final night on the 4th. Hengler's financial troubles finally overwhelmed him in February 1904, just one month after he had loaned Harry costumes for his new pantomime *Babes in the Wood*, when he was served with a summons 'out of jurisdiction' in Manchester for £62.14s in outstanding rates. There had been a history of actions against him for non-payment of rates since 1902 and, in his defence he cited heavy operating costs, dwindling receipts, lack of capital and money lost at Chester Race Course![10] In July he was finally declared bankrupt.

~

Hengler's name disappears from the Manx newspapers after 1904 and consequently we get only fleeting glimpses of Harry's winter sojourns in Glasgow and elsewhere with the circus. Haydn continued to deputise for Harry at the St. Matthew's Church Sunday services during the early months of 1905, and on 19th January gave an important recital at the Castle

Mona Hotel, his debut concert in Douglas in his own right after six years of study at the Royal College of Music, followed by intermittent short periods in 1903 and 1904, and the Brussels Conservatoire. It was at this recital that Haydn introduced his wife-to-be Dorothy Court, a future Savoyard soprano, and still at the Royal College, to Douglas audiences, with a new song especially written for her entitled *Cupid's Hunt*. Harry was somehow able to arrange the music for the St. Matthew's Parochial Tea the following year whilst still engaged in Glasgow.

Miraculously, a brief letter from Emma Albani dated December 1908, Glasgow, has survived in one of the Wood family scrapbooks inviting Harry:

> . . . to dine quietly with us on Sunday Dec 20th at 7.00 . . . we shall be so glad to see you. Dear Haydn is leaving tonight so cannot come I am sorry to say . . . yours E. Albani-Gye.

Two further intriguing scrapbook cuttings have also survived. The first, dated 7th November, 1906, from *The Bailee* cartoon supplement, is entitled 'Hengler's Cirque' and consists of a page of cartoon characterisations of the main performers appearing that season including Hengler himself, Whimsical Walker, the equestrienne Miss Amelia and Harry himself. The second is from an unidentified publication and depicts Harry, baton in hand at the rostrum together with the principal characters from a production of *Cinderella* at Hengler's.

Our genial chef d'orchestre

Although Harry's base of operations was the Palace, he was present at the Derby Castle from time to time to direct the dance programmes and conduct the orchestra for stars such as Florrie Forde. As we have seen, there were a number of deputy conductors appointed to direct the Derby Castle Orchestra during the decade, including in 1906 A. J. Graham, a violinist who led the Palace Orchestra for the Sunday Sacred Concerts, Harry Foxall in the 'cosy variety theatre' in 1907 and his colleague Harry Rushworth in 1912, although his tenure was short-lived as he moved to the Theatre Royal, Birmingham, the following year.

Dance competitions open to visiting amateurs only continued to be popular. In 1908 there were two-step and valeta-waltz nights, and in 1913 new dance novelties, the *Ragtime Crawl* and the *Society Glide* invented and demonstrated each night by Mr and Mrs J. B. McEwan. There were no competition entry fees but a prize of £3 for the winners in each dance category was awarded. No doubt Harry stored away his impressions of these Douglas competitions until he became a prime mover in the foundation of the Blackpool Dance Competition in 1920.

~

Conductors' and managers' benefit nights near the end of each season continued to be well-patronised, particularly Harry's. In 1912 the *Mona's Herald* recorded the twenty-first anniversary of his directing the orchestra at the Derby Castle in its report of his benefit night by describing him as 'our genial chef d'orchestre of the P&DC . . . he has given pleasure to thousands by the delightful character of the selections that he invariably provides . . .' A bumper night was promised for his twenty-second benefit night in September 1913, and so it proved to be.

Charles Fox's benefit night at the Palace Coliseum the following year, celebrating his twenty-one years as Secretary and Manager, was an extravagant gala occasion with many visitors from England in the audience, and the surprise guest appearance of Wilkie Bard. At first he pretended not to have turned up, and then appeared from the rear of the audience in oilskins and sou'wester (it was a wild night), vaulted across the orchestra rails and landed on stage crying 'There you are Charlie'. There followed a good deal of patter and banter during which the great comedian paid tribute to Fox's skill in miraculously cramming fifty-two weeks' worth of entertainment into the Island's short summer season. He ended his speech with 'I give you my right hand, Charlie – the best'.

Later that evening over one hundred staff from the Palace and Derby Castle and the Gaiety Theatre enjoyed an excellent supper at Collinson's Cafe when it was revealed that no less than twelve staff members had also served for twenty-one years. Harry was then prevailed upon to stand and take a bow as he had served even longer: twenty-four years. The celebration ended after his Bijou Orchestra of four players had 'rendered appropriate music during the evening'.

~

Harry continued to seek lucrative employment out of season that both extended his range and experience and kept him abreast with new developments in the world of entertainment. Commencing on 29th September 1913 'Harry Wood's Bijou Orchestra' was engaged to provide music at the Gaiety Theatre during its winter season of films or 'picture plays' as they were advertised. The Gaiety began to show films in response to the opening of the first purpose-built cinema in Douglas, the Strand, and the promise of some half-a-dozen others springing up during the winter, and engaged Harry's ensemble to play music which was as far as possible designed to synchronize with the film.

The *Isle of Man Times* devoted several column inches to this new departure at the theatre and made much of the presence of 'a small but highly efficient orchestra to render suitable music, now recognised as a highly desirable adjunct to all picture shows'. Harry led the ensemble which included his nephew Hilton Cullerne, who had just completed his studies at the Royal College of Music, a harpist, pianist and an organist. The selection of music was left entirely in Harry's capable hands '. . . as he is the possessor of what is probably the finest private library of orchestral music in Britain'. Hilton was further asked to play a violin solo during the short interval between films each evening. Harry's involvement with the music at the Gaiety Theatre could have lasted into the early years of the First World War, but he makes no mention of this phase of his career in *Cavalcade*.

~

It was at a meeting of the directors of the Palace & Derby Castle Company in November 1912 that a plan to build a new opera house - essentially a variety theatre on the site of the existing skating rink in the Palace grounds - was first unveiled. The existing opera house, with seating and standing room for only 1,500 people, had for some time been unable to accommodate the huge numbers wishing to see and hear the great stars. The new opera house situated in front of the huge ballroom, with seating for audiences of between 3,500 and 5,000, became known as the Palace Coliseum, and was officially opened amidst great pomp and ceremony on 21st July 1913 by Vesta Tilley, who journeyed from London for the occasion. She received a tremendous welcome from the audience and delivered a short speech during which she recalled many happy memories of the Isle of Man and the Palace and Derby Castle. She joked that she would rather be singing than speech-making, and promised that she would soon return to Douglas '. . . and here's jolly good luck and prosperity to the new Coliseum'.

Harry's first Sunday Sacred Concert at the new Palace Coliseum took place less than a month later. The spacious hall was virtually filled to capacity and the acoustics were said to be significantly better than the Palace Ballroom. All in all, the experiment of using the new hall for concerts was deemed a success. Harry's orchestra performed an even larger role than usual, perhaps in order to thoroughly test the hall's acoustics; the programmes included Rossini's *William Tell* overture, Sibelius' *Valse Triste* – the 'hit' of the concert – a *Fantasie on Leoncavallo's I Pagliacci* and the exciting *Hungarian March* from Berlioz' *Faust.*

The Cavalcade rolls on

Vesta Tilley did not appear in Douglas between 1900 and 1905 because she was by then one of the highest paid music hall artistes, and the Palace & Derby Castle Company were still recovering from the financial restraints imposed after the collapse of Dumbell's Bank. Tilley's fees rose alarmingly from £150 in 1898 to £275 in 1906, when she returned to charm her audiences with new songs and personas. In 1908 an estimated 9,000 dancers and spectators huddled in a crush in the Palace Ballroom at 10 o'clock each evening to hear her sing *I'm the Idol of the Girls* dressed either in 'regimentals' or in a smart and fashionable brown suit, light waistcoat, brown boots and green hat. She also sang *The Seaside Sultan*, a clever and wickedly 'cutting' song about a typical boastful, pretentious but hard-up 'flannelled fool from an office stool' who once a year 'reigns by the gay sea shore':

He is the Seaside Sultan, the Monarch of the Pier.
Of the Promenade he's Shah, of the beach he is the Czar.
All the ladies in his company will lurk
It's an awful blow when he's got to go
Back to work.

A single letter from Vesta Tilley to Harry has survived to give a fleeting glimpse of the relationship between musical director and variety star. Dated 2nd August 1910, it is brief, to the point and entirely professional in tone:

> Dear Mr Wood
> Would you please score the enclosed song for me in the key of Eb. I want it to open with on Monday and I particularly want it done on small sheets.
> Yours sincerely
> Vesta Tilley

The song in question may have been *The Giddy Little Isle of Man* which she is known to have included in her repertoire that year.

Vesta Tilley appeared in Douglas and the new Palace Coliseum in

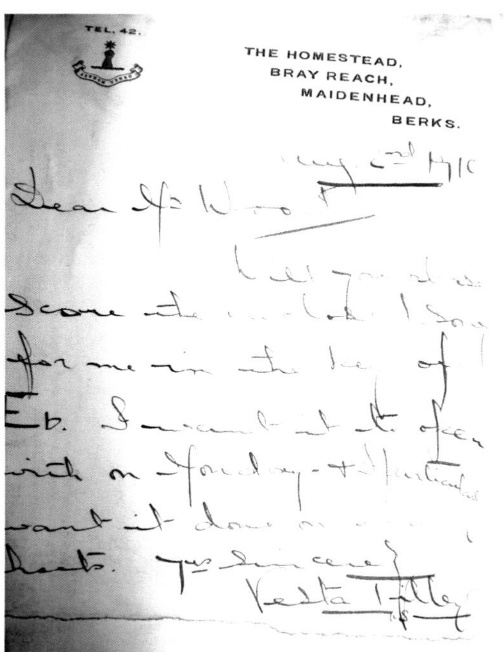
TEL. 42.

THE HOMESTEAD,
BRAY REACH,
MAIDENHEAD,
BERKS.

Letter from Vesta Tilley.

August 1913 for what would be her last appearances on the Island. Her final night attracted the largest crowd ever seen at the Palace, the turnstile having to be re-supplied with small change three times. Harry later recalled that the ballroom was so packed that the dancers 'had no room to pirouette and looked like maggots in a cheese', and recalled that Vesta Tilley brought with her 'the first "dress suit" she wore on stage when she was a little girl, just for my edification'. She apparently introduced a new Isle of Man song which may have been *Seaside Girls* with its chorus altered to make it relevant to the Island:

> Down at Margate (Douglas) looking very charming you are sure to meet,
> Those girls, dear girls, those lovely seaside girls etc

In an act of characteristic generosity, she signed hundreds of copies of her photograph to raise money for Douglas Hospital Day.

Tilley's up-and-coming young rival Hetty King returned to Douglas in 1905 and thereafter appeared at the Palace and the Derby Castle every subsequent year until the First World War. With her jaunty 'masher' act in which she appeared immaculately dressed in top hat and tails, white gloves and smoking a fine cigar, or her famous sailor routine during which

Hettie King and Harry Lauder.

she smoked a foul pipe and sang her best-known song *Ship Ahoy!* or *All the Nice Girls Love a Sailor*, she was a vibrant young talent.

Harry mistakenly recalled in *Cavalcade* that Harry Lauder sang *A Wee Deoch-an-Doris* at the Derby Castle in 1897, but there is no evidence for this. In fact 'London's Favourite and Scotland's Pride' did not appear in Douglas until July 1902 when he was engaged as the resident Scottish comedian during the Glasgow holiday weeks. The artiste who would be soon hailed by many as the greatest entertainer of them all - and certainly the highest paid - rated only the briefest, cursory review. He sang three 'Scotch Airs' and a favourite encore *Risin' ear-rly i' th' mor-rnin', Harry,* 'the crowd joining in the chorus with great energy'. Harry Lauder was engaged again for Glasgow fortnight in 1904, and appeared in the ballroom each evening at 9.45. The reviewers once again failed to recognise the future internationally acclaimed 'Laird of the Halls' and his act was dismissed in a couple of lines because 'he sings and recites in that peculiarly quaint manner which is the delight of the Scotch'. It would be more than a quarter of a century before he appeared in Douglas again.

Gertie Gitana, 'The Star who never fails to shine', appeared at the Palace in August 1911. An astonishingly versatile entertainer (her name means 'Gypsy') famed for her petite figure and sweet child-like voice, she

Wilkie Bard and Gertie Gitana.

was also a tap dancer, yodeller, pantomime star and saxophonist. Her best-known song was *Nellie Dean* which she sang with a simple coyness, quite unlike the crude, boozy manner in which it is frequently rendered today. Her name lives on in cockney rhyming slang: Gertie Gitana – Banana!

Manx cats, Mozart and a 'one-eyed yellow idol' at the Castle

Among the newcomers to Douglas was Wilkie Bard, 'Quaint, Clever and Intensely Funny', who first appeared at the Palace Opera House in August 1901. Popular in provincial halls before going to London, he developed a versatile act perceptively portraying a range of disparate characters: charladies, landladies, policemen and watchmen, before establishing himself as a 'cockney coster comedian'. His best-loved songs were *I want to Sing in Opera* and the tongue-twister *She Sells Sea-shells on the Seashore*. In 1913 he presented his burlesque *Wriggley Rag* which poked fun at the Ragtime craze, and 'new song with local references', *Manx Cat*, or possibly *The Tail-less Cat*. 'No doubt that in a few days it will be whistled all over the town', suggested the *Isle of Man Times*, and published the words of the chorus:

Manx Cat, Manx Cat, why have you got no tail?
You seem all wrong with nothing behind you to steer you along;
Manx Cat, Manx Cat, something you seem to lack,
Without your tail we really can't tell
Whether you're going – or coming back.

Another versatile entertainer, clown, minstrel and eccentric musical comedian, with songs such as *Colonel Nutty of the Nuts* and *If I, If I, If I, If I, If I, If I Do*, was Mozart. Not of course Wolfgang Amadeus, but George Mozart, 'a highly entertaining turn' whose 'little dramas of real life unfold with the aid of his clarionet – in his hands, a living creature - and smart business with his drums'.

Not all the entertainers who filled the Cliff, the Castle and the Palace were singers and comedians. Some were essentially character actors, famous for their dramatic monologues and impersonations. Enter Bransby Williams, 'The Irving of the Halls', a melodramatic actor *par excellence* with a large, imposing stage persona, who flattered his audiences with culture based on a series of vivid and finely-judged portrayals of Dickensian characters and impersonations of great actors and music hall stars. He thus carved for himself a unique niche in the world of entertainment in which his famous recitations were the central ingredient. One of his best-known was *The Green Eye of the Little Yellow God*, written for him in 1911 by J. Milton Hayes which begins with the following evocative lines:

There's a one-eyed yellow idol to the north of Kathmandu,
There's a little marble cross below the town;
There's a broken-hearted woman tends the grave of Mad Carew,
And the Yellow God forever gazes down . . .

Has Anybody Here Seen Florrie

For reasons now unknown Florrie Forde did not appear in Douglas in 1902, and we can therefore dismiss the impression that she was only absent from the Island during the First World War. She returned to the Derby Castle in 1903 and 1904 and sang *Bull and Bush* and *All Aboard for Douglas* and thereafter introduced new songs each summer: *Has Anybody Seen a German Band* in 1906; *She's a Lassie from Lancashire* in 1907; *Oh, Oh Antonio* in 1908 and in 1909, the first and most famous of her 'Kelly' songs, *Has Anybody Here Seen Kelly?* The *Isle of Man Examiner* was quick to appreciate the likely popularity of Florrie's new Manx song:

Florrie Forde and Bransby Williams.

'Among the new songs . . . is one entitled 'Kelly', which having a Manx flavour about it, will surely catch on in the Isle of Man among the visitors, though it is hardly likely to have much vogue elsewhere'. How wrong they were, for Kelly caught on everywhere.

In 1910 she sang *Flanagan* for the first time in Douglas which contained a reference to Kelly in the chorus:

Take me where the folks all cry, K-E-double-L- Y.

Another 'Kelly' song, *Meet me in Kellyland*, appeared in 1911, and *Let's have a Song about the Isle of Man* in 1912 along with *Hello! Hello! Who's Your Lady Friend?* She was by now billed as 'The Greatest Chorus Singer in the World' and although some reviewers observed 'nothing very artistic about her performance' - she was rather portly - hers was a triumph of personality . . . 'and she could make a crowd sing as nobody else could'. Her songs were described as 'melodious', the choruses 'catchy' and her vocal powers seemingly 'inexhaustible': 'What Florrie Forde sings tonight will be hummed or whistled . . . in the street tomorrow'.

And finally, here are three seemingly bizarre acts that one would love to learn more about: Charley Vesty, 'the world's greatest novelty bag puncher . . . the 'Limit' in bag manipulation' who appeared at the Ramsey

Palace in August 1913; the Quaker Dwarf Song and Dance Troupe who appeared at the Marina Pavilion in August 1894, and Sacco, 'the incredible fasting man', whose act consisted of surviving for forty-five days without food. Our present age of entertainment seems bland and colourless in the face of such diversity.

Interlude: Family matters

The first year of Harry's tenure at the Derby Castle was touched by sadness when his mother Sabra Wood died at the Lewisham Hotel, Slaithwaite on 19th June 1902, aged 65 years. Her body was returned to the Island by steamer and was interred with her husband in Kirk Braddan Cemetery. In a service the day after her burial, the minister of St. Matthew's Church, the family parish church, paid tribute to her fortitude in looking after her family after Clement Wood's death barely a year after they moved to the Island.

There are no surviving letters or diaries to shed any light on Sabra's life on the Isle of Man, but we can be sure that she was immensely proud of the achievements of Harry, Daniel and Haydn, and will have attended many of their concerts in Douglas. Perhaps she read in the *Isle of Man Times* or received the news by letter a few days before her death, that Daniel Wood had been chosen to play in the orchestra for the Coronation of Edward VII at Westminster Abbey, for which he received a Coronation medal. In 1904 Daniel was appointed a permanent member of the King's Private Band under the conductorship of Sir Walter Parratt, and played at all the court events that season at Buckingham Palace. On 13th July that year there was a Wood family get-together to celebrate Daniel's engagement to Mary Scholes, and his appointment as principal flute of the new London Symphony Orchestra. There was another joyful family occasion on 6th August 1902, when Harry's younger sister Elise married the Yorkshire musician and singer Walter Gledhill.[12]

There was more sad family news in September 1903 with news of the death of Harry's eldest sister Mary Hannah Cullerne in Slaithwaite, aged just forty. Mary Hannah and her husband Francis Cullerne had taken over the running of the Lewisham Hotel in Slaithwaite when Clement and Sabra Wood moved to the Island. Their youngest son, George (Georgie) Hilton Cullerne, spent some time in Douglas with the Wood family, as did their middle son, Frank Hilton Cullerne, who took violin lessons from Harry, and quickly proved to be a talented and proficient player. He won a scholarship to study the violin at the Royal College of Music, but returned to the Island during the summer holidays to play in Harry's orchestras. He is known to have played violin solos at Harry's benefit concerts in 1910, 1911 and 1912, and in December 1913, he was a guest musician at an 'At Home' hosted by the Mayor and Mayoress of Douglas at the Town Hall. He subsequently enjoyed a varied career as a violinist, conductor and composer.

~

Haydn in the meantime had completed his studies at the Royal College of Music and the Brussels Conservatoire, and in June 1905 had his first substantial orchestral composition, a three-movement suite for orchestra, performed in London at a Royal College of Music Patron's Fund concert. Earlier, on 9th March, whilst spending ten days in London, he performed a fantasia for violin and orchestra based on the Manx national melodies *Illiam Dhone*, *Gwendolen* and *The Cruise of the Tiger* written especially for him by Thomas Dunhill. The Manx melodies that appear in the fantasia were suggested to Dunhill by W. H. Gill after Haydn Wood had earlier introduced him to *Manx National Songs*.

He also began touring throughout Britain with Madame Albani's concert party, and in towns and cities as far apart as Cheltenham and Inverness, Liverpool and Scarborough, he appeared as her resident violin virtuoso, performing some of the most challenging showpieces in the repertoire: Bazzini's *Witches Dance*, Sarasate's *Zigeunerweisen* and Hubay's *Plevna Nota*.[13] Indeed, a significant number of newspaper reviews strongly suggest that the twenty-two year old violinist frequently up-staged Albani, by then at the end of her long and distinguished career, with his display of dazzling aplomb and maturity. During the winter of 1905-6 he toured some of the major Scottish towns and cities with Albani, and in February 1906 joined her concert party for her coast-to-coast farewell tour of Canada.

From June 1907 until January 1908 Albani's tours took her and Haydn to Australia, Tasmania, New Zealand, Ceylon and India. Haydn had developed into a virtuoso of the first rank, 'a born fiddler', whose performances truly astonished those who heard him. As the *Manchester City News* put it: 'To describe Mr Wood there is only one word that will suffice, and that is "genius" . . . such delicacy, such grace, and such mastery of technique one could scarcely conceive imaginable'.

By 1908 Albani, then sixty-one and tired of lengthy tours throughout the British Empire, concentrated on touring in Britain with a reduced concert party consisting of herself, her accompanist and the twenty-six-year-old Haydn, appearing at dozens of concert halls and variety theatres, billed as 'the greatest vaudeville engagement of modern times'. He even conceived the bizarre idea of giving himself a 'foreign' name – 'the famous Russian violinist Herr Zakovsky' – for a few months in the belief that a new persona would lend mystique and panache to his appearances. This ploy worked so well that he was thereafter unable to use the excellent concert notices under his assumed name to further his career.

On 22nd April 1909 Haydn and the Savoyard soprano Dorothy Court were married in St Mary's Church, Westerham, Kent, and, no doubt drawing on the success with Albani, the couple plus a pianist embarked on a thirteen-year career touring the variety halls and theatres of Britain, performing their twenty-minute routine, two or three times each day, with only Sundays free for travelling to the next theatre. Serving his time arduously treading the boards proved to be the ideal way to popularize his songs, and ballads such as *Roses of Picardy*, *Love's Garden of Roses* and *A Brown Bird Singing* became so successful that their world-wide popularity laid the foundations of his future financial security. Clement and Sabra Wood would have been delighted and amazed at Haydn's success, and no doubt would have attributed it to West Yorkshire grit and determination.

~

In 1911 Harry moved from the hurly-burly of the Queen's Promenade to a quieter location above the town at 1, Osborne Terrace, formerly the home of the Manx musical matriarch Miss M. L. Wood. This fine property - the only house occupied by the Wood family that still exists - consisted at the time of a sitting room, dining room, two basement rooms, four bedrooms and three attic bedrooms, kitchen, back kitchen (scullery), coal house, bathroom and two WCs, a large front garden and side garden. Sometime later, the property was extended to

1, Osborne Terrace, Douglas.

include 'out offices' and a large garage. Harry shared this substantial house with his sister Adeline, his nephew Hilton Cullerne from time to time, and two servant girls, the Skillicorn sisters, Ethel and Elizabeth, formerly of the Douglas Industrial Home. More importantly there was enough space to devote two rooms to his ever-expanding music library; Osborne Terrace became the ideal base of operations for the next twenty-seven years.

On 7th June 1913 a rare event occurred in that Harry, Haydn and Daniel Wood were happily all together in the same place at the same time. The occasion was the Epsom Derby, but sadly their horse was disqualified!

Melba! Melba! Who is he?[14]

With few exceptions, the more eminent concert artistes were engaged to appear at the Palace for the well-established Sunday Sacred Concerts whereas the Derby Castle often engaged local or less well-known singers and instrumentalists. In the Isle of Man the distinction between amateur and professional was often blurred as they often shared the same stage. The eminent singers who took part in the Crystal Palace Handel Festivals in 1900 and 1906 include several who appeared regularly in Douglas: Ella Russell, Emma Albani, Clara Butt, Agnes Nicholls, Louise Kirkby-Lunn, Ben Davies, Andrew Black, Kennerley-Rumford, Robert Radford and Charles Santley.

Perhaps the greatest singer ever to appear in Douglas – certainly the one with the greatest reputation for whom the over-used term 'diva' was appropriate – was Nellie Melba, the supreme Australian operatic soprano, the only concert artiste to exceed the substantial fees paid to Vesta Tilley.[15] Six weeks before her first appearance the *Mona's Herald* featured a report in their 'About Men & Women' column concerning Melba's recent performance at Covent Garden, celebrating a twenty-year unbroken association with the opera house during which she missed not one season. 'By general critical consent, too, Madame Melba's voice, after two decades of strenuous work, is as beautiful, matchless, and unimpaired as ever'. In just a few weeks, the audience at the Palace Sunday Concert on 9th August would be able to judge for themselves.

A booking plan for what quickly became known simply as 'The Melba Concert' was published in the local newspapers, and booking opened on Monday 13th July with reserved seats available at a far higher price than usual in the hope of avoiding a loss on the concert. The *Isle of Man Examiner* summed up the prevailing attitude towards high ticket prices in its own inimitably succinct manner thus:

> We in Douglas are exceedingly partial to a combination of the good and the cheap. Yet if a really good thing is to be procured it must be paid for. There is but one Melba.

The Company's gamble paid off. The Palace was full with an estimated five thousand attending, and dissenting voices surrounding ticket prices notwithstanding, the management of the Palace & Derby Castle Company had not witnessed such scenes that attended Melba's appearance with both residents and visitors clambering to obtain tickets.

Melba was supported by her own accompanist and conductor, but Harry directed the specially augmented Palace orchestra in two overtures, pieces from Grieg's *Peer Gynt* suite and two of Mendelssohn's *Songs Without Words*. Melba's programme on this auspicious occasion included Bishop's coloratura aria *Lo, Hear the Gentle Lark* with obbligato flute during which her purity of tone, diction and the flexibility with which she executed the copious trills and roulades that characterise the piece were highly praised. She then sang the popular Scottish ballad *Comin' thro' the rye* 'with a sweetness that enraptured all'. Her second operatic offering was the scene from Act I of Verdi's *La Traviata* that concludes with the brilliantly florid *Sempre Libre*; her final encore was Tosti's affecting *Goodbye!* after which she was recalled four times, and the evening ended with a rousing performance of Elgar's *Land of Hope and Glory*. It was a triumph.

By an intriguing coincidence, Vesta Tilley was also appearing at the Palace that same week and was present in the audience that evening. One cannot help wondering if a discreet meeting took place between the two superstars from such different branches of the world of entertainment, and what they might have talked about. The *Isle of Man Examiner* noted that as Melba left the Palace after the concert she was 'lustily cheered by an immense crowd' who then escorted her to her carriage; Vesta Tilley, departing a short time later, was 'greeted with a somewhat embarrassing cordiality as she passed (through) the gates'.

Melba's second visit to Douglas took place at the new Villa Marina Kursaal 1913 where she gave two concerts on 19th and 21st August. Billed as 'The Event of the Season', her engagement was considered to be 'fraught with financial risk'. Ticket prices were raised throughout the hall with the result that the Tuesday audience was smaller than expected, although Thursday's was 'a capital house', no doubt the result of a reduction in some ticket prices. Melba included some of the songs and arias from her earlier Palace concert, and as before brought her own accompanist with her. She was given a tremendous reception and was recalled again and again after she had sung *Comin' thro' the rye* and Maud Valerie White's *John Anderson, my jo*, which brought a tear to many an eye and a lump to many a throat.

Whilst all agreed that at fifty-two years of age Melba was still in magnificent voice, her concert sustained a loss for the Villa Marina Kursaal of some two hundred pounds.

~

Madame Albani's first Sunday Concert under Harry's baton took place on 9th August, 1903, when she sang arias by Mozart and Handel and Bruch's great scena of clan insurrection and ultimate redemption, *The Fiery Cross*, derived from Scott's *The Lady of the Lake*. The Palace orchestra was praised in the *Isle of Man Times*: 'we do not remember the Palace orchestra at such a pitch of excellence before'. On Sunday 7th August 1904, all three Wood brothers took part in Albani's concert before an audience estimated at between three or four thousand. Daniel played the flute obbligato in the famous aria *Sweet bird that shun'st the noise of folly* from Handel's *Il Penseroso*, and 'a buzz of suppressed excitement went round the Palace as Haydn Wood commenced the violin obbligato in the Bach-Gounod *Ave Maria*'.

She returned to Douglas later that month and appeared at a Sunday Concert together with the bass Robert Radford and Haydn Wood, 'the rising young violinist'. An anecdote deriving from this concert appeared in the *Isle of Man Times* a few days afterwards with the heading 'Madame Albani and the slum child'. It concerned a poor boy 'with a dirty face and hands and wearing ragged clothes' who presented his 6d at the entrance to the Palace and attempted to obtain entrance to hear Albani sing. He was turned away, but returned a little later having washed himself in the sea, was admitted by the management who had by this time heard of his plight, and was given a good seat and a programme. The *Isle of Man Times* declared that Albani had no more fervent admirer in the audience that day than the little boy from 'the Douglas slums'. There is no way of knowing how much of this heart-warming Dickensian tale is merely apocryphal, but a few days later a Mr. Dibb from Douglas wrote to the editor offering to secure the boy's financial future.

'Goodbye forever! Goodbye, Goodbye, Goodbye!'[16]

Albani appeared twice at the Sunday Concerts in 1905 in late August and early September, and her last appearance in Douglas took place on 12th August 1906. Her programme included her favourite Mozart and Handel arias and Tosti's *Goodbye* and *Home, Sweet Home* which, as always, left the audience 'much affected'. A few days after her concerts in Douglas in 1904 the *Isle of Man Times* had published a short interview entitled 'Madame Albani on the beauties of Manxland':

> . . . I leave the Isle of Man tomorrow . . . but I go away with the deepest regret, and I shall so long to come back again . . . what a lovely place your Island is! I have travelled a great deal, and seen many picturesque lands; but I have never seen any place more beautiful than Manxland.

Louise Kirkby-Lunn was the leading English mezzo-soprano, famous for her roles in *Carmen*, *Mignon*, *Lohengrin* and *Rigoletto*. She appeared at Covent Garden and the New York Metropolitan Opera House, with the Carl Rosa Opera Company at the Queen's Hall concerts, and many Promenade Concert Seasons under Henry Wood, and was greeted with

Louise Kirkby-Lunn.

stamping, clapping and cheering from the Palace audience on her first appearance in 1907. One reviewer wrote that 'no more artistic singing can have been heard at the Palace concerts'. The audience agreed and many of them left 'with lumps in their throats' after she sang Handel's *Ombra mai fu*. The reviewer also praised Harry's 'powerful and beautifully balanced orchestra . . . a revelation of light and shade'.

The Australian contralto Ada Crossley – the veteran of five Royal Command performances for Queen Victoria - first appeared in Douglas in 1898 and most years thereafter up to the First World War. She was praised in the newspapers for her personal charm, the beauty of her sympathetic voice in popular ballads and for the 'artistic excellence of her interpretations'. The contralto Phyllis Lett also appeared in Douglas the year after her Albert Hall debut in Mendelssohn's *Elijah*, and for many seasons before the war intervened. Two other singers, the contraltos Fanny Bouffler and the Wolverhampton-born Elizabeth Dews were both favourites with Douglas audiences. Certain local singers, most notably the soprano May Clague, a four times Manx Music Festival Gold Medallist, who appeared in 1911-12 and again in 1914, were always afforded a warm

The young John McCormack and Barton McGuckin.

Manx welcome, although their fees were lamentably lower than those of artistes from Britain.

There were also well-loved and highly-regarded veterans and newcomers among the tenors, baritones and basses who appeared in Douglas at this time. The young John McCormack, billed as 'a tenor in the Italian style', appeared at a Sunday Concert at the Palace in 1908 with contralto Maud Wright, with whom he sang a duet from *Madame Butterfly.* He also sang the *Flower Song* from Carmen and, as an encore Clutsam's *I Know of Two Bright Eyes*:

> I know of two bright eyes, watching for me.
> I know of two white arms, waiting for me.
> I know of cheeks that burn to greet me when I return.
> For Myrra, Oh Myrra, I soon will come to thee.[17]

Did anyone who heard this affecting ballad predict that in a few short years the young Irish tenor would become a household name? Two other Irish tenors appeared during the period: the splendidly-named Barton McGuckin, 'a rousing Handelian', and the leading Irish operatic tenor, Joseph O'Mara, who was reputed to have over sixty roles in his repertoire.

It may be stated without fear of contradiction that the concert artistes, the divas and the prima donnas who appeared in Douglas in the decades before World War I were among the finest in the British Isles, and many of them enjoyed fabulous European and world-wide reputations. One example will suffice to underline the point: an Elgar Festival took place at Covent Garden over three days in March 1904, with Hans Richter conducting the Hallé Orchestra of one hundred players and a Manchester chorus of two hundred and seventy-five voices; of the seven distinguished soloists, six: Clara Butt, Louise Kirkby-Lunn, Agnes Nicholls, Andrew Black, David Ffrancon-Davies and Robert Kennerley-Rumford had performed at the Palace under the baton of Harry Wood.

'Oh, Yes It Is!' Harry in Pantoland.

One of the most prestigious musical events in 1902, and a considerable feather in Harry's cap, was the lavish production of the three-act pantomime *King Gob-ne-Geay* at the Gaiety Theatre in February. There were evening performances from Tuesday 4th to Friday 7th with a Saturday afternoon children's matinee. The not inconsiderable proceeds of some £200 went to the St. Matthew's Church new organ fund, a fund which Harry had instigated.

Described as a 'Manx Fairy Play' and a 'New and Original Grand Manx Fairy Extravaganza', *King Gob-ne-Geay*, or *The Magic Cup* and the *Buggane of St. Trinians*,[18] with play and lyrics by William Hanby[19] and music composed, arranged and adapted by Harry, had been in rehearsal since November 1901, and by mid-January all manner of witches, sprites, hobgoblins, gnomes, demon bats, Manx cats and fairies could be glimpsed making their way to the stage door of the Gaiety Theatre. The *Isle of Man Examiner* enjoyed privileged access to a dress rehearsal early in February and reported:

> . . . that the operetta (sic) was gone through without a hitch . . . the principals were word-perfect and the prompter's services were never in demand . . . the smoothness and precision with which the various evolutions (transformations) and dances were carried out was as remarkable as it is creditable to all concerned, and particularly to the untiring musical director, Mr Harry Wood and his ubiquitous lieutenant Mr W. J. Fell, stage manager.

The colourful costumes were designed by Miss Hastings and Mr H. Skelly of the Empire Theatre, London and, together with the up-to-date scenic and stage resources of the Gaiety Theatre, 'combined to produce a series of spectacular effects undreamt of in our theatrical philosophy'. Harry's sister Adeline helped to devise and develop some of the dances and took the role of Dame Qualtrough. She sang *Hush, Little Darling* which

Harry's sister, Adeline.

the *Isle of Man Examiner* considered to be one of the best features of the production. *King Gob-ne-geay* was no formless jumble of anything and everything linked together with music hall songs and patter, local 'in-jokes', minstrel songs and acrobatic displays, but a real Manx fairy play 'with a lucid, consecutive and well-written story'. Nothing finer, it was suggested, had ever been seen in Douglas.

The first performance was announced in The *Mona's Herald* and audiences were promised 'Manx Songs! Manx Choruses! Brilliant Costumes! Charming Effects! Marches and Tableaux!' There was a large chorus of fishermen, fishwives, dairy maids, old Manx women and farmers and set-pieces including a Cutlass Drill, a Demon Band, Torch Bearers, Country Dancers, buglers and drummers, plus a 150 strong children's chorus recruited from Douglas schools. The orchestra of eighteen musicians was under the direction of Harry himself and, most importantly considering the time of year, the audience was assured that 'the theatre will be heated for these performances'.

The 'pretty and tuneful' music Harry produced for this 'Phantasmagoria' included an overture, and popular Manx songs such as *Ramsey Town, Hunt the Wren, Mylecharane, The Sheep Under the Snow* and *The Maid of Port-y-Shee* from *Manx National Songs*, probably in the arrangements he made for the ground-breaking concert of Manx music in 1897. He also adapted short pieces by other composers, and composed original new music including a storm, an Anvil Chorus, a Witches Gavotte, a Coconut Dance, a Demon Dance, Fanfares and a Final Chorus. He may have written the new topical song *The King of Mannin Veen*, sung by Alister Proctor, and a love song, *Ah! Do not fear*, for Princess Gwendolen, sung by Miss Dorothy Hawnt. For the revival in November that year he wrote the still popular song *I'm A Native of Peel* for the character Philly the Desert, the King's right hand man, based on the character of Phillip

Cain of Baldwin, a well-known singer of traditional Manx songs, sung by a well-known entertainer and versatile comedian, the Douglas Harbour Master George E. Kelly, who also sang *The Maid of Port-y-Chee*. Much of the music for the pantomime, including the overture, is lost.

~

No less a person than Miss M. L. Wood sent her appreciation of Harry's efforts in a letter dated 9th February:

> My dear Mr Wood
> I must send you a line of congratulations upon the success of Gob-ne-geay. You must have worked very hard to have got such good results. Your orchestration was so pretty and piquant and the band very good. I have never seen an electric illuminated baton before . . .
> Yours very sincerely

The *Isle of Man Examiner* report of 8th February reflected the style of most of the reviews:

> . . . a triumphant appearance at the Gaiety after many weeks of rehearsal . . . the best and most unique entertainment of its class ever seen on a Douglas stage . . . the music is pretty and tuneful . . . the dialogue is 'Gilbertian' in character . . . and brimful of humour . . . there were many striking scenes such as the Buggane's Haunt in Act I with witches and sprites jumping over the fire.

Other local newspapers were generally enthusiastic, for it was hoped that the success of the pantomime would give 'a much-needed impetus to talent lying dormant on the Island and arouse an interest in Manx folklore'. Although the efforts of William Hanby and Harry were much praised, one reviewer could not hold back his personal rider, referring to them as 'not quite Manx!'

King Gob-ne-Geay was performed twice more that year on 12th and 13th November at the Gaiety Theatre, and Haydn Wood returned to the Island to lead the orchestra. A charming note dated 22nd October from two little girls - Rene Curphey, aged 10 and Eva Quayle, aged 11 - to Harry has survived in one of his scrapbooks:

> 108 Bucks Rd, Douglas, IOM
> Dear Sir
> I shall be glad if you can find me and a friend a place in King Gob.ne.Gay
> Yours Truly

More Tricks, Traps and Transformations.

William Hanby and Harry Wood – dubbed the Manx 'Gilbert and Sullivan' - collaborated in a second 'childrens' extravaganza', *Babes in the Wood, from a Manx Point of View* which was performed between 9th and 13th February, 1904, at the Gaiety. The new pantomime was eagerly anticipated after the great success of *King Gob-ne-Geay*, and once again large forces were employed including twenty local principals and a chorus of 150 portraying market girls, farmers and huntsmen, yokels, pierrots and pierrettes, policemen, schoolboys and girls and assorted fairies. Haydn travelled from London to lead the orchestra of twenty-five players under Harry's direction for all five performances.

The *Isle of Man Examiner* expressed itself in poetic terms in an effort to encourage people to secure their tickets in good time:

Let us turn for a while from the world and its strife,
To the innocent pleasures which make for our good;
Go and see these sweet Babies depicted in life,
In that charming erection of 'Hanby and Wood'.

Audiences were promised sparkling and witty dialogue abounding with local references and jokes and 'free from the inane vulgarity too often present in modern pantomime', as the dastardly plot of the wicked Baron Kiannoortys and his robber cohorts Blib and Blob is ultimately thwarted by the Fairy Queen. In the time-honoured pantomime tradition, vice was punished and virtue rewarded. The music would be refined, artistic and appropriate and would feature 'all the latest popular songs' from the London pantomimes including *Pansy Faces* – sung by a children's chorus nodding their heads rhythmically in time with the music - *There's a Girl Wanted There* and Vesta Tilley's patriotic song *The Anglo-Saxon Language*. Harry also adapted some 'hit' songs from the publications of Francis, Day & Hunter, Bert Feldman & Company and Frank Dean & Company.

As in the case of *King Gob-ne-gaey* the music Harry produced for *Babes in the Wood* is no longer extant, so we have no way of knowing what was newly-composed or arranged and adapted from the works of others. The *Isle of Man Examiner* observed that the music was:

> . . . refined and artistic, and so appropriate to the text, that one is almost inclined to ask whether the music was written to suit the words, or the words to suit the music.

Thus we are left wondering which songs were sung by local soprano May Fielding in the role of Princess Imogene, 'whose voice was exploited to the full by Harry Wood's arrangements', and we would dearly like to know what the 'excruciatingly funny song and chorus' *We're Doing No Work Now* was like, and did it 'convulse the youngsters' as promised. Adeline assumed the role of Miss Vere de Girton – 'lively if se-vere' – the 'embodiment of the New Woman!'[20] and described as '. . . a real comedienne who possess the rare quality of humour'. Her 'Coon duet' with the Princess, *I'se a-waitin' for yer, Josie*, was considered to be 'the gem of the entire performance'. Other songs and duets included the Baron's *On the day, His day's work was done* and *My Gals a high-born Lady*. The Prince's songs *If you loved me* and *A Little English Girl* sung by principal boy Miss Minnie Walsh were much enjoyed.

One new song Harry wrote for the production can be identified and is still popular today: *The Pride of Port-le-Murra*, sung in the Anglo-Manx dialect by George E. Kelly in the role of Baron Kiannoortys, which 'brought the house down'. The reviewers were especially enchanted with the *Fairies Dance* in the Fairy Dell with its cascade of real water, and praised Adeline's own dancing, remarking that it was 'much above the amateur standard'.

~

One would not expect anything in this harmless enchantment from the world of make-believe to alarm the theatrical censor, but the words of a popular song in *Babes* were altered at the request of the local 'foolish examiner of plays', as the newspapers referred to him, because Superintendent Boyd of the Manx Constabulary objected to the words of the chorus of policemen *We are Bobbies of Malew* and seemingly 'took childish offense' lest the song depicted his 'force' in a comic light:

We are Bobbies from Malew
(We're from Malew, we're from Malew)
And we know a thing or two
(Thing or two, thing or two)

The first line was duly altered to 'We are Watchmen staunch and true'. The censor struck again later in the show when a further word was ordered to be deleted from the Lieutenant of the Watch's song in Act II, after he objected to the word 'scatter' in the line: 'They wait our near approach and scatter'. 'Why', asked the *Isle of Man Examiner* 'should the heads of the Manx Police Force be so petulantly sensitive . . . no objection was ever raised to Gilbert and Sullivan's policemen's chorus in *The Pirates of Penzance*?' Needless to say, such priggishness was soundly derided in the local newspapers.

Babes in the Wood was a spectacle that exceeded all expectations and a personal triumph for Harry and William Hanby. The proceeds were again donated to St. Matthew's Church new organ fund.

The Manx Music Festival comes of age

The Manx Music Festival continued to go from strength to strength, expanding its scope and introducing a number of new competitions, and continued to enjoy the patronage of the Lieutenant Governor Lord Raglan and Lady Raglan, both enthusiastic supporters and regular attendees at the classes during the decade before the First World War. It was during this period that the Festival was extended to three days, and more ambitious choral works were selected for the combined choirs' performance at the Festival concert. On these occasions Harry himself conducted the opening hymn, an overture and a closing march, whilst the chief adjudicator normally directed the orchestra and choirs in the chosen choral work each year. Harry's orchestra was, as usual, selected from his most experienced students, local amateurs and a number of professionals from 'across the water', who were engaged when players could not be found on the Island.

The festival in March 1902 was held in the Palace Ballroom for the first time, and Harry's Special Orchestra opened the festival concert with the overture to the pantomime *King Gob-ne-Geay* and closed the proceedings with Hermann Starke's march *With Sword and Lance*. The combined choirs performed Mendelssohn's setting of Psalm 95, *Come let us sing*, Harry's pupil Kathleen Rydings played a capriccio for violin and joined another of his pupils, Athol Blakemore, and an accompanist in a trio. Miss M. L. Wood's choir sang the *Spinning Chorus* from Wagner's *The Flying Dutchman* after which she was accorded an ovation.

In the aftermath of a fine performance of John Francis Barnet's 'spirited, fanciful and melodious' cantata *The Ancient Mariner* (after

Coleridge's poem) the following month, there were calls for a non-competitive Manx Music Festival along the lines of the Birmingham and Leeds Festivals. For this performance F. C. Poulter directed Douglas Choral Union, soloists and orchestra in the Palace Ballroom; Harry led the orchestra and conducted the miscellaneous orchestral pieces in part two of the concert including Beethoven's overture *Prometheus*, the *Grand March and Chorus* from Wagner's *Tannhäuser*, and a violin solo played by Haydn Wood. Some 2,000 people attended and £170 was raised for the Town Nurse Fund. The suggestion that the Island might inaugurate and host a major music festival annually or bi-annually was not pursued.

~

The choral stakes were raised considerably in March 1904 when the combined choirs, four of them each with around fifty singers (including members of Miss Cannell's and J. D. Looney's choirs), conducted by adjudicator Dr Haydn Coward, performed Elgar's ballad for chorus and orchestra *The Banner of St. George*, a work noted for its uniquely Elgarian orchestral colouration and fine choral writing.

In 1905 the combined choirs performed *Spring* from the first part of Haydn's oratorio *The Seasons* with Harry's orchestra led by Harry himself and conducted by adjudicator R. H. Wilson, the chorus master of the Hallé Concerts in Manchester. The overture was Beethoven's *Prometheus*, Haydn Wood played a violin solo and Adeline was placed second in the instrumental trio class. The following year J. E. Quayle led the orchestra under Harry's baton in Schubert's overture *Alfonso und Estrella* and a closing military march. The choirs performed the hymn – really a cantata - *God Thou Art Great* by Louis Spohr, a composer whose reputation once rivalled that of Mendelssohn's in England.

By the time of the sixteenth Manx Music Festival in March 1907 new 'special' vocal classes had been introduced with gold medals presented to the winners, the precursor of the later prestigious Cleveland Medal competition. Harry's orchestra was led by J. E. Quayle in Balfe's overture *The Siege of Rochelle*, Mendelssohn's Psalm 42 and the Spanish military march *Cadiz*. The Festival concert will be remembered chiefly because the three thousand-strong audience was the first to sing the *Manx National Anthem*, arranged and adapted by W. H. Gill, with Harry's students' orchestra and the choirs conducted by Harry himself. The anthem is based on the traditional Manx song *Mylecharane*, adapted by Gill to fit the words '... with a boldness and presumption to do for our nation what far abler hands ought to have done long ago'.

~

The Manx Society Trophy was presented for the first time in 1908, followed by the Manchester Shield for village choirs, given by the Manchester Manx Society, and the Liverpool Manx Society Shield for the main choral class. Harry's students' orchestra and the combined choirs performed Somervell's cantata *The Power of Sound*[21] and Harry himself conducted a closing march by Sousa. The combined choirs performed Brahms' *Song of Destiny* in 1909 under the baton of Cyril Rootham, the composer and organist of St. John's Chapel, Cambridge, and in 1910, Stanford's dramatic nautical ballad of the Spanish Armada, *The Revenge*, together with a specially written an a capella part-song by Haydn Wood entitled *The Phynodderee*, a Manx fairy goblin, who 'once was lord of a fairy clan, in the Isle of Man'.[22] The Vancouver Manx Society Shield was first presented in 1911 and the choirs performed Parry's *Blest Pair of Sirens*. The year 1912 was another vintage one with Vaughan Williams, no less, conducting the combined choirs and orchestra in Coleridge-Taylor's *Hiawatha's Wedding Feast*; Harry conducted the march *Old Comrades* at the close of the Festival concert. Frederic Cliffe's *Ode to The North-East Wind* was given by the choirs in 1913 with a popular military march to close with as usual.[23]

~

Not directly a part of the story of the Manx Music Festival, but related to it, was 'A unique event in Manx history': the launch in 1904 of the Manx Music Scholarship to the Royal Academy of Music, worth £50 per year from the Baume Trustees. The scholarship had been under discussion since 1902, and Miss M. L. Wood, Mrs Laughton and Harry himself may have contributed to the total scholarship fund; they were each present at the decisive meeting presided over by A. W. Moore, the Speaker of the House of Keys. Known as the Baume (Manx) Scholarship, the competition for an award was governed by twenty-three conditions of which the following were the most significant:

> Only children of one or two Manx parents were eligible.
> If not, the parents must have resided on the Island for more than five years.
> If not, then the candidate must have resided on the Island not less than 5 years.

If not, then any candidate outside the Isle of Man, one or both of whose parents were born on the Island.

The preliminary examination would take place in Douglas and the primary examination in London. Harry's violin pupil Samuel Robinson (later known professionally as Orry Corjeag) was the first recipient of the scholarship.

Harry Wood's student orchestra

Apart from the Manx Music Festival, Harry's students' orchestra continued to appear regularly at local events both large and small. One of the larger-scale events was advertised in the *Isle of Man Times* as 'Harry Wood's Grand Orchestral Concert at the Gaiety Theatre' and took place on 5th March 1903. The orchestra was enlarged to forty players and joined the guest contralto Margaret Vereker in *Land of Hope and Glory*. Other local singers took part together with one of Harry's star pupils, the young violinist Sam Robinson, who played a taxing virtuoso piece, Rode's *Variations in G major*. Harry expected much from his pupils and the programme was ambitious and challenging: 'the charm of variety' pleased the audience although the reviewer thought that the concert was too long, particularly the instrumental solos.

In 1910, Douglas Choral Union, conducted by T. P. Faragher, with an orchestra of experienced pupils led by Harry himself, performed Mendelssohn's unashamedly melodramatic descent into the world of Gothic horror, the secular dramatic cantata *Die erste Walpurgisnacht*, at the Gaiety Theatre. This enterprising departure from the well-tilled soil of *Elijah* was based on Goethe's poem of the same name and is centred on a May Day conflict between Christians and Druids. Rarely performed today, it is a suspenseful and eerily atmospheric work, and contains some of the composer's most imaginative and powerful choral writing.

Harry's students' orchestra of twenty-nine musicians took part in his brother Haydn's Grand Concert at the Gaiety Theatre on 23rd November 1911, which was styled 'A Night with the Stars!' It featured the soprano Dorothy Court (Mrs Haydn Wood) and supporting artistes in a selection of light music miniatures, marches and dances. What was a rather mixed bag also featured gymnastic displays, a Pierrot Party, The Georgia Nigger Minstrels, a one-act play entitled *A Pair of Lunatics*, with Adeline Wood in the cast, (a 'Coon' Song and Clog Dance was especially written for her by Haydn Wood), various sideshows and a picture gallery. A similar occasion in 1912 featured a new two-step by Harry based on Florrie Forde's song *We must have a Song about the Isle of Man.*

In 1912, Harry's two-steps *We Must have a Song about the Isle of Man* and *We All went Marching Home Again*, and the *Up-to-Date 1912-13* barn dance were featured alongside overtures by Thomas, Suppe and Balfe, selections from popular operettas and musical comedies and novelties such as the entr'acte *Teddy Bears' Picnic* and *The Grizzly Bear Rag*. Adeline, ever eager to 'don the motley', took part in two one-act farces and Harry's friend and fellow Slaithwaite ex-patriot G. H. Wood took part in an entertaining comic duologue.

The Villa Marina Kursaal[24]

Between the years 1898 – the year of the Great Amalgamation – and 1913, the Palace & Derby Castle Company was the main provider of musical entertainment in Douglas, with little significant competition. This highly satisfactory situation changed in 1911 with the opening of the Villa Marina Gardens '. . . in the rough . . . still under transformation, yet with sylvan swards and glades', and significantly, with a local band in attendance, which attracted thousands of visitors that first summer.[25]

In February 1912, the Corporation's Lettings of Site(s) for Performance Committee decided to 'seek out and engage the finest band available to make music in the grounds',[26] and after some deliberation awarded the contract to Herr Simon Wurm's Imperial Viennese Orchestra.[27] Numbering some twenty musicians and comprising elements of a typical military band and theatre orchestra, Herr Wurm's ensemble was the only true spa-style band ever to perform regularly in Douglas, and a far cry from the much-ridiculed itinerant German bands that plagued the promenades with their raucous racket every summer. Wurm himself was a flamboyant character who sported a luxuriant 'Kaiser Bill' moustache, and a violinist who often directed the orchestra from the rostrum, violin in hand; many of the band members also sported mustachios and wore 'Ruritanian' - style uniforms.

Wurm's concerts were very well patronised - over five hundred people attended the inaugural one in May, 1912 - and throughout June and July the average attendance was over one thousand. Reviews were mainly positive, many of them acknowledging that the Town Council had at last engaged 'a band of real musical artistes' . . . playing music of a very superior order'.

Despite there being a certain amount of 'childish malice' directed at

The opening of the Villa Marina Kursaal.

the orchestra, and some unsavoury play on the name 'Wurm', at the Palace & Derby Castle Co Shareholders' meeting in November 1912, the Imperial Viennese Orchestra was re-engaged for the 1913 season and was in attendance for the Grand Opening of the Villa Marina Gardens for Whit-week on 10th May. On Saturday 19th July the official opening of the completed Villa Marina Kursaal took place amid much pomp and circumstance and culminated in a grand evening concert with guest artistes Carrie Tubb, soprano, and Joseph O'Mara, tenor, and featuring music by Wagner, Gounod, Liszt and Bizet. In his speech, Lord Raglan made the point that part of the success of the Villa Marina Kursaal was that it catered for:

> . . . a class of holiday-maker whom we in Douglas have hitherto been neglectful of. Large numbers of our visitors care nothing for dancing and variety turns . . . nevertheless, they appreciate entertainment more staid and perchance more elevating in character . . .

The implication was clear: the Palace and Derby Castle catered for the northern working classes but the Villa Marina Kursaal provided high class concerts and sophisticated entertainments for gentle folk. Harry probably winced when he read the speech in full a day-or-so later; Charles Fox, who always maintained that Douglas Corporation had acted beyond its remit by allowing entertainments to flourish at the Marina in direct competition with the privately–owned venues, will have been apoplectic with rage.

At the end of the 'bumper' 1913 season as the re-engagement of Wurm's band was being agreed upon for the following year, it must have seemed that Douglas could proudly stand alongside Scarborough, Llandudno and Harrogate as having a first-rate, spa-style orchestra in its spectacular Kursaal. As we shall see in the following chapter, though, the good fortune of the Villa Marina Kursaal, and consequently Herr Wurm's band, would be short-lived, overtaken by cataclysmic international events barely perceived by many that glorious summer.

'Melodious Manxland . . . the birthplace of popular songs'

Beyond his prowess as a conductor, performer, composer and arranger, Harry's most significant skill was his ability to forge meaningful, lasting relationships with those artistes, musicians, writers, composers and theatre managers who could be most useful to him in his career. Crucially, he also enjoyed long and fruitful associations with four eminent music publishers: Francis, Day & Hunter,[28] Bert Feldman & Company,[29] the Lawrence Wright Music Company and H. Sharples & Son (Blackpool 1920) Limited. He therefore played a pivotal role in the three-way symbiotic relationship between performing artist, musical director and music publisher that was at the heart of Douglas being recognised throughout the publishing world as a key centre for the transmission of popular songs.

Hitherto, most variety artistes performed original songs with which they alone were associated, the sole performing rights of which they purchased outright from the composer or song writer often for as little as a pound or two. The ownership of these songs was jealously guarded and sheet music copies usually had the following instruction printed at the top of the front cover: 'Not to be Sung in Music Halls or Theatres, with the exception of Pantomimes, without Mr Leno's or Miss Tilley's (or whoever's), written permission'. Vesta Tilley always regretted not buying *Daisy Bell*, the song that made Katie Lawrence famous, as she considered it contained 'the best music hall chorus ever written'.

David Day of Francis, Day & Hunter was the first publisher to introduce

Bert Feldman and David Day.

the idea of a royalty payment to artistes, composers and writers in the late 1890s, and the idea was soon taken up by Bert Feldman & Company. The composer and/or song writer would now receive a royalty on potentially thousands of sales if a song was really popular, and the publisher could potentially hold the rights to the most popular songs for years.

~

Arthur Q. Moore writing of the 1920s maintained that:

> Go where you will, you will never hear spontaneous community singing on such a wholesale scale as in Douglas, where groups of laughing young men and women march arm-in-arm along the promenade . . . singing aloud the choruses of the seasons' song 'hits'.

In *Cavalcade* for the year 1899, Harry adds a note to explain how in his estimation Douglas came to be known as 'The Birthplace of Popular Songs':

> During the last two or three years . . . until 1914 . . . it was in Douglas where all the popular songs first saw light and we thank the firm of Francis, Day & Hunter for this fact. When I began conducting at Derby Castle in 1892, this firm sent me in manuscript, the piano, and in some cases the orchestral parts of the songs which they thought would be popular with the visitors. I put the choruses of each of

> them into my lancers, schottisches etc, and these were played nightly throughout the season. We very soon heard the songs the visitors liked because we could hear them singing them on the promenade, and in fact everywhere.

Writing many years later, John Abbott wrote the following in his book about the firm of Francis, Day & Hunter:

> Before World War I the Isle of Man was the ideal summer spot for starting off the season's hits. Billy Murphy and Will Letters (lyricists and composers) were there early in the season playing and singing in any hotel or pub where there was a piano and in which they could gain entry. Florrie Forde, who was a regular at the Palace Theatre, certainly started off Flanagan, take me to the Isle of Man again and Has anybody here seen Kelly.[30]

Harry confirmed that at the end of each summer season the most popular new songs found their way back to England in time to feature in innumerable Christmas pantomimes. It was precisely by this process of musical osmosis that a hitherto little-known song Harry introduced into a military two-step in 1913, became the most iconic of all First World War marching songs: *It's a Long Way to Tipperary*.[31]

'Catches of the Season'

Harry was especially canny in identifying which of each season's new songs would become hits, and helped to promote these songs in his popular sets of lancers which he wrote every year for the Derby Castle and Palace ballrooms. Essentially publisher themed song-medleys, his 1893 lancers, for example, had included Leslie Stuart's *Soldiers of the Queen* and the 1910 lancers featured no less than twenty pantomime songs including *Ship Ahoy*, *Let's all go down the Strand* and *I Can Picture Polly putting up the Holly*. The 1913-14 military two-step *Anywhere in Manxland* included Florrie Forde's *Hold your hand out, naughty boy*, and the 1914 military two-step included her latest 'hits' *Hello! Hello! Who's your Lady Friend* and *I'm Off to Kelly's Isle*. In the years just prior to the start of World War I, Harry began to introduce American themes into his dance-medleys such as the barn dance *Little Miss USA* which included such catchy numbers as *They all do the Wibbly Wobbly Walk* and *Everybody's doing it at the Seaside*; *Mickey Rooney's Ragtime Band* showcased *Kitchy Koo* and *Ragtime Cowboy Joe* among others.

~

According to the *Isle of Man Times* it was Harry who first brought Bert Feldman to Douglas, in 1907, and their relationship seems to have been cordial both professionally and personally. Harry takes up the story in *Cavalcade*:

> It has been his good fortune to publish many of the songs sung by that 'Chorus Queen' Miss Florrie Forde. Mr Feldman visits the Island every summer for some weeks, and now, both he and the natives consider him a Manxman. He is very popular in the Island because he has a happy and most genial disposition, and all our folks know that he has done everything he can to make our 'Lil' Manx nation' a favourite resort. 'Long Live The King of Songs'.

The faintly adulatory tone of this note conceals the generally held view that Feldman was a hard-headed businessman, aggressively promoting his publications, though generally fair in his dealings with his biggest stars, and may be credited with bringing American-style 'song plugging' to Britain with such 'hits' as *A Bird in a Gilded Cage* and *The Teddy Bears' Picnic*. He was also one of the first publishers to recognise the emerging talent of Irving Berlin, and the first to publish *Alexander's Ragtime Band* in England.

Harry's first meeting with David Day of Francis, Day & Hunter is also referred to in *Cavalcade*:

> Early this season . . . Mr David Day, a founder of the firm Francis, Day & Hunter, publishers of songs for variety artistes particularly, brought Mr Tom Barrett who uses the non-de-plume (sic) 'Leslie Stuart' to Douglas on a visit. Mr Day asked the manager of the Derby Castle and myself to supper in order to meet Mr Barrett, who had brought four new songs of his which were in manuscript (ie unpublished). Each of these songs proved immensely popular.

The four songs in question were *The Soldiers of the Queen*, *Sweetheart May*, *The Willow Pattern Plate* and *Little Dolly Daydream*, and Harry was correct in his estimation that all would become among the best-loved songs of the era. Leslie Stuart[32] had given an interview to the *Manxman* in September 1897 during which he revealed that his most lucrative song to date was *Louisiana Lou* which had earned him over £100,000 in royalties, and that his *Soldiers of the Queen* was selling three thousand copies each week. Asked what he thought his next successful song would be, he named *Little Dolly Daydream* written for the famous 'blackface' singer Eugene Stratton. By the time his hugely successful

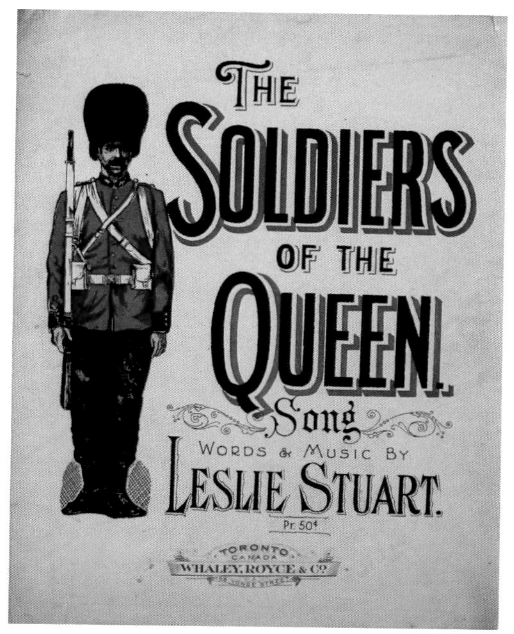

musical comedy *Floradora* was given at the Grand Theatre, Douglas in 1900, Leslie Stuart was 'well-known and highly esteemed in the town'.

Florrie Forde sings Tipperary for the first time in Douglas

History was made when the great chorus singer and Douglas favourite stepped onto the stage at the Derby Castle on Monday 21st July, 1913, and sang *It's a Long Way to Tipperary* for the first time. Harry recorded the event in *Cavalcade* in his usual dry, economical style:

> Florrie Forde sang It's a Long Way to Tipperary for the first time at the Derby Castle. We played the chorus of this song in my Lancers. We played it continuously from Whit-week to the end of the season. It was uproariously acclaimed at every performance.[33]

A brief recollection in the *Isle of Man Times* pasted into one of Harry's scrapbooks for 1913 reads as follows:

> Harry Wood's band played Destiny Waltz at the Derby Castle on a summer night as 'the moon sailed across the Irish Sea, shedding its radiance on that romantic realm'. At 10.00 Florrie Forde appeared and sang It's a Long Way to Tipperary . . .

Harry continued his own recollections of the first performances of Tipperary in *Cavalcade* in 1914:

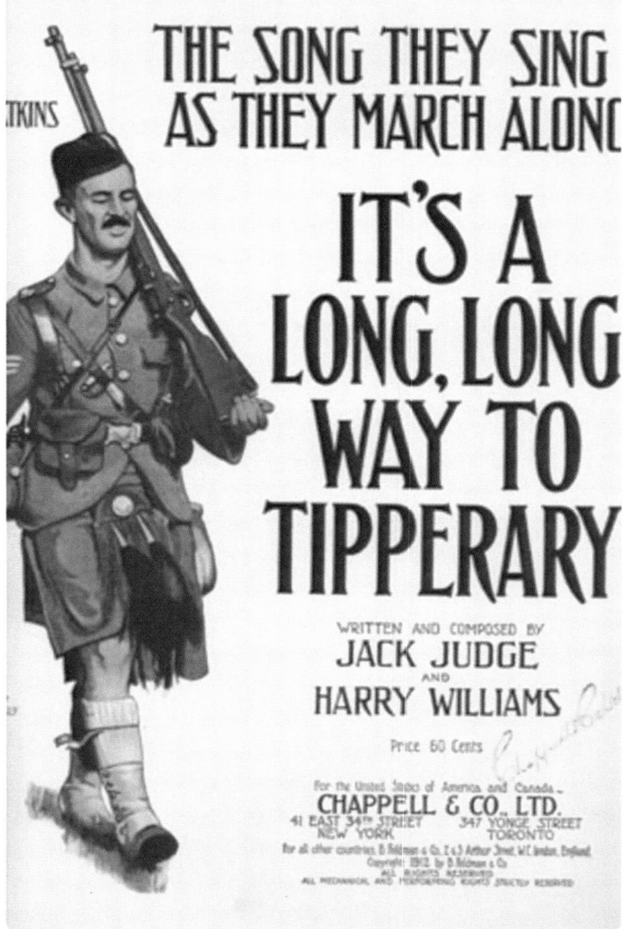

> It is a fact that in 1913 the Battalion of the Liverpool Scottish Territorials were encamped on the Island for some weeks and most of them came to the Castle and join'd merrily in singing the chorus of Tipperary. The result was that when this Battalion was ordered out to the front it sang the chorus of Tipperary as a marching song. They did this also when they arrived in France. The other regiments took it up with the result that this song is known universally. No wonder they call Douglas 'The Birthplace of popular songs".

However, things did not start quite so smoothly, because for some unknown reason, Florrie Forde did not like the song, initially refused to sing it, and took a good deal of persuading before she agreed to include it in her act. Two items of communication between the publisher Bert

Feldman and Harry Wood survive to reveal the behind-the-scenes story of *Tipperary* and Florrie Forde.

Undated card from the London office of Bert Feldman:

> Bay Hotel
> My dear Wood
> You can do me a great favour by getting F Forde to sing 'Tipperary'.
> She will be guided by you.
> See you at 3 o'clock

A letter dated 17th June from Bert Feldman, Metropole Hotel, Blackpool:

> My dear Wood
> I have just ascertained Florrie Forde's address. Hippodrome, Preston. I should take it as a great personal favour if you would write her your views regarding 'It's a long way to Tipperary'. I hope to return to town tomorrow and will attend to the several numbers I promised you . . . All good wishes and many thanks for all your favours.

In a note attached to a letter to Bert Feldman dated April 28th, 1927, Harry adds a further post-script to his account of the events surrounding *Tipperary* and Florrie Forde that summer:

> Mr Feldman gives me credit for persuading Miss Florrie Forde to sing his publication It's a Long Way to Tipperary at Derby Castle, Douglas, Isle of Man. At the first rehearsal in 1913, she said she would not sing this song. I told her that the M.S. had been sent to me at the beginning of the season – that I liked it so much that I had arranged it as a Military Two-step. It was such a favourite with the dancers that I purposed (sic proposed) playing it every night whether she sang it or not. This fact persuaded her to sing the song and she did well with it. Mr Feldman admits that he has made £100,000 by the publication of this song. As we all know, it was a popular ditty in the Great War.

The Military Two-step in question was *The Wedding Glide*, and Tipperary was the third of seven songs in the medley. One last reference was added at the foot of the above note:

> Liverpool Territorials who were camping at Ramsey heard this song at Derby Castle and made it their marching song. Later on – in 1914 – they again sang it & it became so famous with all armies.[34]

As 1913 slipped quietly into 1914 few people will have imagined that in less than a year the whole of Europe would have turned itself on its head and that the places of entertainment in Douglas would be resonating to deeper, far more sinister notes.

Chapter 5

War, and Dancing at the Winter Gardens

1914-1918

There is every reason to believe that had it not been for the outbreak of war on 4th August, the summer season of 1914 would have broken all records for visitor arrivals in Douglas. Throughout the season the local newspapers were upbeat and refused to take seriously the dark forebodings that permeated all aspects of life elsewhere in Europe. The weather was glorious, the boarding houses were full and large crowds flocked to the Palace, Derby Castle, the Gaiety and Grand Theatres nightly and took advantage of the many delightful excursions available to all parts of the Island during the day. As one newspaper wrote with touching optimism:

> It is both early and dangerous to prophesy, but really the indications point to Mr Charles Fox, the manager of the Palace Company (sic), being in a position next autumn to present to his shareholders another record balance sheet.

The Manx Music Festival of 1914 was enlivened by the presence of Elgar as the adjudicator of the choirs and conductor of the combined choirs' Festival concert piece, on this occasion his own patriotic ballad for chorus and orchestra, *The Banner of St George*. Cast in two scenes and an epilogue, and composed the year of Queen Victoria's Jubilee, the ballad is seldom revived today despite the fine choral writing and characteristically brilliant orchestration. It tells the story of St. George of Cappadocia, selected as England's patron saint during the thirteenth century, who slays a dragon with his sword Ascalon, rescues the fair Sabra and promptly leaves 'to bear the cross in other lands'. Shapcott Wensley's text has been described as risible, but these stirring words from the Epilogue, a much-derided 'jingoistic' hymn to Britain's prestige in the world, still have the power to move:

> Great race, whose empire of splendour,
> Has dazzled a wondering world!
> May the flag that floats o'er thy wide domains
> Belong to all winds unfurled.

Elgar praised the Manx choirs and supported the call for a Manx National Choir in his speech declaring that 'You have the material for it to take its place among the great choirs of the world'.[1] Hilton Cullerne played a violin solo at the Festival concert but we learn little of the contribution of Harry's orchestra other than a brief and enigmatic note in Lady Elgar's diary where she describes the orchestra as 'extraordinary'.

One of the highlights of the summer season was the Douglas Carnival, which featured a great many sports events including a marathon at Belle Vue, golf tournaments, processions and parades of all kinds. These included a fancy-dress parade led by the Volunteer Band, illuminations and fireworks on the promenades, a motor car and motor cycle and side car parade, and an aviation display by Messrs Salmet and Raynham, who flew over Douglas Bay and the surrounding countryside at a height of 1,000 feet.

~

The entertainments enjoyed by the visitors the week that war was declared were as varied as ever. At the Palace Coliseum - 'the biggest shillings-worth in Manxland' – R. A. Roberts 'the great protean actor' entertained audiences with his dramatic sketch *Dick Turpin*, and a farce 'of quaint deception', *Ringing the Changes*, during which he assumed all five roles with a series of lightning-quick costume changes 'that are as uncanny as they are clever'. The supporting acts included Yettmah the Magician, Belle Sylvia, billed as 'the lady baritone' and James A. Watts who presented his subtle burlesques of great singers including Caruso and Maud Allen. The male impersonator Hetty King sang *I'm Going Home by Rail* and Ernie Lotinga & Company presented a dramatic sketch entitled *Blue Bottles*.

Harry's Bijou Orchestra provided dance music in the Palace Ballroom during the first week of August, which featured society dances such as the *Maxixe Brasilienne*, the *Hesitation Waltz*, *Royal Boston* and the *Hungarian Rag* and vied with the familiar and entrancing Shadow Dances and fancy-dress evenings in popularity. As July eased into August the Cinema Theatre (formerly the Opera House) showed *The Price of his Honour* and *With Scott in the Antarctic* followed by a biopic about the French boxing champion Charpentier. At the Derby Castle 'lovers of the light and fantastic have indeed had a gay week in dancing to a fine range of dance music excellently provided by Mr Harry Wood's all-British orchestra' which included the season's newest dance sensations *The Harvard Waltz* and the *Castle Walk*.

The biggest star at the Derby Castle was, of course, Florrie Forde - 'a fine figure, a dominating yet sympathetic and genial personality' - who appeared every evening in the grand ballroom for three weeks at the end of July and the beginning of August. Her quick changes of costume before every song was a special feature of her appearances, and that season she sang *Mr Kelly's Isle*, *We all come fra' Lancashire*, *In the Sunny Summer Time*, *When Irish Eyes are Smiling* and of course *Tipperary*. A special prize of £5 was to be awarded to whoever could provide the best extra couplet for the chorus of *In the Sunny Summertime*. That year she mingled with the crowds before and after her performances, collection box in hand, selling autographed postcards in aid of a local charity, and made the following observations during an interview, revealing candid insights into her legendary generosity and great popularity on the Island:

> I've set my heart at getting at least £20 for the Isle of Man Hospital . . . I am not so sure that I shall do it; but it won't be for want of trying.

Asked if the couplet competition was proving a success, she responded:

> Most certainly . . . and the proof of it lies in the fact that we have received more than double the quantity of couplets received up to the same day last week, and they are of better quality, too.

When asked what prompted her to offer a prize for new and original couplets for her song when her lyricist could easily provide them, she replied:

> Probably he could, but many brains must have different ideas, and I think it is a very good idea to have the public supply a little of their own amusement. Besides, almost every human being loves a game of chance, and the chance of winning £5 for two short lines is a good one – better odds than you could get on a race-course.

Asked whether *In the Sunny Summertime* would become popular she replied:

> Oh, undoubtedly; the audience takes up the chorus immediately. That's a pretty sure sign.

When asked if all her audiences took up the choruses as they do at the Derby Castle she said:

> Well, Derby Castle is different to anywhere else. You see we are all there for the purpose of singing a jolly chorus; and (I) am always careful in choosing those with the right swing. Still, wherever I sing,

> the audience always takes up the chorus.

She went on to define the main ingredients for a popular 'hit':

> Directness, simple sounding words, easy rhythm, and a good last line. Add to these a good melody, and the right singer, and the song becomes popular.

'That sounds easy' suggested the reporter, and was invited to have a go at writing some words for a new couplet. To his credit, he had a go, but only managed to produce the following:

> As you look at the ships,
> You can eat tripe and chips,
> In the Sunny Summertime!

As always, Florrie Forde's appearances at the Derby Castle attracted bumper houses, and before long *If Its a Lady, Thumbs Up* and *We All Come fra Lancashire* could be heard sung and whistled on the promenades. Among the supporting artists were Ernest Shand, styled 'The Prince of Comedians' who amused audiences with a sketch about a curate dancing a Tango, and the youthful and talented Mona Vivian who delighted the crowds with 'her exceptional abilities as a singer and fanciful dancer'. Florrie was succeeded by Wilkie Bard, said to be 'in great form', and other supporting turns including the 'sensational feats' of Professor Edward Wulff's Flying Trapeze Terriers and Little May, the 'Marvellous Juvenile Dancer'.

The Sunday Sacred Concert in the Palace Coliseum on 2nd August featured the great contralto Louise Kirkby-Lunn, who sang arias by Bizet and Gounod, the tenor John Harrison, who sang the lovely aria *Waft Her, Angels* from Handel's *Jephtha* and the young Tasmanian violinist Joyce Brown, who played two movements from Mendelssohn's violin concerto. Notwithstanding the 'serious news which had come in during the day concerning Britain's likely involvement in a war of unprecedented magnitude', the concert was attended by 4,000 people who enjoyed a programme that concluded with Tchaikovsky's *1812* overture - 'rendered in a magnificent fashion' - after which Harry was called to the rostrum twice amid 'an outburst of enthusiasm'.

The other Palace & Derby Castle Company venues were also busy and attracting large and eager crowds. The Gaiety Theatre hosted the George Edwardes Company in the three-act musical comedy *The Marriage Market*, which was soon replaced by the tense naval drama *Sealed Orders*, which undoubtedly better reflected the mood of the moment. The Grand Theatre offered Fred Karno's new homely Lancashire comedy *Wakes Week*.

The Villa Marina Kursaal and the fate of Herr Simon Wurm's Imperial Viennese Orchestra.

Earlier, in January 1914, a very acrimonious debate had taken place during a meeting of the Douglas Town Council, over the question of whether a British or foreign band be engaged for the forthcoming summer season. Two members of the Committee threatened to resign over the issue, but the 'supporters of alien musicians' won the day by fourteen votes to six, it being grudgingly accepted that the re-engagement of Herr Wurm's orchestra would ensure that there would be good music from 'an efficient band' at the Villa Marina Kursaal. Another objection was that Wurm's 'Teutonic instrumentalists' were not Viennese at all, but came from all over the world. The irony of this view would however be lost before the end of the season in the confusion and turmoil surrounding the unfolding tragic international events.

The Sunday concerts continued to draw enthusiastic audiences as did the thrice daily concerts in the Villa Marina Gardens, or 'on the green,' as the attractive area was sometimes referred to. The programmes were as varied as the previous two seasons, and often themed: 'Gilbert & Sullivan Nights', 'Humorous Nights', 'Popular Classical Nights' occasionally featuring heavy-weights Wagner and Tchaikovsky, 'Patriotic Nights', 'Scotch', 'Irish', 'Ragtime Nights' and 'Request Nights'. There were always supporting variety entertainments, occasional 'Song Nights' with local singers, firework displays and children's carnivals. At the beginning of August the *Isle of Man Times* noted that: '. . . Herr Simon Wurm's orchestra has now been brought up to full strength . . . every seat was filled and on Sunday the band received quite an ovation'.

All was normal at the Kursaal the evening of the day of the declaration of war as the audience 'rocked with laughter' at Will Evans Company's side-splitting sketch *Harnessing a Horse*. The *Isle of Man Examiner* recorded that the programmes of music during the first week of August were '. . . discreetly selected . . . both classical and popular', perhaps indicating that Wagner and other German composers had already begun to disappear from the selections. Just one week later the same newspaper was at pains to reassure the public:

> In order to remove misapprehension it is well to state that the fine

> band which Mr (no longer 'Herr') Simon Wurm controls includes but one member of German extraction, and he is a naturalised Englishman of twenty years standing, is married to an English woman and has a residence in England.[2]

By the middle of August the name 'Imperial Viennese Orchestra' disappeared from all posters and newspaper advertisements for the Kursaal, and the band was henceforth billed as 'The Famous Douglas Corporation Band . . . under the experienced direction of Mr Simon Wurm'. At this early stage in the conflict every concert opened with the Belgian national anthem, and whenever the Russian national anthem was played, the audiences rose to their feet and applauded vociferously.

The local newspapers were not slow to catch the mood of the times, or perhaps create the mood: 'An English band and an English conductor . . . no Germans need apply' demanded the *Mona's Herald* on behalf of the citizens of Douglas, and also led mounting calls for the name Kursaal to be 'dropped'.[3] During the final week of August the *Isle of Man Examiner* noted that although the thrice daily concerts were still attracting fair audiences 'in glorious weather' the 'depressing effect of the season's slump' in visitor arrivals was beginning to bite.

The Douglas Corporation Band continued to be 'congratulated upon the excellent standard of their judicially selected programmes' for the Sunday concerts, but the reviews often failed to mention Simon Wurm at all. The final reference to him occurred in an *Isle of Man Examiner* review of the daily concerts in the grounds during the gloriously warm final week of August:

> The Douglas Corp Band under the experienced direction of Mr Simon Wurm provided a rich treat by delightful interpretations of classical and popular compositions.

By the beginning of September, Wurm's name had quietly disappeared from all advertising and reviews, and on 3rd November Harry Wood's name appears in connection with the Villa Marina for the first time when his 'select orchestra' provided the music for an American Tea for King and Country. On 12th September the *Isle of Man Examiner* published a poem reflecting on the Villa Marina by 'Musician' during which the author bemoaned the depressed state of the resort and looked back to those 'hours of bliss that filtered by'.

There was one further reference to Herr Wurm and his orchestra the following year when the *Isle of Man Times* picked up a strange after-echo of the pre-war years by noticing that tickets on Douglas trams still bore the following advertisement: 'Herr Simon Wurm and the Imperial Viennese Orchestra at the Villa Marina, morning, afternoon and evening'.

An Island at war

The *Isle of Man Times* had demonstrated little or no presage of the horrors and depravations of war unfolding in Europe and about to impact on Island life in its local news columns, but with the declaration of war the holiday season came to an abrupt halt during a period of exceptionally glorious weather, and Douglas rapidly became a ghost town. The prospect of a record season for visitor numbers was dashed as holiday makers immediately began to leave the Island amid rumours of steamer cancellations and food shortages. Some 416,500 visitors had been recorded up to August, and the Villa Marina, which had just recorded a rise in takings, was now anticipating serious losses. Boarding house keepers, hoteliers and many other businesses that relied heavily on the holiday trade were anticipating a lean time, even if few understood just how devastating the effects of the war on their livelihoods would be. The next few years were nothing short of catastrophic for the Island and Douglas in particular.

As the nine largest Steam Packet vessels were requisitioned leaving the three smallest steamers to ply the Douglas to Liverpool route, it seemed as if the Admiralty had arbitrarily, but effectively, 'stamped out' the summer season with their dire warnings of impending U-boat attacks. The *Mona's Isle* began to bring Manx workers home from the Barrow shipyards and the only visitors to the Island were either Manx or those with Manx connections.

Controversially, the Lieutenant Governor Lord Raglan weighed-in advising holidaymakers to return home as soon as possible and urging hotel and boarding house keepers to sell up and seek work elsewhere, displaying either a disheartening lack of empathy or a harsh but realistic response to unprecedented events, depending on your point of view. The Isle of Man Volunteers were mobilised with over four hundred Manxmen responding to Kitchener's call to arms at the newly-opened recruiting offices in Douglas. Within a year The Loyal Manx Volunteer Association would become the Loyal Manx Volunteer Corps and re-organised for home military duties. Over 8,200 Manxmen enlisted - 82% of the Island's male population - from a total population which has been estimated at around 50,000. In total, 1,165 men and women would ultimately give their lives, and 987 were wounded.

Cunningham's Holiday Camp was commandeered as a temporary internment camp and by September two hundred enemy aliens were interned there. This number grew to three hundred by November, but the less than ideal conditions led to a riot and the death of five internees. Later that month, the first enemy aliens were interned at the new Knockaloe Camp near Peel. A large number of horses were commandeered affecting the operation of the Douglas Bay Tramway, and gas lighting on the Douglas promenades was extinguished so as not to attract German surface raiders and U-boats. The initial brave optimism that the Kaiser would be beaten by Christmas 1914 soon gave way to the realisation that the war would be long and bloody with unimaginable sacrifices being demanded of those in the trenches, at sea and eventually in the air, while those at home would have to cope as best they could.

~

Many regular variety stars began to cancel their engagements including Vesta Tilley at the Palace and Hetty King at the Derby Castle, who along with other artistes could not come to new arrangements with the management in the matter of their fees. Charles Fox, the manager of the Palace & Derby Castle Company appended the following note to a page in the company account books: '. . . refused (to) agree to suggested reduction in terms - Bad business owing to war'.

Wilkie Bard was one of the few stars who appeared at the Palace after war was declared, and was re-engaged for a further first week from 17th August. He was supported by J. H. Scotland, a popular singer of old dialect songs, Henry Hilton and his 'Startling and Sensational Mysteries' and Miss Daisy Stratton, a 'dainty comedienne and charming vocalist'. Another was the Scottish character comedian and singer Neil Kenyon whose monologues in the broadest dialect and tuneful songs such as *Simple Sandy* were enlivened by 'excellent patter'. Regarded by many as a rival to the great Harry Lauder, he 'kept the house in roars of laughter' with his impersonations of a Porter, a Cabbie and a 'Hielander fond of a "smae" scotch'. The Royal Bioscope kept audiences amused and informed with the latest animated daily news features and the newest Keystone comedies. For the few visitors still on the Island with a taste for the bizarre and melodramatic the Grand Theatre presented a one act dramatic episode depicting the horrors of a Chinese opium den and the misadventures of a white opium slave, peopled with characters such as Hung Kow and Sun-Kee.

~

The Sunday concerts at the Palace continued for a while with artistes of the calibre of the coloratura soprano Mignon Nevada and the bass Robert Radford, in patriotic programmes which included Sir A. C. Mackenzie's overture *Britannia*, Arne's *Rule Britannia* which 'had everyone standing and singing loudly with tremendous spirit', and *Land of Hope and Glory* to end with. The Sunday concert on 16th August featured the contralto Phyllis Lett, who also sang *Land of Hope and Glory* to great effect, with supporting soloist Harry's nephew Hilton, 'a youthful but very accomplished member of the orchestra', who performed two movements from Mendelssohn's violin concerto'. With only one singer available Harry's orchestra bore the brunt of the adventurous programme which featured Auber's *Masaniello* overture, Tchaikovsky's *Capriccio Italien*, and the *1812* overture as a grand finale. The tenor Lenghi-Cellini, Thorpe Bates and John Coates all cancelled their engagements at the end of the month owing to travelling difficulties. One of the last concert artistes to appear at the Derby Castle until the end of the war was Harry's brother Haydn

Munitions girls at the Derby Castle.

together with his wife, whose 'charming soprano voice . . . and delicacy of expression immediately found favour'.

Harry's Palace Grand Orchestra of forty 'All British' performers took part in a sumptuous concert on 23rd August in the Palace Ballroom which ended with a national fantasia entitled *Albion* featuring a number of well-known patriotic tunes. The Palace Ballroom stayed open with a small orchestra of twelve players for dancing until the third week of September; the Palace Coliseum closed its doors in mid-August and the Derby Castle in early September. It was the end of entertainments at the two main Douglas venues until the cessation of hostilities. A page in the company's account books listed the advance bookings for 1915-16 naming a number of artistes who would not return to the Island until 1919: Vesta Tilley, who effectively retired at the end of the war and never returned to Douglas, Florrie Forde, Mark Sheridan, Wilkie Bard, George Formby Senior, Tom Foy and Ernest Shand to name just a few.

'The only visitors in substantial numbers are German!'

Under the heading 'A Quiet Time on the Island', the *Isle of Man Times* commented on the lack of visitors in 1915 and wryly remarked that, in common with north of England holiday makers before the outbreak of war, these 'unwelcome visitors' (mainly German internees and prisoners of war) also required housing, feeding, clothing and guarding! The situation was worse than that experienced by other resorts such as Llandudno, Southport or Rhyl because of the obstacle to travel presented by the Irish Sea, although the writer did concede that some country lodging houses were doing a modest business and parents with children were making the best of the fields and beaches. The Tynwald Court Scheme for the relief of boarding house keepers was deemed only a partial and inadequate solution, and consequently met with almost universal condemnation.

The winter of 1914-15, the first depressing winter of the war, saw some enterprising local conductors and musicians doing their best to lift everyone's spirits and provide at least a little cheer for the soldiers and sailors returning from France on leave, by assembling ad-hoc bands and orchestras for various events at the Villa Marina. By February 1915 the appointment of a Villa Marina band for the coming season was high on the agenda of the Promenades Committee of Douglas Town, and applications were formally invited. It was hoped that a local man would come forward and be preferred to 'his rivals across the sea', and in mid-

March Harry's long-standing colleague F. C. Poulter was appointed as the musical director. Very much in his favour was the fact that Poulter would be available all year round; furthermore, he was cheaper than his nearest rival and 'would spend his money in the town'. It was a fair and just decision, for Poulter had served the musical life of Douglas unstintingly for many years and this would be the perfect opportunity for him to fully display his talents.

The Grand Opening of the Villa Marina for Whit-week with the new Douglas Corporation Orchestra, conductor F. C. Poulter, was announced in the *Isle of Man Examiner* at the end of May. There would be a grand opening concert on the 22nd and Grand Patriotic Concerts at 3.00pm and 7.30pm on Whit Monday, which happened to be Empire Day. Thereafter there would be concerts in the grounds each day during the mornings, afternoons and evenings, and local concert parties would provide light entertainment during a short season which lasted until 6th June. Later in the season there were gramophone recitals and a series of concerts given by the Band of the King's (Liverpool) Regiment stationed at Knockaloe Internment Camp in aid of Noble's Hospital. These were the musical highlights of a bleak period when the once vibrant Villa Marina was often given over to anxious and sometimes heated public meetings concerning the course of the war, shortages and other hardships experienced by Islanders.

~

The 24th Manx Music Festival took place between 23rd and 25th March, 1915. The combined choirs, Charles Tree, baritone, and Carrie Tubb, soprano and Harry's orchestra gave a 'magnificent rendering' of Stanford's swashbuckling nautical ballad for choir and orchestra *The Battle of the Baltic* directed by the adjudicator J. A. Roberts at the Festival concert. Lord Raglan used the festival stage to deliver a recruitment speech.

The Palace Ballroom and Coliseum opened for Whit-week with 'Harry Wood's Famous Orchestra' and local singers May Clague and Percy Shimmin, violinist Hilton Cullerne, and a vaudeville entertainment entitled Pierrot, Pierette and Piano. Such concerts as there were naturally began to take on an overtly patriotic flavour with *Land of Hope and Glory* featuring as a grand finale in many of them. There was dancing to Harry's Bijou Orchestra at the Palace during the August Bank Holiday when over 1,000 mainly young people danced to 'merry Manx music' on the famous polished dance floor. Alexandra Day was celebrated with a concert in the

Villa grounds given by Harry's Students' Orchestra at which Hilton, now Private Frank Hilton Cullerne appeared as the violin soloist having recently enlisted in an Officer Cadet Battalion at the age of twenty-two.

Hilton was again the soloist at a garden party in the Palace grounds at the end of August in aid of the Isle of Man Branch of the Earl Roberts Disabled Soldiers' and Sailors' Fund. Harry's orchestra played music by Mendelssohn, Puccini and Haydn Wood and in the evening there was dancing and a fancy-dress carnival. Hilton was proving to be a popular local soloist and was engaged in September to play a selection of solos at a Grand Concert at the Villa Marina with the Douglas Festival Choir, the Festival Ladies Choir and the Douglas Male Choristers conducted by Noah Moore, and again in October with his own ensemble at a Teachers' Fete and concert at the Villa Marina, when over five hundred people enjoyed a programme including a march based on the song *Tipperary*, and Harry's new *Loyal Manx Volunteer Corps Regimental March*.

Harry was not formally associated with the Villa Marina in 1915 and initially played a relatively minor role in its wartime fortunes. This would change the following year - presumably he was still contracted in some way to the Palace & Derby Castle Company in 1915 - but in any case he had by the summer become involved in quite another venture.

Private Wood goes to war.

Harry Wood was forty seven years old in 1915, and as a consequence of the closure of the Palace and Derby Castle his talents as a musical director were much less in demand. Still recognisable as the genial, avuncular, popular, highly respected figure he had always been, he was also a portly one, for physical exercise and Harry Wood were strangers. We cannot imagine him pulling on his boots and setting off for a bracing tramp along the steep costal paths, nor exploring the hidden, secret places of the Island, stick in hand, day sack on his back. He needed something to do other than teaching and maintaining his personal music library, so when the call to arms rang out, Harry did not hesitate, but laid aside his baton and violin, donned a coarse khaki uniform and marched forth to do his bit to vanquish the Kaiser's armies. Not in the footsteps of Guy Mannering perhaps, but rather in the footsteps of Captain Mainwaring.

The first reference in the local newspapers to Harry Wood, soldier of the King, comes in a brief report of a special service in the Villa Marina Gardens on Sunday 26th September, when His Majesty's Forces from the internment camps took part in a Divine Military Service with the Douglas

Harry Wood (front left) with the L M V C.

Festival Choir, the Festival Ladies Choir and the Douglas Male Voice Choristers, and a small orchestra conducted by Private Harry Wood. Over 2,000 people attended including members of the National Reserve and the Loyal Manx Volunteer Corps.

Harry's obituary states only that he was a member of the Loyal Manx Association and 'did duty at the Douglas Internment Camp'. From the Headquarters at the Drill Hall, Douglas, Harry's duties may indeed have involved guard duties at the Douglas Internment Camp, escorting internees to and from the camp to the harbour or guarding the war signals stations or cable landing station. He registered with the Douglas Registration Authority in compliance with the National Registration Act of 1915, and was listed as a 'Professor of Music', height 5' 2", grey hair and blue eyes. The terms and conditions of his service were laid down in Government Circular No. 139, dated 28th May, 1915, from which the following extracts are taken:

> The Loyal Manx Volunteer Corps
> 1. The Lt. Governor has approved of the Loyal Manx Association being affiliated to the Central Association of Volunteer Training

Corps to be known in future as the Loyal Manx Volunteer Corps (LMVC).
2. The Corps is to undertake to perform special duties at Douglas Detention Camp. 300 members will wear recognised uniform at Government expense.
3. The members of the Loyal Manx Volunteer Corps may wear their uniforms in their daily occupations.
4. A Government ration allowance of 1s daily per man will be given to those who perform Camp guard duty. The sum of 2d may be retained to defray incidental expenses.
5. Travelling expenses of men proceeding on guard duty will be defrayed by the Government.
By Order
B. E. Sargeaunt[4]
Government Secretary

On 26th July Harry Wood received the following summons:

LMVC, Tynwald Section

Dear Sir
A meeting of the above Section will be held at the Camp Guardroom tomorrow at 8.30pm sharp to appoint a Section Commander of the above Section the undersigned having been appointed Platoon Commander.
S. T. Shippam
Section Commander

Naturally enough some locals poked fun at this 'Dad's Army' of clerks, professional men and businessmen, mostly over the age of military service, and one can see why from a series of photographs, four of which show Harry in uniform at an LMVC campsite near Port St. Mary, standing by his tent or looking particularly uncomfortable in a knees-bend, arms-stretch exercise drill. By the end of 1915 there were some six hundred and ninety men in the LMVC divided into seven district divisions, .and Lord Raglan paid tribute to them during his Manx Music Festival speech that year: 'For every man drilling in the LMVC camp, as many as nine others were standing idle, some of them laughing at those who were serving'.

~

No doubt Private Wood, meticulous in all things, also paid scrupulous attention to the condition of his equipment as prescribed in the following list headed:

Regulation Equipment for Camp
Extra shirt and socks; Towel, Comb, Brushes (hair and Boots); Soap;
Overcoat; Leggings and extra boots; Blacking; Bathing Drawers;
Rags and grease for cleaning arms and equipment.

Surprisingly Harry proved to be an above average shot as his surviving LMVC Tynwald Section shooting scores demonstrate. His instructors recorded that he was 'an enthusiastic member of the Corps', and achieved an average score of 95 across three disciplines: 2nd class, 1st class and marksman in both deliberate and rapid fire exercises.

Periods of training varied in length from an occasional evening or a day or two in Douglas, to several days under canvas. On Saturday 31st August, 1915, the two hundred men of the LMVC Douglas Division left for a few days training at a camp at Port St. Mary near the Perwick Bay Hotel, in poor weather with frequent heavy downpours, under the command of their District Commander, none other than Charles Fox, manager of the Palace & Derby Castle Company, and Harry's employer in more joyous times. The following morning after settling in, Commander Fox and his men attended Divine Service at Kirk Christ, Rushen, and in the evening, the service at the Wesleyan Church, Port St Mary.

Private Harry Wood under canvass.

The daily routine was arduous. Reveille was at 6.30am followed by hot coffee and biscuits. Harry and his comrades then had to endure a period of 'Swedish' drills before breakfast was served.[5] Thereafter, the day would be taken up with musketry, shooting practice or scouting near the coast in the vicinity of Cregneash village and the Chasms. Lunch was taken at 1.00pm and tea at 5.00; the last post was sounded at 10.00pm followed by lights out fifteen minutes later. Camp life was not all drills, kit inspections and hikes across the heather. On the Wednesday evening of the training week there was a Smoking Concert at the Perwick Bay Hydro where Harry, a pianist, a concertinist and a drummer contributed to a convivial evening of songs and instrumental pieces including his own *LMVC Regimental March*.

There is little more to be learned about Private Harry Wood's war as his No. 2 company was merged with the No. 1 company and a new third company and demobilised in December 1916. Hilton Cullerne, however, joined the King's Liverpool Regiment, rose in the ranks from Private to Lieutenant and was later mentioned twice in despatches for 'outstanding conduct'. From the beginning of September 1918 until the end of January

Adeline Wood in 1915.

1919 Adeline, then aged thirty-eight, was a member of the Women's Army Forage Corps, a civilian women's army raised in 1915 under the control of the Army Service Corps, whose specific task was to source forage (hay) for the army's horses. A forage corps normally consisted of six 'land girls' under the command of an ASC sergeant, but as most horses were at the front Adeline could have been engaged in supplying the internment camps with provisions, acting as a clerk, thatching haystacks with the land girls or even driving military transport on the Island.

The last reference to Harry's war service comes from 1919, when he received a letter ordering him to present himself for a medical examination at the recruitment office in Douglas on 27th July at 2.30pm. As he was engaged at the Winter Gardens, Blackpool at the time, he requested that he be allowed to attend in Preston, and scribbled the following note at the foot of the letter: 'To be medically examined I had to travel to Preston from Blackpool. I did not receive my train fare because I was a "Volunteer". I was not conscripted'. Genial Harry Wood had been more than happy to do his bit as a loyal volunteer part-time soldier on the home front, but his sense of fair play was offended if he felt he was being taken for granted or treated with less than respect.

'... a cloud of misery and mourning'[6]

Christmas 1915 was a very low point in the war with many more people facing severe financial hardship, increasing dissatisfaction with the ultra–conservative and autocratic Lieutenant Governor, Lord Raglan and with the government in general. 'At the beginning of 1916 few would have predicted that it would be a year of such agitation, or that the stalemate at home would be, in its way, as bad as the stalemate at the front'.[7] Boarding house keepers and others dependent on a thriving tourist industry were facing another disastrous season; some residents refused to pay their rates and by October goods were being seized and auctioned. Lord Raglan was absent from the Island for nine months due to illness and was booed at the Tynwald ceremony in St. Johns upon his return. The news from the front was especially grim, as the full horror of the carnage of the Somme campaign began to filter home.

~

Yet for Harry the New Year proved to be the busiest of the war so far as he once again plunged enthusiastically into local musical affairs. Hilton and Adeline took part in a variety show in March at the YMCA Pavilion,

Lord Raglan in masonic regalia.

Knockaloe, supported by officers and staff of the camp, and Adeline appeared in a short farce entitled *The Area Belle* at the Shrove Tuesday St. George's Church Parochial Tea. The month ended with the sad news of the death in Manchester of Oliver Gaggs, the composer of the famous *Hi! Kelly Polka*, and one of the most popular of all the Douglas musical directors.

The 25th Manx Music Festival took place between 4th and 6th of April, and Harry led his orchestra in a performance of Stanford's choral song *The Last Post* conducted by H. A. Branscome of Liverpool. There were one hundred and eighty-three entrants that year, a new class, Patriotic Song, was introduced and a cantata *Allen-a-Dale* was performed on Children's Day.

The round of local concerts continued unabated, and for some of them Harry managed to organise a band of twelve players including Kathleen Rydings and the newly-promoted Lance-Corporal Frank Hilton Cullerne; 'a most admirable little orchestra' wrote the *Mona's Herald*. The

Villa Marina Gardens was the scene of a children's outdoor entertainment in July in aid of Belgian children that began with a procession in a variety of fancy-dress costumes: Charlie Chaplin, clowns, Morris dancers, Irish dancers, sailors and hornpipers, chimney sweeps and minstrels which attracted a large crowd including the novelist Hall Caine. Noah Moore acted as master of ceremonies and Harry directed his orchestra in a selection of National Anthems of the Allies.

A plucky venture

The 1915 summer season at the Villa Marina, with the Douglas Corporation Band under the baton of F. C. Poulter, had been hastily organised and was short-lived. Following a farewell concert in June, Poulter disappears from the story of the Villa Marina as a conductor until 1918, but not as a player.

1916 was the only year during the war that Harry played a significant role in the entertainments at the Villa Marina. Negotiations between Douglas Corporation and Fred Buxton, a highly-regarded local entertainer, entrepreneur, singer, composer and manager of the popular Pierrot Village on Douglas Central Promenade, concluded in May with Buxton being declared the Responsible Manager for the forthcoming season.[8] It was generally viewed as a 'brave enterprise' and a 'plucky venture' on Buxton's part and not without financial risk. There would be concerts, variety entertainers, cinema pictures and dancing, and Buxton appointed Harry to organise and conduct an orchestra of six players to be known as the

Buxton's Pierrot Village.

Villa Marina Bijou Orchestra. The gates were unlocked, the barbed wire was removed from the grounds and encouraging numbers of people began to visit the 'ideal retreat from these scorching days' once again.

The mid-summer daily timetable of programmes was a packed one, with the Bijou Orchestra appearing in the afternoon in the gardens if fine and in the Grand Hall if wet, at the bandstand in the early evening and for dancing at 7.45pm. For Harry, with years of experience at the Derby Castle and the Palace, this was business as usual. The twice-daily Sunday concerts continued to flourish and often featured the Douglas Festival Choir and Ladies Festival Choir conducted by Noah Moore, together with instrumental solos from Hilton and others. Excerpts from Mendelssohn's *Elijah*, Stanford's *The Last Post* and a performance of Coleridge-Taylor's *Hiawatha* were among the popular and challenging works presented during the season, and Fred Buxton himself sometimes appeared as a tenor soloist during the afternoon concerts. By the height of the summer of the grimmest year of the war so far, the local newspapers were declaring that 'truly, the Villa Marina has made life more tolerable'.

The climax of the season was Fred Buxton's Complimentary Performance, a benefit night at the end of a special Gala Day on 31st August, designed 'to enable Mr Buxton to recover the slight loss sustained in running the Villa Marina during the summer'. The highlight of the evening concert was the first known performance of Harry's *Manx Melodies, The Cushag*, a skilful medley of twenty-one popular Manx traditional melodies arranged for orchestra, mainly taken from *Manx National Songs*.[9] The season ended at the end of September with a traditional Manx Mhelliah, and all present were in agreement: there had been much to enjoy during the sombre summer months of 1916, and the Villa Marina had truly established itself as 'the rendezvous for soldiers returning home'.

As the autumn drew on Harry once again threw himself into a round of private teaching and local small-scale engagements although even these were fewer in number than in previous years. Early in October Douglas Town Council informed Fred Buxton that there would be no decision concerning entertainments at the Villa Marina during the winter until the 17th of the month, and that no decision concerning the 1917 summer entertainments would be taken before 1st January. The third year of the war ended amidst further objections to Sunday entertainments at the Villa Marina and uncertainty about the following season.

Harry Wood goes to Blackpool

A brief note in one of Harry's scrapbooks confirms that he relinquished his teaching post at King William's College when 'war measures' forced him to leave the Island in 1917, but it is not known precisely when he began to travel regularly to Blackpool. The formal letter of engagement as Musical Director of the Blackpool Winter Gardens Orchestra was dated 28th April, 1917, from John R. Huddlestone, the General Manager of the Blackpool Winter Gardens and Pavilion Company Limited, following an interview on the 19th:

> Dear Mr Wood
> I have pleasure in engaging you as Musical Director of the Winter Gardens Orchestra for the season from May 28th to Sept 29th, and to assist me generally in the musical arrangements.

His principal tasks were to conduct the orchestra in the Empress Ballroom, select the music for the dance programmes and to forward names to the management of musicians he wished to engage. His salary was £10 per week. His acceptance of the terms and conditions was sent a few days later from the Sheffield Hippodrome on old note paper headed Hengler's Circus, which might indicate that he was once again providing music for Hengler in the early part of the year.

News of Harry's appointment in Blackpool reached the Isle of Man during May and was recognised as a prestigious and demanding position:

> There is no fear but that Mr Wood will discharge the duties attached to the post with the same splendid acceptance to his employers and the public as has distinguished his services in Douglas . . . although not Manx by birth he has been a resident for over thirty years, and is both respected and esteemed by Manx people.

Another letter from this period survives, dated 19th June, from the Town Clerk's Office, Douglas, thanking Harry for the payment of his rates and including news from home:

> You have a fine programme at the Winter Gardens and I hope you have a most successful time . . . things in Douglas are a little quieter than last year. Mr Buxton is doing well at the Villa Marina although his music is confined only to dancing. Needless to say, you are greatly missed.

~

The Blackpool Winter Gardens in 1917 was a large entertainment complex in the centre of the town behind the famous Tower, a short distance from the sea front. It was originally opened in 1878 and encompassed 'a concert room, promenades, conservatories and other accessories' designed to provide a pleasant lounge in poor weather. By the time of Harry's tenure it had expanded to include the magnificent Empress Ballroom, one of the largest in the world (Harry always believed that the Palace and Empress Ballrooms were of equal size), an Opera House or theatre designed by Franck Matcham - who also designed the Gaiety Theatre in Douglas - a grand glass and steel Pavilion and a sumptuous Indian Lounge, whose decor was intended to reflect the extravagance of the British Raj.

Harry's orchestra was known variously as The Winter Gardens Grand Orchestra, The Bijou Orchestra and The Syncopated Orchestra, and the surviving programmes reveal that the weekly schedule of evening dances, revues, shows and concerts was extremely demanding. The first surviving programme for the Empress Ballroom which bears Harry's name covers the last week in July, 1917, and reveals that there was dancing every evening, three rotating weekly programmes and a Grand Naval and Military Revue entitled *For Freedom* until October. One hundred and fifty children took part in this patriotic extravaganza for which Harry himself

selected, arranged and conducted the music.

Harry's new dances for the period included the waltz *Spirit of Spring*, the Schottische Medley on Feldman's songs, an Anglo-American one-step, *Some Reel* with a hint of Dixie in the introduction, his 1917 Lancers and a waltz on themes from a current revue *Let the Great Big World Keep Turning*. In addition to his own compositions Harry introduced dances and other pieces by Daniel and Haydn Wood into his programmes.

~

For a few years after the war waltzes, schottisches and lancers remained as popular as they had been earlier in the Edwardian age, but as Harry noted in *Cavalcade* in 1919:

> It will be noticed that the dance programmes from now onwards have changed drastically. During the war period the Schottische, Barn Dance, Lancers, Veleta-Valse and Military two-step have been superseded by the Fox-trot, One-step, Two-step, Rags, Tango, Maxixe etc.

The change in dance styles could be said to have begun when Irving Berlin's 'jazzy' *Alexander's Ragtime Band* first appeared in Britain in 1911, and gained impetus during the war with the flood of American soldiers and American dance music into Europe. Philip S. J. Richarsdon, editor of the influential magazine *The Dancing Times*, wrote the following about the years 1918-23:

> With the coming of the Armistice, highly syncopated music from America was supreme, and American bands were all the rage.

The change is noticeable in the titles of dances old and new: the waltzes *Missouri* and *Little Grey Home in the West*, the *Russian Rag* and *Ragging Thro' the Rye*, the *Gaby Glide* and *Tipperary* one-step, the fox-trots *Spookville Chimes*, *Say it With Music* and *When the sun Goes Down in Dixie*, the *El Chocla* tango and the maxixe *Amapua*, a kind of Brazilian two-step tango.

The Kursaal and the Kaiser, 1917-19.

Back in April 1917, whilst Harry Wood was finding his feet and establishing himself in Blackpool, Douglas Town Council once again entered into negotiations with Fred Buxton concerning the letting of the Villa Marina for the summer, and it was agreed that providing no losses were incurred, the resort would be made available for 'high-class

Frederick Buxton.

entertainments'. Some committee members were against the use of the main hall, the former Kursaal, but reluctantly agreed to sanction 'some little entertainments providing that there would be no loss to the town'. In May Fred Buxton was once again appointed as the Responsible Manager of the Villa Marina, and charged with organising the entertainments for the summer season.

He immediately engaged F. C. Poulter to form a Bijou Orchestra which contained many of Harry's most experienced musicians from the previous season including Nancy Cowell, 'cello, and J. T. Wood, cornet. Evening dance programmes commenced on Whit Monday, and the Sunday concerts shortly afterwards. The café was well-patronised during the day, and Buxton himself often appeared in his sketch 'John Bull in story and song' during the evening dance programmes when young ladies easily outnumbered the young men - many of whom were in khaki and some of whom were wounded - on the dance floor.

The 26th Manx Music Festival took place between 27th and 29th March. The bass Robert Radford was appointed to adjudicate the vocal classes, but in the event, his place was taken by the tenor Henry Turnpenny. J. A. Roberts, organist, conducted the combined choirs in a 'magnificently rendered' performance of Hamish MacCunn's cantata *The Wreck of the Hesperus*.[10] Harry travelled to the Island to recruit and lead the orchestra and arrived in Douglas only just in time to 'fulfil his duties' as Lord Raglan quipped in his speech: 'Perhaps the German fleet has come out to try to capture Mr Harry Wood on his way to the Island'. Despite the privations of war, the Festival attracted 252 entrants and Miss M. L. Wood received her customary rousing reception at the Festival concert.

~

Of course, the war could never be banished from the thoughts of those at home on the Island for long, even if the pall of gloom could occasionally be lifted by a visit to the Villa Marina. There was a sharp intensification of the deprivations afflicting the Isle of Man in 1917, and a consequent hardening of attitudes towards the government and its entrenched lack of response to taking measures to alleviate the sufferings and hardships that were the daily concerns of the Manx people. The reality of the nightmare in Belgium and France was brought home at the third war anniversary United Religious Service in August, when it emerged that there had been 509 fatalities amongst the 1,333 Manx casualties of the war so far.

In January 1917 the loss of the *Ben-my-Chree*, the pride of the Steam Packet fleet, during the Gallipoli campaign was keenly felt, but news the following month of the heroic action of the captain and crew of the paddle steamer *Mona's Queen* in ramming a German submarine whilst on patrol in the English Channel, 'warmed the cockles of the Manx heart', to paraphrase Churchill's statement following the Royal Navy's plucky action against the *Graf Spee* in 1939. The exploits of the *Ben-my-Chree*, *Mona's Queen* and *Tynwald* during the war were later commemorated in the shanty *Steamers Three*, with music by Miss M. L. Wood and words by 'Cushag', the poetess Josephine Kermode; the final verse pays tribute to all Manx sailors, 'faithful and true':

There are hearts of oak in ev'ry fleet,
But a good Manx sailor is hard to beat.

On the financial front the Villa Marina receipts were down on the previous year as the expense of running and maintaining the venue continued to be high. Carnivals and dance competitions continued to attract crowds as August slipped into September as did the end-of-season Mhelliah on 4th October. In November Fred Buxton's petition to the Promenades Committee to manage the Villa Marina for dancing on Thursday and Saturday evenings during the winter was granted provided that existing bookings were honoured. On 12th November the Villa Marina hosted the 5th Annual World Manx Association T. E. Brown Festival and the year ended with a 'Monstre' whist drive and dance on Boxing Day.

Discontent boiled over into direct action during 1918 when the Island was paralysed by a General Strike called in protest at the ending of the flour subsidy and the government's failure to progress an Income Tax Bill. There was an overwhelming response from all manner of workers culminating in a huge public meeting held on the foreshore near the Villa Marina. Lord Raglan finally gave in on Tynwald Day resulting in the subsidy being extended, and a lower rate of income tax for the Island being agreed by both houses.

The signing of the Armistice on 11th November was followed on the Island by a Service of Thanksgiving at the Villa Marina on the 17th, during which Lord Raglan, Sir Hall Caine and Bishop Denton addressed some 3,500 people. Lord Raglan tendered his resignation as Lieutenant Governor to the Home Secretary on 24th November, after sixteen restless and, at times, turbulent years during which he resolutely refused to consider any kind of political reform for the Island. 'The great dictator' had gone, and the Islanders patiently waited to hear who would be the next Lieutenant Governor, nervously hoping 'that whoever it is should be someone who is sympathetic to the constitutional, judicial and social reforms so long promised . . . and so long postponed'.

~

At the Villa Marina the final year of the war commenced with dancing two nights a week, and in early February a 'Tank' Ball with fancy-dress costumes and masks was held to raise money for an Isle of Man sponsored tank. At the end of February 1918 tenders were once again invited for the provision of music at the Villa Marina for the forthcoming season, and Fred Buxton's appointment as Responsible Manager at the Villa Marina from May until the end of September was confirmed, notwithstanding the predictable objections from some council members to Sunday entertainments.

The season proper commenced at Whitsun with dancing each evening to F. C. Poulter's small orchestra (with no 'Hunnish' or Austrian entertainers engaged), cinema pictures nightly, including, in August, *The Manxman*, based on Hall Caine's novel of 1896[11] and filmed on the Island the previous year, and Sunday *al fresco* vocal and instrumental concerts in the gardens afternoon and evenings. Harry's 1918 novelty ballroom dance was *The Tank's Saunter Dance*, news of whose popularity in Blackpool reached Douglas early in 1919. Together with his 1917 lancers *Manx Melodies*, the *1918 Up-to-Date Lancers* and four new waltzes including *The Bells of Dawn*, it was among the most popular dances of the season.

Chapter 6

Douglas open for business again!

1919-1927

> 'This weekend the Island enters upon its first holiday season proper since the memorable 4th of August, 1914, when Germany thought fit to defy the world.'

The Steam Packet Company was 'straining every nerve' in preparing to cope with an anticipated rush of returning visitors in 1919, but it was not possible at this stage 'to place the ships on their pre-war footing as far as quality and quantity'.[1] The *King Orry*, *Mona's Queen* and *Peel Castle* were overhauled and ready for service, joining the smaller vessels *Tynwald*, *Douglas* and *Fenella* which had continued in service on the Douglas to Liverpool route throughout the war. Everything was in readiness to welcome the holiday makers to the Island once again, with the Saturday before Whit-week witnessing a surge of visitors. Douglas strove valiantly to reclaim its reputation of 'dear but delightful', and visitor numbers recovered well immediately after the war reaching a respectable 334,300 even in 1919. Hotel and boarding house keepers were desperate to recover their severe losses, and a close examination of their tariffs shows that Douglas represented good value as a holiday destination, especially for families and young people, for whom crossing the Irish Sea added a dash of adventure.

~

The Palace Ballroom, newly painted and redecorated, opened on 7th June for the first time since it had been acquired by Messrs Vickers Ltd., (Aviation Dept) during the war for the manufacture of balloonettes, or airbags inside the envelope of an airship. Harry presided over a large orchestra of twenty-five players, and J. H. McEwan, the resourceful Master of Ceremonies, introduced freshly-devised new dances such as the Maxina and The Real Jazz.

'JAZZ! JAZZ!! JAZZ!!! Everybody's Doing It! at the Palace', blared the advertisement in the *Isle of Man Times*, leaving no-one in any doubt that a new jazz age had arrived.

Punch as always caught the mood:

Terpsichore, tired of the Trot,
And letting the Valse go to pot,
In the glorious Jazz
Most undoubtedly has
Discovered the pick of the lot.

The first Saturday of the season got under way with a Special Grand Dance Fete, a Fancy Dress Carnival with £10 prizes and a series of dancing competitions with prizes ranging from 10s to £2. Harry's dance programmes included his new waltz *Exquisite*, *Victory Lancers* and *Up-to-date 1919 Lancers* and his arrangement as a waltz of Haydn Wood's most famous song *Roses of Picardy*, the most poignant of all the songs to emerge from the war. The 'modern' dances styles were represented by the jazz fox-trot *Hullo! America*, *The Bing Boys on Broadway Lancers*, the American jazz fox-trot *Going Up* and the American jazz one-step *Jazzin' thro' the rye*. The high reputation of the Palace orchestra had been maintained and was adjudged of be the equal of the Palace orchestras in pre-war days. As one visitor wrote: 'The Palace on a holiday night is a sight calculated to make even Diogenes dance!'

Sunday concerts began again on Whit Sunday 8th June in the Coliseum with Dilys Jones the favourite contralto of the Queen's Hall concerts, Henry Brearley, tenor, and the 'cellist Edwin Hatton 'of Beecham's orchestra' as the first soloists. The orchestra was augmented for the Sunday concerts by incorporating players from the Derby Castle band as it had been before the war, and was conducted on a regular basis by Harry's leader and deputy conductor A. J. Graham in his absence. The Palace Coliseum opened for the season on Whit Monday with a 'first class variety programme' featuring J. H. Scotland, singer and actor; The Violas, 'in mental Mystery . . . who are opportune now that the world and his wife, including Sir Conan Doyle . . . are troubling themselves with the occult';[2] The Frisco Five, 'adepts of the Jass'; The Goodwins, lady comedy jugglers; and the Davina Trio, (soprano, 'cello and piano) three talented young Manx artistes.

~

The Derby Castle opened for the season on Monday 14th July with dancing to Harry's orchestra in the ballroom and a variety show starring 'the great little comedian' Sydney Swain and his 'revusical vaudeville party' The Electric Sparks in the variety theatre.

Other Douglas entertainment venues now hastened to open their

Queen's Promenade in the 1920s.

doors for the season. At the Villa Marina, under the management of the newly-appointed Noah Moore, Mr Fred Winterbottom's Grand Municipal Orchestra began to play selections of light music afternoon and evening in the grounds, 'rendered in a very acceptable fashion', whilst Feldman's songsters entertained the crowds with all the latest songs. From the week beginning 7th July F. C. Poulter's Bijou Orchestra was engaged for the dancing programmes in the Grand Hall.

At the Grand Theatre Frederick Buxton presented a twice-nightly variety show including a revue entitled *Frills and Fancies*, 'not just any "go-as-you-please show", but (a show) with a reputation, having come from London and the largest provincial theatres'. Despite reservations about the nature of revues, *Frills and Fancies* held the stage until the autumn: 'We want to forget the past . . . and revue seems to fit the bill for those who seek for light and love and laughter' said the *Mona's Herald*. 'Popular prices' attracted audiences to the Gaiety Theatre to see Harry Leslie's Company of entertainers in *The Seven Comedy Cadets* and more musical comedies, farces and dramas were promised during the rest of the season.

At the Strand Cinema *The Lone Star Ranger*, based on the novel by Zane Grey in which a Texas Ranger triumphs over cattle rustlers, was shown in June followed by Charlie Chaplin in *Police*, his recently-released fourteenth film in which he plays an ex-convict hoodwinked by a fake parson: 'A riot of fun; every foot packed with mirth' according to the advertising 'blurb'. *The Silver King* was showing at the Pier Pavilion and was billed as 'a pathetic story told with Dickensian humour'. Harry would surely have recollected the story in its original play version of 1882 when it was in the repertoire of the Theatre Royal, Huddersfield. The new 'movies' being shown at the Empire Theatre were 'edifying, informative and humorous' according to the previews. Lilian Gish starred in *The House Built Upon Sand*, a romantic comedy, supported by two short comedies *A One Night's Stand* and *A Saucy Madeline*, starring the veteran of hundreds of silent films, Heinie Conklin.

Buxton's Amusement Resort on Central Promenade featured concert party afternoons and evenings and in the mornings during wet weather. Buxton also had premises in Ramsey and at the open-air baths in Port Erin.

For those wishing to visit the many secret and hidden places around the Island, the Isle of Man Railway Company's revised summer timetable was an essential guide. Silverdale, described as 'an old-time village' set in a wooded and flowery glen, and Glen Wyllin, with footpaths descending through woodland to the coast, attracted those seeking picnic spots near the sea. Laxey Glen Gardens boasted extensive walking trails, boating, swings, games, *al fresco* dancing and 'catering arrangements of great excellence'. Douglas Head continued to appeal to those seeking spectacular views, the facilities of a fine hotel and unsophisticated entertainments, although one visitor went too far in suggesting that many travellers considered the four-mile tram route along the cliffs to Port Soderick 'beats the famous Monte Carlo Corniche hollow'.

War's embers

If the tourist and entertainment industries quickly began to recover from the war years, for many Islanders the post-war recovery was a slow, drab process with the constant backdrop of rising unemployment, rising prices, particularly food, and low wages colouring everyday life during a period of civil unrest, marches and public meetings. The stock of affordable housing 'fit for heroes' was meagre, although from 1922 post-war housing schemes did get underway, modern houses began to be built and council estates were laid out. As the decade wore on apartment blocks began to appear in Douglas, although many of the unemployed could barely afford even council rents. The up grading of a large area of old Douglas from the Victoria Pier to the railway station, including much of the area around North Quay where the Wood family had first settled, got underway with some urgency. As many as thirty public houses, including the Black Lion, were swept away in what was considered to be essential slum clearance to make way for more direct access to the piers from the western approaches. The once-lively district had fallen into disrepute as a squalid ghetto of dingy, narrow streets with some of the poorest, most cramped and dilapidated housing in the town.

Profitable holiday seasons were essential to the economic well-being of the Island but only operated fully for four to five months of the year. The traditional industries of mining, fishing and agriculture were either in recession or in decline, and there was a substantial fall in the population of the Island from a high of just over 60,200 in 1921 to a little over 49,300 during the early 1930s. There was a significant growth in the development of new roads and public transport; indeed the post-war years were something of a boom time for the Isle of Man railways with a steady increase in passenger numbers for both the main services and the Manx Electric Railway Company. There also developed an 'almost suicidal' spirit of cut throat competition among the charabanc owners, so that by 1923 some Island tours priced at £1 in 1920, and lasting six or seven hours at a crawling speed of around 12 mph over some very bumpy roads, could be purchased for as little as 7s 6d.

The new Governor, Major-General Sir William Fry, arrived on April Fool's Day 1919, and was officially installed at Castle Rushen two days later. He was not a civil servant but a soldier, a veteran of the Afghan and Boer wars, Deputy Director of the Territorial Army and in charge of the military administration of Ireland in 1916. Furthermore, his appointment was limited to seven years only, a significant victory for the reformers. Generally viewed as a fair-minded 'honest broker' and sympathetic to those who had suffered hardships during the war, he was largely successful in dealing with the problems of the Island's war contributions, the salaries of government officials, the rent controversy, and in 1920, the presenting of a healthy budget to Tynwald. In the turbulent post-war period, Fry's was a steady hand on the tiller. His successor, His Excellency Sir Claude Hamilton Hill, was installed at Castle Rushen in May 1926; a proven, able civil servant and administrator in India, he displayed tact and dignity in all matters during the period of the General Strike in Britain, which also had a detrimental effect on the Island.

Home and away

Within Harry's long and varied career, the nature and scope of entertainments went through several stages of development from the peak of Music Hall between the 1880s and the First World War and the coming of the age of Variety, to the newest form of mass entertainment, the Revue. Music hall had been vital, authentic and ranged from the sublime to the surreal, but was also tawdry, boisterous and unsophisticated; Variety was altogether smarter, appealing to both sexes, no longer dominated by comic and chorus songs but featured a blend of individual acts supported by a first rate band. Revue was essentially a show with a theme, an actual production rather than a collection of acts, featuring song and dance numbers, sketches, 'transformations', with elaborate scenery and the all-important grand finale with all the acts taking part. In other words, a variety show that just stopped short of being a musical. Many songs from 'hit' revues ended up in dance sequences such as Harry's *Hullo! Ragtime* and *Hitchy Koo.*

The Winter Gardens' *Little Miss 1918 Revue* with music selected, arranged and adapted from the lists of six different music publishers by Harry and John Tiller, boasted magnificent costumes, wonderful scenery and 'new electrical effects'. There were ten leading roles supported by the Tiller Troupe, the Military Maids, the Twelve Manchester Mites and the Winter Gardens' Gentlemens' Chorus and the Winter Gardens' Grand Orchestra conducted by Harry.

The Empress Ballroom was requisitioned by the Admiralty for war production in 1918, and the dance programmes transferred to the Indian Lounge. Lavish productions were still possible and one of the grandest was the Winter Gardens' Grand Ballet and Revue entitled *Some Show,* which featured music selected from the newest publications of Bert Feldman & Co, the Star Publishing Co and Francis, Day & Hunter. The high point of the revue was a Grand Eastern Ballet set in London, Paris and Baghdad with such song delights as *Yacki-Hacki-Wicki-Wacki-Woo!* and a finale *When the Boys Come Marching Back* which depicted the entry of the British Army into Baghdad.

Variety thrived during the cinema age and the early radio years, survived another war and enjoyed a new lease of life in the television age, but Revue gradually faded between the wars and quickly became outmoded even as a summer seaside entertainment.

Harry and the internee

In January 1919 Harry received a letter from one Charles P. Shaak in Blackpool regarding his father who was interned at Knockaloe Internees

"THE MANCHESTER MITES."

Camp,[3] near Peel, asking him if he could assist in obtaining his father's release home to Blackpool rather than being sent to Germany:

> He is 53 years old and has lived in Blackpool for over 30 years and during which time he has never had any connection with Germany. He has four British born children the eldest of which has been serving with His Majesty's forces in France. My father renounced Germany over 25 years ago and of course has papers to that effect. There have never been any complaints against him and therefore we do not wish him to be sent into Germany but home to us in Blackpool. I am sure you will do your best for me and I hope that you will be able to help me to secure fathers release.

Harry's response to this letter has not survived, but a few days later he received a brief note from Arthur Brittain, deputy manager of the Palace & Derby Castle Company, informing him that:

> Mr Shaak has been interviewed and has a good case. He will have to

> make application to the Assistant Commandant of the Camp to be kept back until such time as the Government decide what is going to be done with those who do not desire to go to Germany.

In fact, there were a large number of internees in Mr Shaak's situation who had lived in Britain for a number of years and had no real connection with Germany. They were housed in a separate compound awaiting a decision about their individual cases. Only sixteen per cent of those who wished to take up residence in Britain again after the war were eventually permitted to do so.

'His part in the institution of the first Blackpool Dance Festival cannot be exaggerated'.[4]

Exactly who first suggested that Blackpool should host a dance festival in 1920 is not known, but it is generally assumed that the idea developed during conversations between Harry Wood, Nelson Sharples of music publishers Messrs Sharples & Son Ltd., of Blackpool and John R. Huddlestone, manager of the Winter Gardens. It was to prove a winning collaboration of talent, experience and business acumen.

The core of the Dance Festival was to be the novelty or sequence dance competition. Long before the war two novelty dances become sensationally popular in Blackpool: the valeta and the military two-step, which flourished because they found favour with the dance teachers' associations who were happy to promote them. It was hoped that composers and choreographers would be encouraged to compose and develop new dances each season with the most popular ones published along with a guide to the steps. Harry himself composed some of the Blackpool Winter Gardens' Trophy Dances such as the novelty two-step *The Festival*, which won the Gold Medal at the first festival, the waltz *Elita*, the one hundred guinea Trophy Prize Dance at the first festival, the *New Empress Tango*, *The Royal Empress Tango* and the *New Empress Waltz* with steps invented by the resourceful A. E. Brown, the Winter Gardens' Master of Ceremonies.

The inaugural Festival took place during Easter week 1920 with James Finnigan, a Master of Ceremonies at the Empress Ballroom since 1902, in the role of chairman of adjudicators. The aim that first year was to discover three new novelty dances from three competitions: waltz, two-step and fox-trot, held over three days. On a fourth and final evening the winning dance was chosen and the inventor presented with the Sharples Challenge Shield.

Some dance teachers and their associations were initially lukewarm about the venture and refused to support it, but most came round following the success of the first season, at the conclusion of which Harry was presented with a silver cup and gold pencil on behalf of the teachers' associations who passed the following resolution:

> We wish to place on record our hearty and sincere thanks, first to Mr John Huddlestone for the splendid and generous hospitality he has displayed in our interests and we trust that in future years the Festival will prove the huge success it so rightly deserves; and secondly to Messrs Sharples & Son, Ltd., for their generous gift of a trophy which we are sure will be very much appreciated in the dancing world . . . We place on record our unanimous approval of the Festival as an Annual function for the Dancing World of Great Britain . . .

~

With his vast experience and reputation for judging the public taste and mood and selecting the most appropriate and up-to-date music for his programmes, Harry clearly relished this new phase in his career as the following letter from the commander of a military hospital in the area suggests:

> On behalf of the boys in the HS American Base Hospital, thank you for introducing the American One-step into the Winter Gardens programmes, and giving up so many encores to allow more time for dancing.

In March 1923 Harry presided over one of the most unusual evenings of his entire career. The event was advertised in the Blackpool Gazette and Herald as a 'Big Football Social Dance Marathon in the form of a football match' at the Winter Gardens in aid of Blackpool Football Club. Harry and his 'Merry Musicians' played a substantial programme of forty waltzes, fox-trots, lancers and novelty dances in an evening divided into four sequences with the 'kick-off' at 8pm and the 'final whistle' at 2.00am. The dance was well-supported and £75 was given in prizes.

Never shy about maintaining his public persona, Harry took part in the Blackpool Carnival in June 1923, which was held over eight days and attracted over two million visitors to the town. The carnival was heralded as 'the greatest event of its kind . . . bigger and better than anything before'. There were processions, pageants, a Carnival King and Queen, grotesque

Harry at the Blackpool Carnival, 1923.

figureheads and decorated carnival cars. A photograph survives showing Harry standing in a decorated car dressed as an Indian Prince complete with turban and gaudy tunic. To mark the occasion he composed The Winter Gardens Carnival Dance: *Blackpool's Dustless Breezes*[5] with words by John R. Huddlestone, which won first prize and became 'a terrific success in the Empress Ballroom that season'. The introduction in march tempo contains a parody of the Yorkshire 'anthem' *On Ilkla Moor baht 'at* with the words *On Marston Moss bewt 'at*. The following year the carnival was sadly marred by drunkenness and violence, but in 1925 the famous illuminations were switched on for the first time since 1914.[6]

As the newer, more exotic dance styles began to establish themselves in Blackpool their provenance was hotly debated, as the following extract taken from *The Ballroom* in 1925 demonstrates:

> Some protagonists believe it (the Tango) originated in the third-rate cafes of Buenos Aires; others are certain that it was first danced in the orange groves of Seville. One ingenious commentator has proved – to his own satisfaction if to no one else's – that it came from the Congo! So far, Blackpool remains silent on the matter, but I should not be surprised to hear from some indignant Blackpudlian that it was invented on the floor of the Winter Gardens Ballroom!

An indication of Harry's personal popularity comes from the

HARRY
WOOD
THE GENIAL
MUSICAL
DIRECTOR
OF THE WINTER GARDENS.

Blackpool Daily Chronicle which in 1925 published a page of cartoons entitled 'Sketches at Blackpool' depicting some of the season's most popular personalities. Prominent on the top row was 'Harry Wood, the genial Musical Director of the Winter Gardens, along with Mrs Hardman, the 'Donkey Woman'; the beach entertainer 'Blind George' with his concertina; 'Doodles' the Tower Circus clown and a trio of 'Sandgrownuns', members of the lifeboat crew.

The relative merits of Blackpool and Douglas as entertainment resorts were discussed – not for the first time - in a piece entitled 'Blackpool versus Douglas: a comparison', which appeared in a Manx newspaper in 1926. Blackpool, with a resident population of 90,000, received as many visitors in one week as Douglas, with a resident population of around 20,000, received in an entire summer season. Although the Lancashire resort could not compete with Douglas and its environs for scenic beauty, its indoor amusements were open all day and were hugely patronised; matinees were not a feature in Douglas except in poor weather. The article conceded that given the overwhelming number of visitors to Blackpool – many of them day trippers - Douglas nevertheless fared well, and was certainly the worthy runner-up, or second best 'watering hole' in the United Kingdom. An important factor common to both Douglas and Blackpool - as opposed to the 'staid and starchy' southern resorts - was that they were both associated in the minds of their mainly northern visitors with 'jolly and carefree holidays'.

The *Keith Prowse Courier* in 1925 acknowledged Harry's role in popularising Blackpool:

> Harry Wood is to Blackpool what Blackpool is to Lancashire - an ever shining bright star in the hearts of thousands. As an exponent of dance music Mr Harry Wood has practically no equal in this country, he knows instinctively what tunes will appeal . . . the musical fare is one of the chief attractions to the town.[7]

However, Harry's tenure as musical director of the Winter Gardens came to an end in 1927, precipitated by a change of management and the possibility that the Dance Festival could be cancelled that year. In the event the *Dancing Times* stepped into the breach and sponsored a slimmed down northern festival with a Fox-trot competition only; the Challenge Shield was not presented. Harry resigned his position and Hermann Darewski took over as musical director, a post he would hold until 1940.

In March Harry received a letter from Jackie Blackburn, an old schoolfriend, saying that she had just heard that he was leaving the Winter Gardens that year:

> You will be missed . . . by the millions who have demanded encores . . . It is a long time since I heard you sing 'Pop goes the Weasel' at the Mechanics School, in dear old Slawit, and John Sugden patted you on the head and said 'Well done Lad'.

Harry's name would now be exclusively associated with Douglas.

The times they are a-changin'

There was pride and joy in June 1919 when the plucky and heroic Steam Packet vessel *Mona's Queen* returned from war duty and recommenced the Liverpool-Douglas service, but alarm in 1921 when the *King Orry* - which had led the German High Seas Fleet into captivity at Scapa Flow in 1918 - ran aground in thick fog in the Mersey off New Brighton in 1921, happily without incurring serious damage or loss of life. In 1923 the SS *Douglas* was not so lucky and sank in the Mersey after colliding with another vessel. The Douglas Detention Camp was finally evacuated March 1919, and the last 175 prisoners were escorted to Peel en route to repatriation in October. In 1923 the Knockaloe estate was purchased for the development of an experimental farm.

Harry's nephew, Lieutenant Frank Hilton Cullerne of The King's Liverpool Regiment, returned to the Island and once again took up his violin to restart, develop and expand his promising career interrupted by war. However, this joyful news was tempered by the deaths within a short space of time of some of Harry's friends and colleagues. F. C. Poulter, perhaps Harry's closest colleague for whom he had enormous respect, died suddenly from a seizure at his home in Douglas on 15th July 1919, barely a week after taking up his baton at the Villa Marina once again. There were many tributes to F. C. Poulter but the brief reminiscence in 'Notes and Notions' by 'Tedimus H' of the *Isle of Man Examiner* seems particularly fitting:

> When I first visited your Island he was pianist at the Pier Pavilion, and his high-class playing was ever a source of pleasure to picture-goers. Then, later, as pianist and conductor of the Villa Marina Orchestra, he performed wonders in keeping up the spirits of the people during the dark days of the war. . . his loss to the Island is a national one.

J. D. Looney, music teacher at Douglas Grammar School, died suddenly on 26th May, 1920. A member of the Manx Music Festival committee for many years, he enjoyed a high reputation as a singing teacher and choir master. His choirs had won major awards in Douglas, Morecambe and Blackpool in 1907. '. . . a great shock to Manx people, and particularly to such of them as are interested in music'.

Fred Buxton, the ebullient entertainer and entrepreneur, died on 14th September that same year, and the acknowledged 'Mother of Manx Music', Miss M. L. Wood, passed away on 4th January, 1925. A highly respected music educator for over 60 years and the founder of the Manx Music Festival, a window was unveiled in her memory in St Matthew's Church.

The keenest loss for Harry personally was G. H. Wood, who died in February 1925. Born in Slaithwaite, West Yorkshire, but no relation to the family of Clement and Sabra Wood, George Wood had for fifty years been secretary, manager and director of the Isle of Man Railway Company. Arguably, the two Yorkshiremen, albeit in totally different spheres, had touched the lives of more people in wholly positive ways than any legislator, politician or churchman of their age.

In 1927 the ties with Harry's youth in Yorkshire were loosened a little more with news of the death of his brother-in-law Francis Henry Griffiths Cullerne, the father of his nephew Hilton, who with his elder sister Mary Hannah, had taken over the Lewisham Hotel after the Wood family moved to the Island. A more severe blow was struck in November with the unexpected death of his younger brother, the flute virtuoso Daniel Wood, in London at the early age of fifty-five. Harry had received an urgent telegram four days earlier informing him that Daniel was seriously ill and asking if he and Adeline would be travelling to London to be with the family, but it is not known if he did.

The Manx Music Festival

The Guild went from strength to strength, unaffected by post-war deprivations. The bass Robert Radford had been unable to participate in the 27th Manx Music Festival in 1918, and his place was taken by the bass Franklin Clive of the Royal College of Music. C. H. Moody, the organist of Ripon Cathedral, conducted Stanford's Irish ballad for chorus and orchestra *Phaudrig Crohoore* with the combined choirs and the new Douglas Amateur Orchestral Society, who also performed Beethoven's *Prometheus Overture* and Elgar's *Pomp & Circumstance March no. 1* directed by J. E. Quayle.

The prize-giving evening during the first peace-time Festival in 1919 was enhanced by the presentation of the Manchester Manx Society medal for services to the Manx people during the war. The warmest applause was reserved for Miss M. L. Wood in recognition of her efforts 'in keeping the home fires burning' in challenging times. The number of entrants reached a very heartening 2,000 in 1920 and 2,252 in 1922 with the inauguration of the Saturday evening Children's Festival Night. Fred Buxton's son, Douglas, made his debut as a tenor that year.

A significant development occurred at the 1923 Festival in April, when the Cleveland Medal donated by the Manx Society of Cleveland, Ohio, was contested for the first time by the winners of the six solo vocal classes. The adjudicator on this occasion was the popular Australian bass-baritone Peter Dawson of world-wide renown, and the worthy winner was the Manx bass Allan Quirk, whom Dawson considered was capable of developing into a great singer.[8]

Away from the Island, Manx choirs continued to enjoy some spectacular successes at other music festivals. In 1924 the Douglas Ladies Choir conducted by Noah Moore won the Dawnay Shield at the London Music Festival and returned to London later that year to make a 'wireless' broadcast in the presence of Queen Mary which was heard by an estimated three million people. In 1925 the same choir won the Wallasey Music Festival, with the Island's Mixed Choir being placed second in their class. That year the Manx Music Festival witnessed a significant rise in the number of entrants with a very healthy 2,913 taking part.

Harry's role in the post-war Festival was far less significant than during the decade before the war, although he continued to support it. The responsibility for providing an orchestra for the Festival Concert passed to his old colleague J. E. Quayle and his Douglas Amateur Orchestral Society, and later during the 1930s to Kathleen Rydings and her Manx Amateur Orchestral Society together with smaller ensembles of professionals from Liverpool and elsewhere.

Unfinished business

One of the most pressing issues in Douglas was a satisfactory resolution of the question of the Palace & Derby Castle musicians' rates of pay. During late 1919 and early 1920, Charles Fox, the manager of the Palace & Derby Castle Company, entered into discussions with the Amalgamated Musicians Union whilst Harry sought information about musicians' rates of pay from other northern theatre managers and musical directors. Despite the perception that 'Isle of Man terms were better than Blackpool',[9] Harry always considered that Isle of Man rates of pay were on the low side, particularly at the Derby Castle and Palace Opera House, and suggested that rates of pay for the Douglas resorts should be in line with theatres in England, but certainly not higher: 'Why on earth should Douglas pay more than the other places?' asked Harry in a letter to Fox.

The final settlement between Charles Fox and the Palace & Derby Castle Company, and the AMU for professional players from England was outlined in a letter dated 2nd February 1920:

> Conductor: £6; Leader: £4 15s; principals or 1st desk players: £4 10s; 2nd desk players: £4 7s 6d.

Sunday performances received an additional 15s for each performance or £1 5s for two performances and a rehearsal. Working hours would be twenty-six and a half hours per week, with a statutory fifteen-minute break between shows if shows were twice nightly. The differentials in pay between English professional musicians and locally engaged musicians, who received a lower rate were preserved, and the Douglas theatres were brought in line with others in the north of England.

We get a further insight into the kind of remunerations Harry himself received from the Company accounts: Harry Wood, Grand Theatre Wages £50 per week, rising to £55 6s 3d in 1929 and £56 in 1930. As the Grand Theatre was part of the Palace & Derby Castle Company, perhaps Harry was sometimes engaged as the musical director for pantomimes or operettas.

Song 'plugging' returns to Douglas

The music publisher Lawrence Wright visited the Isle of Man during July and August 1919, an event recorded by Harry in *Cavalcade*:

> During the war Mr Lawrence Wright served his King and country in the navy. He came to Douglas in 1919 and I saw him at a rehearsal where Miss Florrie Forde was singing, and he wore his naval uniform.

Lawrence Wright, who also wrote popular dance music under the *noms de plume* Horatio Nicholls and Gene Williams, was partly responsible for introducing the 'curse' of song plugging to Douglas. In due course both Wright and Bert Feldman opened a number of music-selling shops, or demonstration stations as Harry refers to them, whose activities created a noise nuisance and were opposed by the traditional music shops; the resultant storm of protest led to a High Court injunction in 1923. Despite the fact that song-plugging shops opened onto the street and frequently held up to a hundred people bawling out the popular songs of the day, the publishers were found 'not guilty' of using their singing halls in Strand Street as unlicensed concert rooms, as the 'entertainment' was a commercial enterprise for the sole purpose of selling sheet music. Needless to say, the music outlets were popular with visitors and, as Harry recorded in *Cavalcade*, 'in this way the "Wright songs" soon became the "Right songs"'.

~

New dances were introduced into the programmes at both the Palace and Derby Castle ballrooms for the season by their respective Masters of Ceremonies, J. B. McEwen and T. W. Dey: the *Dazzle* fox-trot, *Manhattan* one-step and the *Yale* fox-trot; the *Castle* two-step, the *Derby* fox-trot and the Blackpool Winter Gardens Challenge Trophy Dance, *The Festival* two-step.

'Douglas in Revelry for a week' reported the *Isle of Man Times* as 'six days of innocent revelry' got underway for the Douglas Victory Carnival

Week beginning 14th June, 1920. It was hoped that with many attractions on offer the event would encourage visitors to come earlier in the season. Two warships, HMS *Vendetta* and *Verdun*, anchored in Douglas bay; the electric illuminations on promenades were said to be 'indescribably picturesque', with many hotels and boarding houses suitably festooned with flags and bunting. 'Confetti battles' which included 'flinging handfuls of confetti into the face of the first girl you meet' were encouraged by local newspapers; there was a Grand Fancy Dress Parade on the Wednesday in atrocious weather followed by a Fancy Dress Ball at the Palace that evening with the crowds dancing 'elbow to elbow' in the packed ballroom. Feldman's Concert Party presented a burlesque entitled *King 'Orrible*, and Douglas Town Band and the Volunteer Band gave a series of *al fresco* concerts. To complete the festivities there were sporting events with the naval crews taking part, golf tournaments, a mid-week Carnival Dinner and each day at dusk the spectacle of the bay exploding into light with firework displays.

~

Harry had enjoyed a brief brush with the film industry when his small ensemble provided music for the 'silents' at the Gaiety Theatre, Douglas, before the war, and in November 1920 a letter reached him at the Winter Gardens from the Secretary at the Official (Tourists) Information Office of the Isle of Man:

> My Board will shortly release a number of copies of a new Manx Scenic film, and it has been suggested that Manx music be sent along with these, a preference having been made in favour of your orchestral settings to Manx National and other songs, played, I believe, at the Palace during the past summer.

The 'orchestral settings' in question were of traditional songs from *Manx National Songs* that Harry had earlier arranged under the name *The Cushag*. The letter continued:

> If you have this music in volume form, (ie sets of performing parts) or at all convenient for the orchestras usually found in picture theatres, I should be glad if you could let me have 25 copies, or sets, as the case may be.

As *The Cushag* existed only in manuscript Harry went to the trouble of ascertaining the costs of producing sets of performing parts, but four days later he received the disappointing news that, as *Cushag* had not yet been published, and that copying the performing material would take several weeks, the Board had reluctantly decided to look elsewhere.

Here we are! Here we are! Here we are again!!![10]

Florrie Forde was the first big variety star to appear in Douglas after the war for a three-week engagement in July and August 1919:

> . . . perhaps the most popular personality the past twenty years of music hall has produced. Time cannot stale nor custom wither her infinite variety, nor can any reasoning account for her phenomenal success.

She had been appearing at the Derby Castle the week war was declared, and here she was five years later at the Palace for Glasgow Fair week 'as sonsie and buxom as ever'. Some variety stars from the heyday of music hall continued to appear in Douglas immediately after the war: Wilkie Bard, Little Tich and Hetty King, but only Florrie continued to appear season after season between the wars; her relationship with the Isle of Man, its people and its visitors was special and unique.

In the years immediately after the war she continued to sing wartime favourites such as *Pack Up Your Troubles* and *Mademoiselle from Armentieres*, but she gradually let go of her 'Kelly' songs and introduced new songs with contemporary themes, such as *Hold My Hand I've Got The Wind Up* about a young girl taking her first flight, which mirrored her own experience of a flight she made from Douglas beach during her stay. The instant success of *Yes! We Have No Bananas* in 1923 prompted a competition at the Derby Castle for the best performance of the chorus. The competition was so popular that it became a regular feature of her Douglas seasons. The competition song in 1925 was perhaps the silliest song she ever performed: *A n'egg, some n'ham and a n'onion*.

Whilst the newspapers devoted many column inches to her extravagant dresses and hats, they also paid tribute to her great endeavours on behalf of her favourite Manx charities, notably her annual charity fete inaugurated in 1924 when, at her own expense, she organised stalls in the Palace grounds selling all manner of items to raise money for the Lifeboat Institution, Noble's Hospital and the Isle of Man Children's Home. What the *Isle of Man Examiner* referred to as 'Miss Florrie Forde's Act of Grace' occurred in 1927 when she erected a white memorial tablet in Kirk Patrick Churchyard over the grave of an 'Unknown British Sailor' washed ashore near Peel in 1918, inscribed with the words:

'Some Mother's Son'.
Erected by Florrie Forde, 1927.

She visited the grave every year leaving a bouquet of red and white roses, and installed a collection box at the gate to take care of the maintenance of the site.

Only one item of correspondence between Florrie Forde and Harry Wood has survived in the shape of a brief note posted a few days before Scotch Week, 1930:

> Dear Harry Wood
> All being well will be with you on Monday morning. Please let me know to the Castle Mona the times of rehearsal.
> Sal and obbli
> Yours sincerely
> Florrie Forde

Harry and Florrie in the Palace grounds during the 1920s.

Florrie continued to wield her spell throughout the 1930s with songs such as *I'm Fair, Fat and Forty* and *Riding the Range in the Sky*, and so large were the crowds attempting to hear her that she was granted the honour of performing in the Derby Castle Ballroom rather than the smaller variety theatre. In 1934 7,000 fans joined in the choruses and she seemed overwhelmed by her reception: 'I never have happier times anywhere than in the dear little Isle of Man', she once confided to an *Isle of Man Examiner* reporter.

Throughout her career Florrie was one of the Island's most loyal ambassadors and lost no opportunity to extol its many virtues and defend it against its critics. In 1938 a letter campaign in the *Isle of Man Examiner* to have the Freedom of the Borough of Douglas conferred on her began to gather pace. After all, argued her admirers, had she not done as much for Douglas as Gracie Fields had achieved for Rochdale? Inexplicably, the Town Council rejected the idea; thus not for the first time the Island had missed an opportunity to give and receive honour.

~

Florrie Forde was by any measure the best-loved variety artiste ever to appear in Douglas, but others followed in her wake including Wilkie Bard, part jester and part clown, whose thumbnail sketches of everyday life continued to appeal to both 'the highbrow and the man from Owdham'. His 'mini-plays' were likened by some to Dickens and Kipling, and were a far cry from the crude horseplay and manic knockabout antics of Nervo and Knox or the simple slapstick routines of Norton and Gold. Cruickshank, 'the Fool of the Family' returned in 1919, 1920 and 1923, and perched on a high stool dressed in a costume redolent of the commedia del'arte, entertained the crowds with such songs as *The Old Brass Bottle*. A taste for American-style popular songs such as *I Want to be in Dixie* characterised the act of Jen Latona, although she was frequently asked to sing the saucy *Everybody's Doin' it at the Seaside*. The veteran of two Royal Command performances, Harry Weldon, appeared at the Derby Castle in 1920 and 1922 with his famous football match sketch *Stiffy the Goalkeeper*, and his much imitated assumed speech impediment consisting of a long whistle before the letter 'S' as in 'Sno use'.

Among the supporting acts the ventriloquist Arthur Prince and his Jolly Jack Tar companion, Sailor Jim, appeared on stage dressed as an Admiral to the accompaniment of his signature tune *A Life on the Ocean Wave*, and amazed audiences with his trade-mark feat of drinking a glass of beer at the same time as conversing with Jim. The musical novelty duo Moss and Maachah, 'Gypsy Violinist and Danseuse', appeared in exotic outfits whilst the more soberly dressed young Manx Davina Trio (soprano, 'cello and piano) delighted audiences with their blend of ballads, Manx songs and light classical favourites.

Illusionists such as the Violas and their 'Mental Mysteries' appeared on the same bill as bizarre novelty acts such as Norman Osborne's 'Ventriloquial Fishing Scena', Griff, the 'Soap Bubble Juggler' and Marcelle and Partner, a sea-lion act billed as 'almost human'. Hoop manipulators, a comedy bric-a-brac act, Czech dancers, American whirlwind cycling troupes and concert parties all vied with each other to please the crowds in those first anxious years after the war.

~

Some of the best-known songs of those years came from American-born Ella Shields, who was habitually greeted by a storm of applause as she appeared on stage dressed immaculately as 'a man about town' singing her 'swell' song *I'm Burlington Bertie from Bow*, the wartime hit *Oh! It's a Lovely War* and *If You Knew Susie*. In 1923 she sang a new song with local appeal, *I've Been Over to the Isle of Man*, and the *Mona's Herald* wrote that along with Vesta Tilley and Hetty King, she was '. . a good

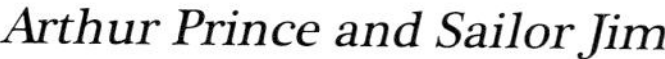

Arthur Prince and Sailor Jim

Cruikshank.

representation of that species of man known as 'the dude.' Hetty King herself appeared at the Villa Marina in 1923 together with her bright and breezy songs such as *Ship Ahoy* and the patriotic *There's a Ship That's Bound for Blighty*. Since the retirement of Vesta Tilley - now Lady de Frece - she could reasonably claim to be the world's greatest male impersonator.

Nellie Wallace, 'The star with lack of star quality', first appeared at the Palace in 1921. With a nose like Mr Punch, a receding chin and prominent teeth, she couldn't compete with the more glamorous stars of the era and instead developed her own brand of eccentric comedy. Her familiar prop was a mangy stole which she referred to as 'me bit of vermin', and her mildly-risqué catch-phrases 'Ridicu'larse' and 'Tretcher-arse' could soon be heard around the town. The equally eccentric Little Tich returned to Douglas in 1921 and made his last appearance there at the Palace Coliseum the following year. Although he no longer performed his crippling 'big boot' dance, his audiences still roared with laughter when his face hit the stage when taking a bow.

Scottish new-comer Will Fyffe first appeared in Douglas in 1922. Plump, and with a twinkle in his eye, he was a superb character-actor; his impersonations of a doctor, railway guard or most memorably a drunken Scotsman singing *I Belong to Glasgow*, the song rejected by Harry Lauder that made his name, Fyffe could just as easily switch to a sentimental ballad that would move his audience to tears. He returned to Douglas in the 1930s and was ultimately saluted as a comic genius. Another Scottish comedian, Neil Kenyon, had bravely appeared in Douglas in September 1914 when most variety artistes had already cancelled their engagements. His stories and monologues in the broadest Scottish dialect imaginable including *The Postie of Dunrobin*, and his much-requested song *Simple Sandy* endeared him to all who heard him.

~

Another variety star who was almost as well known for her costumes as Florrie Forde, was Lily Morris, the bouncy comedienne with a huge national and international reputation. She appeared at the Palace and Derby Castle in 1924, 1926 and 1927 with her best-known songs *Don't Have Any More, Mrs Moore* and *Why am I always the Bridesmaid, Never the Blushing Bride*? Her songs were considered to be 'of the rougher type' and her act a throw-back to the music hall. Dan Leno Jnr appeared at the Palace in 1925 with *Whatever Happened to the Manx Cat's Tail*, but could only 'strive to emulate his famous father'.

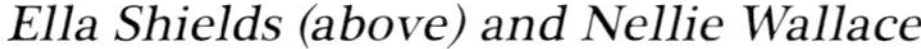

Ella Shields (above) and Nellie Wallace.

One of the most memorable acts to appear in Douglas was Datas 'The World's Greatest Memory Man' (real name William Bottle) who astonished audiences at the Palace in 1925 with prodigious feats of memory and his catch-phrase 'Am I right, sir?'. He maintained that he could answer any question put to him by a member of the audience, a claim Manx journalist Arthur Q. Moore was able to confirm after attending one of his performances in London. Moore was amazed when Datas was able to name the first Isle of Man Steam Packet Company vessel and its launch date, (it was *Mona's Isle*, 30th June, 1830) and truly astonished when the entertainer proceeded to name all the Company's vessels up to that time. When asked how he had acquired such arcane knowledge, Datas replied that when sailing to the Island for his many engagements he used to pass the time studying the Steam Packet brochures and timetables.

Many more acts are forgotten today and one would like to know more about 'The Tossing Testros', Sydney Swain and the Electric Sparks, The Mizumo Troupe, 'Like wise men from the east they came' and Cornalla and Eddie in their 'screaming burlesque' Toss 'em and miss 'em. The name of Dorothy Ward, 'The Queen of Song', however, lives on through her songs *Take Me Back to Dear Old Blighty* and *That Wonderful Mother of Mine*, which opens with the following affecting lines:

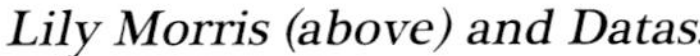

Lily Morris (above) and Datas.

The moon never beams without bringing me dreams
Of that wonderful mother of mine.

The passing of an old friend.

The hope that the first season after the war at the Palace might equal the triumphs of the immediate pre-war seasons were dashed abruptly in the early hours of Tuesday 13th July 1920 when a 'devastating demon fire' broke out in the area of the band room. A local 'bobby' on a cycle patrol near Onchan Head was the first person to witness a rapidly growing 'flare in the sky' and to raise the alarm at around 3.15am. The fire brigade arrived at the Palace between 3.30 and 4.00am by which time the fire had taken hold 'and burned fiercely with flames leaping hundreds of feet into the air'. Tons of glass fell and shattered on the ballroom floor and residents of the nearby Palace View Terrace were instructed to move some of their possessions into the street.

The manager Charles Fox and the his assistant manager Arthur Brittain arrived at the scene just as it became clear that the ballroom could not be saved, and the efforts of the emergency services were being re-directed to saving the Palace Coliseum and Opera House, which was largely achieved after several tense hours. There was happily no loss of life or injury, but Marcelles the performing sea lion, who had been sleeping in the Coliseum dressing room, was peremptorily dragged to safety by his keeper. Some of the personal possessions of those artistes currently appearing at the Palace were lost, together with a quantity of music and all of the instruments belonging to the members of Harry's orchestra left in the band room overnight.

An emergency meeting of the directors was called later that morning and they voted to erect a large wooden platform for dancing in the Palace grounds as soon as possible. Dancing and dance competitions recommenced on 19th July, which to an extent rescued the season from disaster. Even the weather was kind and settled and as Harry noted in *Cavalcade*, the *al fresco* dance floor 'was crowded nightly by the visitors'.

It was two weeks before the debris was removed from the site and all that was left standing was the southern gable end and brick walls; the Coliseum suffered some slight water damage. The overall cost of the fire was estimated at £50,000 and although some loss of revenue was inevitable, the fear that the other venues would become too congested to be able to operate comfortably and safely with the Lancashire wakes weeks and the Glasgow holidays imminent, did not materialise. The Palace Ballroom, the 'largest and most popular amusement resort in Manxland', was the one entertainment facility Douglas could ill-afford to lose at this time, but it was quickly announced that a new Palace Ballroom would rise from the ashes in time for the 1921 season; and so it proved to be.

In the meantime the Company continued to expand and flourish and in November added the Grand Theatre and Buxton's Pierrot Village on the Central Promenade to its portfolio of entertainment venues in Douglas. Ironically the *Mona's Herald*, reporting on the 'enormous crowds' at the Palace a mere two days before the fire, was reflecting that 'it is a great pity that the places of amusement are not capable of expansion'. Among the many messages of support was one from King George V who was visiting the Island with Queen Mary that week, and 'expressed his sympathy with the people of Douglas and the Company in the loss sustained by the disastrous fire'.

Harry's Palace Orchestra was heard at a series of popular *al fresco* promenade concerts every Sunday afternoon throughout the season in 'the charming grounds under the shady trees'. At the Sunday Sacred Concert on 5th July, Harry's best known and most popular orchestral work, *The Cushag*, based on his selection of traditional Manx melodies, was first given in its full orchestral version. The *Isle of Man Times* wrote the following appreciation:

> Mr Harry Wood has done much to popularise himself in the opinion of the little Manx nation, and he must be quite the best known

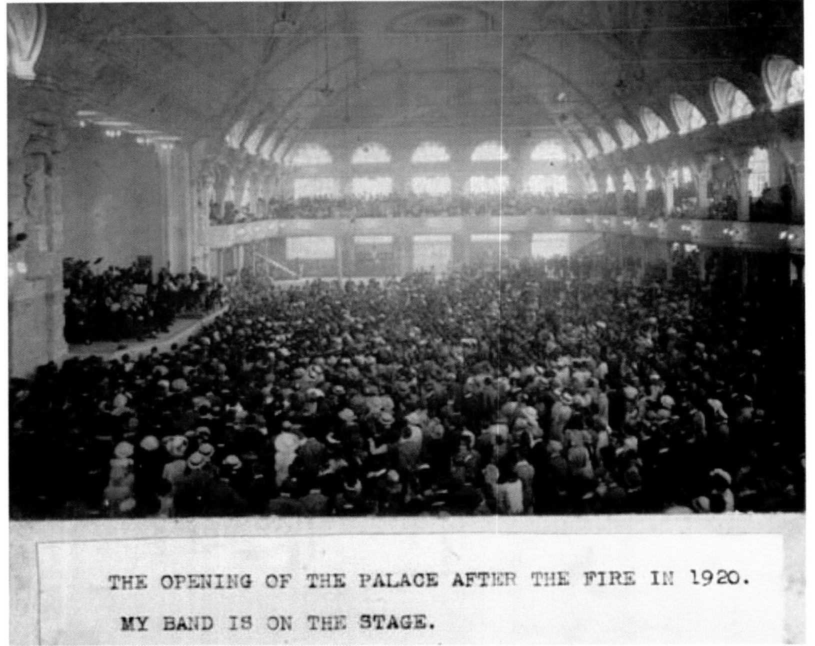
THE OPENING OF THE PALACE AFTER THE FIRE IN 1920.
MY BAND IS ON THE STAGE.

> figure in Manx musical circles. That being so, local music lovers are bound to appreciate the selection, The Cushag, which Mr Wood has arranged for full orchestra . . . it is hoped that the Manx people will make a special effort to be present to listen to their native airs rendered by what is undoubtedly one of the finest orchestras in the kingdom.

Harry conducted *The Cushag* again at the Manx Celtic Concert at the Palace Coliseum on Sunday, 19th June, 1927, as part of the celebrations surrounding the first Manx Homecoming organised by the World Manx Association, and still referred to as The Great Homecoming.[11] Three hundred visitors arrived from Canada and America, some Manx born, others of Manx descent, many of whom had never seen the Island before. They attended many receptions both large and small all over the Island, most notably the Tynwald Day Fair, a gathering at the Nunnery and a gala in the Villa Marina Gardens. There was music and impromptu concerts wherever the visitors went, but the concert at the Palace Coliseum, organised by Harry himself, was the largest and most prestigious and featured 'Manx Vocalists, Manx Music and Songs'. It included two compositions specially written and adapted for the occasion: John Edward

Quayle's Fantasy-overture *Mannin*, a fine tone poem based on two traditional Manx melodies, and Harry's newest arrangement of *The Cushag* which now included four vocal soloists and choir.

The very full programme also included two shorter orchestral pieces by J. E. Quayle, John Foulds' *Keltic Suite* with its haunting Celtic Lament, and Harry's Regimental *March of the Manx Volunteer Corps* with four traditional Manx melodies woven into the texture. Haydn Wood's stirring song *A Health to All Who Cross the Main* for baritone, choir and orchestra conducted by Haydn himself provided a rousing and moving finale. The visit of the Homecomers had been marked by high emotion and a great outpouring of warmth from the Islanders, summed up in the final words of the song:

A Health to all who cross the Main;
And if you love us - come again.

Harry's work has seldom been performed complete since the 1920s. However, selections taken from *The Cushag* appeared on many occasions in the programmes of the Douglas Amateur Orchestral Society and its successor The Manx Amateur Orchestral Society up to the late 1950s. In September Harry had the pleasure of conducting the premier of another of his shorter orchestral works, the march *The Sergeant Major's Parade*, at a Garden Party in the grounds of Noble's Hospital.

The White Palace

The new Palace, known locally as 'The White Palace' and increasingly as 'The Palace Lido', was officially opened at a grand ceremony on 18th July, 1921, one year and two days after the fire that had destroyed the old Palace the previous season. Eight thousand invited guests were present including a number of local dignitaries, the Attorney-General, the Vicar-General, the architect, company directors, Florrie Forde and Bert Feldman. The ballroom looked magnificent with its 'splendid decorations, chaste and beautiful design and comely accessories' and with a larger lower promenade and more spacious upper gallery was generally considered to be 'even more resplendent' than the old Palace. Indeed, 'without equal in the land'.

John A. Brown, the Chairman of the Directors, introduced the Lieutenant Governor Major-General Sir William Fry who recalled the deep sympathy expressed by His Majesty the King for the loss of the Palace Ballroom the previous year, and reminded everyone of His Majesty's consoling message, the main thrust of which was His Majesty's fanciful belief that the Island had been:

> ... laid out by Nature as the pleasure ground for Lancashire ... In this Island you get the fresh air, beauty of scenery, sea breezes and all that the dwellers in the towns of Lancashire require for their annual holidays; and it is up to you people here to provide the people of Lancashire with what they require in the way of entertainment.

Ada Mylchreest, the Manx contralto.

These sentiments were doubtless well meant and the Governor won enthusiastic applause for repeating them. The implication that the Island existed mainly to provide entertainment for the fun-starved working classes of the industrial north of England apparently went unnoticed. When the official business of the day concluded, there followed a short celebratory concert, the highlight of which was the appearance of Ada Mylchreest, the eminent Manx contralto, who sang *Land of Hope and Glory* and *God Save the King* accompanied by Harry's orchestra. The evening ended with two dance demonstrations by the Palace Master of Ceremonies, the 'elegant' J. B. McEwen: the new vocal dance *Amazon*, and the *Highland Fling* with McEwen attired in full highland dress.

Non-stop dancing at the Palace

In order to facilitate the smooth running of the dance programmes at the Palace and Derby Castle whilst Harry was engaged in Blackpool for part of each week, the Company engaged a number of deputy conductors, including his nephew Hilton, during the summer of 1922 before he took up his engagement on the trans-Atlantic liner RMS *Laconia*.

In 1923, the Palace advertised an innovative new concept, one that was perfectly in tune with the spirit of the times and would change the nature of dancing and the orchestras or bands forever: 'Two Bands, one syncopated, one conventional, 40 dances, non-stop dancing from 7.30 –

11.00'. Two bands were placed on opposite sides of the ballroom, the Palace Orchestra conducted by Harold Jones alternating with J. A. Leigh's Popular Jazz Band. In fact there were three resident bands as Leon Moore's Syncopated Orchestra provided more strenuous fare for the young and energetic in the 'new and cosy' Hall of Jazz. The roaring twenties had arrived in Douglas and the town was caught fast in the grip of an unprecedented dance craze. By 1923 Douglas was dancing to a different beat than it had in 1913.

In 1926 Charles Fox, his perceptive ear always to the ground, ruefully observed these changes of fashion and observed that 'dancing has become more akin to walking or running, and (is) much less graceful than (in) former times. Even the waltz, the foundation of all real dancing, and now known as the modern waltz, has altered in method and tempo'. As for the schottische, polka, the lancers and the barn dance, they were as 'extinct as the dodo', displaced in people's affections by the 'all-conquering fox-trot, the one-step and the tango'.[12] New dances seemed to appear in Douglas every season: the Paso Doble in 1926 and the following year the Charleston and the Black Bottom. Writing in 1932 Arthur Q. Moore (*Fifty Years of Manx Amusements*, a series of articles in the *Mona's Herald*), reflected on what he perceived was the increasing lack of variety in the dance programmes of the 1920s. Compared with the older dances which could be easily learned, 'modern steps are complicated to all but the most expert dancers' and he doubted that many in Douglas possessed 'the American sense of rhythm' or were 'blessed with the Latin temperament'.

Reflecting on the new-style, quick-fire dance programmes with up to forty dances in three hours, Charles Fox wrote: 'one third of that number would have sufficed in the old days. Fox estimated that over 500 new dance tunes were being 'manufactured' each week at this period. Before the war the dances were fewer and longer, but the music was distinctly better'. Nor was Fox a devotee of the 'discordant noise' of the popular traditional jazz bands and charted their waning influence as they transformed themselves from 'Jazz' to 'Syncopated' and from 'Syncopated' to 'Symphonic'.

In 1923, Harry Wood's Orchestra featured on the logo at the top of an *Isle of Man Times* Derby Castle advertisement and the following year was billed as 'Harry Wood's Melodic Syncopators' in an evening of non-stop dances and a Felix Walk novelty dance competition. By 1927 J. A. Leigh's Syncopated Five had become the Syncopated Seven, the London Syncopated Five appeared at the Villa Marina and Harry Wood's orchestra of twenty-three performers was billed as 'The Best and Biggest Symphonic Band in Great Britain', although it would be some years before saxophones, banjos and sousaphones would appear in his bands. Douglas may not have been in the forefront of the new craze for dancing, but nor was it trailing in the wake of the new trends, and a measure of the popularity of dancing in Douglas was the opening of a new dance venue, the Palais de Danse, by the Strand Cinema Company in 1927, which featured Jack Kerr's Continental Band. Apparently modelled on the leading London dance halls, it was hoped that the new venue would prove to be a fashionable rendezvous, brightening Douglas' winter months.

'Syncopated Dance Music on the Sabbath'.

It was not only those directly involved in the entertainment business that raised questioning voices in the face of the relentless chugging rhythms of the new dance music. 'Are we becoming less religious?' This was the question posed by the *Mona's Herald* in its review of a Sunday concert at the Palace in August 1925, when the familiar, comfortable ambience of these popular events was apparently shattered by a 'daring experiment', namely the appearance of Jack Hylton's Band playing the 'latest rag-bob of dance music . . . not the pleasantest surprise for a large proportion of normal Sunday concert-goers'.

According to the reviewer a few people showed their antipathy and left the ballroom whilst others 'looked dubious . . . obviously debating in their hearts whether it was "right" or not'. Strict Sunday observance, 'when no music other than sacred was permitted in the home' was on the wane, but nevertheless:

> . . . the majority of the older generation of Manxmen . . . had inherited a deep-rooted religious faith that sat four-square against any innovation which threatened to infringe on the sanctity of the Sabbath . . . the day to be guarded jealously against intrusion by everyday affairs.

The contention that the moral dilemma expressed in the review was the result of a chance conversation with 'a white-haired old man, living in a quiet backwater of the Island' sounds contrived; the more so when the elderly Manxman reportedly 'shook his head as if weary' and with an inexpressible sadness in his voice said: "they can't even leave Sunday alone nowadays . . ."

The audience, however, was thrilled by the band, including a clergyman and his wife who 'applauded every item until they must have been weary', especially their performance of the *Toy Drum Major*, for which the band wore toy helmets, and an arrangement of *I Gonna Bring a Water Melon* in the styles of Wagner and Edward German. When the reviewer eventually got round to discussing the concert, he was full of praise for Harry's orchestra and their performances of Dvorak's overture *Carnival* and Tchaikovsky's *Capriccio Italien*, both colourful and challenging orchestral showpieces; he had nothing to say about Stiles-Allen's performance of Weber's great scena, *Ocean, Thou Mighty Monster*, baritone Horace Stevens' rousing *Arm, Arm ye Brave* from Handel's *Judas Maccabeus* or the encore, the charming donkey duet *Trot Here, Trot There* (*De Ci, De Là*) from Messager's delightful operetta *Veronique*.

Famous Conductor in adventure at sea.

In September 1922 Harry and a companion were involved in a bizarre adventure at sea with potentially disastrous consequences. The story appeared in the *Ramsey Courier* a few days after the events unfolded:

> Mr Harry Wood, conductor of the Empress Ballroom Orchestra at the Blackpool Winter Gardens, saw his nephew Hilton Cullerne off to New York at the start of an Atlantic crossing on the new Cunard liner *Laconia*.

Hilton had been appointed principal conductor of the ship's orchestra, and Harry was part of a small send-off party unfortunately still on board the RMS *Laconia* when she sailed. The sea was 'rough and choppy', and the group was compelled to remain on board and return with the pilot after the liner had got beyond the Mersey Bar. The sixty-year-old Harry and a companion had to climb down a rope ladder, swinging alarmingly over a 'black and angry sea', but eventually made it into the small row boat, very wet and shaken. However, the pilot still couldn't pull away as they had left their umbrellas on board! Harry was given a reviving glass of whisky and eventually disembarked at the New Brighton landing stage after a delay of seven hours, just in time to catch the last train to Liverpool.

The Golden Age of the Orchestral Concerts

Just as the repertoire for the dance programmes became infused with colourful and exotic new fashions, Harry enlivened and refreshed the repertoire for the classical afternoon concerts and the Sunday Sacred Concerts. Harry's experience in Blackpool, where the concert or 'classical' programmes were far more extensive and wide-ranging, provided the

Harry's nephew, Hilton Cullerne (violin).

impetus for a complete review of the concert selections in Douglas, a significant feature of which was the inclusion of more challenging classical overtures and concert pieces.

Whilst popular light overtures such as Suppe's *The Jolly Brigands* and Offenbach's *Orpheus in the Underworld*, and marches and march medleys such as Hubert Bath's *Admirals All* and Aubrey Winter's *Martial Moments* - which featured no less than twenty-one popular military march tunes - continued to appear on concert programmes, Harry increasingly introduced challenging works from the standard orchestral repertoire, such as Dvorak's *Carnival* overture, Liszt's *Les Preludes* and Wagner's *The Ride of the Valkyries*, which reflected well on the quality of his orchestra. These mainstays of the classical repertoire rubbed shoulders with comparative rarities such as the overtures to Rossini's *Tancredi*, Lortzing's *Der Wildschütz* and Mendelssohn's concert overture *The Fair Melusine*. There were selections from Sullivan, Offenbach *et al*, and from wartime hit shows such as *Chu Chin Chow*, and Harry included music from the world of Grand Opera and *verissimo* such as Meyerbeer's *Dinorah* and Puccini's *Madame Butterfly*.

Whenever possible, Harry introduced pieces by Haydn Wood and occasionally Daniel, and Manx pieces by local composers such as J. E.

Quayle and George Tootell, such as the latter's charming *Manx Scenes: Crag and Sea*, *At the Trysting Place* and *A Manx Wedding*.[13] Of course there were occasional hiccups, as Harry relates in *Cavalcade*, although it did provide him with the opportunity to introduce a faux-Manx tune into his concerts:

> Owing to difficulties with the Performing Rights Society I was unable to play Delibes' Pizzicato from the ballet Sylvia. So I turned this beautifly (*sic*) measure 'upside down' and entitled it: A Sprightly Measure or Tapplyn Jiargey (The Red Cap . . . The Lil' Fella). This is a Manx title.

Harry's career was gradually overshadowed and eventually overtaken by the burgeoning career of his brother Haydn. The popularity of the iconic First World War song *Roses of Picardy* secured Haydn's financial future, but from the 1920s he became increasingly highly regarded as the composer of several attractive, melodious and beautifully-crafted light classical orchestral pieces inspired by the Island and its rich store of traditional melodies.

Between 1919 and 1927 Harry introduced a number of Haydn's orchestral works into his programmes: the rumbustious *May-Day* overture; the suite *Harvest Time*; the suite *Three Famous Pictures* and a musical jest, the *Variations on a Once-popular Humorous Song*, a whimsical piece based on the old music hall song *If You Want to Know the Time, Ask a P'liceman*. Intermingled with these fine works were trifles including *entr'actes* from some of the shows Haydn was engaged in writing at this period, ballroom dances derived from his famous songs and an arrangement of *Roses of Picardy* for a musical saw!

Sunday Concerts in the Palace Coliseum

A measure of the quality of the concert singers who appeared in Douglas between the wars can be gauged by examining the list of the sixteen great singers who took part in the first performance of Vaughan Williams' Serenade to Music at the Royal Albert Hall in October 1938. Nine were familiar to Douglas audiences: Isobel Baillie, Lilian Stiles-Allen, Eva Turner and Elsie Suddaby among the sopranos; Margaret Balfour, Astra Desmond and Muriel Brunskill, contraltos; the tenor Walter Widdup and the bass Norman Allin. As time went on some of the fine singers who had appeared in Douglas before the war were engaged again: the mezzo-soprano Louise Kirkby-Lunn, the contralto Phyllis Lett, the tenors

Guiseppe Lenghi-Cellini, Ben Davies and John Coates, the baritones Charles Tree and Kennerley-Rumford and the bass Robert Radford. Lenghi-Cellini was a notable Duke in Verdi's *Rigoletto*, whilst John Coates was a leading English tenor, a popular figure at many regional music festivals, and equally at home in opera, oratorio and on the concert stage.

The first Sunday Concert after the war took place at the Palace Coliseum on Whit Sunday 3rd June 1919 and set the tone for the wonderful concerts to come. The contralto Dilys Jones sang the aria *Che Faro* from Gluck's *Orfeo*; the Yorkshire tenor Henry Brearley sang the ever-popular *Where'er You Walk* from Handel's *Semele*, and the popular Scottish bass J. H. Scotland sang an aria by Handel and *Old Barty*, the whimsical tale about a colourful, old, village church odd-job man. Harry's orchestra played Ansell's nautical-medley overture *Plymouth Hoe* and a selection from *The Gondoliers*.

The Canadian operatic soprano Pauline Donalda appeared at the Palace Coliseum in August 1919 together with the bass Robert Radford. Considered by many to be the natural successor of Albani, she excelled in roles from Massenet, Gounod and Puccini. The contralto Astra Desmond, the veteran of countless *Messiahs*, who had sung the part of the Angel in Elgar's The *Dream of Gerontius* under the composer's baton, became a Douglas favourite following her first appearance in 1920.

In the midst of the excellent programmes at the Palace, the rival Villa Marina pulled off a distinct coup with the engagement of Dame Clara Butt for two appearances in August 1924 together with a concert party of five singers and instrumentalists including her husband, the baritone Bertie Kennerley Rumford. The *Isle of Man Examiner* called the occasion another 'red letter day in the history of concert-giving in the Isle of Man' and referred to Butt's 'unique personality and abnormal voice' thereby adding to the thousands of column inches devoted to her in the world's press. The Marina was barely two-thirds full for her opening night, the consequence of the vastly inflated ticket prices, but she was encored several times after she sang the moving hymn *Abide With Me*. Her second appearance was well attended, and at the end she signed autographs at 2s 6d each with the proceeds going to the Three Arts Women's Employment Fund.

Mignons, Margueritas and Mimis

Among the most popular singers who appeared in Douglas was Muriel Brunskill, who appeared frequently at the Three Choirs, Handel,

The sopranos Isobel Baillie and Lilian Stiles-Allen.

Norwich and Leeds Festivals and was recognised as a fine interpreter of Bach; Margaret Balfour, another renowned Angel in Elgar's *Gerontius*; the sopranos Lilian Stiles-Allen, whose physique was not suited to the opera house but who performed widely on the concert stage in such works as Delius' *Mass of Life* and Schoenberg's *Gurre-Lieder*, and Carrie Tubb, who had appeared at the first Douglas Amateur Orchestral Society concert in November 1918.

A dramatic soprano with a huge international reputation, a magnetic stage presence and one of the most powerful voices ever heard in Douglas, the Australian Elsa Stralia looked every inch the prima donna. Florence Austral, the celebrated Wagnerian soprano, was considered by Melba to possess 'one of the wonder voices of the world'; the steely power of her high notes must have penetrated every square inch of the Palace Coliseum. Clara Serena, tall and graceful in stature, and another fine dramatic contralto from 'down under', appeared in May 1923, and subsequently in the 1924, 1925 and 1927 seasons. In arias and scenas by Rossini, Meyerbeer and Verdi her voice was described as 'gloriously full and pure', her interpretations 'superb' and the delicacy of expression, 'flawless'.

In 1925 the huge voice of the Russian prima-donna Tatiana Makushina soared over the Palace Ballroom in *Elizabeth's Greeting* from Wagner's

Tannhäuser, but was held in reserve during Vuillermoz' exquisite *Jardin d'Amore* and an aria from *Carmen*. She then utterly charmed the audience with two English nursery rhymes, *Dr Foster* and *Mary Had a Little Lamb*, set whimsically in the style of Handel.

'Never Sing Louder Than Lovely'[14]

In great contrast to these heavy-weights, four English sopranos quickly became Douglas favourites following their debuts. Elsie Suddaby, the leading British lyric soprano between the wars, was affectionately known as 'The Lass with the Delicate Air' (from the title of Michael Arne's song of 1762). The *Isle of Man Examiner* painted a delightful picture of her at the Palace Coliseum in 1923 as 'a very sweet, dainty, and charmingly child-like, young soprano' with a voice that 'soars away and loses itself in the blue as beautifully as any lark's'. In a long and distinguished career Bella (later Isobel) Baillie, the well-loved Scottish soprano, renowned in opera, oratorio, lieder and especially English music, reputedly sang *Messiah* over 1000 times, including twenty-six performances with the Halle Orchestra and thirty-three with the Royal Choral Society at the

The lyric soprano Elsie Suddaby.

Royal Albert Hall. Dora Labbette, unforgettable as Mimi in Puccini's *La Boheme*, a fine Juliette in Gounod's opera and enchanting in Debussy's *Pelléas and Mélisande*, appeared regularly at the Villa Marina Sunday concerts throughout the 1920s and '30s. Reviewers were bewitched by her diminutive poise and charmed by the purity and youthfulness of her voice. The Parisian-born English coloratura soprano Mignon Nevada appeared in Douglas in August 1935; her light, agile voice made her utterly beguiling in the title roles in Thomas' *Mignon* and Delibes' *Lakmé*.

Siegfrieds, Nemorinos and Rudolfos

The years between the two world wars were exceptionally rich in tenors. Guiseppe Lenghi-Cellini was a frequent visitor to the Palace Coliseum and sang many of the best-loved arias in the repertoire: The *Flower Song* from Bizet's *Carmen*, *Una furtiva lagrima* from Donizetti's *Elisir d'Amore*, *M'appari tutto amor* from Flotow's *Marta* - said to be Caruso's favourite aria. Lenghi-Cellini always included favourite songs and ballads such as Haydn Wood's *Fleurette* and Dvorak's *Songs My Mother Taught Me* in his programmes. The Welsh tenor Ben Davies was peerless in Handel and sang the sublime recitative and aria *Deeper and deeper still/ Waft her, Angels* from *Jephtha* at a Sunday concert in August 1920. Another Welsh tenor, Tudor Davies, was engaged in August 1923 as 'the new Welsh tenor' on the strength of his appearance as Rudolfo opposite Dame Nellie Melba's Mimi in the famous Covent Garden *La Boheme* of 1922. Harry assembled an augmented orchestra of forty players for this concert.

Lauritz Melchior.

Lauritz Melchior, the great Danish quintessential Wagnerian Heldentenor from the 1920s until the 1950s, performed only once in Douglas at a Sunday concert at the Palace in August 1923. He sang the *Prize Song* from *The Mastersingers*,

Ujarak's Leaving from Hakon Børresen's opera *Kaddara*, (a story set in Greenland with, uniquely I should imagine, a cast of Eskimos) Ireland's evocative song *Sea Fever* and Frank Bridge's *Love Went-a-Riding*. The orchestral pieces were also impressive: music from *Lohengrin* and *Tannhäuser*, and the ballet from Meyerbeer's *Le Prophète*. Frank Mullins, 'The English Wagnerian' and a member of the Beecham Opera Company, sang the *Prize Song* from *The Mastersingers* in August 1920, in a strenuous programme which opened with Harry and his orchestra playing the *Tannhäuser* overture and included the soprano Carrie Tubb singing Weber's great scena from *Oberon*, *Ocean! Thou Mighty Monster*.

The voice of John Coates was not as large as those of the Wagnerians, but nevertheless his repertoire ranged from Purcell and Bach to Wagner and he overcame his limitations with a combination of a striking stage presence and flexible vocal expression. In August 1919 he sang an aria that could have been tailor-made for him, *Onaway! Awake, Beloved!* from Coleridge-Taylor's *Hiawatha*, and songs by Elgar, Frank Bridge, Ireland and Edward German.

Mephistos, Figaros and Wotans

At the age of thirty, the bass Norman Allin was one of the up-and-coming singers whose careers had been interrupted by World War I. He was best-known to British audiences for his performances in oratorio, most notably *Messiah*. At his fourth appearance at the Sunday concert series in September 1923 he was acclaimed as England's foremost bass, with a voice that was 'magnificently solid, strong, deep and true'. Robert Radford, another Beecham Opera Company bass, sang Vulcan's Song *Where Brazen Hammers Sound* from Gounod's *Philemon and Baucis* in August 1919, along with Huhn's ever popular *Invictus* and Frederick Keel's defiant war song *Tomorrow*. Radford returned to Douglas the following year and sang Méphistoféles' *Serenade* from Gounod's *Faust*, F. H. Cowen's *Onaway! Awake, Beloved!* and Oley Speak's famous setting of *On the Road to Mandalay*. One can only imagine the relish with which he delivered Kipling's gritty lines:

> Ship me somewhere's east of Suez, where the best is like the worst,
> Where there aren't no Ten Commandments an' a man can raise a thirst.

The Australian bass-baritone Peter Dawson possessed a dark-timbred voice with an incredible range which ensured that he was equally at home

Peter Dawson.

in the world of opera as on the concert stage. Between 1904 and 1955 he made hundreds of recordings (some say as many as 2,000), so that by the late 1920s there was hardly a home in Britain that did not own one of his gramophone records. Such was his popularity, that he was perhaps second only to John McCormack in the affections of the public. He appeared at the Villa Marina Sunday concerts many times between the wars singing operatic favourites such as the *Largo al factotum* from Rossini's *Barber of Seville*, songs like *Drink to Me Only* and popular encores notably John L. Hatton's *Simon the Cellarer*, *The Floral Dance* and James L. Molloy's *The Kerry Dance*. Dawson was unmatched in Handel and in English songs and ballads, and was awarded more double encores than any other singer who appeared in Douglas. His perfect diction and congenial, easy-going personality won over audiences and critics alike. Audiences invariably refused to let Dawson leave the stage until he had sung several encores, which meant that on many occasions his programmes consisted of some dozen-or-so arias, song and ballads. From the management's point of view, Peter Dawson was very good box office!

~

A number of fine instrumentalists appeared in Douglas during the 1920s including the pianists Myra Hess in 1924 and Benno Moiseiwitsch in

1925. Billed as 'England's Leading Lady pianist', Hess captivated her audiences with her 'consummate artistry', her reserve, charm and 'pleasing stage presence'. She was a celebrated interpreter of Bach, Mozart, Beethoven and Schumann and became an iconic and much respected figure during World War II when she instigated her famous National Gallery lunchtime concerts - some 1,700 in six years - starting during the London Blitz. Her recording of her transcription for piano of Bach's *Jesu, Joy of Man's Desiring* achieved 'classic' status.

Ukranian-born Moiseiwitsch was pre-eminent in Rachmaninov, Tchaikovsky, Scriabin and other Russian Romantics and his playing combined fiery brilliance with lyrical elegance. So enthralled were the audience, that their applause did not erupt for fully half-a-minute after he lifted his hands from the piano at the end of Chopin's *Nocturne* in F sharp major. He was recalled several times, and eventually had to decline to play further encores.

The Wood brothers take to the air-waves

Music by both Haydn and Harry featured in three notable broadcast concerts in 1925 and 1927. At a time when the very future of broadcasting was still under consideration, the BBC broadcast a three-hour concert of Light British Orchestral Music on 30th March, 1925, performed by The Wireless Orchestra conducted by Charles Ancliffe, Haydn Wood and Dan Godfrey Jnr. many of whose pieces featured in the programme. Tynwald

Moiseiwitsch and Myra Hess.

Day, 5th July 1927, should feature prominently in the story of the Island's musical culture, for on that day the first-ever broadcast of Manx music took place from the Manchester studios of the BBC. The soloist was the popular Manx soprano May Clague, supported by Hugo Teare, who gave what Harry described as 'a descriptive chat' about 'The lil' Islan''. J. E. Quayle conducted his recent tone poem *Mannin*, and Harry conducted two selections from his *Manx Airs*.

The following week there was a further unrelated broadcast from Belfast featuring Harry's *Manx Airs*, as *The Cushag* was now commonly known, and George Tootell's *Manx Scenes* played by the BBC's regional orchestra. Also taking apart were three Manx singers all of whom had earned plaudits at the Manx Music Festival: Allan Quirk, Margaret Christian, Henrietta Smith (Mrs Quintin-Smith) and the talented pianist Mary Towler. The performers were part of a delegation led by the Mayor of Douglas, Alderman A. B. Crookall, MHK, whose address on the subject of the Island was well received. This long-anticipated broadcast was unhappily spoiled for many listeners by severe atmospheric interference and intrusions from news bulletins broadcast from Dublin. Disappointingly, George Tootell's *Manx Scenes* became a casualty of the perils of broadcasting in 1927 and was not heard.

~

Harry faithfully charted all the changes of styles and fashions in popular songs and dances in *Cavalcade* but offers few clues as to his personal likes and dislikes. Did he, like Charles Fox, consider that the golden years at the Palace and Derby Castle lay in the past? Did the 'cheerful and popular musical wizard' prefer the old-style lancers, waltzes and schottisches to the racier fox-trots, Charlestons and tangos? Whatever his private views may have been, he will have been fully aware of just how quickly the world of entertainment was moving forward.

He has been our guide through some of the most turbulent years in the story of the Island's entertainment story, and the decade 1917-27 when he was engaged simultaneously in Blackpool and Douglas, was the most demanding of his career. His obituary in the *Isle of Man Times* states that 'Mr Wood used to cross to Douglas each weekend (from Blackpool) to conduct the orchestra at the Palace on Saturdays and Sundays', an arrangement that probably began in 1919 when the Palace and Derby Castle re-opened after the war, and continued until 1927. Now, at the age of sixty-five he may have been quite content to return permanently to

Music publisher and composer Lawrence Wright and Harry Wood outside the Castle Mona hotel.

Douglas and the Palace, surrounded by his musical, Masonic and Rotarian friends and looked after and supported by his sister Adeline. As he embarked on his last decade, there would be many more challenges ahead as the Island got fully back into its stride as an important holiday destination.

Chapter 7

'Ard Vainstyr Kiaullee'

1928-38

On St. Patrick's Day, 1933, Douglas Rotary Club hosted a 'Rale Ould Manx Fest' at the Sefton Hotel in Harry's honour at which he was feted as 'Ard Vainstyr Kiaullee', 'The Master Musician', in the souvenir programme. The large banqueting hall was transformed into a baronial chamber and illuminated by candlelight. It was an evening of toasts, responses and addresses accompanied by a plentiful supply of 'shag' tobacco, stone jugs filled with buttermilk (Bainney-Gear) and a roast of beef heralded by a trumpeter.

The music for the evening was organised by Harry himself who played the violin in a trio which also featured his valuable Broadwood piano. The pieces included an arrangement of his own Manx Airs, together with English, Scottish and Irish Airs, Haydn Wood's *Manx Rhapsody*, and popular 'classics' such as Boccherini's *Minuet*. The convivial evening concluded with robust communal singing of hunting songs, and ballads such as *My Grandfather's Clock* and *Drink to Me Only*.

Where are the songs of Yesteryear?

After the First World War not only did new dance styles begin to rapidly replace the old-time waltzes, lancers and schottisches, and dance bands, but orchestras had to evolve in order to meet the challenges of the new music. We have also seen how the nature of variety entertainment changed as the music hall stars of the past either retired or adapted to the demands of the new variety and cinema age. Harry was sixty years old in 1928, in reasonably good health, and seemingly as energetic and enthusiastic as ever to adopt and embrace the new trends of the entertainment revolution.

As the heady 1920s lurched into the 1930s many began to develop warm nostalgic feelings for the pre-war days. During the summer of 1929 the Examiner's special correspondent submitted a wistful report for his 'A London Cooish' column, outlining musical events of interest to Manx readers and bemoaned the fact that 'every year songs with a typical seaside flavour become scarcer and the average American chorus ditty, which has replaced the hearty British number, bears no logical connection with the holiday spirit'. In his opinion the current hits did not compare with *She's A Lassie from Lancashire* and *I Do Like To Be Beside The Seaside*. He concluded: 'What, I wonder, does Miss Florrie Forde think about it?'

Let the people sing!

There were still occasional dissenting voices and resentment aimed at the influx of holiday makers every summer, typified for some by the noise issuing from the 'song-plugging' rooms in Strand Street, the singing room at the Douglas Head Hotel and the many little white booths along the promenades where indefatigable songsters plugged the latest hits to crowds who jostled around the platforms.

The music publisher Bert Feldman defended the 'song rooms' in the *Mona's Herald* in April 1932, maintaining that the Isle of Man:

> has yet to learn the art of free entertaining particularly for those visitors who are short of cash. The severe criticism of the song plugging rooms is outweighed by the innocent pleasure they give.

One important reason for the rise in popularity of the singing rooms was the town's poor reputation for entertainment during spells of poor weather: 'A decidedly depressing spot to be' was one visitor's opinion. With few morning band or orchestral concerts, and the premier venues not opening until after lunch, the singing rooms provided both shelter and entertainment. Ted Judge, known as Manxland's Super Song-Plugger', and brother of Jack Judge the composer of *It's A Long Way to Tipperary*, attested to their popularity. He had occupied the spacious singing room at the Douglas Head Hotel for fifteen summers and claimed to sing 30,000 choruses each summer, or some fifty songs every two-and-a-half hour session. He emphasised Douglas's vital role in popularising popular songs throughout Britain:

> Douglas has always been the birthplace of song hits. If the holiday-makers show a preference for any particular song, that song is destined to be sung in pantomimes all over the country . . .

The Island 'where trippers really trip'[1]

Although there was a disappointing slump in overall visitor numbers in 1930-32, 1933 was the first of three consecutive 'bumper' years, reviving memories of the record-breaking years just before the First World War. 'Douglas for Happiness', recommended one article in a London newspaper, where 'people walk along the Douglas roads with linked arms . . . and

Queen's Promenade in the 1930s.

singing as they go'. Ironically, the Isle of Man Publicity Board decided in 1930 that as most visitors came from Lancashire, Yorkshire, the Midlands and Scotland, a London office could no longer be justified.

Of course, there was much more to a holiday on the Isle of Man than 'belting out the season's "hit" songs on the promenades', for Manxland had even more to offer than in earlier decades, and a much-improved transport infrastructure to enable people to reach even the remotest corners of the Island. In 1930 the June Effort Committee – of whom Harry was a member – was tasked with encouraging holiday makers to visit the Island earlier in the season, and engaged the services of an unlikely ally, the 'Queen of Crime', Agatha Christie. The famous mystery writer accepted a fee of £60 to write a short story entitled *Manx Gold* which was serialised in the Manchester *Daily Despatch* and distributed in pamphlet form throughout the Island's hotels and guest houses. The mystery contained four clues as to the location of four gold snuff boxes each containing a £100 token. Only three snuff boxes were ever detected.

~

Most visitors still arrived at Victoria Pier courtesy of the Steam Packet

Company's extensive fleet of passenger ferries, and in 1930 a new, even more luxurious vessel was added to the fleet, the *Lady of Mann*. Launched to coincide with the celebrations surrounding the company's centenary, she was capable of holding over 2,500 passengers, and with an average speed of twenty-two knots on the crossing from Fleetwood, was soon hailed as 'The Pride of the Fleet'. In 1934 another new vessel was added to the Liverpool to Douglas route, the *Mona's Queen*. With graceful lines and the characteristic white hull, she and her sister ship the *Ben-my-Chree* were reckoned to be the finest short-crossing passenger vessels in the world.

There was also a marked increase in the number of visitors who could afford to fly to the Island. The short-lived Hall Caine Airport, three miles from Ramsey, opened in 1935 and some 2,000 passengers took advantage of the services from Blackpool, Liverpool, Carlisle and Glasgow that summer. More significantly, the following year the Air Ministry granted an open licence to operate an approved airport at Ronaldsway.

~

From a high of 54,000, August Bank Holiday had settled to around 40,000 visitors by 1934, with the Steam Packet Company operating some two dozen sailings during the holiday weekend. The resident population of Douglas was around 20,000, so it is remarkable that 30,000 attended the outdoor service at Kirk Braddan Church that holiday Sunday.[2]

There was a record-breaking Scottish 'invasion' in July 1935 when 12,000 arrived for their traditional Manx week, an invasion that was calculated to be worth £100,000 to the Manx economy. On one day in August that year the Douglas Corporation horse trams and buses carried an incredible 82,000 passengers.

'For sheer industrious love-making, Douglas is supreme'.

The Manx experience as a whole was far more visitor friendly than for those coming to the Island a generation earlier. Even those visitors who disembarked early in the morning found that the arcades in the Pier buildings and the seats under the Villa Marina colonnades were accessible for shelter and even 'forty winks' before the boarding house owners could be roused. The shops were able to stay open for as long as they wished, although some Sunday restrictions still prevailed. Hotel and guest houses were far more flexible and many remained open until 11.00pm in order to accommodate those guests who had spent the evening dancing in the

Palace or Derby Castle ballrooms, enjoying the variety shows in the theatres or visiting one of Douglas's superb modern cinemas.[3]

On sunny days the beaches were packed with families, and for the more energetic there was tennis, golf and open-air swimming. The smaller towns of Ramsey, Port Erin, Peel and Castletown also benefitted from the tourist boom helped by inexpensive rail travel, the Manx Electric Railway and the fiercely competitive charabanc companies who guaranteed that everyone would be safely back at their accommodation by six o'clock in time for their evening meal.

For those visitors for whom a week in Douglas meant a daily stroll along the promenades, taking advantage of the sea air, the wonderful vista of the bay and the entertainments that could be enjoyed there, the new much wider Loch Promenade, which stretched from Victoria Landing Pier to the War Memorial near the Gaiety Theatre, with the benefit of six sunken marine gardens, a rose garden, and a children's boating pool and fountains, was completed in 1934.

The *Mona's Herald* August Bank Holiday revue of 1932 describes the Douglas experience perfectly:

> In the afternoon, glorious sunshine flooded the Island, and the

Outdoor Sunday service, Kirk Braddan.

> holiday crowds made the most of it. Hundreds bathed from Douglas beach, and a host of others esconsced (sic) themselves in deck chairs on the sands. The promenades were thronged, and a large number found enjoyment at the orchestral concert in Villa Marina Gardens. At Port Skillion, after enjoying a plunge in the baths, groups of bathers were to be seen on the roofs of the bathing huts, basking in the sunshine. Sun-bathers were everywhere on Douglas and Onchan Heads.

Although the menace of German bands, Italian hurdy-gurdy players and the manic beach preachers of the pre-war years had largely disappeared, a fresh nuisance arrived on the Island in 1928 and created an unwelcome din to rival even the noise issuing from the singing rooms: the raucous toy trumpet known as the 'Tommy Talker', the perfect instrument for the late-night reveller, whose tuneless blaring was soon heard all over the town. In 1933 a more serious scourge visited itself on the Island in the shape of pick-pockets, noticeably on the passenger ferries. These criminals, it seemed, travelled with the holiday makers from Manchester or Liverpool and took advantage of the holiday euphoria to cover their crimes.

~

Just a mile-or-so outside Douglas, Bellevue, the former exhibition park-cum-fairground-cum-race course, had been acquired by Douglas Corporation who planned to transform it into the King George V Park. One commentator looked forward to a time when the once-popular recreation ground would again ring to the sounds of merry laughter 'or witness Florrie Forde place her two bob on Lucky Jim'

Douglas retained its special place in the affections of holiday makers from the north-west of England up to the Second World War, as one visitor's appreciation of his visit entitled 'A Gay Time in the Isle of Man' published in *The Southport Visitor* and reprinted in the *Isle of Man Examiner* demonstrates:

> . . . an excursion by rail followed by pleasant and aimless wandering among the beautiful glens and hills, returning late afternoon for dinner, followed by a visit to a cinema or to the Derby Castle to join in the rollicking songs of Florrie Forde. Douglas has everything for modern holiday seekers.

Another contented holiday maker summed up his typical day in

Douglas on a postcard home:

> For sheer industrious love-making, Douglas is supreme. The chat at breakfast; the excursion; the voluptuous Waltz at eventide followed by a stroll along the promenade and intrigues and amours at the boarding-house.

Douglas' cheap and modern boarding houses catered for hundreds of people in a home-from-home atmosphere:

> Dear steady-going elderly married couples, elderly bachelors, genteel old maids, damsels sly and shy, young men bold, and the enfant terrible. All contribute to the gaiety of the whole.

Ee, what a to-do![4]

Some entertainers who appeared in Douglas during the 1930s were now familiar to audiences from their comedy films, and enjoyed radio and television careers after World War Two. Rob Wilton, the Lancashire–born comedian famous for his monologues portraying incompetent officials such as *The Day War Broke Out* and *The Fireman*, topped the bill in 1924, 1933-4 and again in 1938. He was a popular radio star during the 1930s and '40s with his best-known character the J. P. Mr Muddlecombe. Will Hay, star of stage, radio and the silver screen, and billed as 'the famous schoolmaster comedian', first appeared in Douglas as the star of Will Hay & Company in 1933 Arthur Q. Moore in the *Mona's Herald* described his sketch St. Michael's as 'a rich subtle comedy . . . a joy to watch and hear'.[5]

Robb Wilton and Will Hay.

Ted Ray, considered by his peers to have been the greatest ad-libber in the business, appeared in 1934 as the 'ultra-modern' comedian in an act peppered with fast-and-furious quick-fire gags. Early in his career his act included playing the violin badly - something he had in common with Jimmy Wheeler and Jack Benny - and was sometimes billed as 'Nedlo, The Gypsy Violinist'.[6]

Hylda Baker, the diminutive Lancashire comedienne whose 'novel songs and witty patter went down well' in 1936, had been on the stage since the First World War, but didn't become a household name until the mid-1950s after she introduced the tall, silent stooge, Cynthia, as the foil in her act together with the catch-phrase: 'I said, "Be soon", didn't I?' "Beee Soooon!" '

Novelty acts could still produce a surprise or two, and few were more intriguing than Liverpool-born Madamoiselle Veronica, 'a charming young danseuse', who was better known as a champion 'high-kicker' who had kicked her way to two world championships: one hundred kicks in fifty seconds and two thousand in forty-five minutes. Her legs were apparently insured for £1,000 each! The ventriloquist Arthur Worsley had an unusual gimmick: he hardly ever spoke himself! Instead, with a dead-pan expression, he allowed the bullying and hectoring from his dummy Charlie Brown to dominate the performance with his demanding 'Look at me when I'm talking to you'.

Frank Randle and Sandy Powell.

Wilson, Kepple and Betty & Norman Evans.

~

There was, however, an unsettling notoriety about Wigan-born Frank Randle who appeared at the Derby Castle in June 1935 billed as London's new star comedian. He had begun touring the north of England around 1928 and quickly developed a subversive edge, sometimes appearing on stage carrying a workman's red warning lamp and shouting: 'Look what some dam'd fool left in t'road'. His characteristic stage persona was that of a toothless, scruffy belligerent drunk and although he later developed a range of characters, he often appeared swigging from a flagon, his belches growing ever louder as he exclaimed: 'By gum, there's 36 burps to the bottle'. If only he had confined his 'orificial' noises to just belching! His Derby Castle appearances, though, were uncontroversial and he was fondly remembered for his sketches *The Seaside Boatman* and *Horace the 82 Year Old Hiker.*

A more endearing personality was Rochdale-born Norman Evans, who appeared in Douglas in 1937, and introduced his best-known character, the gossip Fanny Fairbottom, the local heroine of his sketch *Over the Garden Wall.* Talking about 'her at number seven' Evans delivered the ultimate gossip's line:

> The coalman was never far away. I mean – don't tell me it takes 35 minutes to deliver two bags of nuts!

Another much loved northern comic was Sandy Powell who was a frequent visitor to Onchan Head Pavilion during the 1930s with his revue Sandy Powell's Roadshow. From 1928 he had been the popular star of BBC radio's first regular variety show Sandy's Hour, and was never known to tell a risqué joke; his catchphrase, 'Can you hear me, Mother?' could be heard at the start of each episode.

Still fondly remembered and much imitated today, Wilson, Kepple and Betty created a wonderfully eccentric 'silent' act entitled 'Cleopatra's Nightmare' during which they sand-danced to Luigini's *Ballet Egyptien* dressed in long tunics and fezzes. Among the purely musical turns, Teddy Brown loomed large in every way. Billed as The World's 'Greatest' Xylophonist - he weighed twenty-four stone - he showered his audiences with constant comic patter whilst astonishing them with his phenomenal virtuosity on his six octave instrument. Comedy pianists proliferated, but Freddy Bamberger, 'Jest-er Piano Player', who performed piano stunts and tricks at the piano in the manner the young Mozart was said to have accomplished in London in the 1760s, such as playing through a cloth over the keys, was among the most accomplished and entertaining.

'Speak of Me As I Am'.[7]

With the appearance of Paul Robeson at the Villa Marina in 1929 and 1931, and Sir Harry Lauder at a Highland Gathering at the Nunnery in 1932, it must have seemed as if the age of the great international entertainers had returned. Robeson's reception on his first visit to Douglas was a tumultuous one, which he acknowledged standing by the piano with a quiet dignity, patiently waiting for the hall to settle. At 6' 3" his appearance was imposing and his quiet and modest demeanour strangely magnetic; as the *Isle of Man Examiner* wrote: he 'possesses the supreme gift of sincerity'. Robeson sang twelve Spirituals with 'perfect naturalness and without the slightest affectation'. There was barely a sound from the large audience during the slave song *Water Boy*, and all present were deeply moved when he sang *Were You There When They Crucified My Lord?* The climax of the evening came when he sang the song everybody wanted to hear, *Ol' Man River* from Jerome Kern's hit musical of 1927, *Show Boat*.

Now billed as 'The world's greatest negro actor vocalist', Robeson returned to the Villa Marina in July 1931 with a huge programme of twenty-two Spirituals and other songs; once again the finale was centred on *Ol' Man River* but the audience, who could not get enough of that 'beautiful bass-baritone voice, rich and of immense resonance', would not let him go

Paul Robeson.

until he sang several other encores and a double encore to finish. It could be argued that Paul Robeson's concerts were the greatest musical events featuring any artist in either the variety or classical fields on the Isle of Man. His artistry transcended musical genres and he left audiences acutely aware that they had witnessed something very special indeed. A great man had communicated his deep humanity to them in a variety theatre in Douglas through the medium of his wonderfully unique voice in the way that only music can: straight to the heart.

The 'King of Mirth' holds court.

Another event which attracted a huge crowd, estimated at 13,000, was the fifth annual Highland Gathering at the Nunnery Park on the 18th July 1932. The 'big scoop' was the surprise appearance of Sir Harry Lauder, now in semi-retirement, but persuaded to cross the briny and re-visit the scene of some of his earliest appearances.

The purpose of his visit was to witness and to an extent take part in a colourful pageant of his life from pit-boy to knighthood. The show, performed outdoors in brilliant sunshine, was titled 'The King of Mirth', and featured the songs which had made him famous, sung by a choir of over 100. In addition there was a mini-Highland Games, pipe band competitions, Scottish dancing, and a special kilted military band from the Glasgow Corporation Gas Department. At the conclusion there was a grand march past by all those taking part, but not before Sir Harry, together with his famous gnarled stick, had been persuaded to tell stories about his life 'with much banter' and conduct the crowd singing *Keep Right On to the End* of the Road, 'filling every word with meaning'.

In an interview with an *Isle of Man Examiner* reporter, the great entertainer recalled his visit to the Island in 1904 and remembered the horse trams and the wonderful sweep of the bay. What became known as the 'Sir Harry Lauder Gathering' made a substantial profit of £200. No other Highland gathering, before or since, equalled it in scope.

A charm offensive

More popular than even Dame Clara Butt, and a household name through hundreds of recordings, the Irish tenor John McCormack - now styled Count John McCormack[8] - returned to the Island and the Villa Marina in 1932, twenty-four years after his last appearance in Douglas. The *Isle of Man Examiner* congratulated the management for its 'commendable boldness' in bringing to the Island 'such top-notchers' and predicted that McCormack's appearance would break all Villa records.

This indeed proved to the case. The Villa Marina was fuller than at any time during its nineteen-year existence; the alcoves and balconies were fitted with extra seating and some people had to stand or squat in the aisles throughout. Hundreds were turned away. *The Isle of Man Times* caught the mood:

> His style is the mirror of the man. He has no mannerisms such as custom associates with a virtuoso. He simply walks on, takes up a restful position against the famous Steinway piano he takes with him on all his engagements, and just sings . . . he can infuse into a song more feeling than any other singer one has ever heard . . . The notes flow in a liquid stream; every word is heard distinctly . . .

The deepest appreciation was reserved for the Irish ballads and folk songs, and for the encores *The Rose of Tralee, I Met Her in the Garden Where the Praties Grow, The Last Rose of Summer* and most of all for *I Hear You Calling Me*, the affecting ballad that launched his career. McCormack appeared in the Villa Marina again in 1933, 1934 and 1935, and on all occasions the hall was full to capacity. Even though he sang twenty or so songs the audiences clamoured for more.

At his final concert in 1936 he sang Ernest Charles' moving love song *When I Have Sung My Songs to You*:

When I have sung my songs to you, I'll sing no more;
T'would be a sacrilege to sing at another door.
We've worked so hard to hold our dreams, just you and I;
I could not share them all again, I'd rather die.

~

Heddle Nash.

In August 1930, Tom Burke, 'The Lancashire Caruso', appeared at the Palace Coliseum for his only appearance in Douglas that season. An ex-boy-miner from Leigh in Lancashire, a fine cornet player and composer of popular songs, he was revered for the great passion and expressiveness that imbued every note he sang. Unsurprisingly, a huge crowd filled the Palace Coliseum to hear this archetypical working-class lad made good. Heddle Nash, the lyric tenor, or 'tenore di grazia', appeared at the Palace Coliseum in 1935 and 1936. For many he was the quintessential, unsurpassed Gerontius and was known to thousands through his appearances in oratorio, on the concert stage, regular radio broadcasts and his many recordings.

The dramatic soprano Eva Turner, the 'Queen of Grand Opera', came to the Palace Coliseum in July 1933 and attracted one of the biggest crowds of the season. Her singing was said to be an inspiration, and her programme a strenuous one: Bantock's orchestral song *The Lament of Isis*, the great scena, *Ocean, Thou Mighty Monster* from Weber's *Oberon*, *One Fine Day* from *Madame Butterfly*, and a number of encores including the lighter songs and ballads *The Pipes of Pan* from the *Arcadians* and the affecting *Homing* by Teresa del Riego.

The Palace was again filled to capacity in July 1936 when Mary Jarred appeared with the tenor Heddle Nash. Hers was 'a contralto voice of distinction' and she captivated her audience with *O Peaceful England* from

Fritz Kreisler.

German's *Merry England* and Sullivan's *The Lost Chord.* She was so popular with Manx audiences that she was invited to sing at the Manx Music Festival concert in 1937.

Music of almost unbelievable beauty

Yet another red-letter day for the Villa Marina was Sunday 24th July 1932 when the great Viennese violinist Fritz Kreisler was engaged for an evening recital. It was the first visit to the Island of the internationally acclaimed 'superstar' who was as admired in America, the Far East and Australia as he was in Europe. Expectations naturally ran high, and were exceeded:

> We often hear of people entranced by beauty, but that was literally true when the greatest violinist of our time filled the Royal Hall with golden melody. Row upon row of motionless figures sat wrapt – intent, with eyes riveted upon the tall, powerfully-built man upon the platform, whose magic fingers called forth from the violin music of almost unbelievable beauty.

Kreisler's playing was without extravagant gestures or distracting mannerisms, and if the audience was tense and hushed, enthralled and spellbound, he, too, seemed lost in his art and unconscious of everything around him during a demanding two-hour recital. The delightful salon-pieces *Liebesfreud* and *Schön Rosmarin* won him sustained and thunderous applause.

John Dunn, a violinist highly-regarded by Manx audiences, appeared many times, and although his choice of pieces in 1920 was described as 'heavy', Sarasate's *Zigeunerweisen* won the audience over and brought the house down. Albert Sammons was another welcome visitor to the Sunday concerts, and came with a huge reputation, partly the result of his association with Elgar, whose violin concerto he first played in 1914. 'Hooking a Big Fish' was how the *Isle of Man Examiner* described his engagement at the Palace Coliseum in 1923.

Two brilliant, but very different, musical personalities left their mark on the Douglas concert scene during this period: the Portugese 'cellist Guilhermina Suggia, billed as 'the world's greatest lady 'cellist' and Beatrice Harrison, a member of a notable musical family. Suggia's playing was as revelatory as her stage presence was commanding. Tall, slender, dark-haired, olive-skinned and temperamental by nature, her playing was as exuberant and flamboyant as her long luxurious gowns, her fashionably-styled hair and artfully applied make-up.

Beatrice Harrison gave the first performances of Delius' 'cello concerto, his double concerto for violin and 'cello, and the premier outside London of Elgar's 'cello concerto, the work with which she was most associated. Her atmospheric 'live' recordings made in the garden of her house in Oxted accompanied by nightingales were extremely popular.

The Wood brothers take to the air waves . . . again

As Harry's career entered its final decade, his brother Haydn's entered its most productive period. Haydn had retired from the life of a touring concert violinist around 1925 and emerged fully as the composer of beautifully written lyrical orchestral music. His music was increasingly performed and broadcast in concerts largely devoted to his music, and Harry, too, enjoyed a measure of success with his *Manx Airs* which were broadcast a number of times during this period.

On the 3rd January, 1928, the BBC broadcast a programme devoted to Haydn's music with the composer himself conducting the Wireless Symphony Orchestra, from a London recording studio. The programme included his festive overture *May-Day*, the *Variations on a Once Popular Humorous Song*, the suite *Three Famous Pictures* together with *entr'actes* and songs. Haydn originally conceived the variations as a musical joke based on the old music hall song *If You Want to Know the Time, Ask a P'liceman*, and deliberately chose a song from the Victorian age that only the older members of any audience would remember 'as one of the tunes that held sway before English popular songs had succumbed to the lure of jazz'.

This broadcast concert was more or less repeated at the Palace Coliseum on Sunday 22nd July at the first all-Haydn Wood concert on the Island, at which he appeared as a violin soloist and the composer and conductor of a number of his works.

~

Harry's nephew, the violinist Hilton Cullerne, was also making a name for himself on the Island in 1928, for in early May his band was chosen as the favourite among those short-listed to provide music in Mooragh Park, Ramsey for the season. Ramsey Town Commissioners and the Development Association confirmed the engagement of Hilton's band of six players, known as the Ramsey Municipal Band, before the middle of the month. The ensemble that appeared for the afternoon concerts was a highly flexible group of multi-instrumentalists including Hilton in the role of violinist and conductor, a second violinist, a pianist, a 'cellist, a trumpet player and a percussionist. For the evening dance programmes the band altered its line-up to feature a violin, saxophone, banjo, piano, trumpet, percussion and 'effects'. Under Hilton's leadership the band was a popular success and soon began to attract visitors to the town to listen to the thrice-daily concerts of light overtures and selections each morning on Court House Green, at Mooragh Park in the afternoons and for dancing at the Electra Grounds each evening.

In January 1929 Haydn put forward to the BBC a proposal for a Wood family concert; nothing came of the idea but Harry's *Manx Airs* were broadcast from Manchester on 5th November. On Sunday 17th August the following year Harry directed a Haydn Wood concert at the Palace, with Haydn performing his virtuosic gypsy piece, *La Vie de Boheme*, and conducting some of his orchestral works including the fantasy-overture *Harlequinade* and the suite *Three Famous Cinema Stars*.[9]

It was in 1931 that Haydn began to write a series of orchestral works based on Manx traditional melodies and evoking Manx history, folk lore, myths and the wonderfully varied countryside. Harry wrote warmly in *Cavalcade* about his younger brother's love of 'these beautiful tunes' and of the evocative orchestral works that he incorporated them into: *A Manx*

Rhapsody (1931), the rhapsody *Mylecharane* (1931), *Mannin Veen*, (Dear Isle of Man, 1932-3) and *King Orry* (1938), a particular favourite of Harry's, and first broadcast in May 1938. The popular *Manx Overture*, 'The Isle of Mountains and Glens', is not actually based on authentic Manx melodies, although the whole work is imbued with a strong Manx flavour, the happy result of Haydn's long association with the Island's traditional music.

~

The BBC broadcast three musical events on their National and Northern Regional programmes in 1931, giving the Island and its culture a tremendous publicity boost at the start of the holiday season. The first of these, an illustrated talk on Manx music and folklore entitled 'Ellan Vannin', was broadcast from Manchester on 28th June, and was a prelude to the much more significant broadcasts which took place between 4th - 6th July to herald the start of the week-long Celtic Congress held in Douglas that year. Fifty delegates arrived in Douglas on Saturday 4th July and attended a civic reception at the Villa Marina that evening. On Sunday afternoon the delegates travelled to Lezayre Church near Ramsey to take part in a service conducted in Manx Gaelic, and that evening were present at the Palace Coliseum for a Grand Celtic Concert.

A feature of the concert was the choice of vocal soloists from all the Celtic regions: Megan Thomas (Wales); Ada Mylchreest (Isle of Man); Mabel Ritchie (Cornwall and Brittany): Alec Macrae (Scotland) and Gabriel Lovell (Ireland), each of whom sang a selection of traditional songs in their ancient languages. Ada Mylchreest received the warmest welcome and sang five traditional Manx songs; Harry conducted the Palace orchestra which was augmented for the occasion with players from the Hallé orchestra.

B. E. Sargeaunt from the Celtic Congress Committee wrote to Harry shortly after the concert thanking him for 'all you did to make the concert such a great success . . . the orchestral numbers were excellent, and I have nothing but praise on all hands'. There were many other letters of congratulation from listeners for whom the broadcast brought back happy memories of the Island.

~

Further concerts in Douglas featuring Haydn's music occurred between 1932 and 1935. The *Homage March*, *May Day* overture, *Apollo* overture, *A Manx Rhapsody*, the suite *In An Old Cathedral Town* and the waltz *Joyessness* were performed in 1932. The following year *Mannin Veen* was performed for the first time in Douglas along with the *Intermezzo: Roses of Picardy* and two movements - Andante and Finale - from his violin concerto played by the Spanish virtuoso Antonio Brosa, with both Harry and Haydn taking it in turns to conduct the Palace Grand Orchestra.

In August 1933 a Haydn Wood Concert was broadcast from London, with Reginald King and his orchestra performing *A May Day Overture*, *Three Famous Pictures* and *Mannin Veen*, 'the composer's most recently published work'. Three days later *Mannin Veen* received another broadcast performance from the hands of Reginald Dixon at the organ of the Tower Ballroom, Blackpool. A selection from Harry's *Manx Airs* was performed by the Scottish Studio Orchestra and broadcast in the late afternoon of 18th December.

~

A similar but much more prestigious concert to that of the Celtic Concert of 1931 took place at the Palace Coliseum on 1st July 1934, when the Wood brothers once again shared the rostrum for a concert featuring the music of three Manx composers – Haydn, Harry and J. E. Quayle – which was broadcast on the BBC North Regional Programme.

The BBC came to the Island at the invitation of Charles Fox, Manager of the Palace & Derby Castle Company, and although the first part of the concert featured music by Rossini and Verdi, the longer broadcast part consisted exclusively of Manx music by Manx composers, and therefore can be said to have been the first such musical event ever broadcast from the Isle of Man. The concert was a great success and generated many letters of appreciation. A photograph taken at the time shows Harry on the rostrum and Haydn at the front of the stage with the four soloists, and orchestra of twenty players and a choir of twenty-five.

The vibrant murals of the Scottish artist Anna Zinkeisen (who also painted murals on the liners *Queen Mary* and *Queen Elizabeth*) were the inspiration for Haydn's suit Frescoes which was broadcast on the first Sunday of the new year, 1935, conducted by Joseph Lewis. He apparently admired the murals, having observed them at Chappell's music publisher's offices in London, and wrote the three movement suite with the following titles: *Waltz Vienna 1913*, a nautical scene *Sea Shanties* and a march, *The Bandstand, Hyde Park*. In July that year he and Dorothy spent three weeks in Douglas with Harry and Adeline, playing golf and catching up on old friends.

The bands play on

In the years immediately after the war the Palace and Derby Castle Orchestras were essentially the familiar 'theatre' style bands of twenty to twenty-five players incorporating a modest body of strings supported by single or double woodwind and brass instruments, a percussionist and piano accompanist. A few of Harry's draft programmes from 1919-20, and later printed programmes from the 1931 seasons of Sunday afternoon concerts in the Palace gardens have survived and show that the music he selected for these al fresco concerts and Sunday Sacred Concerts remained unchanged in style and content between the wars.

However, Harry makes clear in *Cavalcade* in 1919 that as the new jazz-influenced dance styles grew in popularity and began to replace the earlier lancers, schottisches and waltzes, the dance bands also began to evolve in order to do justice to them: 'The orchestration of the original Fox-trot and other new dances had no saxophone parts in them. Later on a saxophone part was added and finally the four saxophones were used'.

The 1920s saw the rise of the 'syncopated' bands and as early as 1926 the following bands all appeared in Douglas: Al Davidson's Claribel Band at the Villa Marina, Jack Howard's Band, Fred Sakers' band from *No, No Nanette* and J. A. Leigh's 'art and antics' Band at the Derby Castle. The following year Harry's Derby Castle band was advertised as The Castle Syncopated Orchestra.

In May 1928 in a season's preview entitled 'What Will Manxland Hear This Season?', Arthur Q. Moore reported on a 'chat' he had had with Harry just a week or so earlier about his new 'Super-Syncopated Band' that would be playing in the Palace Ballroom that year. They both agreed that the traditional dance orchestras of the pre-war years often struggled to be heard in the vast, cavernous cathedral-like space of the ballroom, and furthermore many subtle details of orchestration were practically inaudible. He referred to Harry's new band as a 'melody band', which is to say that in response to the new dance styles the instrumentation of the band would emphasise melody and rhythm at the expense of fine orchestral detail.

~

Two undated photographs of Harry standing with his new band support A. Q. Moore's impressions of the changing face of dance bands. The first, dating from about 1924-6 shows a band in transition. Nineteen

The Palace band in the 1920s.

players are shown although not all their instruments are visible. On the front row are seated four violinists in more or less their traditional dance orchestra position, and next to them two tenor saxophones (a baritone saxophone can be seen on a stand), a banjoist and a flautist. Behind the front row can be seen two more violinists, a sousaphone player, two trumpet players, two trombonists and a second sousaphone player. At the rear stand two lady percussionists and a pianist. The inclusion of two sousaphones - American marching band bass instruments - is a strong indication that Harry wished to emphasise the bass line in the dance numbers and make it more audible for the dancers in a way that a 'cello and double bass could never do.

The second photograph is headed 'Harry Wood's Palace Band' and shows a larger ensemble of twenty-three players against a Grecian backcloth with some significant changes in its make-up and seating arrangements. The front row of the band was very different with two alto and two tenor saxophones, a musical saw, a banjo, two trumpets and two trombones. A middle row features a sousaphone, two banjos and one ukulele, three violins, a further trombone and a second sousaphone. The back row has five players, one a pianist and the others percussionists who between them played the timpani, side-drum, bass drum and cymbals, xylophone, glockenspiel, dulcitone and tubular bells. As A. Q. Moore put

The Palace band in the 1930s.

it, it was a band 'long renowned for its grand tonal effects'.

The new 'Super-Syncopated Bands' were the ideal ensembles to accompany the new dance styles but lacked the flexibility needed to adequately perform the light classical selections that were the core of the afternoon concerts and the larger-scale classical and sacred pieces so characteristic of the Sunday concerts. Harry's solution had always been to supplement his Palace and Derby Castle bands with local professionals and experienced amateur musicians for the 'classical' concerts.

The issue arose again in 1935 when Promenader in the *Mona's Herald* suggested that 'Douglas no longer boasted an orchestra capable of doing full justice to a classical programme of music'. Promenader's point was not that dance band players were technically incapable of performing a classical work, but that dance bands, with their pared down wind and brass sections, were not the appropriate ensembles for such 'symphonic' repertoire. Doug Swallow, the conductor of the Palace dance band replied:

> Up to now Palace Sunday concert audiences have been very pleased with the band's items, and bands come to Douglas to please the visitors, who keep the Island going.

He then – unwisely perhaps - issued a challenge:

> If Promenader cares to send me a request for any piece of music, that piece will be played at the following Sunday evening concert – providing I receive the request in good time.

Promenader responded that he would be very interested to hear Doug Swallow's interpretation of Wagner's *The Ride of the Valkyries*, and the work was duly scheduled for performance at the Sunday concert on 4th August. Many in the audience clearly knew about the challenge and turned up in good numbers to hear Wagner's 'terrifying trifle'. The orchestra numbered just seventeen players, and although Promenader remained unconvinced that they did anything like justice to the piece, he conceded that the attempt had been 'plucky', and congratulated Swallow and his musicians on almost certainly being the first dance band to ever perform it!

~

During this last decade of Harry's long career, several new-style bands and smaller ensembles were engaged at the Palace and Derby Castle, the Palais de Danse (on the site in Strand Street, Douglas, occupied by Woolworth's for many years) and the Villa Marina: Jack Kerr and his 'Famous Continental Band' at the Palais de Danse; Doug Swallow's band in the Derby Castle ballroom: Ivan L. Huckerby's band in the Palace Coliseum; the Tom Katz Saxophone Six and Reg Roney's London Band in the Derby Castle variety theatre; and Bert Relphs' Band in the Palace ballroom. Billy Cotton's Astorians Band appeared in 1934, and in 1937 Joe Kirkham and his band were engaged at the Palace ballroom and for the Sunday concerts. Another regular musical director at the Palace was Ernest Arnold, who by 1938 had been engaged there for seventeen seasons. Like Harry, he was a conductor, composer and arranger and conducted many of the Palace revues.

~

Harry had always been open to new ideas in order to keep the dance programmes fresh and up-to-date. One such innovation was outlined in *Cavalcade* for the year 1929:

> This season we always played three Fox-trots one after the other. In one number (set) we played the first Fox-trot quickly, the second slowly and the third quickly. In the next set we played them vice versa.

The variety shows, too, evolved to respond to audiences' expectations, and in 1933 the entertainer who was quickly dubbed 'Variety's Ringmaster' and 'the man who brought variety back to Manxland', Will Dalton, presented his first new-style brand of non-stop variety to the Derby Castle. In a fast-moving show that normally featured ten stars, his innovation was to present a blend of acts, each one related to the previous act and the one that followed, with no act lasting longer than fifteen minutes. 'Speed is essential' he told a reviewer from the *Mona's Herald*, and 'humour the keynote'. Dalton recognised that 'variety succeeds in Douglas because the people appreciate the panorama of tastes'; holiday makers demanded entertainment that was 'Fast, Funny and Thrilling', and he insisted that, during the Derby Castle's greatest period of post-war prosperity, only the best talent in the business would do.

Manxland's King of Music

In September 1931 Harry was given the opportunity to reflect on his forty-seven years' music-making in Douglas in a long interview the *Examiner*. This took place in the library at 1, Osborne Terrace, which the reporter described as 'a veritable encyclopaedia of the various personages and places which have loomed large in the development of the town's musical activities'. Harry looked back to a time 'when Sir Harry Lauder hadn't been heard of!' and in showing the interviewer the many old photographs of the Falcon Cliff, the Derby Castle and the Palace and the many variety artists who appeared at these resorts over the decades, and recalled his own debut at the Falcon Cliff as a sixteen-year-old solo violinist in 1884.

The reporter remarked upon the tied-up bundles of old programmes from the Sunday Sacred Concerts at the Palace from the time when Harry first directed them in 1902, and of course the thousands of individual sets of orchestral parts in his library which in themselves reflected all the changes in the styles and fashions of popular music during the period:

> In short, Mr Wood possesses priceless relics of days that are gone – but if forgotten today by most people, they are not so by Mr Wood, who possesses a remarkable memory and can recall incidents both grave and gay – of thirty and forty years ago! Out of the distant past, he can almost bring to life the artists who made our grandparents rock with laughter . . . there is no doubt that Mr Wood's association with Douglas justly entitles him to be described as 'Manxland's King of Music'.

The reporter concluded:

> . . . like many others who have played a very commendable part in the development of the Island as a popular pleasure resort, Mr Wood is not a Manxman . . . but who would deny that after so long a connection with Manx people and business, he is not wholly Manx by adoption.

Still busy after all these years

Harry's days continued to be filled with activity, and as the years flew by were increasingly punctuated by reminders of the past. In 1928 both he and Haydn donated one guinea each to the memorial fund for Florence Laughton, for thirty years the hard-working secretary and treasurer of the Manx Music Festival, who had died the previous year. For although Miss M. L. Wood, the 'Mother of Manx Music', was the inspiration and guiding light behind the Festival, it was Mrs Laughton's immense tact and resourcefulness that ensured that everything ran smoothly behind the scenes.

The year 1929 was barely under way before there was a death in the family: Harry's younger sister Sophia died in Douglas at 1, Osborne Terrace in February after a short illness, aged fifty-eight years, and was buried in Kirk Braddan cemetery.[10] In March the following year Harry's eldest brother John, who never visited his family on the Island, died in Slaithwaite aged seventy-two. In April news reached Harry of the death of the great Canadian operatic soprano Emma Albani; her death will have brought back memories of her many wonderful appearances in Douglas before the First World War.

In addition to his everyday duties as musical director of the Palace & Derby Castle Company, Harry continued to play the occasional violin solo at local concerts and increasingly gave lecture recitals. In August 1929 'Mr Harry Wood's String Quartet' gave a chamber music recital at the Sefton Hotel for Douglas Rotary Club. After Harry's introductory talk the quartet played pieces by Mozart, Grieg, Beethoven, Boccherini and William Wolstenholme, a well-known blind organist from Blackburn, whom Harry described as 'the gradely Lancasheer Lad'. In drawing the recital to a close, Harry made the point that attractive popular pieces like Boccherini's famous Minuet would not live much longer in the face of the 'canned' and 'mechanised' music that he felt prevailed at that time.

In August 1930 'Harry Wood's Piano Quartet' - four wind instruments and piano - played at a Rotary Club luncheon, and in March the following year Harry attended a Rotarian ‘big do’ in March and was the recipient of an amusing piece of doggerel written by the headmaster of a Douglas school:

A charming girl met Harry Wood
(Who would have been good if he could)
Would Harry please lend her
Help with her suspender?
Would Harry? My Word, Harry would!

Rotary Club social events were clearly convivial occasions, with or without music.

~

Only one piece of correspondence from any of Harry’s finest violin pupils has survived, an undated letter from Kathleen Rydings:

Laxey Lodge
9 Avondale Road
Onchan
Isle of Man
Dear Mr Wood
Many thanks for your letter. I shall be pleased to play at the Gaiety for the week starting July 12th. Of course you will let me know later about rehearsals.
I started at the College three weeks ago. Again, many thanks for giving my name to the Principal.
Best wishes
Yours sincerely

The letter has a rather formal feel to it considering that Harry and Kathleen had been musical colleagues for forty years. The college referred to is almost certainly King William’s College at Castletown where Harry had been the violin teacher up to 1917; the letter was probably written around 1937 when her name appears in the college records as a teacher for the first time. Now that Harry had ceased giving private violin lessons, Kathleen Rydings was the most experienced and influential string teacher on the Island, and a stalwart of the Manx Music Festival, entering not only string soloists, duos and trios, but her two string orchestras consisting of her most able pupils.

~

The main event of 1932 was the three-day visit of HRH Prince George, the youngest son of King George V and Queen Mary, who made history by flying himself to the Island in a two-seater light aircraft. His visit included a Royal Musical Reception at Government House. The programme chosen by Harry was a light one and featured Haydn Wood's *A Manx Rhapsody* and selections from Noel Coward's *Cavalcade*, Lehar's *Frederica* and Edward German's *Merrie England*. Lady Hill, the wife of the Lieutenant Governor, wrote to Harry a few days later thanking him for 'his choice of music presented so excellently by the musicians'. The day after the reception the Prince presented the T.T. race prizes at the Palace Ballroom in front of an audience of 9,500; the front of the specially-printed programme shows the prince addressing the crowded ballroom with Harry's orchestra visible in the background.

Harry does not seem to have resumed his private violin teaching after the war - he would hardly have had time - but he was always supportive and encouraging to young musicians. In May 1933 he was invited by B. E. Sargeaunt, the Attorney General and Isle of Man representative of the Associated Board of the Royal Schools of Music, to present the certificates to successful candidates at the Grand Theatre. Harry congratulated the young musicians and spoke of his forty years as a musical director, his large collection of music and recalled that he received his first music certificate at Leeds Town Hall in 1883.

In October 1933 Sir Claude Hill left the Island after seven and a half years as an 'efficient and industrious' Lieutenant Governor and his successor, Sir Montagu Butler, was installed in November. A popular figure, he would later oversee plans for the defence of the Island in the event of war, namely air-raid precautions and the formation of an anti-gas brigade.

Harry and Adeline travelled to their sister Elise's home in Golcar near Huddersfield for Christmas 1933 which meant he was able to take part in the celebrations surrounding Slaithwaite Prize Band's great victory at the Crystal Palace Brass Band Competition and to present the trophy and a new cornet to the band president. He later delighted the bandsmen with dialect tales of old 'Slowit' and memories of the early days of the band when his father Clement was their conductor.

'Maybe I'd better best be goin' not, better'n I?'[11]

Harry was sixty-six years old in 1934 and Adeline twelve years younger. Haydn and Dorothy celebrated their Silver Wedding on 23rd March, and the following month the *Mona's Herald* (quoting from a *Melody Maker*

The King of Swing.

article headlined 'Mr Harry Wood to take things easy'), announced that after forty years of service he would be retiring 'from active dance band conducting'. The Palace Ballroom dance programmes for the first five weeks of the summer season would be under the direction of Bert Relphs, and thereafter Douglas Swallow would be taking charge. Henceforth Harry would confine himself to directing the orchestras in the Palace and Derby Castle variety theatres.

Harry's social and charity activities continued to keep him occupied even if he was less concerned with the day-to-day organisation of the Palace and Derby Castle orchestras and bands. In May 1934 he donated five guineas to King William's College new Barrovian Hall Fund, and later that month he was present at the annual Douglas Rotary Club golf fixture.

Trial by Air

With more and more visitors coming to the Island by air during the 1930s it is not surprising that Harry would eventually take to the air himself. In what one supposes was his first ever flight, Harry and three friends took a short trip by sea-plane from Port Erin Bay during the summer of 1933 or '34. The flight took them over the monument on Bradda Head and across to the Calf of Man on a 'rather windy day'. After a bumpy landing back on the beach Harry summed up the experience as 'A wonderful incident, which none of us will ever forget'. However, he noted at the foot of his observations about the flight that during the summer of 1936, the very same plane crashed into the sea on a journey from Jersey to England and everyone was drowned: 'A tragic ending'.

Back on *terra firma* three happy events took place during Harry's Christmas holiday in Yorkshire in 1934. He gave a lecture with slides about the Isle of Man at a local school which was reported in the *Colne Valley Times*, where he was described as 'Manx by reason of his choosing the Isle of Man as the land of his adoption'. It seems that both the Isle of Man and his native Yorkshire had difficulty in deciding whether to claim him for their own!

Two days later he conducted Handel's *Messiah* in Slaithwaite Parish Church with the augmented Philharmonic Society choir, four local soloists and a solo trumpeter. The performers entirely filled the choir stalls and part of the central aisle; the congregation was very large and a collection at the close of the evening yielded £14 11s 2d. The performance was said to be 'devoid of fireworks, but nevertheless impressive and sincere'.

On Sunday 30th December the annual musical service took place at the Parish Church, organised by Harry with the participation of the Slaithwaite Prize Band and a large choir. The band requested that two pieces be included in the programme: Daniel Wood's *Maritza* and Haydn's *Prelude*. The following Wednesday Harry hosted a suitably seasonal supper and get-together for the band at his old home, the Lewisham Hotel, his annual 'thank you' to the band for giving their services so willingly at the annual musical service. What memories will have been revived of weekly rehearsals, social gatherings, triumphs and disasters and tales of old bandsmen long since departed. Would the band be available for next year's service? The answer, a resounding Yes! Before returning to the Isle of Man Harry was able to announce to the band that he had received an assurance from the BBC in Manchester that Slaithwaite Prize Band would be engaged to give a broadcast concert from Leeds in February 1935.

~

Harry naturally kept in contact with his oldest Douglas musical colleagues, and they still sought his advice from time to time, as a letter from the composer, violinist and conductor John Edward Quayle dated 30th March, 1935 shows:

> Summerland, Brunswick Rd
> Dear Harry
> Many thanks for your very kind note of appreciation. I am glad to know that you liked the Variations. It is rather curious that you should have referred to the Orchestra. I struggled (or strained) to write them for orchestra and had scored some half dozen for you but found that the medium did not fit somehow, hence the organ.
> I agree with your view as to the Comparative Merits of the organ and the orchestra.
> Kind regards
> Yours sincerely.

Harry had been a patron of J. E. Quayle's old orchestra, the Douglas Amateur Orchestral Society, and in October 1937 he received a letter from the orchestra's secretary asking if he would extend his patronage by allowing his name to go forward for election as a Vice-President, for '. . . the members are keen to keep alive an interest in instrumental music'. This was an ideal close to Harry's heart from the earliest years of the Manx Music Festival.

In April, a few weeks before the commencement of the 1935 summer season, Harry received a letter from J. B. McEwan, currently engaged at the Norwood Ballrooms, Glasgow, informing him that after twenty-eight years of 'dance-demonstrations dances' at the Palace and Derby Castle he and his wife wished to retire. He expressed the hope that in the future he would continue to visit Douglas 'for old time's sake' and to meet up with Harry and his many other friends.

~

Later that month Pauline, the daughter of Harry's late brother Daniel married Jacques Gorowski, but it is not known if Harry and Adeline attended the wedding. By the second week of May it was 'business as usual' in Douglas and Harry entered into discussions concerning incidental music for a new play, *Illiam Dhone* by Henry Hanby Hay. Harry was confident that Haydn would be willing to compose the *entr'actes* and interludes required, offered his own services as musical director and

Harry and Adeline, Haydn and Dorothy.

suggested that the Douglas (Manx) Amateur Orchestral Society would happily agree to take part: 'I think that the music and orchestra will cost you nothing'. In the event, the Legion Players whom he recommended might do justice to 'the great work', declined to take part as they lacked the requisite number of acting members at that time.[12]

In July 1935 Haydn and Dorothy travelled to the Island for their annual three-week summer holiday, having made a detour to Blackpool *en route* where Haydn conducted a substantial concert of his music with the North Pier Orchestra, consisting of no less than fourteen works.

In November Harry was able to congratulate the Colne Valley Male Voice Choir on their success at the Blackpool Festival: 'Bravo and Bravo Again! Guid owd Slawit' he wrote. Shortly afterwards he and Adeline travelled to Yorkshire for their annual Christmas holiday with their sister Elise in Golcar, and on 29th December took part in the annual musical service at the Parish Church. In addition to the usual Christmas musical fare, the Slaithwaite band played an arrangement for solo cornet of Haydn's *Roses of Picardy*, and his *Homage March*, together with the *Largo* from Dvorak's symphony *From the New World* and Sibelius' *Finlandia*: 'A rare musical treat'.

Harry was involved with a second music service at Slaithwaite Parish Church on Sunday 17th January during which his vesper *Holy, Holy, Holy* was sung by the choir. The following Thursday Harry hosted his annual supper for Slaithwaite Prize Band in the band pavilion, and to everybody's delight gave his customary witty after-dinner speech during which he recited the band favourite, *Mi Father's Owd Trombone*.

Whilst Harry was still in Yorkshire, the news of the death of King George V on 6th January, 1936, was broadcast to the world.

~

According to figures obtained by Promenader in the *Mona's Herald*, August 1935, visitor numbers were down on the previous year and he anticipated 'the annual wail of our local dismal jimmies', with 'our own folk seizing the opportunity to extol the virtues of the Island's rival resort - Blackpool'. According to Promenader, enterprising Blackpool was Lancashire's Big Bad Wolf: 'that all-devouring monster who can swallow up a million holiday-makers whilst we are counting our thousands'. As he disembarked from the *Lady of Man* at the end of a short tour of the rival resort, his spirits rose as he surveyed Douglas bathed in sunshine, and he fell into conversation with a young man on his first visit to the Island: 'Isn't it wonderfully clean-looking after Blackpool!' Promenader's final thought for 'the dismal ones': 'They can find themselves in many a worse place than Manxland in summertime . . .'

~

Away from the hurly-burly of life on the Island as the summer season approached, the rise of Hitler and the possibility of war started to be taken more seriously. A National Defence Commission from the Island entered into talks at the War Office in London to consider the Isle of Man's possible role in any conflict. Although the government did not believe that the Island would become a target for invasion, the Island's strategic position in the Irish Sea meant that it would quickly become a significant element in Britain's overall defence planning, particularly after Prime Minister Chamberlain's limp Munich Agreement with Hitler in September 1938.

An unpleasant foretaste of the horrors to come occurred in Douglas in July 1936 when a group of Germans from the liner *Monte Pastoral* marched along the promenade wearing Nazi insignia and gave a Nazi salute at the War Memorial. The party then travelled to the site of the Knockaloe Detention Camp near Peel and visited the graves of German prisoners who died there during the First World War. The following year the appearance of two Messerschmitt Bf 108 'Typhoon' sports and recreational aircraft at the London – Isle of Man Air Race caused a few eyebrows to be raised, particularly as the aircraft bore swastikas on their tail fins. One of the German competitors was declared the winner in controversial circumstances and reportedly declared, 'It is better to race in peace than in war'.

~

In September 1936 the *Isle of Man Examiner* noted that 'Mr Hilton Cullerne concludes his engagement as leader of the Gaiety Theatre Orchestra and has been engaged by the orchestra of Sadler's Wells Theatre, London, for the coming season.'

Further invitations for Harry to speak on various musical matters also came along during the autumn of 1936. The Isle of Man Natural History and Antiquarian Society asked him to present a lecture-recital on Manx music early in 1937, but he declined as he would be in Yorkshire at that time. In November whilst in Yorkshire, he gave a lantern lecture detailing how the Isle of Man had celebrated various Coronations and other Royal events over the decades, during which some of Haydn Wood's songs were performed by Philip Taylor, a young cornet player from Slaithwaite Prize Band. Just before Christmas the *Radio Times* listed the first broadcast performance of Haydn's *Manx Overture* given by the BBC Orchestra conducted by Joseph Lewis, a great advocate of his music.

Harry was unwell over Christmas that year and the annual music service at Slaithwaite Parish Church was postponed until 3rd January. Whatever the nature of his illness, Harry was well enough to arrange the music and conduct the Prize Band as usual before a packed church of some 1,600 people, with many places taken thirty minutes before the service began. Harry hosted his annual band supper on 7th January, and once again he was prevailed upon to recite *Mi Father's Owd Trombone* during an evening of music, songs and sketches devised by band members.

~

The year 1937 marked the 70th anniversary of the composition of Johann Strauss' *Blue Danube* waltz, and Harry talked about his enthusiasm for the music of the Strauss family, and the waltzes in particular, during an interview in the *Isle of Man Times*. He revealed that his private music collection contained no less than forty-seven waltzes, that the *Emperor Waltz* was the great favourite at the Palace, and that *Tales from the Vienna Woods* was his personal favourite. He also recalled that when he introduced the *Blue Danube* waltz into his Blackpool Winter Gardens concerts it created 'quite a sensation among the young dancers who did not know it!'

On 12th May, Albert, Duke of York was crowned King George VI, an occasion which was celebrated with great enthusiasm throughout the Island, and which happily coincided with the arrival of a large party of 'Homecomers' from America and Canada on the liner *Athenia*. All school children received coronation mugs and medals, and many towns and villages staged their own carnivals; the Lieutenant Governor, Sir Montagu Butler, undertook an eighty- mile tour round the Island to see the displays and pageantry for himself.

On Sunday 25th July the Colne Valley Male Voice Choir - very much Harry's local Yorkshire choir – appeared at a sacred concert at The Palace, Douglas. The conductor George Stead wrote to Harry a few days later thanking him for the invitation and for organising the concert. About this time he received an undated letter informing him that he had been unanimously elected as the choir's patron. In October Harry wrote to the choir congratulating them on winning their class at the Blackpool Music

Festival with a very challenging piece of little-known early Wagner, the Pentecostal cantata *Das Liebesmahl der Apostel*.

In September Harry and Adeline, Dorothy and Haydn holidayed together and enjoyed 'a most delightful tour up to John O'Groats', a round trip of over 1,400 miles, organised by Dorothy with Haydn elected to undertake the driving. Their tour took in Loch Lomond, the Pass of Glencoe and a distant view of the Orkney Isles. Harry was back in Douglas just as the new Lieutenant Governor was installed, Vice-Admiral the Hon. William Spencer Leveson-Gower, whose wife was the elder sister of Queen Elizabeth, later The Queen Mother.

The last year

The year began with the sound of deep, solemn brass chords from the opening of the overture to Verdi's opera *Nabucco* from a packed Slaithwaite Parish Church at the beginning of the annual musical service. Harry conducted the Slaithwaite Prize Band in the overture, an extract from Schubert's *Unfinished* symphony, Haydn Wood's *An Evening Song* and Mendelssohn's *Cornelius March*. The band's young star cornet player Master Philip Taylor played some arrangements of Haydn's songs, and the traditional carols were lustily sung by the large choir and congregation. Harry's sister Elise contributed an additional charming verse for the carol *Merry Bells* especially for the occasion:

> Wise men came with gifts resplendent, to the babe the star foretold.
> To a manger in a stable, brought they frankincense and gold.

Although nobody in the audience could know, they had witnessed Harry's last Christmas musical service in the town of his birth.

Harry and Adeline, Haydn and Dorothy and Hilton Cullerne were together again for the annual Douglas Rotary Club dinner at the end of January. A substantial six-course feast was followed by toasts and speeches and Harry was elected President of the club. Hilton played two of Haydn's most attractive violin pieces, *Slumber Song* and *Elfin Dance*, with Haydn himself accompanying on the piano, followed by two of his songs, *Ship o' Mine* and *The Sea Road* sung by Rotarian Fred Craine. The evening ended with the traditional communal sing-song.

Shortly afterwards Hilton left for South Africa to take up an appointment with the South African Broadcasting Company in Cape Town. He never saw his uncle Harry again.

~

Harry's *Manx Airs* was performed by The Band of His Majesty's Scots Guards during a Douglas Gas Light Company Exhibition staged at the Palais de Danse, Douglas in mid-February. At the conclusion of the afternoon concert Harry made a brief speech of thanks and congratulation:

> I want to thank Capt. Dowell for the excellent manner in which he conducted the Manx Airs, because some of them are rather quaint. Everything came out 'A.1. at Lloyds'.

Early May brought with it encouraging news of Hilton's first broadcast from Cape Town during which he played several of Haydn's short violin pieces. A number of Haydn's orchestral works were heard on Sunday 8th May in a broadcast on the National wavelength conducted by the composer himself, including the tone poem *King Orry*, the overture *Harlequinade*, the *Variations on an Original Theme* and the *Scherzo in the Olden Style*.

Cavalcade

In early May Harry completed the personal musical record he began the year before. This document is the most valuable primary source of information about Harry's years as a musical director in Douglas. It consists of 48 pages of manuscript typed throughout in capital letters, with occasional pasted-on corrections, amendments and additions, and covers the period from 1888 until 1938. The title page of which reads:

> Cavalcade of Popular Music, Song and Dance
> in Douglas, During the Last Fifty Years.
> Compiled by Harry Wood,
> Musical Director, Palace & Derby Castle Ltd,
> Douglas I.O.M.

Below the title Harry wrote the following dedication:

Presented to Charles Fox, (Managing Director of the Palace & Derby Castle Coy. Ltd.) by the compiler Mr Harry Wood, May 23rd 1938.

On the last page he wrote:

> Conclusion:
>
> (I) thank Charles Fox Esq., J.P., Managing Director of the Palace and Derby Castle Limited, for giving me the opportunity of compiling this record of popular music, sung and played in Douglas, during the last fifty years.
>
> Also thank Fred Day Esq., chairman of Francis, Day & Hunter Ltd., music publishers; Bert Feldman Esq., Head of the firm of Feldman & Co, music

publishers; Lawrence Wright Esq., The Lawrence Wright Music Co. Ltd; Messrs Campbell Conneley Co., music publishers; Will Dalton Esq., Joe Kirkham Esq., for the great assistance they have rendered me.

H.W. 7/5/38.

~

On the evening of Tynwald Day, Harry's *Manx Airs* was played by a small orchestra led by Kathleen Rydings at a Grand Concert in the Royal Hall at the Villa Marina. Local soloists sang selections of traditional Manx songs and the Woodside Ladies Choir performed excerpts from Dr George Tootell's cantata *The Legend of Man*. The evening was presided over by Miss Mona Douglas, poet, novelist and folklorist, the honoured doyen of Manx culture.

In late July 1939 Haydn and Dorothy arrived on the Island for their annual four-week holiday with Harry and Adeline, catching up with old friends, sight-seeing, including a visit to Harry Kelly's cottage at Cregneash, and playing golf. In an interview with an *Isle of Man Times* reporter shortly after their arrival, Haydn said that he always looked upon the Island as home, and recalled his first journey from the Island to study at the Royal College of Music in London many years before. He had shared his train compartment from Liverpool with another young musician, a composition student named Herbert Ferrers, who later became a well-known composer. Tragically, his companion became blind in adulthood, and in a characteristic act of generosity Haydn was busy that summer orchestrating his opera *The Blind Beggar* for him.

The reporter commentated that hardly a day went by without some of Haydn's music being heard on the radio, but Haydn reflected with sentiments that Harry would have agreed with, that although *Roses of Picardy* had sold some one and a half million copies in the twenty-one years since its composition:

> I don't think there is a public for popular songs like there used to be. People haven't got pianos in their homes as they had in the days when they used to make music for themselves. All they do now is turn a knob and listen to anything they like.

Haydn further suggested that although musicians and composers could earn an income from performing rights, broadcasting fees and from writing film scores:

> . . . it does not compensate for the old days when music used to sell

> in tens of thousands of copies. Today a 2s song that sells 20,000 copies is considered a big success.

Haydn's own songs, however, continued to be as popular as ever, and that year the popular bass-baritone Peter Dawson had broadcast two of the latest ones: *Dawn Over London* and *A Bird Sang in the Rain.* Haydn also revealed that he had written a new choral ending to his tone poem *Mannin Veen* which had already been broadcast over two hundred times.

In conclusion, the *Isle of Man Times* suggested that Haydn was a 'Jekyll and Hyde' character, 'a composer who writes serious works on an ambitious scale in one mood, and in another, ballads which vie with dance band tunes in popular appeal.' At the same time the *Colne Valley Guardian*[13] posed the question: was Haydn Wood 'A Manx Yorkshireman or a Yorkshire Manxman?' and after coming to no particular conclusion declared that 'What the Brontë sisters did for Haworth and Thomas Hardy did for Wessex, Haydn Wood has done for the IoM'.

The annual conference of Rotary International took place in Douglas in September, and on the Sunday evening there was a concert at the Villa Marina during which Harry Wood's *Manx Airs* were played by a quartet led by Kathleen Rydings. It is not known if Harry himself was present.

Illness and death.

It was during what was to be the last family summer holiday on the Island that Harry began to exhibit the first signs of serious health problems and made it clear that he felt unequal to the task of organising, rehearsing and directing the annual Christmas musical service in Slaithwaite. A photograph of Harry and Haydn in the music library at Osborne Terrace is revealing as it shows Harry looking far from his old ebullient self, with a noticeably puffy face and unhealthy colour possibly indicating high blood pressure. Photographs of Harry in his library dating from about 1936, and Harry and Haydn in the garden at Osborne Terrace show that whilst he had certainly put on a little weight he still retained his familiar twinkle in the eye and jovial expression.

A further intimation that all was not well comes from an undated letter from (Lieutenant-Commander) Alfred J. Parkes of Ballaugh, the immediate Past-President of the Douglas Rotary Club:

> My dear 'Harry', I cannot tell you how dreadfully sorry I am to learn that the doctor (Dr Lionel Wood) will not permit you to be present at our annual dinner, nor will that sorrow be confined to myself. We

Harry and Haydn in the music library of 1, Osborne Terrace.

> shall miss that happy smiling countenance that has always contributed so much to the happiness of the evening, but it would be unpardonable selfishness on our part were we to press you to adopt any live action that might prove detrimental to your health and well-being.

The occasion that Harry was forced to miss was the highlight of the Rotary International Conference weekend. The conference began with a civic reception and dinner in the Royal Hall of the Villa Marina, and concluded with a grand concert given by Margaret Minay, soprano, Rotarian Douglas Buxton, and a supporting comedian and conjuror. A selection from Harry's *Manx Airs* was performed in an arrangement for strings and piano by a small ensemble led by Kathleen Rydings. Thereafter Harry's name is absent from the local newspapers for the first time in fifty years until the sad events of just a few months hence.

At the end of September the *Isle of Man Examiner* included a brief report from the Transvaal Manx Association Annual Supper during which fond memories of the Island were relived as a small orchestra played one of Harry's sets of lancers. On 20th October he received a birthday greetings telegram from his family in Yorkshire.

~

Towards the end of November Harry left the Island for what would be the last time. In the company of Adeline, he travelled to London to stay with Haydn and Dorothy for two weeks although he was far from well. He and Adeline left London for Yorkshire sometime during the first two weeks of December and stayed with their sister Elise and brother-in-law Walter Gledhill in Golcar near Huddersfield. Soon after his arrival his health took another turn for the worse and by the middle of the month alarming news reached the Isle of Man: MR HARRY WOOD GRAVELY ILL.

According to the *Isle of Man Examiner*[14] he had suffered a sudden attack, either a seizure or a stroke, on Saturday 10th December and lay unconscious amid considerable apprehension from friends and family concerning his recovery. Haydn rushed up from London to Yorkshire, local medical specialists were in attendance and Harry's doctor in Douglas was consulted.

Cavalcade of Music Ended[15]

Harry died on Christmas morning after suffering a further attack at his sister's house surrounded by his family. The Rev. J. Greenwood, Pastor of Golcar Baptist Church, conducted a brief service at the house on the morning of 28th December, followed by a full funeral service at the parish church of St. James', led by the vicar, Canon W. H. Verity, who also officiated at the graveside.[16] The church organist played Mendelssohn's *O Rest in the Lord* at the commencement of the service and Handel's *Largo* at the close. The principal mourners were Adeline Wood, Walter and Elise Gledhill, his niece Miss May Wood and Haydn and Dorothy Wood. Arthur Brittain represented the Palace & Derby Castle Company along with Will Dalton, the theatrical manager. Other mourners included the conductor and officers from the Slaithwaite Prize Band and representatives of the Slaithwaite Philharmonic Society, the Huddersfield Permanent Orchestra, the local Musician's Union and members of the Colne Valley Freemason's Lodge and Golcar Central Liberal Club. There were a great number of floral tributes including a wreath from the Palace & Derby Castle Company.

Announcements of Harry's death and tributes to him began to appear in the Isle of Man newspapers almost immediately with the *Mona's Herald* taking the lead with a full and well-considered obituary beginning with the following lines:

> It is with deepest regret that we record the death of Mr. Harry Wood,

> one of the Island's best-known and most respected personalities . . . at the age of 70.

Readers were reminded of his association with music in Manxland for over half a century and how Harry's 'unfailing cheerfulness and kindly consideration' endeared him to all who met him, and how 'a marvellous capacity for making friends had gained the affection of vast numbers of holiday makers from all parts of the Kingdom'.

The *Isle of Man Examiner* opened its equally thoughtful obituary with the following announcement:

> Manxland mourns the death of one of its most distinguished adopted sons in the person of Mr Harry Wood . . . one of the outstanding personalities in the musical life of the Island.

Compiled by that doyen of observers of the Island's entertainment world, Arthur Q. Moore, the obituary indulged in some gentle nostalgia by evoking 'memories of an age whose mode of life may seem quaint against this era of rhythm and rush, and of the times when the waltz held sovereign sway', and recalled the countless occasions when '. . . the jovial little man - known affectionately as "Harry" to all - beamed down upon the dancers from the platforms of the Palace and Castle ballrooms'. The piece concluded with a attribute to Adeline '. . . who for years was his inseparable companion, and a never-failing source of help to him in his brilliant career'.

The *Ramsey Courier* described Harry as 'one of the best-known musicians in the North of England in the days before wireless made conductors household names'. Not for the first time his charitable work was alluded to, and the report closed with the following assessment of Harry the man:

> His friendliness and kindness were his chief characteristics, and he will be greatly missed by a host of friends.

The *Isle of Man Examiner*'s Roving Reporter's 'News, Notes and Gossip' column offered a newspaperman's view of the courtesy and consideration Harry extended to local reviewers:

> Not the least of those who will miss the popular musician's cheery smile and presence are the journalists who have had to interview him from time to time in the course of their work. Unlike some celebrities . . . Harry Wood was never too busy to turn down a newspaperman's request for information; and indeed, he often went

> to a great deal of trouble and research to ensure the information being accurate.

The *Isle of Man Times* in an informative article in the 'At Random' series entitled 'From Yorkshire to the Isle of Man . . . Island's links with Slaithwaite', described Harry affectionately as 'The Fairy God-father of Manx Music', and then marvelled that from Slaithwaite in Yorkshire's bleak Pennine moors should come two families 'which have left their mark on Manx affairs'. The two families were those of Harry Wood, and George Henry Wood, the manager and director of the Isle of Man Railway Company. The article stated that, although not related, the two families had been friends, and from the time when Harry was resident in Douglas they enjoyed a musical evening every Friday when professional engagements permitted.

A Life Devoted to Music.

Tributes to Harry's long and fruitful career in Douglas from those who worked closely with him soon began appear. Among the first was a letter from Charles Fox, Manager of the Palace & Derby Castle Company, to Adeline:

> Belle and I deeply sympathise with you Haydn and the family in your great loss. Harry was a loyal and greatly esteemed friend whose place will never be filled. For forty years he and I worked together with complete understanding and his unremitting zeal and service to the Palace Company will long be remembered by all who were associated with him in that work. His passing will leave a gap in the musical life of the Island while his many personal friends will greatly miss his kindly and genial personality.

In December the government official Bertram E. Sargeaunt wrote to Adeline in an equally personal vein:

> I know how devoted you were to each other and what a terrible blow it must be. All of us who are interested in music will miss him more than words can express. He was always so helpful and willing and so deeply interested in anything to do with music.

Letters from Yorkshire demonstrated that Harry had not been forgotten in his native Slaithwaite. On the day of Harry's funeral, the secretary of the Colne Valley Male Voice Choir wrote the following to his brother-in-law Walter Gledhill:

> It was with very sincere and deep regret that I learned this morning of the death of our dear friend and Patron Mr H. Wood. He will be very badly missed by all with whom he came into contact for both his genial personality and his musical ability.

Perhaps the most poignant good wishes were written on a card from a small boy, the son of a neighbour in Golcar, sent from the Royal Infirmary, Huddersfield:

> 'Please tell Mrs Geldhill how very sorry I am to hear of the death of her brother Mr Harry Wood. I am sure though that God will help her and all his relations in this time of great sadness and bereavment. (sic)
> Signed Donald Byrne, 292 Scar Lane, Golcar.

Harry's first Slaithwaite violin pupils from the early 1880s had not forgotten him either, as an appreciation of his life sent to the *Huddersfield Daily Examiner* during the last days of the year shows. Edwin Stead, one of Harry's first pupils, wrote about their long friendship and said how he used to walk from Meltham to Slaithwaite for his violin lessons and recalled once playing a piece for Harry's father, 'usually called CLEM'.[17]

~

On Sunday 1st January, 1939, the annual musical service that Harry had so often organised and directed, and which meant so much to him, took place in St James' Church, Slaithwaite, led by the Rev. Verity. The hymns included *O Love That Will Not Let Me Go*, *Hark the Herald Angels Sing* and Harry's own setting of *Holy, Holy, Holy*, and the Slaithwaite Band gave a heart-felt performance of Grieg's *The Death of Åse* from *Peer Gynt* and Haydn Wood's ceremonial march *Homage*.

Three weeks later the *Isle of Man Times* reported that Haydn and Dorothy were staying with Adeline back in Douglas, that both were well 'but feeling the passing of Harry Wood keenly'. Further tributes continued to appear during the early months of 1939 including one from the *Dancing Times* acknowledging Harry's role in establishing the Blackpool Dance Festival. Before January was out Harry's estate had been assessed and valued at £10,700 and probate granted to Adeline.[18] After attempting to settle Harry's affairs Haydn and Dorothy left Douglas for London on 1st February.

Adeline continued to involve herself socially in local affairs though doubtless with a heavy heart and with less enthusiasm than before; in

January 1939 she received the following letter from the Ellan Vannin Club thanking her for:

> Your kindness in handing over the shares held by your brother in the Ellan Vannin Proprietary Co for the benefit of the Club. Harry had endeared himself to all and his bright and happy disposition was a real inspiration; he was first one of those splendid men, who, in knowing and meeting, made one feel all the better by contact and association and we are the poorer by his going from us.
> SJ Kaye Hon. Sec.

Harry Wood's Treasures

Adeline had been named executrix of Harry's will, and with Haydn's advice and support, undertook the daunting task of dealing with his extensive music library together with a number of antique, rare and valuable musical instruments. What happened to Harry's library of some 6,000 pieces of music, programmes, playbills and photographs charting his career on the Island remains a mystery to this day, but at least some clues as to the whereabouts of his collection of musical instruments have come to light.

The following advertisement appeared in the *Isle of Man Times* in early February:

> To Be Sold (miscellaneous)
> FOR SALE a Chappell Boudoir GRAND PIANO, in excellent condition, and an early Broadwood GRAND PIANO. Dated 1804; also a unique set of musical GLASSES (note: A glass harmonica which Harry once played at a concert in Douglas.) in mahogany case, a museum piece, the property of the late Mr Harry Wood. For particulars apply Blakemore's, Victoria Street.

It would seem that none of these fascinating instruments were sold, for shortly afterwards Adeline offered the Broadwood piano to the Manx Museum, who declined to accept it on the grounds that it was not of Manx manufacture.

~

The *Colne Valley Guardian*[19] informs us that sometime during the late spring or early summer of 1939, Adeline presented the Ravensknowle Memorial Museum, Huddersfield,[20] with the following antique musical instruments: a hurdy-gurdy; an early 19th century keyed cornet which was played in the first Slaithwaite band when Harry's grandfather, and later father, were the conductors; a serpent, which may have been owned by one Ralph 'Raife' Sykes, shoemaker and lamplighter of Slaithwaite; an ophicleide played 'at local sings' by one Haigh of Scapegoat Hill and an 1804 Broadwood piano, described as 'very narrow from front to back' and in perfect playing condition.[21]

The whereabouts of Harry's valuable Italian violins, a number of violins that once belonged to A. W. Moore, and a three-quarter size violin by Thomas Perry of Dublin, which both Haydn and Hilton Cullerne had played when students, is unknown.

One artefact that Harry had been very proud of owning because it provided a direct link to his family in Yorkshire, was a sundial fashioned from an ancient pillar which he believed might have been either a Roman milestone or the base of a column from the Slack Roman fort or way station at nearby Outlane near Huddersfield.[22] In reality the stone pillar, which bore a faint carving of a Christian cross, was probably the shaft of a 16th century preaching cross, and for centuries had stood opposite the Slaithwaite Manor House, where Harry's mother Sabra had been born. The stone pillar was given to the Wood family by Lord Dartmouth in 1931 and transported to the Island where it stood on the front lawn at 1, Osborne Terrace. In March 1939 Adeline presented the milestone with the sundial on top to the Colne Valley Council and paid for its packaging and transportation. In compliance with Harry's wishes the stone pillar, standing between four and five feet in height, was erected on a small triangular piece of lawn in the grounds of Slaithwaite Town Hall. The pillar and sundial were later moved back to the grounds of Slaithwaite Manor House, but the sundial is now missing, either lost or even stolen since.

~

The Wood family home in Osborne Terrace was put up for sale by public auction in May 1939 and offered as suitable as a private residence, medium sized boarding house or company house. Harry's old home did not sell at that time and appeared regularly in the auctioneer and estate agent H. J. Johnson's advertisements for sale by private treaty from June until early February 1940 when it appears to have been sold to Mr A. Smith, a senior ledger clerk. It is not known for how much Harry's house sold, but the adjacent property was sold for £990 during this period.

Adeline would have been relieved to be back in Yorkshire with her sister Elise and the rest of the family. Her life in Douglas had been inextricably linked with Harry's; they had been very close, and with him gone, she must have felt very isolated despite all the friends they had made on the Island. It was probably sometime during this turbulent period that Harry's music library was either dispersed or disposed of.

Aftermath

There was one happier piece of family news that reached Douglas during the first bleak month of the New Year: Gilbert Scholes Wood, Harry's nephew, the son of his late brother Daniel, passed his final Law Society examination at the age of twenty-three.

Music by both Harry and Haydn featured strongly during a five-day exhibition in mid-February at the Palais de Danse in Douglas. The occasion was another in a series of exhibitions under the auspices of the Douglas Gas Light Company which included demonstrations of cookery using the latest gas appliances. The company manager and engineer A. Ronald Bissett devised and produced a colourful pageant of music, dialogue and various tableaux telling the story of the development of science throughout the ages, and promised 'one of the most spectacular and interesting entertainments seen for a long time'.

The production consisted of seven scenes, including *The Cavalcade of Ships* and *The Cavalcade of Gas*, and huge panoramas depicting *The Cavalcade of Creation*, and *The Cavalcade of the Sea* which both featured music by Haydn Wood. Music by Harry accompanied *The Cavalacade of Coal*, which presented a replica of a working mine, complete with men toiling at the coal face, and a cage carrying miners to and from the surface, in a production that featured local singers and an Industrial Orchestra consisting of six local musicians.

~

Haydn visited the Island for the last time before the outbreak of World War II in April 1939 to conduct his cantata *Lochinvar* with the combined choirs at the Manx Music Festival concert. The event was broadcast and a surviving photograph taken at either the rehearsal or performance shows Haydn standing before an orchestra and choir of some two hundred performers. Harry's former pupil Kathleen Rydings can be seen in the second row of the first violins.

Florrie Forde appeared for the last time in Douglas in 1939 for a four-week engagement during July and August and revived many old favourites, including *Bull and Bush*, *Goodbye-ee* and *Tipperary* together with *The Umbrella Man*, *Count Your Blessings*, *Cheerie O* and the hit of

The irrepresible Florrie Forde with Eva Kane, Billy Danvers, Gracie West and Ethel Revnell at an open-air pantomime at the Falcon Cliff Hotel.

the season *Boomps-a-daisie*. Harry's place on the rostrum was taken by the ever-reliable Bert Noble. History was repeating itself, as it is apt to do: Florrie Forde was once again at the Derby Castle on the eve of war.

The end of an era

Haydn, Dorothy and Adeline spent some of the war years in the Bideford and Westward Ho area of North Devon and were active in local concerts. As time went on some of the personalities great and small, and family members who had featured in Harry's life for decades, began to fade from view. The sudden death of Charles Fox, the Chairman of the Palace & Derby Castle Company Ltd., at a nursing home in Manchester in August was announced at a gloomy Company shareholder's meeting at the Derby Castle in November 1939 amid speculation as to what would befall the vast entertainment complexes in the coming years.

Florrie Forde died in harness on 18th April 1940 after entertaining troops in Aberdeen. Harry's nephew Hilton married Irene Finnemore of Pietermaritzburg, Natal, but died suddenly in 1942 in South Africa, following a period of ill-health related to rheumatism, the result of his

First World War service.

Bert Feldman died in 1945 having lived out his last years in a Blackpool hotel. Mrs A. M. Rushworth died in Douglas that same year; she had been Harry's accompanist for the Sunday Sacred Concerts for many years. Adeline died at her sister's home in Golcar on 10th September 1948 after a long illness, and was buried in Slaithwaite. Dorothy Wood died in London in 1958 and Haydn in a London nursing home on 11th March 1959. The last of Clement and Sabra Wood's children, Elise Gledhill, died on Boxing Day 1966 at her home in Golcar, which was also the year that the Lewisham Hotel finally closed its doors.

Epilogue

In December 1937 the *Mona's Herald* published a review of a radio broadcast entitled 'Scrapbook for 1913'. The programme presented a series of snapshots 'of that wonderful year' with the closing scene set on the Isle of Man, and drew an evocative picture of that summer season a quarter of a century earlier:

> with a thousand couples dancing in the Derby Castle ballroom to the music of Harry Wood's Destiny waltz. Outside, the moon-lit sea could be heard gently lapping on the shore of the perfect crescent of Douglas Bay, and at 9.50 Florrie Forde comes into the ballroom to sing It's a long way to Tipperary. They would all be singing it soon . . .

That is how I like to imagine Harry Wood, the genial musical director at the height of his popularity during the most successful summer season in the Isle of Man on record. As his father Clement Wood might have said: 'Well done, lad!'

Notes

Chapter 1

1. The Lewisham Hotel, situated on Station Road, Slaithwaite, was demolished in 1969, and there is now a bungalow on the site. An unobtrusive oval plaque mounted on the original stone wall bordering the Lewisham Hotel along Station Road, commemorates the birthplace of Haydn Wood.
2. John William Wood (1857-1930) may have been a bandsman in the Slaithwaite band, which held its practises at the family home, the Lewisham Hotel. He is not known to have visited the Isle of Man, and no photograph of him exists.
3. Mary Hannah Wood (21st Feb 1862 - 1st Sept 1903), was another musical member of the Wood family who played the piano. She married Francis Henry Griffiths Cullerne (1859-1927) in 1882, and they took over the running of the Lewisham Hotel when Mary Hannah's parents and younger siblings moved to the Isle of Man in 1886.
4. Slaithwaite from Old Norse: 'Timber-fell clearing', *English Place Names,* The English Place Name Society.
5. The Huddersfield Narrow Canal, constructed between 1794 and 1811, runs between Huddersfield and the Ashton Canal, Ashton-under-Lyne and was limited to boats less than 7 ft wide. Slaithwaite is said to be the only village in England that has a canal running alongside its main street.
6. John Sugden*, Slaithwaite Notes of the Past and Present,* John Heyward, Manchester, 1905, Hardpress reprint, covers many aspects of Slaithwaite life from the mid- nineteenth century to the early Edwardian period, including the mills, the churches, the pubs, the bands, workers, local characters, education, sport, crime, country matters, holidays and many other topics.
7. William Walter Legge, 5th Earl of Dartmouth (1823-1891), a Conservative politician and Lord Lieutenant of Staffordshire.
8. The nineteenth century textile industry employed children as cotton piecers or scavengers to lean over the looms to 'piece' or repair the threads. Other members of the Wood-Sykes family also worked in the textile industry as cotton teazers, twisters and spinners.

9. John Schofield, born c. 1768, Mallingfield, died May 24th, 1843, 'after fifteen days of illness' according to the lost diary of Clement Wood, which covered the years 1856-72, extracts of which were published in the *Colne Valley Guardian* on 28th August, 1936.
10. Mrs Susannah Sunderland, nee Sykes, (1819-1905), the legendary West Riding soprano, was born in Brighouse, and soon made her name as a chapel soloist following her first public appearance in 1833. Her nickname, the Yorkshire 'Queen of Song', was given to her after she appeared before Queen Victoria at the first Leeds Music Festival in 1858. She was a founder-member of the Huddersfield Choral Society in 1836, and a respected singing teacher. A flourishing music festival, The Mrs Sunderland Festival, founded in 1889 in Huddersfield, still bears her name today.
11. Extracts from Clement Wood's diary (lost) appeared in the *Colne Valley Guardian* on 21st November, 1934; 28th August, 1936 and on 26th November, 1936: *Slaithwaite Brass Band*, Mr Harry Wood's Reminiscences.
12. Humphrey Wood (c. 1831-54) was at one time either the owner or landlord of the Lewisham Hotel. His relationship to Clement Wood is uncertain.
13. Sykes, John, *Slawit in the Sixties, Reminiscences of the Moral, Social, and Industrial Life of Slaithwaite and District in and about the year 1860*, Schofield and Simms, Huddersfield, 1926.
14. Harry Wood's Engagements Diary covers the period from June 1878 to September 1885.
15. According to the official Slaithwaite Guide for 1936, the Feast - known locally as 'Sanjimis', an obscure local name derived from St. James - inevitably became an excuse for three or four days 'of eating and drinking large quantities of roast beef and home-brewed beer, accompanied by pickled cabbage and plum pudding'.
16. George Haddock (1823-1907) was a member of an influential Leeds musical family, a highly respected violin teacher who was reputed to have taught over 4,000 pupils, including, briefly, the young Delius around 1869. He was a member of the Hallé Orchestra for over twenty years, and later the Liverpool Philharmonic. His family owned one of the finest private collections of Cremonese violins including the 'Red Diamond' Stradivari (1732), the 'Emperor' Stradivari (1715) and a Guarneri del Gesu (1734). His son Edgar was the founder and first

principal of the Leeds College of Music in 1873, later the Yorkshire College of Music & Drama.

17. The Slaithwaite Spa and Baths leisure complex was developed in 1825 by local businessman Richard Varley, and founded on two mineral springs of sulphur and chalybeate containing salts and iron. The site was bisected by the River Colne, with the baths and other public rooms where the 'smoking concerts' took place on the near side of the river, and the numerous 'lovers' walks, shady nooks and bowers, leisure gardens and bowling green . . .' on the far side.

18. See Harry Wood Engagements Diary, 5th September 1885: '*Miss Ann Armitage, a girl who had lived at our house for some years, and Miss Anne Day, one of our servants, went home this morning, they had been on a visit to the Island (Isle of Man) for a few days. They enjoyed themselves very much*'.

19. Edgar Ward was the first musical director at the Falcon Cliff, and was succeeded by a series of eminent conductors: Dick Ball, Oliver Gaggs, Charles Reynolds, John Greenwood and F.C. Poulter.

20. Lester Barrett (1855-1921). Real name Stephen Barrett, brother of T.A. Barrett aka Leslie Stuart, composer of the song *Lily of Laguna* and the 'hit' musical *Floradora*. One of Barrett's most popular songs was C.W. Murphey's *Kelly the Carman*, the first of a series of 'Kelly' songs associated with the Isle of Man.

21. Bessie Bellwood (c.1856-1896), real name Kate Mahoney, was born in Cork. A ballad singer turned comedienne, her career was somewhat eclipsed by the rise of Marie Lloyd. She was famed for her portrayals of colourful working class characters, and for her vibrant, quick-fire repartee with her audiences, when she frequently 'gave as good as she got'.

22. J. Sydney Jones' son, also James Sydney Jones, but known simply as Sydney Jones, played the clarinet with Harry in the pit, and later achieved great acclaim for the shows *The Geisha and San Toy.*

23. Born George Henry Snazel (1850-1912). A bank clerk turned singer who insisted on the professional name Mr G.H. Snazelle. He was famed for his monologues and yarns. Sir Thomas Beecham referred to him as 'that inveterate old joker'. His stage persona may have brought the term 'Snazzy' into the language.

24. Edward de Jong (born Deventer, Holland, 1837; died Sulby, Isle of Man,

1920) was one of the original members of the Hallé Orchestra and in 1870 he inaugurated his Popular Saturday Concerts in Manchester with an orchestra of 60 players. He was appointed musical director at the Derby Castle in 1888, and that year engaged Harry Wood as a first violin and repetiteur violinist.

Chapter 2

1. Origin obscure. Sir Walter Scott in *Guy Mannering* (1815) writes 'Because the Hour's come . . . and the Man'. I prefer P. G. Wodehouse in '*Aunts Aren't Gentlemen*': 'And the hour . . . produced the man'.
2. D.F.E. Sykes, *The History of the Colne Valley*. F. Waller, Slaithwaite, Yorkshire, 1906.
3. Sir Spencer Walpole KCB, FBA, D.Litt. 'A man without prejudice, of modesty, candour and wide interests' as A. W. Moore described him. A scholar and notable historian.
4. Sir Thomas Henry Hall Caine (1853-1931), 'The Manx Novelist', did much to promote 'the little Manx nation' through his writing and many visitors came to the island to seek out the places described in his novels. Born in Runcorn, he spent much of his boyhood on the Island, and after a period as a journalist in Liverpool, purchased Greeba Castle. He represented Ramsey in the House of Keys, was knighted in 1918 and made a Companion of Honour in 1922. His novels were translated into 20 languages and his 1894 novel The Manxman is widely regarded as his finest work. The praise heaped on his work - and the adulation afforded to him personally during his lifetime - was, perhaps, undeserved, but so is the neglect that he has fallen into since.
5. Maurice Powell, *Hear the Little German Band* . . . Kiaull Manninagh Jiu, 2015, manxmusic.com and Manx National Heritage Manuscript Collection, MS 13670.
6. From the Italian 'canaglia', a pack of dogs; the lowest class of people. Lazzaroni, homeless beggars or casual workers from the Hospital of St. Lazarus where some of these 'idlers of Naples' took refuge. Hokey-pokey men were ice cream street vendors.
7. The Black Lion Hotel was established in 1846 and formerly known as Cowin's Black Lion Inn; Sabra Wood became the licensee in 1887 following Clement's death. From 1889 it was known as Rushworth's

Black Lion Hotel.

8. Richard (Dick) Ball. Violinist, composer and musical director. He conducted a military band at the Derby Castle in 1883, and was conductor at the Falcon Cliff in 1886.
9. The designation Valse is frequently used by Harry Wood in *Cavalcade*, and Valse appears on many publications, in concert advertisements and reviews. I have chosen as far as possible to use the designation 'Waltz', being more common in English speaking countries.
10. Elizabeth Dews studied at the Royal College of Music and made her London debut at St James' Hall in 1891. She appeared frequently at de Jong's Free Trade Hall concerts in Manchester, and festivals in Leeds, Birmingham, Glasgow, Edinburgh and Dublin.
11. *The Death of Nelson*, from John Braham's 1811 opera *The Americans*, was a great concert-piece for Victorian tenors. Braham was England's most famous tenor in the first half of the century, eclipsed only by the arrival on the scene of the great Sims Reeves.
12. The best-known setting of Eliza Craven Green's poem *Ellan Vannin* has music by J. Townsend. The setting by Dr. Fred W Friend (c.1880, pub. by J. Brown & Son, Douglas) was popular for a time, but is rarely heard today.
13. The 'arry' character may have derived from the song of that name popularised by the serio Jenny Hill in 1882, in which the pretentious social aspirations of clerks and shop boys is mocked.
14. See *Oliver Gaggs, the man who wrote the HI! Kelly Polka*, in A Supplement to New Manx Worthies, by Maurice Powell, Culture Vannin, manxmusic .com, 2014. Oliver Gaggs produced four further very popular dances for the 1888 Falcon Cliff season: the vocal schottische *The Manx Herrin*', the *Douglas Head Waltz*, the *Sweet Mona Waltz* and the *Kippers Polka*.
15. Charles Reynolds (1843-1917) was an oboe and cor anglais player, composer and conductor, and a principal oboist with the Halle Orchestra under Richter, and under Max Bruch at the Liverpool Philharmonic Orchestra. He was a renowned teacher and taught the young Leon Goosens, the doyen of English oboists. Goosens recalled that '. . . he was a very dear man . . . very portly . . . and chewed charcoal biscuits because of tummy trouble'.

16. See Ounsley, Karen Esme, *Bands and Orchestras in the Major Northern Seaside Resorts of England 1865-1911*, PhD thesis, Hull University, 2009. The Derby Castle bands before Charles Reynolds in 1886 included one conducted by W. Short for whom Oliver Gaggs wrote his Derby Castle Grounds galop in 1877; 'a beautiful string band' conducted by Edward Beedon Redfern, whose players included Charles Reynolds as the oboe soloist, in the Sunday concerts of 1877; Dick Ball's band of 1882, and military band of 1883, which gave morning and afternoon concerts and played for dancing in the evenings, and Arthur Grimmet's band of twenty players of 1887. Manx Sun, 29th August, 1887.
17. Maurice Powell, *The Origins of 'Hi! Kelly'*, Culture Vannin, manxmusic.com, 2017.
18. *Cavalcade of Popular Music, Song and Dance in Douglas, during the last 50 years*, Harry Wood, May 1938. The first entries date from 1888.
19. This process was apparently known as 'Plebiscite E'. During the week, dances were awarded marks by the audiences, and a final selection was made from the most popular ones.
20. Meyer Lutz (1829-1903) was a German composer of light music for the theatre, operettas, cantatas and songs. The burlesque, or 'spoof' on Gounod's opera *Faust*, was first performed at London's Gaiety Theatre in October, 1888, and was one of many such 'travesties' in vogue at this period such as *Carmen Up to Date* and *Cinder Ellen Up too Late*.
21. *My Bohemian Life*, Leslie Stuart, ed. Andrew Lamb, Fullers Wood Press, 2003, and *Leslie Stuart, The Man Who Composed 'Floradora'*, Andrew Lamb, Routledge, 2002. He later wrote the popular songs *Lily of Laguna, Sweetheart May, Little Dolly Daydream, Soldiers of the Queen, My Little Octoroon* and the *Coon Drum-Major* for Eugene Stratton.
22. A well-loved ballad by Stephen Adams, real name Michael Maybrick (1841-1913), who was organist and conductor of the Liverpool Choral Society, and whose best-known work is the sacred song *The Holy City*.
23. See 'What the Island gave the visitors 65 years ago', IoMT, November, 1954.
24. Frederick Vetter (1844-1920), violinist, concertina virtuoso and conductor. He was 24 years with the Hallé Orchestra, and well-known in the Manchester area. Like Oliver Gaggs, he was a distinguished brass band contest adjudicator, and adjudicated at the British Open

Brass Band Championships on a number of occasions. In 1906 he was the adjudicator at the second Concertina Band Contest held at Belle Vue, Manchester. He died in Toronto, Canada.

25. Belle Vue Gardens was situated in the general area of the present-day National Sports Centre, 'ten minutes walk via either Peel Road or the Nunnery Grounds' or a short 'omnibus' ride from 'The Clock'.

26. An Orchestrion was a large mechanical musical instrument which reproduced the sounds of a wind orchestra, including percussion, by means of revolving cylinders, with the sounds projected through a series of differently voiced pipes.

27. Frederick Charles Poulter (1858-1919). Pianist, organist, accompanist, teacher and multi-instrumentalist originally from Sheffield, he was bandmaster of the Isle of Man Volunteers, conductor of Douglas Town Band, organist of St. Thomas' Church, Douglas, and conductor of the Douglas Choral Union. He was the musical director of the Falcon Cliff orchestra during 1893-4. See Maurice Powell, *F. C. Poulter, A Supplement to New Manx Worthies*, Culture Vannin, 2016.

28. The Diorama was a popular theatrical entertainment in Victorian England, and viewed at specially erected, often portable theatres. Invented by Daguerre in France in 1822, it consisted of a 10-15 minute viewing of a picture – often a landscape – which via a system of multi-layered panels and skilfully manipulated lighting, would appear to change, giving the audience the impression of a natural scene.

29. Miss Clinch took part in a performance of a work by Charles (Jean Baptiste) Dancla (1817-1907) that appeared a number of times in the programmes of the students' concerts played by Harry's most advanced pupils. The 'violin duet' performed at the first student's concert was performed again in April 1900 at Harry Wood's Grand Concert at the Grand Theatre, Douglas, with soloists Haydn Wood and Kathleen Rydings, one of his most successful pupils.

30. John Edward Quayle (1869-1957). A most important figure in Manx music in the first half of the 20th century. Violinist, organist, conductor, and a significant Manx-born composer of such fine orchestral works as *The Magic Isle* and *On Maughold Head*. See Maurice Powell, John *Edward Quayle, Supplement to New Manx Worthies*, Culture Vannin, manxmusic.com, 2013.

31. The Misses Mew. Three very accomplished musical sisters: Miss Amy

Mew, later Mrs Harry Rushworth, the well-known accompanist at many of the Sunday Sacred Concerts at the Palace; Miss Nellie Mew, later Mrs T. Clague, and Miss Blanche Mew, a violinist who studied with Emile Sauret for a time, who left the Island and became a journalist. Both Nellie and Blanche were talented violinists and played in Harry Wood's 4th Annual Orchestral and Operatic Concert of 1893, the 5th Annual Students' Orchestral and Choral Concert of 1894, and the 6th Annual Students' Concert in 1895.

32. Sissie Rowe, daughter of Capt. Richard Rowe, mines captain and owner of Laxey Glen Flour Mills. His large warehouse at Laxey harbour was the venue for many local concerts and meetings.

33. The Isle of Man Industrial Home was founded in 1868 as the Douglas Industrial Home for Orphan and Destitute Children and from 1882 was housed at Strathallan Hall, Onchan, (demolished 1960) and later Glencrutchery. Ninety children were cared for on a self-sufficient basis including the operation of a market garden, glass houses and paper bag-making.

34. The Cullerne branch of the Wood family is almost as interesting as the Wood family itself. Frank Hilton Cullerne (1892 - 1942), the second son of Francis Henry Griffith Cullerne and Harry's eldest sister, Mary Hannah, lived with Harry in Douglas intermittently after his mother's death in 1903. Harry gave him violin lessons, and at the age of 15, he won an open scholarship to the Royal College of Music. Four further children were born to the Cullerne's at the Lewisham Hotel, Slaithwaite: an older brother, Harold, born 1891, an architect, who emigrated to Canada in 1912, and played the flute with a short-lived sixty-piece orchestra founded by the Vancouver Symphony Society in 1919, which disbanded in 1921. Among others, he designed the Hollywood Theatre, one of Vancouver's Art Deco treasures of the 1930s, which still stands today. A younger brother, George (Georgie) Hildred, born 1897, lived with the Woods in Douglas from time to time (see 1901 census), possibly because his mother in Slaithwaite did not enjoy good health. After two years in Australia, he emigrated to Canada in 1922, and enjoyed a variety of careers including insurance salesman, farm worker, fisherman, tallyman at a salmon canning factory and book keeper. He was also a proficient, self-taught banjo and banjolele player. All three brothers saw service in World War I. Two daughters, Elsie

and Doris, born in 1894 and 1895 respectively, barely survived infancy. (I am most grateful to Marjorie Cullerne - the daughter of George Hildred Cullerne - for the above information about her family.)

35. Samuel Robinson (born c. 1884) known as Orry Corjeag, was fortunate to enjoy the patronage of Lady Raglan, the wife of the Lt. Governor. He studied at the Royal Academy of Music, and from 1907-9, was a member of the Hambourg Quartet, whose viola player was the young composer Eric Coates. Over a brief span the quartet gave concerts in London and toured to South Africa. Orry Corjeag saw distinguished service during WWI, and later became leader and deputy conductor of the Carl Rosa Operas Company. He married the 'cellist Dorothy Marno.

36. Henri Josef Baume (1797-1875) was something of a shady character. Diplomat, spy, debt collector to the Prince Regent, possibly even a murderer known as the 'Islington Monster', a wealthy refugee from France who moved to the Isle of Man during the 1860s, an eccentric, a miser and recluse, who left his considerable fortune made partly in property on the Island, to Douglas charities at his death, including King William's College, and £300 in trust for talented musicians to study at the Royal Academy of Music.

37. Kathleen Rydings (1887 -1961). See Maurice Powell, *A Very Gifted Manx Lady*, Wibble Publishing, 2014.

38. The Minnehaha Minstrels were established in Manchester as a charitable organisation; their act was a blend of old Negro songs, English parlour songs, jokes and banter, clog and sand dancing etc.

39. The new Queen's Promenade ran from McCrone's Slip at the Falcon Cliff to the Tramway Company station, virtually at the gates of the Derby Castle.

40. Charles Blondin (1824-97), born Jean Francois Gravelet, French tightrope walker and acrobat whose legendary crossing of the Niagara Falls took place on 30th June, 1859. After a period of retirement, he reappeared in 1880 and toured throughout Britain, often in pantomimes.

41. Preliminary site clearing had commenced in May in an area to the south side of Parade Street near the Victoria Pier, before all the properties to be demolished had been purchased. The 'gloomy forebodings' of some shareholders and other detractors from the outset proved to be accurate; the project foundered when only £25,000

of the required £75,000 was apparently raised by the Standard Contract & Debenture Organisation who went on to construct the Blackpool Tower in 1894.

42. Dr. Stocks Hammond (1859-97). Popular organist, composer and conductor, Fellow of the Society of Arts, well-known from engagements at Scarborough and Morecambe Winter Gardens. He was an examiner at the Royal College of Music and the founder of the Victoria College Corporation and choir master of St. James' Cathedral, Toronto, Canada, where he died, young, of complications following an operation.
43. Les Petites Jolies Quarttete enjoyed a very long run at the Castle, and were all dance protégés of John Tiller, the Lancashire-born theatre manager, credited with inventing high-kicking precision dance routines.
44. Harry Freeman (1858-1922). His career was based mainly in the Midlands and his most popular songs included The Giddy Little Girl Said 'No' and That's All Rum-Fum-Foozle-Up. In 1890 he became 'King Rat' of the Grand Order of Water Rats entertainment charity.
45. Theo. Bonheur (1857-1919), real name Charles Arthur Rawlings - he is said to used 62 different pseudonyms- was the composer of piano pieces, songs, military marches, polkas and waltzes such as the *Hippodrome Circus March* and the famous Scottish march that became a popular dance, *The Gay Gordons.*

Chapter 3

1. The Queen's Promenade was completed in 1890 and officially opened by the new Lt. Governor, Sir Spencer Walpole, in a ceremony which featured a procession of the entire fleet of tramcars. The official opening of Central Promenade took place on 26th August 1896.
2. The 900ft long Iron Pier was opened in August 1869, re-opened 1882 and closed in 1891. It was demolished in 1894 as part of a promenade widening scheme and offered for sale by tender in 1896 at a guide price of £1300 and bought by a Manchester scrap merchant. See National Pier Society www.piers.org.uk.
3. The Douglas - Laxey Electric Tramway via Groudle Glen opened July 1893. The Snaefell Mountain Railway opened in August 1895, the only one in the world at that time. The Electric Railway finally reached

Ramsey in 1899.

4. Attributed to the genius of French operetta, Jacques Offenbach.
5. Founded 1893 in Manchester, with initial strength in the north of England, sought to improve the low pay and terrible working conditions of theatre musicians.
6. Harry Wood himself received a weekly wage of £2 7s 6d as repetiteur violinist in Fred Vetter's Palace band in 1889. In addition to his weekly wage, 6s per appearance was paid for participation in the Sunday Sacred Concerts during August and September.
7. Harry received £59. 7s 6d from his benefit at the Derby Castle in 1897, but there are few other references in the account books to individual amounts paid to him.
8. The three most popular composers of English operas during the nineteenth century were Michael Balfe, the composer of *The Bohemian Girl*, William Wallace, the composer of *Maritana* and Julius Benedict, the composer of *The Lily of Killarney*. Many of the era's most enduring ballads were drawn from these operas.
9. The Douglas Choral Union eventually became associated with operetta rather than oratorio and other sacred music and survives today presenting magnificent, highly professional shows at the Gaiety Theatre.
10. Like so many aspiring singers of her era, Marie-Louise-Emma-Cécile Lajeunesse, 1847-1930, born in Chambly, Quebec, first won recognition in Italy, and adopted the name of a noble Italian family, Albani. She was the favourite singer of Queen Victoria and Sir Arthur Sullivan, and deserves to be named alongside the great singers of the 1870s and 80s, Patti, Gerster and Melba.
11. Sir Thomas Beecham quipped that Clara Butt's voice could be heard across the English Channel; Reynaldo Hahn called her voice 'thunderous' and 'obscene'; Sir John Barbirolli referred to her as '. . . an oratorio contralto . . . that almost bovine monstrosity'.
12. The range of Santley's voice was said to be from low E to high G. He sang both *Messiah* and *Elijah* at Manchester town hall every year from 1858 to 1907, and was the first singer to be knighted.
13. Born Alan J. Foley, he Italianized his name according to the fashion of the day, as did Albani (Lajeunesse) and Melba (Mitchell). Two of the most inventive examples of this practice were John Clarke of Brooklyn

whose stage name became Signor Giovanni Chiari di Broccolini, and Yorkshire-born Hetty Holroyd, who after emigrating to Australia and the town of Dargo, became Esta D'Argo.

14. A Speaker of the House of Keys and the highly-respected author of many books on Manx life and folklore, A. W. Moore's *History of the Isle of Man* is a standard work on the subject, as is his collection *Manx Ballads and Music*, 1896.
15. The Royal Edition also included volumes of songs of Scotland, Wales, England, Ireland and France and Handel's *Songs from his Oratorios*.
16. From the evidence of the style of the letter and the use of language, Dr Fenella Bazin has plausibly suggested that the anonymous writer may have been none other than T. E. Brown, the Manx National Poet. 'Balldin' is Baldwin, a short distance from Douglas.
17. See Maurice Powell, *A rale Manx Concert*, Kiaull Manninagh Jiu, manxmusic.com, October, 2014.
18. Fishing net buoys traditionally made from sheeps' stomachs.
19. The only Manx melody that Harry is known to have personally 'collected' is a version of the Primitive Methodist hymn, *The Good Old Way*, taken down from the singing of Alister Proctor in December 1895. This version, which later appeared in his *Manx Airs* of 1920 differs from other versions in having sections of alternate 3/4 and 2/4 bars.
20. A *Mhelliah* is a traditional Manx harvest time celebration during which the Queen of the Mhelliah is crowned.
21. Harry Rushworth was a musical director and violinist; his wife, Amy, was one of the three musically talented Mew sisters, and the accompanist at the Palace Sunday Sacred Concerts for many years.
22. From racoon, and normally portrayed as a lazy, good-for-nothing buffoon.
23. The Christy Minstrels were formed in Buffalo, America, in 1843 by Edwin P. Christy. Their routines established the form and content of the minstrel show.
24. Cited in Jacobs, A., *Arthur Sullivan*, OUP, 1986.
25. Maurice Powell, *A Very Gifted Manx Lady*, Wibble Publishing, 2014.
26. The Annual Exhibition was first held in the Masonic Hall, Douglas and then at the Grand Music Hall until 1891, when the directors of the Palace made their ballroom available. Exhibitions of needlework, embroidery, knitting, domestic cookery, drawing, painting, writing,

modelling etc attracted large numbers of entrants from infants to adults. The Exhibition was not re-instigated after WWI.

27. These arrangements of Manx melodies were probably re-cycled from the concerts of *Manx National Music* in 1897.
28. Maurice Powell, ENCORE, the story of the Isle of Man Symphony Orchestra, Manx Heritage Foundation, 2012.
29. Slang, from 'heart-smasher', a young dandified would-be lady-killer who regularly made sly sexual advances to women. Vesta Tilley often impersonated this stock music hall character.
30. Quotation from a song sung by the Yorkshire comedian 'Old George Nicholson', cited in the *IoMT*, 6th October, 1900. G. W. Nicholson appeared at the Derby Castle in 1897 with his song *The Tenor Who Lost His Top Note*.
31. *A Manx Notebook*, Victorian and Edwardian Douglas, The Palace, and 'the strictures of the Rev Thomas Rippon'. Initially vilified for his views, he later became a popular minister on the Island.
32. *The Land O'Cakes and Brither Scots*, an obscure book about Scotland by Alexander Ireland published in 1882 and containing a reminiscence of Sir Walter Scott.
33. Gilbert and Sullivan, *Patience*, 1881.
34. The *Manx Sun*, 6th January, 1894. Oliver Gaggs left the Island to take up the post of conductor at the Blackpool Tower Ballroom early in 1894 owing the sum of £4 to the liquidator; the amount was ultimately considered too small to be worth pursuing through the English courts.
35. The fall of Dumbell's Bank brought financial ruin to many sectors. Five officials were arrested, charged with fraud and jailed after a 15 day trial. Sir Alexander Bruce, the General Manager, escaped justice as he died in July.

Chapter 4

1. 'As you like it', the *Manxman*, 9th June, 1900.
2. Whit-week 1902, *IoMT*, 17th May.
3. The coronation was postponed from 26th June to 9th August because the King contracted appendicitis on 24th June.
4. Edwin Bogetti, born c. 1862. Composer and conductor. He wrote the

popular Derby Castle waltz *Beautiful Mona* when he was conductor there in 1902, but his name ceases to appear in connection with the Palace & Derby Company's orchestras after 1903. His march *United Services* was performed at a concert in the People's Palace, East London, in August 1892. *Dresdina* sold some 17,000 copies each year for a time. The title 'Professor' did not imply that he held an academic qualification from a college or university, as the title was attached to almost anyone who taught music, including Harry Wood.

5. John Philip Sousa, 1854-1932, conductor and composer of many military and patriotic marches. His formed his own band after leaving the USA Marine Band in 1892. His best-known marches are *The Stars and Stripes Forever*, *Semper Fidelis* and *The Liberty Bell*. He initiated the development of the Sousaphone, a large bass brass instrument specially designed for marching bands, in the 1890s.
6. A partial view of one of the library rooms can be seen on two photographs from 1937-8, which show Harry and Haydn Wood at Harry's desk with shelves crammed with music in the background.
7. A verse from a poem entitled '*The Promenade*' by 'An Irish Girl'.
8. *IoME*, 29th October, 1904. Hengler's circus first came to Douglas in 1870 together with twenty horse boxes and operated from a site in Upper Church Street at the rear of the Catholic church. The acts mainly featured horses and ponies, the star of the show being Miss Jenny Louise Hengler, 'Queen of Equestriennes'. In July 1898 Hengler brought with him seventy horses, a troupe of high-leaping greyhounds and 120 performers of which twenty were clowns. The spectacle of the season was the plunge into water of a sleigh drawn by three horses.
9. See *The Victorian Circus* for an illustration of Hengler's most famous 'Water Pantomime' *The Village Wedding* or *Tramps Abroad* at the Victoria & Albert Museum. Depicted is a water-filled arena, boats, bridges, live wild fowl, fisherman and comic policemen chasing tramps into the water.
10. Hengler also owed rates on circus property of £12.16 to the Asylums Board and the School Board in the amount of £24 14s; see also *IoMT*, 7th May, 1904.
11. According to Arthur Brittain, the Secretary of the Palace & Derby Castle Company, in conversation with the soprano Isobel Baillie in 1936, 11,400 people, each paying 1/-, witnessed Tilley's final bow.

12. Eliza (Elise) Beaver (Beever or Beavor) Wood, 1878-1966, an accomplished pianist who was associated with the Golcar Baptist's Womens' Meeting for over twenty years. Her husband Walter John Gledhill, 1872-1941, baritone, appeared at a Palace Sunday Concert the following year taking over at short notice from Fowler Burton as Madame Albani's supporting singer.
13. Albani had first heard the sixteen year old Haydn play at a concert in Douglas in 1898. Her concert party normally consisted of herself and her husband-manager Ernest Gye, a supporting singer, a solo pianist, a violinist Haydn Wood, and an accompanist.
14. The response of a well-known Douglas tradesman who, when asked 'Are you going to hear Melba tonight?' assumed the questioner was referring to an itinerant preacher. Cited in Chats, *IoMT*, 15th August, 1908.
15. Melba's fee for her Palace concert in 1908 was £300; in 1913 her fee for her two Villa Marina Kursaal appearances was £700.
16. Francesco Paolo Tosti, *Goodbye*.
17. From *Songs of the Turkish Hills*, music by George H. Clutsam, lyrics by Abdülmecit, recorded by McCormack in 1912 and 1933.
18. *Gobnageay* – 'mouth of the wind' in Manx gaelic - is the name of a farm near the present-day Creg ny Baa bar public house, near the 35th milestone on the TT course; the *Buggane* is a mythical Manx giant with a mighty voice who according to legend persistently blew the roof off of St. Trinian's church, Marown.
19. William Hanby, born c. 1860, d. 1921. An engineer with the General Post Office; his poetry displays a lightness of touch that often laid bare the foibles and eccentricities of the Manx character in a perceptive yet kindly way.
20. Girton College, Cambridge had been established as a college for ladies in 1873, and by the time of *Babes in the Wood* housed 180 students.
21. Highly regarded during his lifetime for his choral works, Arthur Somervell, 1863-1937, is remembered today mainly for his song-cycles *Maud*, after Tennyson, and *A Shropshire Lad* after Houseman.
22. See Musical Notes, *IoME*, 4th December, 1909. The Phynodderee was a satyr, half beast, half fairy, sometimes malevolent, sometimes benign, whose wickedness could be thwarted by the sound of church bells or sacred music.

23. Frederic Cliffe, 1857-1931, was the Bradford-born composer of two symphonies, a violin concerto and a scena, *The Triumph of Alcestis* for Clara Butt. He was a Professor of Piano at the Royal College of Music for nearly fifty years.
24. German: literally 'Cure-hall', a public room at a health resort or spa, and later generally referring to an amusement park. The Kursaal at Southend-on-Sea in Essex was the world's first purpose-built example and opened in 1901; like the Villa Marina Kursaal in Douglas, it had originally opened as a 'Marine Park and Gardens'.
25. Formerly the property of Henry Bloom Noble, and purchased from his estate by Douglas Corporation for £60,000. The Villa Marina complex was developed at a cost of a further £25,000.
26. Maurice Powell, *The Kaiser and the Kursaal, Herr Simon Wurm's Imperial Viennese Orchestra*, KMJ, 2016, for a fuller account of Herr Wurm's short-lived and turbulent relationship with Douglas Corporation and the Villa Marina Kursaal.
27. Simon or Stanislaus Wurm was also the conductor of the White Viennese Band on Brighton pier during the 1890s, and the young Gustav Holst was one of his trombonists. He was also associated with a Viennese band in the Cantelupe Gardens, Bexhill-on-Sea. Wurm's brother Maurice or Moritz was the musical director of the Red Viennese Band in Folkestone for a period.
28. Francis, Day & Hunter was founded in 1877 by William and James Francis, David Day and Harry Hunter. In 1897 the company established itself in Charing Cross Road, London and helped to create London's own Tin Pan Alley district. *Cavalcade* lists seven songs published by F, D & H sung by Florrie Forde including *Oh! No! Antonio, Has Anybody Here Seen Kelly?*, and *Flanagan*.
29. Bert (Bertram) Feldman & Company was founded in 1896 on the back of one song bought cheaply from an old music-hall comedian. The business thrived when Feldman acquired the English rights to a number of American 'hit' songs in 1907 and again in 1912. *Cavalcade* lists a further twenty-eight songs published by Feldman & Co that Florrie Forde included in her repertoire including *Down at the Old Bull and Bush, I'm Forever Blowing Bubbles* and *Minnetonka*.
30. John Abbott, The Story of Francis, Day & Hunter, Chappell, 1952.

31. Maurice Powell, *Tipperary and the Isle of Man: New Evidence*, Kiuall Manninagh Jiu, Culture Vannin, manxmusic.com, November, 2015.
32. Thomas Augustine Barrett, aka Leslie Stuart, 1865-1928, could be quick-tempered and argumentative, but was easy to appease and generous to a fault. Most people said he was 'as genuine as his music', a 'delightful raconteur and a charming companion'. The name 'Leslie Stuart' apparently derived from two names he noticed on stage door cards: Fanny Leslie and Cora Stuart.
33. *Cavalcade*, 1913, p. 25. Ted Judge, the brother of Jack Judge, the composer of *Tipperary*, confirmed in a newspaper interview in the *Isle of Man Examiner*, 7th August, 1936, that he and his brother first brought the song to Douglas in 1913 and performed it at Cunningham's Holiday Camp during the time that Florrie Forde was singing it at the Derby Castle.
34. The enduring popularity of Tipperary may be gauged from an anecdote from 'Bulletin', the 'voice of the North American Manx Association' dated Winnipeg, Manitoba, 1936: An Irish Engineer, 2000 miles up the Amazon, was astonished to find that the only song the local Indians knew was *Tipperary*.

Chapter 5

1. Cited in Faragher, *With Heart, Soul and Voice*, Leading Edge Press, 1992.
2. According to another source, Herr Wurm's band at one time or another comprised 14 Englishmen, 4 Italians, 1 Russian, 2 Austrians and 1 German musician.
3. The *Mona's Herald*, 21st August, 1914. The Manx Language Society had objected to the name 'Kursaal' from the beginning as it was 'inappropriate and not Manx in character'. A number of Manx names were put forward including 'Halley ny Bingys as Garey ny Ferrishyn' (Hall of Music and Garden of the Fairies), but all were turned down. The name 'Kursaal' was soon dropped from the Villa Marina, but the main hall was not renamed the Royal Hall until the visit to the Island of King George V and Queen Mary in 1923.
4. Bertram Edward Sargeaunt, MVO, OBE, FSA, FRGS, 1877-1978, was responsible for administering the Island's detention camps during World War I. He was a man of great influence in Manx affairs, as well

as an amateur musician and composer, and the author of many perceptive and encouraging concert reviews during the 1930s-50s. His *The Isle of Man and the Great War*, Brown & Sons, 1920, is valuable source of information about the period.

5. A system of daily physical exercises designed for large numbers of people marshalled into serried ranks. See *The Swedish Drill Teacher* by M. H. Spalding and L. L. Collett, 1910, popularised in Britain by Charlotte Mason, educationist and pioneer of home education.
6. The *Mona's Herald*, 5th January, 1916.
7. Smith, C., *The Isle of Man in the Great War*, Pen & Sword Military, 2014.
8. Frederick John Buxton (1868–1920) was born in Nottingham of a family of entertainers and entertainment promoters. He wrote two popular Manx songs: *Come Back to Mona* and *Mona, I Am Coming Back*. His son Douglas became one of the Island's most highly respected singers, singing teacher and choir trainer.
9. *The Cushag, Manx Airs* or more usually *Manx Melodies* was performed again in 1920, and in 1927 for the Great Homecoming Concert with added solos and choral forces, and subsequently became a popular selection with local orchestras. See Maurice Powell, *Harry Wood's Selection on Manx Melodies*, KMJ, manxmusic.com January 2015.
10. Hamish MacCunn (1868-1916), composer of the perennially popular tone poem *Land of the Mountain and the Flood*.
11. When war broke out in 1914, Hall Caine put aside his fictional work and dedicated his time to journalism, letters, articles and public addresses to aid the war effort. In recognition of this work, he received a Knighthood in 1918 and was made a Companion of Honour for his services to literature in 1922.

Chapter 6

1. *The Ben-my-Chree, Empress Queen, Ramsey* and *Snaefel* were lost due to enemy action, and the *Viking, Mona's Isle, Queen Victoria* and *Prince of Wales* were still engaged overseas. The *Hazel*, a vessel of good size with excellent accommodation, was purchased and renamed *Mona*.
2. A reference to Conan Doyle's interest in spiritualism following the death of his son Kingsley at the end of the First World War.
3. A. Shaak, CVO 17843, Camp 4, Compound 5-5B.

4. Obituary of Harry Wood, The *Dancing Times*, 1939.
5 From a quotation attributed to Lloyd George.
6. Annual Lights Festival, as it was known, began in 1879; the first 'modern' display took place in 1912 and lasted for sixty-six days.
7. The newspaper of Keith, Prowse & Co., concert artiste and theatre ticket agents, and publishers of light music, songs and piano music.
8. In 1932 Alan Quirk became the first triple Cleveland Medal winner.
9. Letter from the AMU to Harry Wood dated 20th January, 1920.
10. Charles Knight's popular First World War 'battle cry' made famous by Mark Sheridan.
11. The World Manx Association was founded in 1911 by Richard Cain, of Kirk Braddan, to bring together all the Manx societies throughout the world. Cain and the Mayor of Douglas had travelled to Toronto and Cleveland, Ohio, to help organise the Homecoming, and acted as escorts on the journey to the Island. Maurice Powell, *A Manx Celtic Concert*, Kiaull Manninagh Jiu, June 2014.
12. Charles Fox, Douglas Amusements, their origin and development, paper delivered to the Dilettante Debating Society and published in *IoMT*, 13th November, 1923.
13. George Tootell was as cinema organist of genius in Douglas, and the composer of the Manx cantata *The Legend of Man* and *Manx Scenes and Songs*.
14. The autobiography of Isobel Baillie.

Chapter 7

1. *London Daily Mail*, August, 1930.
2. The *Mona's Herald*, 2nd August, 1932. That year, 110 charabancs, 73 light motor vehicles, 36 horse-drawn carriers, three special trains and several buses helped transport a congregation of some 36,000 to and from Kirk Braddan Church.
3. The premier cinemas in Douglas during the 1930s were the Royalty, the Regal, the Picture House, the Strand Cinema and the 2,000 seat Crescent 'Super' Cinema on the promenade.
4. The catchphrase of Rob Wilton.
5. Will Hay was a polymath who spoke several languages; a violinist,

pianist and a notable amateur astronomer who discovered a white spot on Saturn.

6. His real name was Charlie Olden or 'Nedlo' backwards.
7. The title of a 1998 television documentary about Robeson.
8. McCormack received three papal knighthoods and was made a Papal Count by Pope Pius XI in 1928 for his services to church charities.
9. Musical portraits of Ivor Novello, Delores del Rio and Charlie Chaplin.
10. Sophia Wood, born in 1870, married Joseph Gledhill in 1896. She was an accomplished amateur piano accompanist and lived on-and-off with Harry and Adeline in Douglas and helped with the organisation of his music library.
11. One of a series of Manx sayings jotted down in one of the Wood family scrapbooks.
12. It is not known if Haydn Wood wrote any music for this production. If he did, some of it may have been re-cycled into the score he composed for the Manx Pageant of 1951, known as the Festival of Man or the Manx response to the Festival of Britain. See Maurice Powell, the Festival of Man 1951, Culture Vannin, manxmusic.com September, 2017.
13. *Colne Valley Guardian*, 22nd August, 1938.
14. *IoME*, 16th December, 1938.
15. *IoME*, 30th December, 1938.
16. *Ramsey Courier*, 6th January, 1939.
17. Edwin Stead gave up violin when the Wood family moved to Douglas, but was later engaged by Harry as a trombonist in his Derby Castle Orchestra.
18. *IoME*, 27th January, 1939. London Probate granted to Adeline in the sum of £2,258 4s, 22nd March, 1939.
19. *Colne Valley Guardian*, 28th July, 1939.
20. Known as the Tolson Memorial Museum, Ravensknowle, near Huddersfield.
21. When my colleague Marjorie Cullerne from the Haydn Wood Music Library and Archive, Victoria, British Columbia, Canada visited the museum in 2000, the Broadwood piano could not be located, although the instrument was listed in their acquisitions catalogue.
22. *At Random, IoMT*, 4th March 1939.

Bibliography

Primary Sources

The Haydn Wood Music Library and Archive, Victoria, British Columbia, Canada (HWMLA) (www.haydnwoodmusic.com)

Harry Wood's Engagement Diary, 1878 - 1885.

Harry Wood, *Cavalcade of Music* (1938)

The Wood family scrapbooks including newspaper cuttings, letters, photographs.

Sheet music collection of orchestral music, dances, songs and incidental music by Harry, Daniel and Haydn Wood.

Manx National Heritage Library, Douglas, Isle of Man

The Palace and Derby Castle Engagements books, 4 vols, 1891-1950s (MNHL, MS 11627 and MS 10258); The Falcon Cliff, Derby Castle and Palace Cash Books, Ledgers and Contracts, etc (MNHL, MS **09398**).

The archive of the Palace and Derby Castle Co., Ltd.,

Isle of Man Public Record Office, Douglas, Isle of Man

Other documents pertaining to the formation and ultimate winding up of the Derby Castle Hotel and Pleasure Grounds Company, The Derby Castle Company Limited, The Palace (Douglas, Isle of Man) Limited, The Falcon Cliff Castle and Grounds Company Limited, the Pavilion Limited and Palace & Derby Castle Company can be found in the Public Records Office, Douglas.

Isle of Man Newspapers Online (imuseum.com):

Isle of Man Examiner

Isle of Man Times

Manx Sun

Mona's Herald

Peel City Guardian

Ramsey Chronicle

Ramsey Courier

Ramsey Weekly News

Books and articles

Abbott, J., *The Story of Francis, Day & Hunter*, (London, Francis, Day & Hunter, 1952).

Baker, R. A., *British Music Hall, An Illustrated History*, (Great Britain, Pen & Sword History, 2014).

Baker, R. A., ***Old Time Variety, An Illustrated History*, Great Britain, Pen & Sword.**

Baker, R. A., **Remember When, Great Britain, Pen & Sword, 2011.**

Bazin, F. C., *Much inclin'd to Music, The Manx and their Music before 1918*, (Douglas, Manx Heritage Foundation, 1997).

Beckerson, J., *Holiday Isle, the Golden Era of the Manx Boarding House, 1870s-1970s*, (Douglas, Manx Heritage Foundation, 2008).

Belchem, J. (ed.), *A New History of the Isle of Man, The Modern period, 1830-1999*, (Liverpool, Liverpool University Press, 2000).

Bratton, J. S., *Music Hall, Performance & Style*, (Milton Keynes, Open University Press, 1986).

Cowgill, R. & Poriss, H., *The Arts of the Prima Donna in the Long Nineteenth Century*, (New York, OUP, 2012).

Cowsill, M. & Hendy, J., *Steam Packet 175 (1830-2005)*, (Ramsey, Ferry Publications, 2005).

Cresswell, Y. M., *Living With the Wire*, (Douglas, Manx National Heritage, 1994).

Cringle, T; Kniveton, G. N., (eds.), *Here is the News, A Chronicle of the 20th Century*, Vol 1, 1901-50.(Douglas, The Manx Experience, The Manx Heritage Foundation, 1999/2004.

Davis, R., Those Were the Days, collected images from the Isle of Man's past, (Ramsey, Lily Publications, 2012).

Davis, R., *Those Were the Days*, volume II, (Ramsey, Lily Publications 2013).

Davis, R., Those Were the Days, volume III, (Ramsey, Lily Publications, 2014).

Davis, R., Those Were the Days, volume IV, (Ramsey, Lily Publications, 2016).

Double, O., *Britain Had Talent, A History of Variety Theatre*, (Basingstoke, Palgrave MacMillan, 2012).

Earl, J., *British Theatres and Music Halls*, (Princes Risborough, Shire Publications Ltd., 2005).

Faragher, M., *With Heart, Soul and Voice, 100 years of the Manx Music Festival*, (Burtersett, Leading Edge, 1992).

Frow, G., *'OH, Yes IT IS!'*, (London, British Broadcasting Corporation, 1985).

Gammond, P., *The Oxford Companion to Popular Music*, (New York, OUP, 1991).

Gammond, P., *Your Own, Your Very Own! A Music Hall Scrapbook*, (Ian Allen Ltd., London, 1971).

Gammond, P., *Music Hall Songbook*, (Newton Abbot, David & Charles, 1975).

Gibbons, V. H., *Jack Judge, The Tipperary Man*, (Smethwick, Sandwell Community Library Service, 1998).

Gill, J. F., Clague, J., Gill, W. H., *The Manx National Songbook*, combined edition, (Douglas, The Manx Experience, 2001).

Goodman, A., *Gilbert and Sullivan's London*, (Tunbridge Wells, Spellmount Ltd., 2000).

Hannavy, J., *The English Seaside in Victorian and Edwardian Times*, (Oxford, Shire Publications Ltd., 2003).

Harding, J., *Folies de Paris, The Rise and Fall of French Operetta*, (London, Chappell and Company Ltd., 1979).

Hendry, R., *100 years of Man, 1860-1960*, (Douglas, The Manx Experience, 2007).

Honri, P., *Lions Comiques!*, (Greenwich Exchange, London, 2005).

Honri, P., *Working the Halls*, (Farnborough, Saxon House).

Hoy, M., *A Blessing to this Island, the story of King William's College and*

The Buchan School, (London, James & James, 2006).

Jacobs, A., *Arthur Sullivan,*(Oxford, OUP, 1986).

Kelly, D., (ed), *New Manx Worthies,* (Douglas, Manx Heritage Foundation, 2006).

Kilgarriff, M., *Sing Us One Of The Old Songs, A Guide to Popular Song 1860-1920,* (New York, OUP. 1998).

Kinrade, V. G. C., *Music of the Manx Tourist Industry, 1870-1970,* (M.Phil Dissertation, 2009).

Kniveton, G. N., *Douglas Centenary, 1896-1996,* (Douglas, 2006).

Lahee, H. C., *Famous Singers of Today and Yesterday.* (Reprint).

MacDonald, C., *Emma Albani, Victorian Diva,* (Toronto, Dundurn Press Limited, 1984).

McMillan, R., *A Full Circle, 100 years of the Gaiety Theatre and Opera House,* (Douglas, Keith Uren Publishing, 2000).

Maitland, S., *Vesta Tilley,* (London, Virago Press, 1986).

Major, J., *My Old Man, A Personal History of Music Hall,* (London, William Collins, 2012).

Moore, A. W., *Manx Ballads and Music, 1896,* (facsimile reprint by Llanerich Publishers, Lampeter, 1998).

Mullen, J., *The Show Must Go On, Popular Music in Britain during the First World War,* (Farnham, Ashgate Publishing Ltd., 2015).

Ounsley, K. E., Bands and Orchestras in the Major Northern Seaside Resorts of England, 1865-1911, A Socio-Cultural History, (Diss. November 2009).

Powell, M., *A Very Gifted Manx Lady, the Life of Kathleen Rydings,* (British Columbia, Wibble Publishing, 2014).

Powell, M., *ENCORE! The Story of the Isle of Man Symphony Orchestra,* (Douglas, Maurice Powell, 2013).

Rodgers, K., *Our Heritage . . . This was Our Island, (I),* (Friends of Port St. Mary, 1995).

Rodgers, K., *Our Heritage . . . This Was Our Island, (II),* (1998).

Russell, D., *Popular Music in England, 1840-1914, A Social History*, (Manchester University Press, 1987).

Scott, D., *Singing Bourgeois, The Songs of the Victorian Drawing Room and Parlour*, (Milton Keynes, Open University Press, 1989).

Scowcroft, P. L., *British Light Music*, (Dance Books, 1997/2000).

Smith, C., *Isle of Man in the Great War*, (Barnsley, Pen & Sword Military, 2014).

Smith, I., *Looking Back . . . Isle of Man Holidays*, (Ramsey, Lilly Publications with Camrose Media, July, 2017).

Stimpson, R. & Hall, S., *Knockaloe Internment Camp, 100 Years of History*, (Rmasey, Lily Pubs., 2014).

Sugden, J., *Slaithwaite Notes of the Past and Present*, (Manchester, John Heyward, 1905).

Sykes, J., *Slawit in the Sixties, Reminiscences of the Moral, Social and Industrial Life of Slaithwaite and District in and about the year 1860*, (Schofield and Simms, Huddersfield, 1926).

Taylor, J., *Yesterday's MANN, a photographic study in contrasts*, (Douglas, Manx Industrial Trust Ltd., 1974).

Toulmin, V., *Winter Gardens Blackpool*, (Blackpool Council/ Boco Publishing Ltd., 2009).

Turner, M. R. & Miall, A., *The Parlour Songbook*, (London, Michael Joseph Ltd., 1972).

Traubner, R., *Operetta, A Theatrical History*, (London, Victor Gollancz Ltd., 1983).

Vickers, D., *Songs of The British Music Hall*, (London, Wise Publications, 2013).

Ward Lock, *The Isle of Man*, (London, Ward Lock & Co Illustrated Guide Books, 1925-6 series).

Webber, D. T., & Kniveton, G. N. (eds), *An Illustrated Encyclopedia of the Isle of Man*, (Douglas, The Manx Experience, 1997).

Winterbottom, D., *Governors of the Isle of Man since 1765*, (Douglas, Manx Heritage Foundation, 1999/2012).

Woolley, C., The Revival of Manx Traditional Music, (PhD thesis, University of Edinburgh, 2003).

Woolley, S. & Cowsill, M., Ramsey, *A Collection of Images Through the Years*, (Ramsey, Lily Publications, 2013).

Young, K., *Music's Great Days in the Spas and Watering Places*, (London, MacMillan and Co Ltd., 1968).

INDEX

A

B

C

D

E

INDEX

Z